Online Searching

A Guide to Finding Quality Information Efficiently and Effectively

Second Edition

KAREN MARKEY

ROWMAN & LITTLEFIELD
Lanham • Boulder • New York • London

Credits and acknowledgments of sources for material or information
used with permission appear on the appropriate page within the text

Published by Rowman & Littlefield
An imprint of The Rowman & Littlefield Publishing Group, Inc.
4501 Forbes Boulevard, Suite 200, Lanham, Maryland 20706
www.rowman.com

6 Tinworth Street, London SE11 5AL

British Library Cataloguing in Publication Information Available

Library of Congress Cataloging-in-Publication Data

Names: Markey, Karen, author.
Title: Online searching : a guide to finding quality information efficiently
  and effectively / Karen Markey.
Description: Second edition. | Lanham : Rowman & Littlefield, [2019] |
  Includes bibliographical references and index.
Identifiers: LCCN 2018039719 (print) | LCCN 2018043110 (ebook) | ISBN
  9781538115091 (Electronic) | ISBN 9781538115077 (cloth : alk. paper) |
  ISBN 9781538115084 (pbk. : alk. paper)
Subjects: LCSH: Electronic information resource searching. | Information
  retrieval.
Classification: LCC ZA4060 (ebook) | LCC ZA4060 .M37 2019 (print) | DDC
  025.0425—dc23
LC record available at https://lccn.loc.gov/2018039719

♾™ The paper used in this publication meets the minimum requirements of
American National Standard for Information Sciences—Permanence of Paper
for Printed Library Materials, ANSI/NISO Z39.48-1992.

Printed in the United States of America

For my brother Kevin.
Mother was right about people coming and going in life,
but you remain ever firm, forthright, and faithful.

Contents

List of Figures, Textboxes, and Tables

LIST OF FIGURES

LIST OF TEXTBOXES

LIST OF TABLES

Preface

For everyday people, searching for information usually means Googling and searching the World Wide Web. Web searches are satisfactory for providing information that gives people a working knowledge of unfamiliar, long-forgotten, or difficult topics. Unfortunately, searching the open Web for useful information gets people just so far. That anyone can publish information on the Web makes it risky for people to make decisions about their health, well-being, and livelihood using the information that they find there. People need to access trusted sources of information, where authors, editors, and contributors have the proper credentials to write about topics; where they document their facts; and where what they have to say is objective, accurate, and reliable. Additionally, people pursue lifelong interests in academic fields, disciplines, and professions; they become gainfully employed; and some even achieve world-class expert status in a chosen domain. Becoming a domain expert means developing disciplinary knowledge. For the time being, trusted sources of information and disciplinary scholarship reside in the licensed Web, largely inaccessible to Google and other Web search engines.

Your job as a librarian involves uniting library users with trusted sources of information to answer their questions and satisfy their information needs. This means learning how to become an expert intermediary searcher who is in full command of the wide range of functionality characteristic of the search systems that access licensed databases and of the search engines that access quality information on the open Web. You want to put not only *relevant* information in your users' hands but also information that is *credible* and supports their decision making and intellectual growth so that they can pursue their personal, educational, and professional goals.

Librarians are especially biased toward searching licensed databases. The portal to these databases is their library's website, where self-service access to scholarly, professional, and educational information resides, providing access not only to surrogate records but also to the actual sources themselves in the form of digital full-texts, media, or spatial and numeric data.

Quality information is expensive to produce, and database publishers expect payment from users for publishing, organizing, and making this information available online. Librarians would like to populate their library's website with just about every available quality database known to mankind, but they cannot due to the tremendous expense of negotiating licenses with database publishers and aggregators and subscribing to their licensed databases, so they scrutinize the wide range of available licensed databases, choosing ones that support the interests, preferences, and domain expertise of their libraries' user base. Increasingly, quality content is becoming available on the open Web as a result of the open access movement and the nature of the World Wide Web itself as a low-cost distribution technology.

Underlining the distinctions between librarians and everyday people seeking information is Roy Tennant's oft-cited quip, "Only librarians like to search, everyone else likes to find" (Tennant 2004). I believe that Roy was right about librarians liking to search. Librarians memorize the searching languages of the databases and search systems they use repeatedly on the job and rely on their favorite language as a springboard to understanding a new database's searching language. Unfortunately, their efforts to teach end users how to become expert searchers have always failed (Bates, Wilde, and Siegfried 1995); in fact, studies demonstrate that hardly anyone except for librarians uses searching languages (Jansen and Spink 2006; Jansen, Spink, and Saracevic 2000; Vakkari, Pennanen, and Serola 2003).

I believe that Roy got the second part wrong—people don't want to find; they want to *know*. In fact, they want to know immediately—right there on the spot and without a moment's hesitation—so they can put the information to work, completing the task that prompted them to pause and search for information in the first place. Before people approach librarians, they search many other sources—friends, family members, their personal libraries, Google, Wikipedia, and the Web—for answers to their questions (Fast and Campbell 2004; Head 2007; Kolowich 2011). Some give up along the way, and others persevere. When they ask you—the librarian—to help them, they are approaching you almost as a last resort. Their focus won't be on how you answer their questions; it will be on the *answers you find* to their questions. A few people might want to know how you found the answer, but they won't necessarily attend to online searching details in ways that will enable them to become better searchers. As an expert intermediary searcher, you will walk a curious tightrope, interacting with people who want you to find answers to their questions but restrained about just how much detail you should reveal to them about how you found the answers and whether you should offer to show them online searching basics right there and then that would help to make them better online searchers. The purpose of *Online Searching* is to teach you how to become an expert intermediary searcher who finds quality information online efficiently and effectively so that you can help library users satisfy their information needs.

Chapter 1 sets the stage, describing how and why scholarly information is split between the open Web and licensed databases. Chapter 2 introduces you to the library's website, where end users access scholarly, educational, and professional information online. The next ten chapters (3 to 12) are organized according to the seven steps of the online searching process:

1. Conducting the reference interview, where you determine what the user really wants (i.e., the negotiated query; chapter 3)
2. Selecting a relevant database (chapter 4)
3. Typecasting the negotiated query as a subject or known-item (chapter 5)
4. Conducting a facet analysis and logical combination of the negotiated query (chapter 5)
5. Representing the negotiated query as input to the search system (chapters 6 to 10)
6. Entering the search and responding strategically (chapter 11)
7. Displaying retrievals, assessing them, and responding tactically (chapter 12)

There are so many databases, search systems, and search engines that you cannot be an expert at searching every single one. To quickly come up to snuff, chapter 13 gives you a methodology called conducting a technical reading of a database. Use this methodology to quickly and efficiently familiarize yourself with a database and the system you'll use to search it.

Chapter 14 brings your reference-interview interaction with library users back into focus, where you enlist *their* assistance, making sure the search is on track and retrieving relevant information to satisfy their queries. Use this occasion to teach users something about information seeking so that they can put what they learn to work for themselves in the future. What and how much you teach them requires deliberation on your part, taking into consideration your mode of interaction, the nature of their inquiry, and your assessment of their motivation to learn something about information seeking in addition to answers to their questions. Chapter 15 discusses current online searching trends and issues, and it concludes with a wish list of improvements to today's search systems and databases.

The illustrations that preface selected chapters bear links to explanatory videos. Use a Web browser to navigate to these videos online. These videos are hardly three minutes long, and they capture the essence of that chapter's contents—important information about online searching that you should remember for as long as there are search systems, databases, and library users with information needs.

This book's contents will interest:

- *Students* in library and information studies (LIS) programs who are learning how to help library users satisfy their information needs

- *LIS faculty* who teach the school's online searching course—*this* is your textbook for the course
- *End users* who frequently seek information for serious pursuits and want to know expert searchers' secrets for finding information (you may be college seniors researching senior theses, graduate students researching master's theses and doctoral dissertations, faculty at colleges and universities, or professional-amateurs who are passionate about your avocations)
- *Practicing librarians* who want to upgrade their searching skills and knowledge

COVERAGE OF THIS EDITION

Additions to *Online Searching*'s second edition begin in chapter 1, with a discussion of the origins and genres of social media. Chapter 2 has been considerably revised, using the websites of an academic library (University Library of the University of Illinois at Urbana–Champaign) and a public library (Los Angeles Public Library) to orient you to the wide range of search tools available for identifying sources that have the potential to answer the user's query. Additionally, this revised chapter 2 downplays the distinction between licensed and open access resources in favor of showcasing the library's "everything" search and being explicit about the systems and services that the various players in the information industry market to libraries that make these search tools possible. Added to chapter 3 is a categorization of the queries that users posit to reference librarians, so that you can anticipate which types of queries users are likely to ask you and which are likely to involve online searching. Editorial control is a new dimension in chapter 4's classification of databases, and it is there to remind you to encourage users to perform a critical evaluation of the information they derive from sources in which editorial control is absent. Considerably expanded is chapter 5's discussion of typecasting negotiated queries to ease your transition from presearch preparation to actual online searching. Concluding chapter 5 are new questions and answers to give you experience with the three simultaneous steps of the searching process—typecasting, database selection, and facet analysis and logical combination.

Entirely new in chapters 6, 7, and 8 are demonstrations of how databases are structured for controlled vocabulary (CV) searching, free text (FT) searching, and extended-Boolean searching, respectively. Use these chapters' sample seven-record database, indexes, and queries to perform information retrieval manually. Doing so, you'll understand how online systems respond with relevant retrievals to the search statements you and end users enter into them. In fact, these demonstrations are like opening up the hood and turning over the engine to see what powers your car. Also new to these chapters are discussions of the classic and discovery interfaces of online public access catalogs (OPACs) and which type of searching (e.g., CV, FT, extended-Boolean) is most effective for subject and known-item queries. *Online Searching*'s discussion of FT searching spans two chapters now to focus attention on FT searching of Boolean search systems (chapter 7) and FT searching of such extended-Boolean systems as web search engines, web-scale discovery (WSD) systems, and the OPAC's discovery interface (chapter 8).

Chapter 9 is now emphatic about which CV and FT search features are most efficient for conducting searches that target the one known-item that interests the user. Added are discussions about how digital object identifiers (DOIs) and Open Researcher and Contributor IDs (ORCIDs) figure into known-item searching. Updated are chapter 10's real-life examples of how publication-level and article-level metrics are used to assess research impact. Also added to this chapter are discussions of the specialized and mainstream social networking websites that domain experts use to promote their research, teaching, and services activities. A slightly modified chapter 11 has new search examples for selected strategies. The idea of enhancing chapter 12's tactics table with evaluation tactics comes from Alistair Smith's comprehensive search-tactics literature review, but the actual tactics themselves have been extracted from an empirical study of the criteria searchers use to evaluate information from the Web that my Michigan colleagues and I conducted earlier in this decade (Markey, Leeder, and Rieh 2014). Chapter 13's technical reading has been simplified so that busy reference librarians need only answer three or four important questions about a database and its search system to familiarize themselves with them. The most important modification to chapter 14 is the integration of known-item searching into the discussion of which online searching content is appropriate to teach to end users. Chapter 15's future functionality wish list bears additional features for CV searching and database selection, and its trends and issues have been reworked so that the fake news epidemic becomes a driving force for librarians to redouble their information literacy efforts with end users.

Online searching resides in the crosshairs of technology, where the pace of change is rapid, sudden, and sometimes only a heartbeat away. Be prepared for changes to database interfaces, contents, and search system functionality. Such changes are always likely, and they will affect this book's screenshots of a database or its descriptions of a particular system's features. Such changes also mean that you will find yourself running in place—struggling to keep up with changes to databases and search systems and reflecting them in the instruction you provide to your library's users. What won't change about online searching is the really hard stuff: conducting a successful reference interview in which you gain an understanding of the gap in another person's knowledge that is the impetus for his asking you for help, transforming this into search statements that retrieve relevant information, advising the person about his ongoing search so that he isn't overwhelmed with too much information, and knowing just how far afield you can go in terms of leaving each and every user with at least one information-literacy-oriented tip above and beyond the information that answers their questions so they can apply what they learn to further the search in hand and improve their future searches.

WELCOME TO ONLINE SEARCHING!

As an expert intermediary searcher, you are the linchpin between library users with information needs and useful information that satisfies them. This is a challenging task but one you will be ready to take on as a result of reading this book, searching online to find answers to its many end-of-chapter questions, comparing what you did with the answers given, and sharing what you learn about online searching with your instructor and fellow classmates in class discussions. Let's get started!

BIBLIOGRAPHY

Bates, Marcia J., Deborah N. Wilde, and Susan Siegfried. 1995. "Research Practices of Humanities Scholars in an Online Environment: The Getty Online Searching Project Report No. 3." *Library and Information Science Research* 17 (Winter): 5–40.

Fast, Karl V., and D. Grant Campbell. 2004. "'I Still Like Google': University Student Perceptions of Searching OPACs and the Web." *Proceedings of the ASIS Annual Meeting* 41: 138–46.

Head, Alison J. 2007. "How Do Students Conduct Academic Research?" *First Monday* 12, no. 8. http://firstmonday.org/issues/issue12_8/head/index.

Jansen, Bernard J., and Amanda Spink. 2006. "How Are We Searching the World Wide Web? A Comparison of Nine Search Engine Transaction Logs." *Information Processing and Management* 42, no. 1: 248–63.

Jansen, Bernard J., Amanda Spink, and Tefko Saracevic. 2000. "Real Life, Real Users, and Real Needs: A Study and Analysis of User Queries on the Web." *Information Processing and Management* 36, no. 2: 207–27.

Kolowich, Steve. 2011. "What Students Don't Know." *Inside Higher Education.* http://www .insidehighered.com/news/2011/08//22.

Markey, Karen, Chris Leeder, and Soo Young Rieh. 2014. *Designing Online Information Literacy Games Students Want to Play.* Lanham, MD: Rowman & Littlefield.

Tennant, Roy. 2004. "Five Easy Pieces." *Library Journal* 129, no. 19 (November 15): 25.

Vakkari, Pertti, Mikko Pennanen, and Sami Serola. 2003. "Changes of Search Terms and Tactics while Writing a Research Proposal: A Longitudinal Case Study." *Information Processing and Management* 39, no. 3: 445–63.

Acknowledgments

Despite the passing of more than forty years, I recall the first time that I saw online searching in action. At the time, research was a tedious, time-consuming, and manual process to which researchers dedicated whole days, pawing manually through print indexes and reading hundreds of titles listed under a subject heading in the hope of finding something related to their interests. I worked at the Milton S. Eisenhower Library of the Johns Hopkins University, where our science librarian, the late Edward Terry, was in charge of the library's new online searching services. Ed sat at a computer terminal that was the size of a small desk and showed me how to conduct a facet analysis and combine facets with Boolean operators. Then he put these to work, demonstrating an online search and accomplishing in fifteen minutes that which took a researcher fifteen hours to do. It was nothing short of a miracle! Earning my master's degree in library science at Syracuse University two years later, my teacher, Professor Pauline Cochrane, was one of the first to offer a course in online searching. Students learned how to search the Dialog and Orbit search systems. Pauline gave me a password to test-drive the new BRS search system, and our class visited the law library where a librarian demonstrated the brand-new Lexis search system on a dedicated terminal with special key caps that executed system commands. I am indebted to both Ed and Pauline for getting me started in online searching, an area that has always been at the core of my research and teaching.

Over the years, various book editors have asked me to write a textbook on online searching. As much as I've wanted to write it, I've declined due to the various research projects on my plate. Executive Editor Charles Harmon at Rowman & Littlefield was particularly persistent, but he was also patient and deliberate, approaching me minus the pressure and urgency that I felt from other editors. Finally, I decided the time was right for me to put *Online Searching* on my plate. Throughout both the first- and second-edition writing projects, Charles has been immediate and frank in his responses to my inquiries, his words of encouragement come at the right time, and his suggestions for breaching an impasse are always spot-on. What a pleasure it has been to work with Charles! Also at Rowman & Littlefield, thanks to Michael Tan and Andrew Yoder, who assisted in final editing and production work. My gratitude also goes to Penny Duke, who shouldered the lion's share of the proofing burden so that I could focus on indexing and last-minute substantive issues.

Grateful thanks to William H. Mischo, engineering librarian at the University of Illinois at Urbana–Champaign, who demonstrated Easy Search to me, encouraged my enthusiasm about using Easy Search as a search tool example in *Online Searching*, and shared his knowledge of new information-retrieval tools in the research and development pipeline. Heaps of gratitude go to my University of Michigan (U-M) Library colleagues. So many times I have consulted Librarian Kathleen M. Folger, the U-M Library's chief electronic resources officer, about a wide range of issues, ideas, and facts pertaining to databases and search systems. Her assistance has also been crucial for putting my screenshot-permission requests into the right hands of this and that database publisher and search system supplier. Associate Librarian Shevon Desai, Librarian Karen E. Downing, and Librarian Charles G. Ransom sent me ideas for search topics, and I was inspired by the guest lectures U-M Librarians Kathleen Folger and Scott Dennis gave to my students in SI 620, Collection Development, that overlapped onto online searching. Thanks to the U-M Library's Web systems manager, Kenneth J. Varnum, who walked me through the U-M's new "everything" interface and answered my many questions about its implementation. Worth its weight in gold has been the University of Michigan's Ask-a-Librarian service, with its many nameless, faceless librarians available at the touch of a keystroke via email and chat who have answered my particularly vexing questions about this and that database. Thanks also to City Librarian Director John Szabo and Public Relations and Marketing Director Peter Persic at the Los Angeles Public Library (LAPL), who let me showcase LAPL's website.

For graciously sharing their time and expertise, I thank my colleagues in the U-M's School of Information, especially Clinical Associate Professor Kristin Fontichiaro, Associate Professor Soo Young Rieh, and Associate Professor Qiaozhu Mei, who read selected chapters and gave me useful and thoughtful comments that I put to work to improve the book's content. I salute Christopher Hebblethwaite, coordinator of reference services at SUNY Oswego, who shared search topics and chat transcripts. Serving as a sounding board have been my students in SI 665, Online Searching and Databases, who gave me their reactions to various ideas, with Martha Stuit taking notes for me during class so that I could revisit student input later. On the U-M home front have been our school's staff members, Deborah Apsley, Heidi Skrzypek, Nickie Rowsey, Stacy Callahan, and Barbara Smith, who were important sources of information about the various resources available to me that streamlined writing, editing, and production tasks, and Michael Emery at our school's Neighborhood ITS, who quickly solves all problems related to computers, printers, and connectivity.

Thanks to Cliff Lampe, professor at the University of Michigan, and Darren Gergle, professor at Northwestern University, for being good sports about the comparison of their publication records in the Google Scholar, Scopus, and Web of Science databases. That I am able to showcase research impact metrics in a real-life example makes these metrics more salient and vivid to aspiring expert searchers, whose superiors will soon task them with comparable analyses.

Chock full of screenshots from a wide range of search systems and databases, *Online Searching* both shows and tells how to search online effectively and efficiently. I am grateful to the many publisher, database, and search system representatives who gave me permission to screenshot their online products and services. At EBSCO Information Services, Karen Hedge, Joel Pratt, and Paige Riordan gave me carte blanche to showcase the EBSCOhost search system. Sheila Harris, Heidi Prior, and Ryan W. Roberts at Gale Cengage Learning were also very flexible about me using screenshots to showcase their search systems and databases. Truly, I have been heartened by the positive reception that my screenshot-permission inquiries received and want to convey my gratitude to so many more representatives: William Whalen at Alexander Street Press; Timothy Otto and Jeffrey Clovis at Clarivate Analytics; Barry Bermudez at the Cornell Lab of Ornithology; Rebecca W. Brown and Elizabeth Dyas at Elsevier B.V.; Eric Larson and Nate Vack at Gimlet; Ann Della Porta at the Library of Congress; Fred Marks at Marquis Who's Who; Kimberly Bastian, Corye L. Bradbury, Kim Kimiecik, Lisa McDonald, and Paul Webb at ProQuest; Steven Swartz and Juan Vasquez at SimplyAnalytics; Kate Hutchens at the Special Collections Research Center of the University of Michigan Library; Lynne Raughley at the University of Michigan Library; and Georgiana Gomez and Douglas Ballman at the USC Shoah Foundation.

Bolstering *Online Searching*'s graphical presentation of online searching is its many figures that TattleTail Design executed with care, precision, and attention to detail. Thanks to the Noun Project's (http://thenounproject.com) library of symbols that streamlined TattleTail's production. Especially compelling is *Online Searching*'s series of explanatory videos. Created by Studio Librarian Emily Thompson at the University of Tennessee at Chattanooga, the videos capture the essence of the reference interview, controlled vocabulary, free text searching, and other important online searching concepts and distill them into two-minute videos. A graduate of the U-M's School of Information, Emily has built on what she learned in my Online Searching class almost a decade ago, drawing on her experience as a reference librarian and masterfully applying her creative abilities to telling stories about difficult technical concepts in visual terms so that they are easy for aspiring expert searchers to understand.

1

Online Searching in the Age of the Information Explosion

For most everyday people, online searching means querying Google and the World Wide Web for information. This scenario is actually comparatively new, evolving over the last fifteen to twenty years in response to the rapid growth of web-based information. Online searching has a more than fifty-year history, stretching back to the Cold War, when Eastern and Western Blocs invested heavily in education, science, and technology to keep pace with each other and to keep each other militarily at bay. In the West, the investment gave birth to an information explosion. Scientists and scholars churned out new publications at a record pace, overwhelming librarians, whose nineteenth-century technologies—card files, book indexes, printed loose-leaf services—bogged down under the sheer numbers of new publications issued by science, technology, and scholarly publishers.

This first chapter looks backward at these and other factors that gave rise to online searching to harness the information explosion and forward to advances in new technology that have steered online searching onto its present course. On the surface, online searching seems as simple as one-stop searching in a Web search engine, but it is actually more complicated due to a whole host of factors that collided, resulting in two parallel streams of online searching development and fracturing access to information along quality lines, ranging from scholarship that undergoes rigorous peer review and editorial scrutiny to popular culture tidbits, unsubstantiated hearsay, anonymous postings, speculation, and rumor. How the people you help will put to work the information you find for them affects your decision about which stream of information you should dip into for answers to their questions.

SEARCHING FOR INFORMATION BEFORE COMPUTERS, THE INTERNET, AND THE WORLD WIDE WEB

During the 1960s, the phrase "information explosion" became commonplace for describing the rapid increase in the amount of information available to people from all walks of life (Emrich 1970). Back then, the Cold War was the impetus for the rapid increase in information (Hayes 2010). The heavy investments that Eastern and Western Blocs made in education, science, and technology were first and foremost meant to channel new discoveries into the arms and space races; however, the payoffs were more varied and far-reaching in the West, where investments led to increased student enrollment in colleges and universities, the rise of new private-sector industries, the emergence of new disciplines at the academy, the availability of new jobs for highly qualified graduates, and eventually more discoveries made by scientists and scholars in industry and the academy. Fueling the cycle of discovery and the information explosion generally was the free flow of information, in which scientists and scholars disseminated details about their discoveries in not-so-free scholarly publications.

Searching for Information before Computers

While the production of new knowledge was at an all-time high before computers, keeping abreast of the latest discoveries and finding information generally was tedious, boring, and tremendously time consuming. Let's flash back to the mid-1960s to find out what it *was* like. Your topic is "escape systems from earth-orbital vehicles in emergency situations." You visit the university library; plunk yourself down in a chair at a desk lined with rows and rows of book-length indexes, usually one thick, heavy volume for a year's worth of scholarly publishing on a subject; reach for the volume for 1966, the most recent year; and open it to the Es. Thankfully, "Escape Systems" is an index term. Next, you scan titles listed under this term to determine whether they discuss your topic. Finding no promising titles in the 1966 volume, you grab the 1965, 1964, 1963, and as many volumes as you need until you find enough sources with promising titles. By the way, finding these titles is just the beginning. You have to *write down* (there were no personal computers back in the 1960s!) each title's citation, search the library catalog to see if the library subscribes to the journal, then fetch the right volume from the library bookshelves for the article. If the journal volumes you want are in circulation, you have to start all over again or wait until the borrower returns them.

The Birth of Online Searching

Funding research and development in search of more efficient ways to retrieve relevant information was the US Department of Defense's Advanced Research Projects Agency (ARPA) that issued a request for proposal (RFP) for the development of computer-based online search systems. Lockheed Missiles and Space Company received ARPA funding and gave birth to Dialog, one of the first online search systems. Lockheed implemented Dialog on NASA computers, where it searched a database of citations on foreign technology, defense, and space research topics (Bourne 1980; Summit 2002).

By the early 1970s, Lockheed was exploring the commercial potential of its Dialog search system. Minus a database, search systems have nothing to search. Thus, the key to Lockheed's success was government service contracts from the US Office of Education, National Technical Information Service, National Agricultural Library, and National Library of Medicine that supported the development of the ERIC, NTIS, Agricola, and Medline databases, respectively (Bourne 1980). Over time, the number of databases grew through the efforts of for-profit companies and learned and professional societies that converted their card catalogs, book indexes, and loose-leaf services to databases and licensed them to Lockheed and its competitors.

Online Searching: Initially the Domain of Expert Intermediary Searchers

By the end of the 1970s, Lockheed, System Development Company (SDC), and Bibliographic Retrieval Services (BRS) had become database aggregators, hosting databases from a variety of database publishers and marketing online searching of these databases through their Dialog, Orbit, and BRS search systems, respectively, to libraries and information centers (Björner and Ardito 2003). Only librarians who were expert intermediary searchers were authorized to use these search systems for these reasons:

- Special training was necessary because each search system had its own searching language that operated within a terse command-line interface.
- Online searching was a high-cost enterprise that involved the purchase and maintenance of computer equipment and supplies that few people could afford.
- Search systems billed librarians for every search they conducted, and to pay for these services, librarians had to pass much of the cost of the enterprise on to people who used the services.

Online searching eliminated the most tedious, boring, and time-consuming elements of the task—consulting year after year of book indexes and writing down citations. It also increased the efficiency and accuracy of the results. Manual searches had been limited to the searcher consulting one index term at a time (e.g., "Escape Systems") and visually scanning for text that indicated a citation's coverage of the more complex topic (i.e., "escape systems from earth-orbital vehicles in emergency situations"). In one fell swoop, computers could now search for surrogates bearing multiple index terms (i.e., "Escape Systems," "Earth-Orbital Vehicles," and "Emergencies"), ensuring that retrievals covered all major concepts of the complex topic. This was an almost immeasurable improvement of online searching over manual searching!

The First Search Systems for Everyday People

It wasn't until the early to mid-1980s that everyday people could perform their own searches, first through the library's online public access catalog (OPAC) that accessed its book collection (Markey 1984) and later through the library's CD-ROM search systems that accessed many of the same databases that expert intermediary searchers accessed through the Dialog, Orbit, and BRS search systems (Mischo and Lee 1987).

Back then, search systems had terse, command-line interfaces (Hildreth 1983). They were difficult to search, but it didn't matter to end users. They lined up to search these systems, and even if their searches were not as sophisticated or their results as precise as expert searchers' searches for the same topics, *end users* wanted to conduct online searches *on their own* (Mischo and Lee 1987).

THE ERA OF THE INTERNET AND THE WORLD WIDE WEB BEGINS

The Cold War was also the impetus for the Internet. In the 1960s, scientists and military strategists worried that a Soviet attack could wipe out the nation's telephone system. In 1962, computer scientist J. C. R. Licklider proposed a solution in the form of an "intergalactic network of computers" that would continue working even if attacks on one or more computers succeeded (Hafner and Lyon 1996, 38). ARPA, the same US agency that funded the development of the earliest search systems, funded the building of such a network and named it ARPANET. From the 1970s through the 1990s, scientists in the United States and around the world routinely used ARPANET and its successor, NSFNET, to send messages, share files, and conduct their research on the network's supercomputers.

In the late 1980s, computer scientist Tim Berners-Lee envisioned an online information space where information stored across the vast network of interlinked computers (i.e., the Internet) could be shared with anyone anywhere (Berners-Lee 1999). By the early 1990s, he had prototyped a suite of tools that transformed his vision into reality. Ensuring the success of Berners-Lee's new invention that he called the World Wide Web were computer enthusiasts who set up Web servers, populated them with hypertext documents, and developed free Web browsers that people could use to surf the Web.

Technology Spawns New Communication Paradigms

For everyday people, the Web and the Internet generally gave birth to a *revolution* in human communication. Before their invention, everyday people interacted with one another via the *one-to-one* communication paradigm—writing letters, making phone calls, sending telegrams, or conversing face to face. The *one-to-many* communication paradigm was off-limits to everyday people because of the tremendous expense involved with this paradigm. It was the domain of powerful, deep-pocketed gatekeepers—book, journal, and newspaper publishers; local and national radio and television broadcasters; and film and game production studios—who decided the content the "many" would read, watch, listen to, and play based on their careful assessments of the content's marketability.

The invention of the World Wide Web changed everything, making it possible for *anyone* to publish directly to the Web and communicate almost instantaneously with potentially hundreds, thousands, and even millions of people. By the turn of the century, Web 2.0 introduced a new Web design and development philosophy that spawned entirely new modes of *many-to-many* communication, now called social media platforms. Today's successful social media platforms—Facebook, Twitter, Flickr, YouTube, Reddit, and Instagram—trace their origins to loosely knit groups of like-minded friends, hobbyists, and computer buffs who seized on the informal and ephemeral activities of everyday life—talking to friends, leaving phone messages, showing snapshots, watching home movies, and sending postcards—to solve their information needs, find content, and develop knowledge and expertise. With so many new and compelling ways for both individuals and groups to express themselves and interact with others, the Web grew at an astonishing rate over its twenty-five-year existence, and it is now the dominant communications medium on the planet.

Searching for Information on the World Wide Web

Initially, finding useful information meant clicking on a series of Web page links until you found something of interest. Some people published their saved links, and the popularity of their websites encouraged teams of editors to browse the Web in search of quality websites and share their recommendations in the form of Web directories. Although a few such directories continue to the present day (pages 264 to 265), they were quickly overshadowed by Web search engines that indexed Web content automatically, dispatching Web spiders (also called Web crawlers) to navigate the links between Web pages, finding and indexing new Web content. Their search interfaces consisted of a search box into which people entered words and phrases that described their interests, and they retrieved Web pages bearing these words and phrases.

In the Web's first decade of existence, no one particular search engine was favored by a majority of Web users for longer than a year or two. That all changed in the new millennium, when the Google Web search engine rose to prominence, topping the most-popular list, where it still stands today. Google's initial success at achieving better search results was a result of its PageRank innovation that ranked retrieved Web pages based on the number and quality of Web pages that linked to them.

By the start of the new millennium's second decade, two types of social media platforms had emerged as useful sources of information, knowledge, and expertise: *social network sites*, such as Facebook, Twitter, LinkedIn, and ResearchGate, that encourage interpersonal communication between individuals or groups, and *user-generated content sites*, such as Flickr, YouTube, Wikipedia, Reddit, and GarageBand, where people share text- and media-based content. Compared to search engines, social media got a later start under Web 2.0 technologies, and thus, we can expect a shaking-down period in which both social media types and sites rise and fall in response to user needs.

The Library's Response to the Web's Popularity

Everyday people searched the Web right from the start. The reason was that the Web began a full decade after the personal computer (PC) revolution. People were familiar with PCs as a result of using them at school or on the job, and by the time the Web got started in the early 1990s, PCs were being marketed as an affordable household consumer electronics device. Replacing the PC's command-line interfaces were graphical user interfaces (GUIs) that increased their overall usability.

Noticing that the number of Web queries far surpassed the number of OPAC queries, librarians reluctantly admitted that the Web search engine and the Web had become the search system and database of choice, respectively, for many everyday people seeking information, supplanting the library's longtime role in this regard (Donlan and Carlin 2007; Fast and Campbell 2004; Yu and Young 2004). To win users back, librarians gutted their OPAC's command-line interface in favor of Web browser technology and put pressure on database publishers to phase out CD-ROMs in favor of web-based search systems. It didn't take long for academic and public libraries to transform themselves into places that users could visit physically or virtually through their websites, where scholarly, professional, and educational information resides, not only for access to surrogate records but also for access to the actual sources themselves in the form of digital full-texts, media, or spatial and numeric data. Taking a back seat to searching is the library's social media presence, most useful for maintaining the library's salience among its users regarding resources, programs, facilities, and news (Winn et al. 2017).

Especially in academic libraries, users have found the sheer number of search systems and databases daunting (King 2008). An alternative is the web-scale discovery (WSD) system, one-stop shopping for academic information. Into a Google-like search box users enter their search statement, and the WSD system searches a humongous index bearing content from a wide variety of quality databases. WSD systems are a cutting-edge development for libraries—the new Google for academic content.

THE EROSION OF EDITORIAL OVERSIGHT IN THE ERA OF THE WORLD WIDE WEB

In summer 1993, not long after the Web's inception, *The New Yorker* published a cartoon showing two dogs, one sitting on the floor looking up at the other seated at a PC, saying, "On the Internet, nobody knows you're a dog" (Wikipedia contributors 2018).

Although several interpretations are possible, I have always felt that this cartoon underlines the danger of blindly accepting anything you read on the Web at face value because *anyone* can publish there. That anyone can publish on the Web with a modest investment in the right technology is both a blessing and a curse. With regard to the former, people who want to broadcast messages are able to have their say and reach anyone who cares to read, listen, watch, or play. With regard to the latter, it means that the recipients of web-based communications have to judge for themselves whether the information is trustworthy because there is no guarantee that such gatekeepers as editors, publishers, peer reviewers, broadcasters, or producers are involved in the publication process, making sure authors have the right credentials to communicate their messages and reviewing what they say for accuracy, reliability, and objectivity.

Despite warnings from educators, librarians, and even the mainstream news media about the need to evaluate web-based information, most people pay lip service to evaluation, telling anyone who asks that they recognize its importance. In practice, if people evaluate web-based sources at all, they do so in a cursory manner (Julien and Barker 2009; Metzger 2007). At the time of the 2016 US presidential election, a Pew Research study reported that more Americans (62 percent) got their news on the Web from social media than from traditional, editorial-based news outlets (Gottfried and Shearer 2016). A few months later, the fake news phenomenon erupted (Spohr 2017), not only shocking Americans but also reverberating around the world, zapping people's trust in the people who make, report, and broadcast the news. The issue isn't limited to social media but extends to the world's most established media outlets, particularly where those outlets fall on the political bias spectrum.

Librarians have known for a long time that people sidestep evaluation. In response, librarians have chosen search systems and databases that are safe havens from fake news, misinformation, and fabrication because editors, publishers, peer reviewers, broadcasters, or producers select the information that goes into them and librarians evaluate whether these search systems and databases contain information that is appropriate for their users. Librarians especially scrutinize these resources because access to them isn't free; in fact, according to Kathleen M. Folger, chief electronic resources officer at the University of Michigan (U-M) Library, the largest libraries may pay tens of millions of dollars for safe-haven resources. Thus, librarians want to make sure that what they select and pay for is a good match with their library users' needs and interests.

Librarians negotiate licenses with publishers and aggregators that require them to put authentication procedures in place to allow access to search systems and databases only for their library's cardholders. Thus, when you link from your library's website to one or more specific databases, you are asked to authenticate yourself as a library cardholder by entering your username and password. *Online Searching* refers to the databases at the library's website as "licensed databases," and to the online space in which they reside as the "licensed Web."

If it seems like the publishers of licensed databases are overly concerned about unauthenticated uses of their databases, *they are*, and with good reason. Databases are costly to produce, update, and maintain, and the search systems that access them are costly to build, improve, maintain, and support 365 days a year. Thus, in the absence of license fees, publishers would go out of business.

Not all scholarly, professional, and educational databases require authentication through the library's website. Some are available free of charge on the open Web to anyone with a Web browser and Internet connection. Their publishers realize that access to information has the potential to push back the frontiers of knowledge and improve the quality of life for all, so they make their databases freely available to anyone on the Web. Ultimately, someone has to pay the bills, and thus most open Web databases are funded by governments, foundations, and for- and nonprofit organizations. Librarians add links from their websites to many open Web databases, but before they do, they evaluate them to make sure they provide quality information.

By the midnoughties, both Google and Microsoft had applied their search engines to scholarly, professional, and educational information through their Google Scholar and Microsoft Academic databases, respectively. Searching and displaying retrieved surrogates is free. The moment you click to display a full-text, you enter the licensed Web, where the database publisher's system pops up, asking you to enter your credit card to purchase the source outright or rent it for a limited period of time. Had you initiated your search through your library's website or its WSD system and then retrieved these sources, their full-texts would be free. Of course, the full-texts really *aren't* free. The licenses your library has negotiated with publishers gives you and other library cardholders unrestricted access to scholarly, professional, and educational information. The bottom line is that libraries *subsidize access to quality information* for their institution's users. When you use your library's website or its WSD system, you authenticate yourself, and access to whatever you retrieve appears to be free.

Why Scholarship Isn't Free

As students progress from high school to college and beyond, they learn how to become domain experts in a discipline, profession, or trade. They read textbooks and assigned readings that verse them on the foundations of their chosen domains. Their instructors help them understand, interpret, and apply what they read and transition them to increasingly more difficult and challenging material. In labs, practicums, and internships, they experience firsthand what it is like to be domain experts. To complete assignments, students search for information that gives them ideas and increases the depths of their understanding of a topic. Becoming a domain expert means developing disciplinary knowledge, and for the time being, much disciplinary scholarship resides in the licensed Web, largely inaccessible to social media sites, Google, and Web search engines generally. Your job as librarian is to transition students from their reliance on the open Web to scholarly, professional, and educational information on the licensed Web.

Scholarship (also known as scholarly communication) is the process of sharing new discoveries, theories, ideas, information, and data. Its origins trace back five hundred years to the European Renaissance, when scholasticism gave way to science, technology, and humanism. Scholars wanted to meet like-minded scholars, share their ideas, and build on existing knowledge. They formed scholarly societies and published their research in society-sponsored journals that were issued periodically and distributed to society members. Thus, scholarly societies were exclusive, limiting the dissemination of new knowledge to their own members.

Loosening up scholarship's exclusivity in the United States was a series of events, beginning with the Morrill Land-Grants Acts. Passed by the US Congress in 1862 and 1880, the acts funded universities, required university faculties to conduct research that benefited society, and fueled a surge in the establishment of new publishing venues by both public and private sectors. When the Second World War ended in 1945, veterans cashed in their GI Bill benefits and swamped college campuses, where faculty shortages led universities to embrace tenure to attract faculty and to establish formal promotion and tenure-review processes to select the best faculty. Faculty cashed in, too, competing for federal grants that funded their research and included tuition and living support for the doctoral students who worked on their research teams.

Pressured by the insatiable demands of promotion and tenure committees, faculty publications surged, feeding the demand for new publication venues and swamping editorial offices with journal manuscripts. Commercial publishers realized the opportunity to make a profit, launching new journals and negotiating with university presses and scholarly societies to conduct the business of their scholarly publications. Eventually, commercial publishers gained control of the academic marketplace and increased the cost of journal subscriptions many times over the cost of inflation (Cummings et al. 1992; Guédon 2001; Lynch 1992). Librarians dubbed this a "crisis in scholarly communications" and responded by cutting journal subscriptions and complaining to anyone who would listen that the academy pays several times over for scholarship that emanates from the very place where it is born (Edwards and Shulenburger 2003; Guédon 2001). Let's examine the scholarly publishing cycle to see what motivates their complaints.

At the academy, faculty pursue their research agendas, reading the latest research from sources at the library's website, which helps them generate ideas for research proposals. The academy pays faculty salaries. Some larger grants pay a percentage of the faculty members' work effort, and most grants pay doctoral-student tuition and living support. Faculty seek the most prestigious journals in which to report their research findings because promotion and tenure committees give greater weight to such communication venues.

Faculty submit their manuscripts via a journal management system (JMS) to an unpaid journal editor, who is usually a full-time faculty member at a college or university and whose recompense for serving as editor is the full or partial fulfillment of their institution's service or research commitment. The journal editor uses the JMS to send manuscripts to unpaid peer reviewers, who are also full-time faculty members at a college or university and whose recompense for serving as reviewers partially fulfills their institution's service commitment. Based on one or more reviews for a submitted manuscript, journal editors make decisions about whether to accept or reject the manuscript, including acceptance that is contingent on the author making reviewer-suggested revisions. Accepted manuscripts are already in digital form, so all that remains is for the journal publisher's production assistant to format the article, insert author-supplied figures and tables, and convert the manuscript into the journal's particular style and design. Journal publishers release new full-text issues of journals bearing faculty-authored articles to database publishers, who append full-texts with surrogates bearing citations, index terms, and abstracts. Database publishers license database aggregators to offer online searching of their databases to libraries, or the database publishers themselves offer online searching of their database(s) directly to libraries. Libraries negotiate licenses with database publishers and aggregators so library users can search online databases.

The scholarly publishing cycle has now come full circle, returning to the starting point, where faculty pursue their research agendas, reading the latest research at the library's website, which helps them generate ideas for new research proposals (figure 1.1). Indeed, the academy pays *four times* for scholarship—it pays the salaries of faculty who write the manuscripts, faculty who edit the journals, and faculty who review new manuscripts, and it pays publishers for full-texts that are the scholarship their faculty produce.

The Dream of Unrestricted Access to Scholarship: Open Access Movement

Librarians recognize that the academy pays multiple times for its own scholarship. For a time, librarians put their hopes into technology, thinking that it would lessen scholarly publishing costs for publishers and that publishers would pass the savings on to libraries. Contrary to expectations, publishers have continued to increase prices. Librarians have had little recourse, except to cut more journal subscriptions and licensed databases. Enraged by these cuts, scholars, scientists, and researchers joined librarians

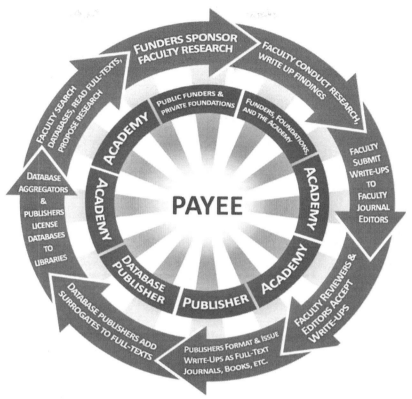

FIGURE 1.1
Scholarly Publishing Cycle

in the search for solutions to the crisis, giving birth to the open access movement, with the goal of unrestricted online access to scholarship.

The open access movement has spawned new publishing models that has thrust the academy into the scholarly publishing enterprise (Borgman 2007; Willinsky 2006). One such model involves the establishment of an institutional repository (IR), a combined search system and online database that a learning institution such as a college, university, or laboratory supports, and where institution members (e.g., faculty, students, researchers) archive digital materials that are the products of their teaching, research, learning, and/or service activities (Lynch 2003). IRs are now commonplace in academic institutions, and people can search them using the OAIster database (http://oaister.worldcat.org) or via Web search engines.

Another model involves the establishment of discipline-specific databases, where experts in a discipline, subject, or field of study archive digital materials that are the products of teaching, research, and service activities. Especially successful in this re-gard has been the arXiv database (http://arXiv.org), where domain experts in physics have contributed scholarship for more than a quarter-century. To defray the costs of hosting arXiv, Cornell University Library receives funding from the Simons Founda-tion and solicits membership fees from academic and research institutions around the world (arXiv 2018).

Dedicated to the open access movement, librarians have been proactive about encouraging faculty to negotiate with publishers, retaining some or all of their legal rights to distribute and use their published scholarship, including posting their pub-lished works on their professional websites and/or in their institutions' IRs. Enter-prising individuals, faculties, and entire research communities have established open access journals (OAJs). OAJs that do not receive financial sponsorship from colleges, universities, scholarly societies, laboratories, etc., levy fees on authors of accepted manuscripts to defray the costs associated with open access (e.g., Web servers, such journal identification numbers as ISSNs and DOIs, and production assistance).

Deciding Whether to Publish on the Licensed Web or Open Web

Since the first OAJs were established, researchers have studied whether scientists and scholars consult them and whether their contents are more likely to be cited than articles from traditional publishers. On both fronts, results are positive and encour-aging (Mischo and Schlembach 2011; Sotudeh, Ghasempour, and Yaghtin 2015); however, when it comes to prestige, traditional journals still hold sway (Nicholas et al. 2017; Tenopir et al. 2016). It may take a decade or more for OAJs to equal or surpass the prestige of traditional journals. Until the balance shifts from traditional publica-tions to OAJs, scientists and scholars are inclined to publish in the former, believing that their peers read and cite articles in their fields' most prestigious journals and that promotion and tenure committees weigh prestige over other factors pertaining to published scholarship. About the only event that could suddenly change the status quo would be legislative policies that mandate immediate publication of research findings that are the result of government funding in open access venues.

Faculty, researchers, and professional practitioners want to publish their scholar-ship in the most prestigious journals and conference proceedings (Lynch 1993). For the time being, these sources reside behind paywalls, where publishers profit from the direct sale of articles to individuals, and on the licensed Web, where libraries subsidize access for their cardholders. Searching the licensed Web is accomplished through your library's website and WSD system. Whether you are a librarian at an academic institu-tion, where students are studying to become experts in a field, subject, or discipline, or at a public library, where people's reasons for searching for information involves aca-demics and the serious personal business of handling their own or a family member's health and well-being, making decisions connected with their jobs, finding employment, and so on, you will want to solve their information needs by retrieving the best and most credible and accurate information for them. Thus, your starting point should be licensed Web resources. This does not mean you should ignore the Web entirely. Google and Wikipedia are great places for people to develop a working knowledge of a topic, and they use them as such (Colón-Aguirre and Fleming-May 2012; Garrison 2015; Head and Eisenberg 2010; Oxford University Press 2017). Additionally, Google Scholar and Microsoft Academic regularly index scholarship published in such open access vehicles as IRs, discipline-specific databases, and OAJs; thus, people who have no access to the licensed Web aren't entirely locked out of scholarly, professional, and educational information.

HIGH-QUALITY INFORMATION IS YOUR LIBRARY'S SPECIALTY

People prefer to conduct their own online searches, and when they reach an impasse, they are much more likely to ask a friend, a colleague, their instructor, or a family member for help than a librarian (Head and Eisenberg 2010; Markey, Leeder, and Rieh 2014; Thomas, Tewell, and Willson 2017). In fact, the librarian is usually the *last* person whom library users consult about their information needs (Beiser and Medaille 2016; Head and Eisenberg 2009). Some people even experience library anxiety, "an uncomfortable feeling or emotional disposition experienced in a library setting" (Onwuegbuzie, Jiao, and Bostick 2004, 25), that prevents them from approaching librarians for help. When library users ask librarians for help, they have probably exhausted the people they usually consult and have searched the open Web. Thus, librarians must be prepared to answer the most difficult questions people have.

People search the Web because it is easy, quick, and convenient (Fast and Campbell 2004; Lawrence 2015; Vinyard, Mullally, and Colvin 2017). They complain about how difficult it is to search the library's search systems and databases—they don't know which database to choose, they can't find the right keywords, they are stymied by their complex and bloated interfaces, they are overwhelmed with too many irrelevant retrievals, and they are stumped about how to narrow their topics (Colón-Aguirre and Fleming-May 2012; Head and Eisenberg 2010; Thomas, Tewell, and Willson 2017). Yet, people sense that the sources they find through the library's search systems are more credible, accurate, and reliable than open Web sources (Colón-Aguirre and Fleming-May 2012; Fast and Campbell 2004; Markey, Leeder, and Rieh 2014).

People want searching the library to resemble Google, consolidating multiple search systems and databases into a single interface, correcting their spelling, and responding with relevance-ranked retrievals to their natural-language queries. Libraries have responded by doing just that—deploying WSD systems that make the experience of searching licensed Web content resemble Google searching.

For the foreseeable future, most high-quality information will reside in the licensed Web. High-quality information *is* your library's specialty. Familiarize yourself with your library's search systems and databases so that, whenever you interact with library users, you know instantaneously which high-quality sources have the most potential for satisfying their information needs.

SUMMARY

This first chapter has a historical bent to it, looking backward at the factors that have given rise to online searching to harness the information explosion and forward to advances in new technology that have steered online searching onto its present course. Online searching was born to harness the information explosion that sparked new discoveries in science and technology to keep the United States and its Western Bloc allies militarily ahead of the Soviets during the Cold War. The first online search systems and databases were expensive and difficult to search, so their users were librarians, who were trained as expert intermediary searchers to search on behalf of others. It wasn't until the 1980s that library users could perform their own searches. Despite the difficulty of querying early search systems, users were delighted to search for information on their own.

The Internet is a byproduct of the Cold War. What made it so usable was Tim Berners-Lee's several inventions that gave birth to the World Wide Web. Infinitely more versatile than the printed page, the Web was an overnight success. Not only could people access information on the Web, but with a nominal investment in a computer, Internet connection, and Web browser, they also could become publishers, posting anything they wanted to say to the Web, communicating instantaneously with anyone who cared to read, listen, look, watch, play, share, or like their messages. Educators, librarians, and even the mainstream news media warned people about the need to evaluate web-based information because of the absence of editorial oversight. The Web grew so quickly that people relied on search engines to find relevant information.

By the early noughties, Google became the Web search engine of choice when the number of Google searches far outnumbered searches of the library's online search systems. This prompted librarians to improve their systems, going so far as to re-invent them in the image of Google with the deployment of WSD systems. On the heels of Google's popularity has come social media, transforming news consumption from a passive to an active medium. In only a dozen years, social media has become the go-to way the majority of Americans get their news. Social media puts the power of publishing and unlimited circulation in everyday people's hands. That social media has been implicated in the fake news phenomenon is due in part to the absence of editorial oversight and the rush to share breaking news with others before evaluating its credibility.

What distinguishes library- from web-based information is editorial oversight. Libraries load their search systems and databases with high-quality information that domain experts have written, their peers have reviewed, and scholarly publishers have issued. Editorial oversight is expensive. Despite the progress of the open access movement toward its goal of unrestricted online access to scholarship, most quality information resides behind paywalls in the licensed Web. Libraries subsidize access to the quality information in the licensed Web for their institution's users. Whether you are helping a youngster find information for a science fair project or a doctoral student conduct a thorough literature search, you will want to solve their information needs by retrieving the best, most credible, and accurate information. Thus, your starting point should be licensed Web resources—your library's gateway to high-quality information.

BIBLIOGRAPHY

arXiv. 2018. "arXiv Business Support and Governance Model." Accessed May 29, 2018. https://arxiv.org/help/support.

Beiser, Molly, and Ann Medaille. 2016. "How Do Students Get Help with Research Assignments? Using Drawings to Understand Students' Help Seeking Behavior." *Journal of Academic Librarianship* 42, no. 4: 390–400.

Berners-Lee, Tim. 1999. *Weaving the Web: The Original Design and Ultimate Destiny of the World Wide Web.* New York: HarperCollins.

Björner, Susanne, and Stephanie C. Ardito. 2003. "Early Pioneers Tell Their Stories, Part 2: Growth of the Online Industry." *Searcher* 11, no. 7 (Jul./Aug.): 52–61.

Borgman, Christine. 2007. *Scholarship in the Digital Age: Information, Infrastructure, and the Internet.* Cambridge, MA: MIT Press.

Bourne, Charles P. 1980. "On-line Systems: History, Technology, and Economics." *Journal of the American Society for Information Science* 31, no. 3: 155–60.

Colón-Aguirre, Mónica, and Rachel A. Fleming-May. 2012. "You Just Type in What You Are Looking For: Undergraduates' Use of Library Resources vs. Wikipedia." *Journal of Academic Librarianship* 38, no. 6: 391–99.

Cummings, Anthony, et al. 1992. *University Libraries and Scholarly Communication.* Washington, DC: Association of Research Libraries.

Donlan, Rebecca, and Ana Carlin. 2007. "A Sheep in Wolf's Clothing: Discovery Tools and the OPAC." *Reference Librarian* 48, no. 2: 67–71.

Edwards, Richard, and David Shulenburger. 2003. "The High Cost of Scholarly Journals (and What to Do about It)." *Change* 35, no. 6 (Nov./Dec.): 10–19. https://kuscholarworks.ku.edu/handle/1808/12546.

Emrich, Barry R. 1970. *Scientific and Technical Information Explosion*. Dayton, OH: Air Force Materials Laboratory, Wright-Patterson Air Force Base.

Fast, Karl V., and D. Grant Campbell. 2004. "'I Still Like Google': University Student Perceptions of Searching OPACs and the Web." *Proceedings of the ASIS Annual Meeting 2004* 41: 138–46.

Garrison, John C. 2015. "Getting a 'Quick Fix': First-Year College Students' Use of Wikipedia." *First Monday* 20, no. 10 (Oct.). http://firstmonday.org/ojs/index.php/fm/article/view/5401/5003.

Gottfried, Jeffrey, and Elisa Shearer. 2016. "News Use across Social Media Platforms." Accessed May 29, 2018. http://www.journalism.org/2016/05/26/news-use-across-social-media-platforms-2016/.

Guédon, Claude. 2001. "In Oldenburg's Long Shadow: Librarians, Research Scientists, Publishers and the Control of Scientific Publishing." Washington, DC: Association of Research Libraries. Accessed May 29, 2018. http://www.arl.org/storage/documents/publications/in-oldenburgs-long-shadow.pdf.

Hafner, Katie, and Matthew Lyon. 1996. *Where Wizards Stay Up Late: The Origins of the Internet*. New York: Touchstone.

Hayes, Robert M. 2010. "Library Automation: History." In *Encyclopedia of Library and Information Sciences*. 3rd ed. Vol. 11, pp. 3326–37. Boca Raton, FL: CRC Press.

Head, Alison J., and Michael B. Eisenberg. 2009. "How College Students Seek Information in the Digital Age." Accessed May 29, 2018. http://www.projectinfolit.org/uploads/2/7/5/4/27541717/pil_fall2009_finalv_yr1_12_2009v2.pdf.

———. 2010. "How Today's College Students Use Wikipedia for Course-Related Research." *First Monday* 15, no. 3. http://firstmonday.org/article/view/2830/2476.

Hildreth, Charles R. 1983. *Online Public Access Catalogs: The User Interface*. Dublin, OH: OCLC.

Julien, Heidi, and Susan Barker. 2009. "How High-School Students Find and Evaluate Scientific Information: A Basis for Information Literacy Skills Development." *Library and Information Science Research* 31, no. 1: 12–17.

King, Douglas. 2008. "Many Libraries Have Gone to Federated Searching to Win Users Back from Google. Is It Working?" *Journal of Electronic Resources and Librarianship* 20, no. 4: 213–27.

Lawrence, Kate. 2015. "Today's College Students: Skimmers, Scanners and Efficiency-Seekers." *Information Services & Use* 35: 89–93.

Lynch, Clifford. 1992. "Reaction, Response, and Realization: From the Crisis in Scholarly Communication to the Age of Networked Information." *Serials Review* 18, nos. 1/2 (Spring/Summer): 107–12.

———. 1993. "The Transformation of Scholarly Communication and the Role of the Library in the Age of Networked Information." *Serials Review* 23, nos. 3/4: 5–20.

———. 2003. "Institutional Repositories: Essential Infrastructure for Scholarship in the Digital Age." *portal: Libraries and the Academy* 3, no. 2: 327–36.

Markey, Karen. 1984. *Subject Searching in Library Catalogs.* Dublin, OH: OCLC.

Markey, Karen, Chris Leeder, and Soo Young Rieh. 2014. *Designing Online Information Literacy Games Students Want to Play.* Lanham, MD: Rowman & Littlefield.

Metzger, Miriam J. 2007. "Making Sense of Credibility on the Web: Models for Evaluating Online Information and Recommendations for Future Research." *Journal of the American Society for Information Science and Technology* 58, no. 13: 2078–91.

Mischo, William H., and Jounghyoun Lee. 1987. "End-User Searching of Bibliographic Databases." *Annual Review of Information Science & Technology* 22: 227–63.

Mischo, William H., and Mary C. Schlembach. 2011. "Open Access Issues and Engineering Faculty Attitudes and Practices." *Journal of Library Administration* 51, nos. 5/6: 432–54.

Nicholas, David, et al. 2017. "Early Career Researchers and Their Publishing and Authorship Practices." *Learned Information* 30: 205–17.

Onwuegbuzie, Anthony J., Qun G. Jiao, and Sharon L. Bostick. 2004. *Library Anxiety: Theory, Research, and Applications.* Lanham, MD: Scarecrow Press.

Oxford University Press. 2017. "Navigating Research: How Academic Users Understand, Discover, and Utilize Reference Resources." Accessed May 29, 2018. https://global.oup .com/academic/content/pdf/navigatingresearch.pdf.

Sotudeh, Hajar, Zahra Ghasempour, and Maryam Yaghtin. 2015. "The Citation Advantage of Author-Pays Model: The Case of Springer and Elsevier OA Journals." *Scientometrics* 104: 581–608.

Spohr, Dominic. 2017. "Fake News and Ideological Polarization: Filter Bubbles and Selective Exposure on Social Media." *Business Information Review* 34, no. 3: 150–60.

Summit, Roger. 2002. "Reflections of the Beginnings of Dialog: The Birth of Online Information Access." *Chronolog* (June): 1–2, 10.

Tenopir, Carol, et al. 2016. "What Motivates Authors of Scholarly Articles? The Importance of Journal Attributes and Potential Audience on Publication Choice." *Publications* 4, no. 3: 1–22. http://www.mdpi.com/2304-6775/4/3/22/htm.

Thomas, Susan, Eamon Tewell, and Gloria Willson. 2017. "Where Students Start and What They Do When They Get Stuck: A Qualitative Inquiry into Academic Information-Seeking and Help-Seeking Practices." *Journal of Academic Librarianship* 43, no. 3 (May): 224–31.

Vinyard, Mark, Colleen Mullally, and Jaimie Beth Colvin. 2017. "Why Do Students Seek Help in an Age of DIY? Using a Qualitative Approach to Look beyond Statistics." *Reference & User Services Quarterly* 56, no. 4 (Summer): 257–67.

Wikipedia contributors. 2018. "On the Internet, Nobody Knows You're a Dog." *Wikipedia, The Free Encyclopedia*. Accessed May 29, 2018. https://en.wikipedia.org/wiki/On_the_Internet,_nobody_knows_you%27re_a_dog.

Willinsky, John. 2006. *The Access Principle: The Case for Open Access to Research and Scholarship*. Cambridge, MA: MIT Press.

Winn, Dee, et al. 2017. "MTL 2.0: A Report on the Social Media Usage and User Engagement of the 'Big Four' Academic Libraries in Montréal." *Journal of Academic Librarianship* 43: 297–304.

Yu, Holly, and Margo Young. 2004. "The Impact of Web Search Engines on Subject Searching in OPAC." *Information Technology and Libraries* 23, no. 4 (Dec.): 168–80.

SUGGESTED READINGS

Gillies, James, and Robert Cailliau. 2000. *How the Web Was Born: The Story of the World Wide Web*. Oxford: Oxford University Press. A history of the World Wide Web, from its Cold War origins to the new millennium, just as Google begins to rise in popularity.

Lamphere, Carley. 2017. "Research 3.0." *Online Searcher* 41, no. 3 (May/June): 30–33. Encourages library users to leave the convenience and ease of Google searching for trusted sources on the licensed Web.

Van Dijck, José. 2013. *The Culture of Connectivity: A Critical History of Social Media*. New York: Oxford University Press. A history of social networking and online sociality.

2

Accessing Quality Information at the Library Website

Not limited to brick-and-mortar buildings anymore, libraries have an online presence in the form of a website, where they extend library services to users whether they are or aren't physically located in the library building, at any time of the day or night and every day of the year. Search is an important website service, and the search tools that libraries provide users at their websites depend on a variety of factors, such as the library's emphasis to access on physical or digital resources; its financial and staff resources for acquiring, deploying, and maintaining these tools; and the expectations that library users have for these tools, especially based on their experience with comparable web-based search tools.

Chapter 2 orients you to the search tools available at the library's website. The design of some search tools can be traced to the first computer applications in libraries, and others are recent developments due to users who want the search for library resources to resemble Google, where they search everything in one fell swoop and the most relevant retrievals are listed first. When it comes to search tools, librarians aren't going it alone. They depend on big-time players in the information industry, such as integrated library system vendors, journal publishers, database aggregators, and web-based discovery services. You can rest assured that librarians have evaluated each and every search tool, making sure their content is in sync with the interests of their libraries' users and provides them with access to quality information.

SEARCH TOOLS AT THE LIBRARY'S WEBSITE
To familiarize you with a library's search tools at a library's website, *Online Searching* features Easy Search at the website of the University Library at the University of Illinois at Urbana (UIUC). Easy Search traces its origins to the federally funded Digital Library Initiative of the 1990s that experimented with "making distributed collections of heterogeneous materials appear [to the searcher] to be a single integrated collection" (Schatz et al. 1996, 28). Evolving considerably over its twenty-year history in

response to new technology, usability findings, and search tool development trends (Mischo, Norman, and Schlembach 2017), Easy Search is a hybrid of federated search (i.e., the system dispatches user queries to multiple-distributed collections and repackages individual results in a way that seems like a single, unified result to the user) and index-based discovery (i.e., the system aggregates content into a single index, searches it, and presents a single result to the user). Easy Search embraces the bento-box approach to displaying retrievals, dividing the Web page into smaller units, and placing retrievals into units named for types of retrievals, such as "Articles," "Catalog," "Subject Suggestions," and "Other Resources."

Figure 2.1 shows Easy Search at https://www.library.illinois.edu. Easy Search dominates the screen due to its placement on the top left of the page, where your attention is likely to rest. To the right of the search box is a pull-down menu that enables you to search encyclopedically or limit the search to a specific subject. Atop the search box are tabs that you can activate to generate retrievals from searches of "Everything," "Books," "Articles," "Journals," or "Media." Navigate to Easy Search, mouse down on each tab, and click the question "What am I searching?" under the search box to find out which sources Easy Search searches to produce retrievals. At the Easy Search interface, you can also choose individually entitled search tools, such as a particular OPAC, database, journal, or reference source, by selecting options in the light-colored menu bar under Easy Search's search box, selecting a listed tool, and interacting with

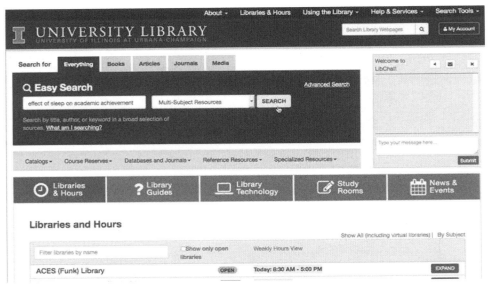

FIGURE 2.1
Easy Search Dominates the University Library's Website at UIUC

Source: Screenshots provided under a Creative Commons Attribution license by the University of Illinois at Urbana–Champaign Library.

your selected tool's native interface. Links to library information and assistance reside on the top-right menu bar and a menu bar that spans the center of the page, and below the fold are links to campus libraries.

While you read about Easy Search and search tools generally, check out your favorite library's search tools by navigating your Web browser to its website. Types of search tools and their names vary from library to library. *Online Searching* gives multiple examples of search tool names but can't be comprehensive because there are so many variations. You'll have to experiment on your own, click on "Help," or ask a librarian at that very library for assistance.

Choosing Easy Search's "Everything" tab produces retrievals from searches of books, journal articles, journal titles, *and* media. Alternatively, you can limit retrievals to books, articles, journals, *or* media tabs by choosing their tabs. Choosing Easy Search's "Everything" or "Articles" produces retrievals from the University Library's WSD system. Few public libraries have a WSD service because their focus is on responding to users' demands for print materials. You probably won't see an "Everything" search on their websites, and if you do see an "Articles" search, then choosing it launches a display of available databases that you choose and search individually.

Public libraries usually spread search tools across several Web pages. Expect their websites to be topped with a search box where users enter a query that produces retrievals through the OPAC's discovery interface. Look for links named "Research," "Online Resources," or "Databases" to access lists of available databases; look for links named "Catalog," "Quick Search," or "Library Catalog" to access the OPAC's discovery interface; and look for links named "Digital Collections," "Digital Library," or "Special Collections" to access the library's digital access management (DAM) systems, with their special functionality for displaying media content.

Figure 2.2 shows the website of the Los Angeles Public Library (LAPL) at http://www.lapl.org. Instead of an "Everything" search, LAPL's website invites you to search the OPAC's discovery interface. Under the search box is the "Go to the Catalog for more options" link that launches the OPAC's advanced search, where you can limit your query to searches of particular fields, such as author, title, subject, or call number. Placing the cursor on the "Collections & Resources" link produces a drop-down menu bearing links comparable to those at UIUC's Easy Search; for example, LAPL's "Research & Homework" is comparable to Easy Search's "Database" and "Journals," and LAPL's "Catalog" is comparable to Easy Search's "Books." Also on this menu is a link to Tessa, which accesses LAPL's rare and historical digital collections, such as "Fruit Crate Labels," "Sheet Music Covers," "Fashion Plates," and "Photo Collection."

On LAPL's "Research & Homework" page, LAPL card holders have three ways of finding a database: (1) limiting the list by a specific subject, (2) limiting the list by the alphabet, A to Z, and (3) browsing an alphabetized list of databases. In figure

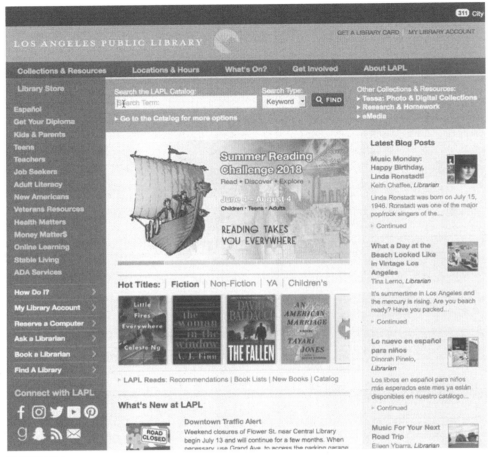

FIGURE 2.2
Los Angeles Public Library's Website, with Links to the Catalog and Library Resources
Source: Courtesy of the Los Angeles Public Library.

2.3, the user selects the specific subject "Business," limiting the full databases list to 34 business-oriented databases (in the bottom center of the page). The user searches databases individually, each database with its own interface and indexed content. Search tools at the websites of academic libraries let their users search databases individually, too.

Easy Search's "Everything" search is the default for searching digital resources at UIUC (figure 2.1). Of course, Easy Search doesn't search *everything*, but it's named "Everything" because the alternative—web-scale discovery system—is library jargon that few library users would understand. "Everything" conveys to users that it is the most comprehensive search that the library's search tools have to offer. To find out what "Everything" searches, click on the "What am I searching?" link under the search

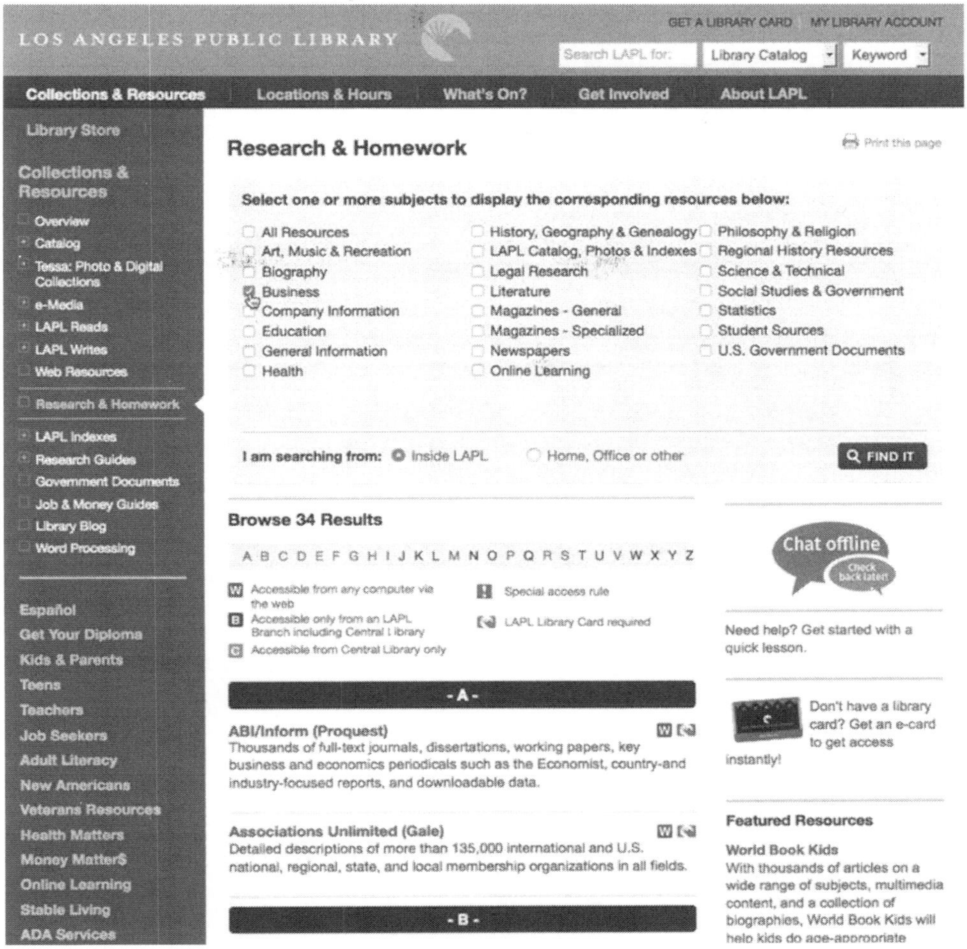

FIGURE 2.3

Limiting Los Angeles Public Library's "Research & Homework" Page to Business Databases

Source: Courtesy of the Los Angeles Public Library.

box. Generally, an academic library's "Everything" search covers journal articles from its WSD system and surrogates from its OPAC. On occasion, "Everything" searches digital content from the institutional repository (IR) and one or more digital collections when a DAM's special display functionality isn't needed (but not at UIUC).

Figure 2.1 simulates how an undergraduate student might search Easy Search's "Everything" option. The searcher enters her natural-language query `effect of sleep on academic achievement` directly into the search box beneath the "Everything" label. To experience a comprehensive search of your academic library's digital resources firsthand, choose its "Everything" search by looking for such names as "Everything," "Onesearch," "One," "Supersearch," or something comparable and entering the same query.

In figure 2.4, Easy Search's "Everything" uses the bento-box approach to report results, giving dynamic suggestions that are tailored to the query's specificity in a "Suggestions" box and placing retrievals from journal articles, books, and one or two especially relevant subject-specific databases on the left, center, and right, respectively. The more general the user query, the more suggestions Easy Search puts into its "Suggestions" box, especially directing users to "Library Resource Guides" and the University Library's "Ask-a-Librarian" online chat for help. Many articles and e-books have links to PDFs, so users can go directly to full-texts instead of lingering over surrogates along the way. "Open Access" designates PDFs free to all users, even users who aren't affiliated with UIUC. When available, altmetric badges accompany article surrogates, revealing the popularity and attention domain experts have given to them. Way beneath the fold under the "Articles" list on the left are article retriev-

FIGURE 2.4

"Everything's" Bento-Box Retrievals

Source: Screenshots provided under a Creative Commons Attribution license by the University of Illinois at Urbana–Champaign Library.

als from the Scopus database. "Subject Suggestions" lists one or two subject-specific databases, a subject-specific library, and a subject-specialist librarian—all sources of more relevant information on the topic at hand. To generate "Subject Suggestions," Easy Search analyzes its retrievals from the WorldCat database; the Library of Congress classification numbers on these retrievals; and look-up tables for databases, libraries, and subject-specialist librarians. On the bottom right are "Other Resources," such as CrossRef, WorldCat, and Google Scholar, that are external to the University Library's digital collections but promising sources for more information on the topic at hand.

In figure 2.4, the moment you click on an accompanying full-text link, such as "Get PDF," "Get Full-Text," or "Publisher Full-Text," Easy Search prompts you to enter your Illinois username and password. You should be able to use any library's search tools, but the moment you click on a full-text link from a licensed database, you will be prompted to authenticate; however, Open Access links designate sources free to all.

"Everything" isn't the only Easy Search option in figure 2.1. Choose "Books" instead, and enter the query `effect of television violence on children`. You can limit the search to "Author" or "Title words" from the pull-down menu, but leave it at the default "Keyword" search for now. Easy Search responds by placing retrievals to the University Library's OPAC and I-Share Catalog in the bento box's left and center units, respectively. (I-Share is a union catalog bearing catalog holdings of Illinois-based research, college, university, and community college libraries.) OPAC retrievals are accompanied by real-time dynamic status indicators for availability, format designation (e.g., book, e-book, journal, DVD, movie, etc.), and direct links to e-books. When you browse beyond the first page of "Library Catalog" retrievals, you leave Easy Search and enter the OPAC's discovery interface.

Choose Easy Search's "Articles" tab to search for journal articles in the University Library's WSD system. Enter the query `effect of television violence on children`. Use the pull-down menu to limit the search to a specific subject area or leave it at the default "Multi-Subject Resources" to search databases that are encyclopedic in coverage. Easy Search responds to the default by placing encyclopedic retrievals and retrievals from the Scopus database in the bento box's left and center units, respectively. PDF and full-text links accompany most articles and e-books, and a few also have altmetric badges. "Articles'" retrievals are the same as "Everything's" retrievals, but "Everything" is more comprehensive, retrieving books and e-books and adding them to the display.

Choose Easy Search's "Journals" to search for journal titles. You won't find journals focused entirely on and named for our two sample queries, so simplify your queries, entering single words, such as `children`, `violence`, `television`, or `sleep`.

"Journals" responds with two reports: (1) journals bearing your entered word in their titles and (2) journal articles bearing your entered word. You'll use "Journals" to help library users find full-texts when their accompanying full-text or PDF links fail to retrieve full-texts automatically (pages 209 to 212) and to browse issues of relevant journals in search of articles on a subject through the journal run (pages 214 to 217).

In figure 2.1, choose Easy Search's "Media" to limit your retrievals to such media as movies, DVDs, music recordings, software, and computer files. "Media" triggers a search of the University Library's discovery OPAC. A "Books" search retrieves these same retrievals, but because media retrievals aren't always listed among the highest-ranked retrievals, the user might miss them.

Figure 2.5 is a schematic diagram of the University Library's bento-box discovery model. It summarizes the full range of Easy Search's response to queries submitted via the "Everything," "Catalog," and "Articles" options. "Books" retrievals omit "Articles" retrievals and vice versa. Easy Search encourages users to search comprehensively, gives them one-click access to actual sources, blends library information and assistance into the retrievals display, and extends retrieval to quality open access resources

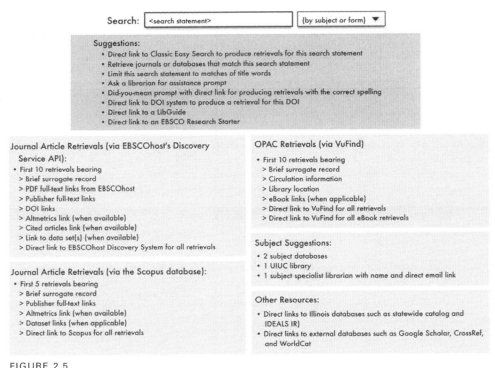

FIGURE 2.5
Easy Search's Bento-Box Discovery Model
Source: Adapted from Mischo, Norman, and Schlembach (2017).

that address the user's interests. Easy Search is in keeping with the trend toward full library discovery, casting a wide net that fills with locally available resources as well as from trusted repositories worldwide (Dempsey 2013).

THE ROLE OF THE INFORMATION INDUSTRY IN THE SEARCH TOOLS ENTERPRISE

Libraries work together with non- and for-profit firms in the information industry to put search tools in their users' hands. It all starts with non- or for-profit vendors who market proprietary and open access integrated library systems (ILSs) to libraries, enabling them to automate their most important functional operations—acquisitions, cataloging, circulation, interlibrary loan (ILL), public access, and serials control. The University Library's ILS is Voyager, originally developed by the for-profit ILS vendor Endeavor Information Systems, which later merged into Ex Libris Group and was recently acquired by ProQuest. Librarians formulate surrogates for book purchases and journal title subscriptions in the cataloging subsystem of their ILS. This subsystem passes completed surrogates to the ILS's OPAC subsystems for indexing and end-user searching. Transforming the ILS's OPAC into a Google-like interface is the OPAC discovery interface, proprietary or open access software offered by non- and for-profit discovery interface vendors. The University Library's OPAC discovery interface is the open source VuFind, originally developed at Villanova University and now deployed at hundreds of libraries worldwide, where everyone benefits from the improvements various library systems staff incorporate into the software. Librarians share their cataloging with libraries worldwide, uploading surrogates from their ILSs into WorldCat, an online cataloging system that is maintained by the nonprofit OCLC bibliographic service. WorldCat serves as a union catalog of OPACs worldwide and an open access database that anyone can search to determine whether a desired source exists and which libraries hold it. Users can place and monitor their own ILL requests through their ILS' interlibrary loan subsystem or through Illiad, software OCLC markets to libraries that integrates with a variety of ILS subsystems, such as OPACs and OPAC discovery interfaces. At UIUC, authorized users log into Illiad to place and view ILL requests.

Search tools for "Articles" comes from the information industry due to decisions librarians made more than one hundred years ago about delegating analytical access to this industry. Providing access to journal articles are database publishers. They specialize in the published literature of a discipline, such as chemistry, education, or psychology, or in a particular genre, such as journal articles, dissertations, or newspapers. They come from the government and for-profit and nonprofit sectors. Especially important are professional societies that have assumed the publisher role, producing databases that serve their membership specifically and entire professions generally. Social media has also given rise to databases, making everyday people database publishers when they contribute citations, media, tags, or biographical information to such websites as CiteULike, Flickr, YouTube, and LinkedIn.

Database publishers employ professional staff to select content and organize it into databases. Database publishers might index all of the articles in a journal or index the journal selectively. For each article, they generate a citation, and most add index terms from a controlled vocabulary that describe its big ideas and an abstract that summarizes its content. Full-texts come from journal publishers or from journal aggregators that journal publishers license to distribute their digital content. Full-texts that are HTML files or PDFs look like a printed page in a journal, magazine, or newspaper. A few databases deliver full-texts in the form of text files that open in the user's preferred word-processing program. Database publishers either offer online searching to their databases via their own search systems, or they license access to their databases to one or more database aggregators. The database aggregator indexes the database and makes it (along with many other publishers' databases) accessible to users via its proprietary search system. Because database aggregators provide access to so many databases, they are sometimes referred to as database supermarkets. Some database aggregators are also database publishers, adding their own databases to their supermarket-like search services.

Libraries are deliberate about the databases they add to their search tools. The process starts with both librarians and prospective database users evaluating the database. Examples of the many factors dominating the evaluation are the database's contents, the range of its functionality, the usability of its interface, its potential user base, and its overall value (Powers 2006). Licensed databases that pass the evaluation proceed to the license negotiation and purchasing steps. The final three steps pertain to both licensed and open Web databases—profiling the database at the library's search tools, marketing it to prospective users, and maintaining it in the library's search tools. Be prepared to evaluate new databases and shoulder responsibilities for profiling, marketing, and maintaining some of your library's databases. At the largest libraries, one librarian may serve as the library's chief electronic resources officer, managing all of the business connected with databases and their evaluation, selection, licensing, renewal, or deselection (Weir 2012).

Easy Search's "Everything" search displays database suggestions that it matches to the user's query and lists them under "Subject Suggestions" on the right center of the screen (figure 2.4). Easy Search users can also select a database by clicking on the "Databases and Journals" link on the light-colored menu bar underneath Easy Search's search box (figure 2.1). This link provides search tools for browsing database names from A to Z, typing in all or part of the database's name, limiting the database list by subject, or by publisher or aggregator (Easy Search uses the term *vendor*). At both public and academic libraries, the user can choose databases individually and search their native interfaces.

When you click on a licensed database's link or request a full-text, the system prompts you to authenticate. The licenses that libraries negotiate with publishers for access to online databases are very specific about who is and who is not an authorized user. Libraries also negotiate with publishers to offer guest access to anyone who walks into the library to search licensed Web databases from their computer workstations. Kathleen Folger, the U-M Library's chief electronic resources officer, asserts that costs can exceed $2.5 million annually for licensed access to the most expensive databases.

WSD systems are an alternative to searching databases individually, and they are particularly attractive to academic libraries because users are able to search a large portion of the library's digital content in one fell swoop—just like how they search Google. Libraries have a choice of three WSD systems: (1) EBSCO and its Discovery Service, (2) ProQuest and its Summon, and (3) OCLC and its WorldCat Discovery. To build and maintain a comprehensive index, WSD-system vendors must cultivate a relationship with just about every publisher on the planet, securing their digital content, preferably *both* surrogates and full-text sources, for WSD systems to index, retrieve, and display. Establishing successful relationships with database publishers may seem simple to do, but such relationships are actually very complicated because the same databases that database publishers license directly to libraries are the databases WSD-system vendors want indexed in their systems. Database publishers know that the WSD system will compete with individual database selection, and they are quick to do the math—counting three WSD systems versus thousands of academic libraries hosting their databases; consequently, when it comes to securing digital content from database publishers, WSD systems fight an uphill battle. They might secure citations only from some database publishers because these publishers want to be exclusive, marketing their databases of citations, abstracts, index terms, author-keywords, and cited references to academic libraries generally. Ultimately, WSD-system vendors are likely to negotiate "some kind of reciprocal arrangement of other incentives" to win over database publishers (Breeding 2014, 13–14). The University Library's WSD system is EBSCO's Discovery Service, covering a large share of the journal articles, conference papers, newspaper stories, and individually authored book chapters in the Library's licensed and open access databases. (The share that isn't included emanates from publishers that don't allow EBSCO to index their digital content, which might include EBSCO's Discovery Service competitors.)

Google Scholar is an open access alternative to an academic library's WSD system, and it serves independent scholars, professional-amateurs, and everyday people who have no access to a library's WSD system. Searching Google Scholar, users benefit from the same search and retrieval capabilities that have made Google the preferred search engine around the world. Google has optimized them so that Google Scholar searches give higher weight to high-cited scholarly sources than to no- or low-cited sources. To populate Google Scholar with scholarly content, Google scours the Web for as much free scholarly content as it can find and, like WSD systems, negotiates with database publishers for access to their content. Google Scholar searches retrieve scholarly sources from both open and licensed Web resources. The moment that you click on a full-text link from the latter, Google Scholar refers you to the full-text fulfillment websites of database publishers and journal aggregators, where you have to enter your credit card number to download full-texts. To make such publisher paywalls transparent to their users, libraries have enhanced Google Scholar with resolver links so that their users can authenticate at their library's website to avoid publisher paywalls for the library's licensed content.

Be forewarned that most library users who come to you for help have already used your library's search tools, particularly its "Everything," "Books," and "Articles" searches. Thus, you'll be fielding the most difficult searches, and to find useful information, you'll have to select the right search tool for the job. You might start by retracing their steps in the most popular search tools (i.e., "Everything," "Books," and "Articles"), but when these fail, you'll have to go farther afield, checking search tools users are less likely to consult, such as the library's DAM, OPAC, and IR. Searching databases individually should be high on your list because their native interfaces give you functionality that's not available via "Everything," "Books," and "Articles" searches. Finding the right search tool to answer a user's query is a difficult task but one that will become increasingly easier as you gain experience using your library's search tools and answering user queries.

QUESTIONS

Here are questions to give you hands-on experience using your library's most important search tools. Answers conclude the chapter.

1. Launch your library's website. Are you searching an academic or public library? Does it feature an "Everything" search? If it does, what is it called? Which sources does it search to produce retrievals? Does it use the bento-box approach to display retrievals? If it does, what are the names of each unit, and what are the sources it searches to produce each unit's retrievals? If it doesn't, how does it order retrievals? How far can you drill down before you must authenticate as a library cardholder?

2. Revisit your library's website. On which link or tab do you click to search your library's WSD system? What is the name of the link that launches the search? How does it order retrievals? If you can change the order of retrievals, what other op-

tions are available? How far can you drill down before you must authenticate as a library cardholder?

3. Repeat question 2, replacing your library's WSD system with its OPAC's discovery interface.

4. Repeat question 2, replacing your library's WSD system with its IR.

5. Revisit your library's website. On which link or tab do you click to display open access and licensed databases? What tools are given to help you select a database? How far can you drill down before you must authenticate as a library cardholder?

SUMMARY

Explore the websites of your academic library and favorite public library to see what search tools they provide users. Do they have tools that are comparable to Easy Search's "Everything," "Books," "Articles," "Journal," and "Media" options? Which sources does each tool search? Which library systems—OPAC, discovery interface, WSD system, IR, and so on—are underneath the hood, powering these tools? What website links provide direct access to individual search tools so you can use their native interfaces, where the real power lies?

Ultimately, the users who consult you for help have searched all the easy search tools. It's your job to dig deeper, and for many user inquiries, this will mean searching sources individually, where you have functionality to search in ways that are out of the reach of easy search tools.

BIBLIOGRAPHY

Breeding, Marshall. 2014. "Library Resource Discovery Products: Context, Library Perspectives, and Vendor Positions." *Library Technology Reports* 50, no. 1.

Dempsey, Lorcan. 2013. "Full Library Discovery." *Lorcan Dempsey's Weblog* (blog), September 15, 2013. http://orweblog.oclc.org/full-library-discovery/.

Mischo, William H., Michael A. Norman, and Mary C. Schlembach. 2017. "Innovations in Discovery Systems: User Studies and the Bento Approach." Paper presented at the Charleston Library Conference, Charleston, SC, November 2017. https://2017charleston conference.sched.com/event/CHp3/a-decade-in-discovery-updating-assumptions-and -conclusions-in-information-access-and-retrieval.

Powers, Audrey. 2006. "Evaluating Databases for Acquisitions and Collection Development." In *Handbook of Electronic and Digital Acquisitions*, edited by Thomas W. Leonhardt, 41–60. Binghamton, NY: Haworth Press.

Schatz, Bruce, et al. 1996. "Federating Diverse Collections of Scientific Literature." *Computer* 29, no. 5: 28–36.

Weir, Ryan O. 2012. *Managing Electronic Resources.* Chicago: ALA Techsource.

SUGGESTED READINGS

Breeding, Marshall. 2014. "Library Resource Discovery Products: Context, Library Perspectives, and Vendor Positions." *Library Technology Reports* 50, no. 1. Find out how librarians dress up searching for academic and scholarly information in the image of Google in this comprehensive treatment of the information industry's discovery products.

Weir, Ryan O. 2012. *Managing Electronic Resources*. Chicago: ALA Techsource. Learn about the job responsibilities of the electronic resources officer, who manages much of the library's business connected with electronic resources.

ANSWERS

1. **Everything search at your library's website.** The "Everything" search tool is more characteristic of an academic library than a public library because of the former's emphasis on digital materials. For the most part, the academic library's "Everything" search covers journal articles from its WSD system, surrogates from its OPAC, and digital content from its IR; however, UIUC's "Everything" goes beyond UIUC, searching such massive encyclopedic databases as EBSCO's Academic Search Premier, Google Books, OAIster, LexisNexis Academic News, Scopus, and WorldCat Discovery for books, e-books, journal articles, newspaper stories, and open access resources. Retrievals are augmented with a variety of full-text links, some links implying one-click access to full-texts (e.g., "PDF full-text," "PDF full-text from publisher," and "Get PDF") and other links implying that full-texts aren't immediately available (e.g., "Request through interlibrary loan," "Full-text finder," and "Look for full-text"). Figure 2.4 shows "Everything's" bento-box approach to display retrievals. Click on Easy Search's "Everything," "Books," "Articles," "Journals," or "Media" tab, and then click on the "What am I searching" link under the Easy Search's search box to find out which sources Easy Search searches to produce retrievals. Drill down to a licensed database or click on a full-text from a licensed database, and Easy Search asks you to authenticate.

2. **The WSD system at your library's website.** Not all libraries have a WSD system, particularly public libraries. On your library's website, look for a tab or link atop a search box with the name "Articles" or "Journal Articles." Figure 2.4 shows "Articles'" bento-box approach to display retrievals. See the answer to question 1 for the drill-down answer.

3. **The OPAC discovery interface at your library's website.** On your library's website, look for a tab or link atop a search box with the name "Catalog," "Library Catalog," "Books," or bearing a name of local significance such as Mirlyn (serving U-M), Consort (serving Dennison University, Kenyon College, Ohio Wesleyan University, and College of Wooster), or Magic (serving Michigan State University).

Easy Search uses the name "Books." Figure 2.4 shows the bento-box approach to display retrievals. Except for e-books, authentication shouldn't be necessary because the library owns books, reports, dissertations, sound recordings, and DVDs.

4. **The IR at your library's website.** IRs are typical of academic libraries, but not all such libraries have an IR. Because the name *institutional repository* isn't likely to be understandable to end users, your IR probably has a name with local significance, such as Deep Blue (U-M), Knowledge Bank (The Ohio State University), and IDEALS (UIUC). A library's "Everything" search might include IR holdings. Mouse down on Easy Search's "Specialized Resources" link on the light-colored menu bar beneath the "Search" button, and select "IDEALS" to access to UIUIC's IR. Open access is fundamental to the IR's mission, so authentication isn't necessary. Accompanying surrogate records are direct links to full-texts.

5. **Databases at your library's website.** On a library's website, look for links named "Databases," "Research," or "Online Journals and Databases." Here are ten database-selection approaches, and your library's website may reveal even more: (1–5) searching by database name, keyword, database publisher, database aggregator, or ISSN; (6–9) browsing lists of databases organized by subject, by database names A–Z, by most commonly used databases, or by genre; or (10) consulting the library's LibGuides especially for specific disciplines or fields of study. Mouse down on Easy Search's "Databases and Journals" link on the light-colored menu bar beneath the search box, choose "Online Journals and Databases" or "Databases by Subject" to get started on database selection. Drill down to a licensed database or click on a full-text from a licensed database, and you will have to authenticate.

3

The Reference Interview

Ultimately, you are learning about online databases, search systems, and searching tools so that you can become an expert intermediary searcher, applying your knowledge to help library users satisfy their information needs. Your interaction with users in which they express these needs is called the reference interview. Taylor (1968) explains, "Without doubt, the negotiation of reference questions is one of the most

Condensing everything that is important about the reference interview is this three-minute video at http://www.onlinesearching.org/p/3-interview.html.

complex acts of human communication. During this process, one person tries to describe for another person not something he knows, but rather something he does not know" (180). Thus, expert searchers must become expert reference interviewers, able to engage in a conversational exchange to determine exactly what the user really wants so they can take the appropriate action. When this action involves online searching, your searches may be familiar, routine, and deliberate, such as searching a familiar reference database to confirm a fact. Other times, you'll conduct a subject search that produces multiple retrievals, none of which answers the user's question entirely, and to generate answers, the user must extract useful information from these retrievals and synthesize what he learns to answer his query.

Initially, it may be difficult to distinguish queries that require in-depth analysis from all the rest of the queries that come your way. Eventually, you will sense the open-ended nature of complex queries, and instead of searching for hard-and-fast answers for them, you will respond with in-depth searches and engage users in the process of identifying relevant retrievals so you can use them to find more information or take the search in new directions.

The reference interview is fundamental to the process of online searching specifically and to interacting with library users generally. Round out your understanding of it by consulting books that focus exclusively on the reference interview (Harmeyer 2014; Ross, Nilsen, and Radford 2009) or the briefer one-chapter treatments of the reference interview in the major textbooks on reference services (Cassell and Hiremath 2018; Smith and Wong 2016). The reference interview is core to librarianship, so prepare yourself to the nines.

MODELS OF THE INFORMATION-SEEKING PROCESS

This chapter's examination of the reference interview begins with information-seeking models. Models are used to shrink real-world situations, processes, and systems down to their essential components. They help us understand complex phenomena and make them easier to study. Presented here are five models of the information-seeking process to help you bridge the gap between understanding this process and being a key participant in it. Because no one model represents the full gamut of information-seeking activities, plug the most relevant model of the five into the situation at hand, and be flexible, able to discard this model and apply an entirely different model to the next situation.

Classic Model of Communication

The classic model of communication is represented as a one-way street involving a sender, message, transmission, noise, channel, reception, and receiver (Shannon and

Weaver 1949, 5). Although this model has been criticized for its one-sided nature, you merely have to turn it on its head to represent communication that is a conversation between two people or an interaction between a user and a search system.

Consider how the typical reference interview unfolds. The sender is an undergraduate student, the message is his query, the transmission is human speech, the noise is one or more factors affecting one or more elements in the chain, the channel is the English language, the reception is hearing, and the receiver is you—the reference librarian. Consider the noise that might affect each element in the chain (figure 3.1). Sender noise may be the student's low-level understanding of the topic he seeks. Message noise may be the student's partial expression of what he wants. Transmission noise may be the student's English-language description of his information needs, trying to put into words something he doesn't know. Reception noise may be actual noise—the hustle and bustle of classes changing that increases the noise level in the library, making it hard for the librarian to hear what the student is saying. Receiver noise may be you, the reference librarian, tired as a result of heavy partying the night before. When the classic model is applied to the reference interview, a host of factors may impinge on the user's query so that its initial expression in the sender's mind will be quantitatively and qualitatively different from its eventual representation in the mind of the receiver. This is especially important when one considers that our scenario's receiver is the reference librarian, who will eventually assume much of the burden of resolving the sender's message by searching for information online.

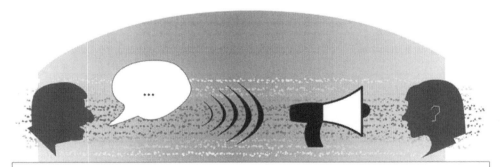

FIGURE 3.1
Classic Model of Communication
Source: Adapted from Shannon and Weaver (1949).

Levels of Question Formulation Model

Putting the queries that users pose to librarians under the microscope is Robert S. Taylor's levels of question formulation model. In an oft-cited article, Taylor (1968, 182) defines four question types, Q1 to Q4:

Q1   Actual but unexpressed need for information (*visceral* need). A conscious or unconscious need that changes in form, quality, and concreteness as the user encounters everyday life.

Q2   Conscious, within-brain description of an ill-defined area of indecision (*conscious* need). This may be a rambling statement, and it is at this stage that the user may talk to someone to sharpen his focus or initiate a search.

Q3   Formal need statement (*formalized* need). The user is able to form a qualified and rational statement in concrete terms. The user may or may not be thinking of the context or constraints of the system from which he wants information.

Q4   Question as presented to the information system (*compromised* need). This is the representation of the user's information need within the constraints of the search system and database.

Taylor's model demonstrates that queries do not pop up instantaneously without some forethought and deliberation on the part of the user. Users experiencing Q1 might not even be aware that they have an information need. They encounter life, various phenomena garnering their attention momentarily and passing away. Their Q2 expressions may range from a patchwork of words and phrases that they can barely put into a sentence to rambling statements that have little focus or substance. When you find it difficult to understand a user's information needs and respond with a plan of action, you may be encountering a user with Q2 needs. The role-playing exercise in textbox 3.1 creates the conditions for you to experience this phenomenon from the perspective of the end user or reference librarian or both.

The Q3 question is a qualified and rational statement of the end user's desires in concrete terms. While negotiation that enables the librarian to develop a full understanding of the user's query might be necessary, it is less protracted than in Q2 questions and transitions in a timely manner to related concerns, such as how much information is needed, how technical or scholarly the information should be, deadlines connected with the project, and so on. Q4 questions are the actual search statements that users or librarians enter into search systems. Taylor's name for Q4 questions—the compromised need—is especially appropriate because it acknowledges that user queries and the search statements that librarians enter into search systems are not one and the same.

HELPING USERS TRANSITION FROM Q2 (CONSCIOUS) TO Q3 (FORMAL NEED) QUESTIONS

To perform this role-playing exercise, work with a partner. One person plays the role of the end user, and the second person plays the role of the reference librarian. You could even switch roles at some point.

Before getting started, the person playing the end user should think about a topic that interests him or her but hasn't had time to pursue in terms of conducting research online. It could be a topic of personal interest or a topic that she or he must write about for another class but hasn't yet started to research. Don't give this much thought, and *don't* spend time searching online in advance.

The end user approaches the librarian and expresses his or her query. The librarian reacts, getting the end user started. Both end user and librarian need to decide what "started" means within the context of the role-playing episode and when to stop. The episode should include these events:

- The end user describing his or her information needs to the librarian
- The librarian listening to the end user and negotiating with the user to arrive at a full understanding of the user's query
- Getting the user started on his or her search for information, which might include user and librarian working together online to find relevant information

When you are done, take a few minutes to answer these questions:

1. (For both) Do you think that the end user's initial expression of his or her query was comparable to the Q2 question that Taylor had in mind? Why or why not? Was it a Q3 question instead? Why do you think it was a Q3 question?

2. (For the librarian) Do you think that you understood the user's query? Why or why not? What strategies did you use to facilitate your understanding? What worked, what didn't work, and why?

3. (For the end user) Do you think the librarian understood your query? Why or why not? How do you think she or he could have done a better job developing such an understanding?

4. (For both) As a result of the negotiation that went on between the two of you, what does the user really want? Are you both in agreement as to what the negotiated query is? (The negotiated query is the librarian's understanding of what the user wants as a result of conducting a reference interview with the user.) Do you detect differences between the initial query and negotiated query, and if you do, what are they?

5. (For both) Did you go online to find relevant information? If yes, did the two of you contribute equally to the finding process, or did one person contribute more than the other? What were your respective contributions during the finding process?

If you role-play in class, be prepared to share your answers to questions in a class discussion.

Search Strategy Process Model

The search strategy process (SSP) model uses genre to rank reference sources so that users' exposure to those ranked early in the process primes them intellectually for the more complex, technical, and advanced sources ranked later in the process (Kirk 1974). Encyclopedias and dictionaries come first because their entries are basic and foundational, intended for readers whose knowledge of a discipline and its topics is elementary. The SSP model recommends the library catalog next, then abstracting and indexing (A&I) sources, and finally citation indexes because increasingly greater sophistication and domain knowledge are needed to understand the sources that these three genres serve up.

Berrypicking Model

Accounting for searches that aren't one-time events is the Berrypicking Model (Bates 1989). This model acknowledges that people search for information repeatedly on the same or similar topics; they apply the sources that they've found to the situation at hand; and, in the course of doing so, their knowledge increases (figure 3.2). As a result, the next

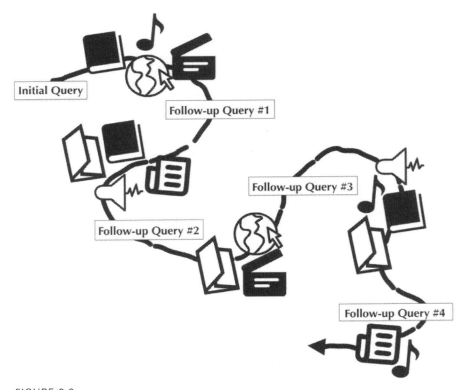

FIGURE 3.2
Berrypicking Model
Source: Adapted from Bates (1989, 410). Created using symbols from the Noun Project (http://the nounproject.com): "Book" symbol by Simple Icons; "Music Note" symbol by Parker Foote; "Internet" symbol by Jaclyne Ooi; "Clapperboard" symbol by Adrien Griveau; "Document" symbol by Claudiu Sergiu Danaila; "Audio" symbol by iconsmind.com; "Newspaper" symbol by Quan Do.

time they search, their follow-up query has changed, which changes the questions they ask librarians, the search statements they enter into search systems, and their relevance assessments of the new sources that their follow-up searches retrieve. This sequence of events may continue for many years, especially in the case of domain experts—scholars, scientists, and veteran researchers—who build on the results of current research initiatives when proposing new research and advising and teaching students.

Information Search Process (ISP) Model

The information search process (ISP) model describes the user's information-seeking experience as an evolving process that involves specific thoughts, feelings, and actions (Kuhlthau 2003). Dividing information seeking into six stages, Kuhlthau (2018) names and describes each stage, along with the feelings users experience:

1. Initiation, when a person first becomes aware of a lack of knowledge or understanding. Feelings of uncertainty and apprehension are common.
2. Selection, when the person identifies a general area, topic, or problem, and his or her initial uncertainty often gives way to a brief sense of optimism and a readiness to begin the search.
3. Exploration, when inconsistent, incompatible information is encountered and uncertainty, confusion, and doubt frequently increase and people find themselves "in the dip" of confidence.
4. Formulation, when a focused perspective is formed and uncertainty diminishes as confidence begins to increase.
5. Collection, when information pertinent to the focused perspective is gathered and uncertainty begins to decrease.
6. Presentation, when the search is completed, with a new understanding enabling the person to explain his or her learning to others or put the learning to use. Accompanied by feelings of relief, with a sense of satisfaction for a search gone well or disappointment if it has not.

Figure 3.3 lists these stages from left to right, along with the feelings people experience at each stage. Between them is the "feeling" space, with the middle, top, and bottom areas representing neutral, comfortable, and uncomfortable feelings, respectively. Flowing from left to right through this space is a purposeful line that represents how information seekers feel at each stage in the process. Notice how this line has several possible ending points, depending on whether people are satisfied, relieved, or disappointed with the overall results.

No one likes feeling uncomfortable, but the ISP model tells us that such feelings are inevitable and experienced more than once between spates of neutral or comfortable feelings (Kracker and Wang 2002; Kuhlthau 2003). Because information seeking is an emotional roller coaster, it may be worthwhile for librarians to tell information seekers to expect ups and downs so that they know what to expect, are less likely to procrastinate, and don't give up when they feel bad.

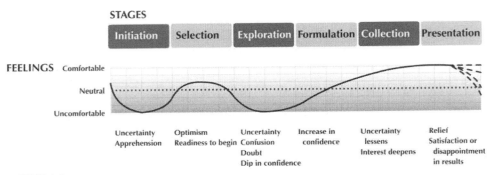

FIGURE 3.3
The Feelings People Experience When Searching for Information
Source: Adapted from Kuhlthau (2003).

THE NATURE OF THE REFERENCE INTERVIEW

The reference interview is a conversational exchange between a librarian and a library user, in which the user is likely to describe something she doesn't know and, thus, requires negotiation so that the librarian is able to determine what the user really wants. The interview usually but not necessarily includes the librarian's search of the library collection for what he believes is relevant information that he passes on to the user, with the expectation that it has the potential to completely or partially resolve the user's unknowable state. The crux of the exchange is the negotiation between user and reference librarian, in which the librarian questions the user to find out what she wants so that he can search library resources for answers. Some reference interviews are brief because the user expresses what she wants right from the get-go, and others are protracted due to the negotiation that is needed for the librarian to develop an understanding of what the user wants and the complexity of using certain library resources to generate usable answers.

Researchers have studied user inquiries, categorizing them and determining which are more or less likely in academic and public libraries (Arnold and Kaske 2005; McKewan and Richmond 2017; Radford and Connaway 2013). Categories, category names, and their definitions vary across studies, but there are enough similarities between studies to suggest that you can expect user queries for the following:

- Subject (also called Research, Specific-Search, or In-Depth). A query that involves a topic for which your searches are likely to produce multiple retrievals, none of which answers the user's question entirely. To generate answers, the user must extract useful information from these retrievals and synthesize what she learns to answer her query. Examples: "What is the effect of television violence on children?" "How successful was President Johnson's War on Poverty?"

- Known-Item (also called Holdings or Citation). A query for a specific source that you or the user knows exists and for which your searches are intended to target *the* one retrieval that the user seeks. This category includes assisting users with formulating complete bibliographic citations because your searches will be targeting one specific source. Examples: "I need to know the name of the journal in which this article was published." "Do you have Richard Flanagan's latest novel?"
- Reader's Advisory. A query that elicits advice regarding library materials that are similar to one that the user really likes. Because Reader's Advisory starts with a Known-Item, it really is a subcategory of the previous Known-Item category; however, distinguishing Reader's Advisory from other inquiries will help you become attuned to them. Examples: "I've read all of Steve Hamilton's books and want to read more like them." "This journal article is pivotal to my research. I wish I could find more like it."
- Reference (also called Ready Reference, Fact-Finding, Facts, or Look-Ups). A query for a fact that needs no additional analysis beyond verification in an authoritative source. Example: "What peaks do I have to climb to become a 46er?"
- Policy & Procedural Matters. An inquiry that involves the library's policy or procedures. Examples: "I want to check these materials out, but I forgot my library card." "Under what conditions do you forgive fines?"
- Technical Assistance. An inquiry that asks for help with hardware, software, or physical resources. Examples: "How do I print this screen?" "How do I cite this blog in my term paper?"
- Directions. An inquiry about a virtual or physical library space. Examples: "How do I find books I can download?" "Where is the washroom?"
- Referrals. An inquiry for information or services provided by another organization. Examples: "Where can I get food aid?" "I need help studying for my GED."

Online searching resolves most queries categorized as Subject, Known-Item, Reader's Advisory, and Reference. Indirectly, it helps you answer inquiries categorized as Policy & Procedural Matters, Technical Assistance, Directions, and Referrals; for example, searching your library's website for answers to a policy matter or searching an application's online technical manual while troubleshooting equipment problems. This chapter's Questions and Answers demonstrate how fluid queries are, beginning as this category and transforming to that category due to your negotiation with users during the reference interview.

Research findings reveal that query categories depend on type of library (McKewan and Richmond 2017). Work at an academic library, and expect about two of every five queries to pertain to Subjects; rare will be Technical Assistance and Reference, accounting for about one of every ten inquiries. Work at a public library, and expect one of every two inquiries to be either Technical Assistance or Policy & Procedural Matters and one of every three queries to be either Subjects or Known-Items; rare will be Reference and Reader's Advisory, accounting for less than one of every twenty inquiries.

Researchers who study the reference interview observe that certain behavioral attributes on the part of the reference librarian are likely to leave library users with positive perceptions of the librarian's performance and of libraries generally. In response, the Reference & User Services Association (RUSA), the division of the American Library Association that specializes in reference services, has published guidelines for the behavioral performance of reference-interview providers that advise them to be approachable, interested, a good communicator, an effective searcher, and capable of conducting follow-up to the original interaction (RUSA 2018).

Study the guidelines, make a mental note of those you know you will accomplish with ease, and capitalize on them initially. As your confidence increases, identify guidelines you know are not your forte, observe how your more-experienced librarian colleagues handle themselves, and model their behavior. Compliment them on their performance, and ask if they had difficulties initially, what they were, and how they overcame them.

PHASES OF THE REFERENCE INTERVIEW

Underlying the RUSA guidelines is a multiphased reference interview, in which the process of online searching is embedded. Figure 3.4 shows the interview's phases along with iterative loops back to earlier phases for searches that fail or get off track.

Library users rate the success of the reference interview less on whether the provided information is useful and on target and more on the quality of their interaction with the librarian, especially whether they would consult the librarian in the future. Librarians rate success based on the quality of the information they provide to users (Durrance 1989; Magi and Mardeusz 2013; Radford 1999).

Greeting Phase

The in-person reference interview begins with a greeting, such as "Hi, may I help you?" The librarian's smile, relaxed demeanor, eye contact, and open body stance all contribute to putting the user at ease and establishing rapport so that the user feels comfortable and the interview begins on a positive note.

Personally, I do not like the greeting "Hi, how may I help you?" because it might suggest to the user that she must know *how* the librarian can help her and, thus, predispose her to phrase her initial question in a way that anticipates what the librarian should do with the query; for example, which database the librarian should choose or which search statements he should enter to produce useful retrievals. Use instead

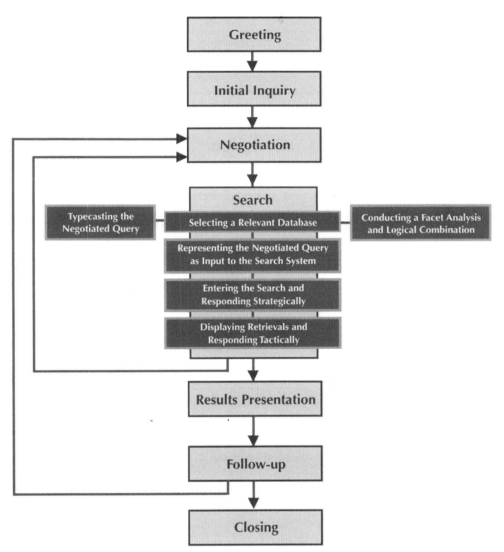

FIGURE 3.4
Phases of the Reference Interview and Steps of the Online Searching Process

a greeting that encourages users to say what is on their mind, to spill the beans, so to speak, so that you can gain an understanding of what they want and use it to initiate the search.

First impressions go a long way toward setting the tone of the interaction yet to come, and thus, your overall demeanor should convey the message to everyone around you that you are approachable, friendly, eager, and willing to help. If you are

working on an unrelated task while you are on duty at the reference desk, make sure
it isn't a task that totally consumes your attention and every inch of the desk in front
of you because users may be hesitant to approach and interrupt you, especially those
who have the slightest inkling of reluctance to ask for help. Because one insignificant
sign of nonapproachability could send them scurrying in the opposite direction, it is
important to send a message that you are ready, prepared, and pleased to help everyone, and it is your job to do so.

If you are helping one user and notice more users approaching, smile and make eye
contact so they know they have been seen. You may be uncomfortable interrupting
the ongoing reference interview to verbally acknowledge them with a comment, such
as "I'll be with you shortly," so a nonverbal signal, such as a nod of the head while you
smile and make eye contact, may be a good substitute.

Library reference staff may have an agreed-upon greeting for answering the phone
at the reference desk that includes the name of the library and varies depending on
how busy the staff member is. If you smile while you answer the phone, your voice is
likely to convey the smile, sending a signal to the inquirer that you are pleased she has
called and are ready and willing to help her. If you can't manage a smile, answer the
phone with an upbeat and enthusiastic tone of voice so that the interaction starts on
a positive note.

Email reference service usually requires users to complete a web-administered form
that asks them about themselves and their query. Referring to the form enables you
to jump-start your interaction with them. Users contacting you via your library's chat
or instant-messaging service might test the waters, asking if there's anyone there or
blurting out what's on their mind.

Initial Inquiry Phase

The interview transitions to the initial inquiry when users make a statement that
describes what they want. Librarians agree that users' initial queries rarely describe
what they really want, and there is a mountain of research that confirms their sus-
picions (Dewdney and Michell 1997; Radford et al. 2011; Ross 2003). Consider this
reference interview:

LIBRARIAN: Hi, may I help you?

USER: I need some books on alcoholism.

LIBRARIAN: Okay. [Types the subject heading "Alcoholism" into the library catalog.] We
have lots of books on alcoholism. It looks like most of them have the call number 362.29.
I'll write that down for you. Take a look at the books there, and you'll probably find what
you're looking for.

USER: Thanks. [Leaves for the bookshelves.]

No negotiation between the librarian and the user takes place. The librarian takes this user's query at face value, checks the library catalog for the right call number, and dispatches the user to the bookshelves, where she can browse books on alcoholism. Let's see what happens when the librarian negotiates the user's initial query.

LIBRARIAN: Hi, may I help you?

USER: I need some books on alcoholism.

LIBRARIAN: We have lots of books on alcoholism. Tell me what it is about alcoholism that interests you. [Navigates to the library catalog just in case.]

USER: Like I'm interested in recovery and meetings and stuff.

LIBRARIAN: Okay. We can look for books that talk about what happens at meetings, how meetings help with recovery.

USER: Yes, meetings. Are there any meetings around here?

LIBRARIAN: Well, let's check a local events calendar for campus and then for Ann Arbor.

This reference interview has a different outcome because the librarian probes the user's interest in alcoholism by saying, "Tell me what it is about alcoholism that interests you," to which the user volunteers more information, first "recovery and meetings" and then "meetings around here." These cue the librarian to what the user really wants—a list of the closest Alcoholics Anonymous meetings to campus, their exact locations, and meeting times. Consider this reference interview:

LIBRARIAN: Hi, may I help you?

USER: Do you have a map of the UP?

Stop right there and ponder the librarian's next step. He could take this initial query at face value, referring the user to the library's map room, where atlases and maps are stored, or to map websites on the open Web. Instead, he probes the user's initial interest in maps:

LIBRARIAN: Sure, but is there something in particular about the Upper Peninsula that interests you?

USER: Yeah. The UP's parks and wilderness areas.

LIBRARIAN: OK. So you are interested in the parks and wilderness areas up north. Anything else?

USER: I'm going birding.

LIBRARIAN: OK. Is there a particular type of forest or wilderness area that is best for birding in the UP?

USER: I want to see a Connecticut Warbler—that's where they nest, up in the UP—and a few other northern species while I'm there.

LIBRARIAN: OK. So you are interested in finding Connecticut Warblers and other birds in the UP.

USER: Yeah.

LIBRARIAN: Let's search the eBird database, where birdwatchers record the species they've seen. Maybe they've reported the bird you want to see, plus its location in the UP.

This second reference interview starts with the user pursuing a map of Michigan's Upper Peninsula (UP) and ends with the librarian and the user searching the eBird database on the open Web for reports of the species that interests the user. The librarian may work with the user for a while, both of them figuring out how to search eBird for a particular species in the geographical location that interests the user. When they do, the librarian is likely to pass the searching task on to the user so she can search all the species that interest her and triangulate an area where she'll see most of the birds that interest her.

Both of these chats capture interactions with users who don't immediately disclose their interests to the librarian. Table 3.1 tells why people aren't forthcoming about their interests. Of these reasons, the user seeking "some books on alcoholism" is probably concerned about self-disclosure, and the user seeking "a map of the UP" probably doesn't think the librarian knows enough about her subject to be able to help her. These are just guesses. You'll never know, and knowing the reason doesn't help you answer the question. The bottom line is that users' initial queries rarely describe what they really want, and as a consequence, you have to negotiate all your interactions with users to find out what they really want.

Negotiation Phase

The negotiation phase is the crux of the reference interview when the librarian determines what the user really wants. Getting it wrong means that whatever you do or advise the user to do may be for naught because both you and the user are on the wrong path toward an answer. As a result, the user might regret her interaction with you, making her less likely to consult you or librarians generally in the future. Even when the user appears confident, assertive, and totally knowledgeable of the topic, you should probe by asking such open-ended questions as "What kind of information are you looking for?" "What specifically are you looking for relating to [topic]?" or "Tell me more about [topic]," just in case the user has something in mind that she is not revealing. Consider this chat between user and librarian:

Table 3.1.   Reasons People Don't Reveal Their Real Information Needs

Overall Reasons	Specific Reasons
The nature of the reference interview	Users' initial inquiries are their way of starting up and getting involved in the interaction.
	Users think they are being helpful by expressing their queries in ways that anticipate the systems that librarians will search to produce relevant retrievals or the genres that will characterize relevant retrievals.
The difficulty of developing a searchable topic	Users express their queries in broader terms than their specific topics, thinking that, if the library has information on the former, they will be able to find information on the latter.
	Users don't know the "enormous extent of information" that is available in the library.
	Users are "just beginning to explore" their topics and are sampling what's available in the library.
	Users don't know whether there is anything to be found on their topic.
	Users asking an imposed query are unsure what the original requestor wants.
The difficulty of expressing one's information needs to someone else	Users don't know what they want, and it is difficult for them to express what they don't know in the course of asking someone else to help them find it.
	Users think that they have to express their queries in ways that anticipate what librarians will do to find useful information for them.
	Users don't realize that even simple requests, such as "I'd like information on football," are bereft of the context that they have in mind. To successfully communicate their needs, they have to add context to their queries; for example, "football in the United States, the college game, injuries, particularly to the head."
The erroneous assumptions users have about libraries and their resources	Users think libraries are information supermarkets, where they are on their own except to ask for directions when they can't find something.
	Users think libraries and their systems are simple and they can figure them out if only they had a few clues about how things work.
	Users don't "volunteer information that they do not perceive as relevant, and they don't understand the relevance because they don't know how the system works."
	Users don't know that the library's mission includes a commitment to service and helping people like themselves find information.
The erroneous assumptions users have about librarians	Users don't know that librarians are there to help them satisfy their information needs.
	Users don't think librarians know enough about their specialized topics to be able to help them.
	Users don't want to bother librarians, who they think have more important things to do.
Users who want to be seen as competent, secure, and knowledgeable	Users avoid self-disclosure, especially if their queries reveal financial, health, or legal issues they are dealing with or sensitive personal matters that they feel expose something about them or make them feel vulnerable.
	Users think that the librarian will consider them to be incompetent, dumb, or worse because they have to ask for help.
	Users think that the librarian will think they are cheating when they ask for homework help.

Source: Adapted from Ross, Nilsen, and Radford (2009, 18).

USER: Hi, I'm looking for something on the Vietnam War.

LIBRARIAN: Welcome to Ask-a-Librarian. What specifically are you looking for relating to the Vietnam War?

USER: Well, I'm interested in the response to the war that old veterans are having.

LIBRARIAN: OK, so how veterans of the Vietnam War are looking back at it in a more current time?

USER: More like the old veterans who are going back to Vietnam. Some just visit, and others actually stay and do good things. I want to know the reasons they go back, OK?

LIBRARIAN: OK, please hold while I look.

The user begins the interaction, telling the librarian she is interested in the Vietnam War. Do not expect the interaction to proceed immediately from initial query to the negotiated query just because you used one open-ended question. It may take several back-and-forth interactions for you to understand what exactly the user wants. Be prepared for reference interviews that leave you hanging, wondering whether you truly understood what the user wanted. In some of these interviews, the user won't know what she wants—she is testing the waters, determining whether there is any information available to warrant her further investigation of the topic and seeing what interests her.

Vietnam War Veterans is an example of an in-depth subject query that may take time to set up and conduct, so you might ask the user whether she is in the library or at home. In the case of the former, invite her to meet you at the reference desk or your office, where you can involve her in the search more directly, negotiating her interests, gathering search terms, getting her immediate feedback on retrievals' relevance, and so on.

Distinguishing features of in-depth queries are their open-endedness—the impossibility of finding one rock-solid answer to the question. Instead, users must gather as much information as possible, study it, and generate an answer or course of action based on their knowledge and understanding of everything they have read. Especially in academic settings, users typically report the results of their analyses in written form—an essay, journal article, or book; however, they could just as well put the results to work—arriving at a decision, making a diagnosis, or building something.

Open-Ended Questions

Open-ended questions are your secret weapon for getting users to open up about their real interests because they are meant to elicit anything *but* the user's yes or no response. Interspersed between several queries in table 3.2 are a librarian's open-ended questions that were instrumental in eliciting a user's negotiated query.

Table 3.2. Open-Ended Questions That Give Rise to Negotiated Queries

User's Initial Query	Librarian's Open-Ended Questions	Negotiated Query
The War in the Middle East	That's a big topic. What specifically interests you about the war?	The book *Three Cups of Tea* by Greg Mortensen and David Oliver Relin
Conversions	When you say *conversions*, what do you mean?	A biography of Thomas Merton
School Lunches	Tell me more about your interest in school lunches.	Do kids ever outgrow peanut allergies?
The Library's History Books	We have lots of history books. What time period in history interests you?	Sherman's March to the Sea
Opera	The library has lots on opera, even recordings. Tell me more.	What singers created the major roles in the Gershwins' opera, *Porgy and Bess*?
Cornwall	What interests you about Cornwall: its history, geography, travel, or something else?	Books like *Poldark*
Jackass Tails	I'm not sure I know what you mean. Tell me more.	Jataka tales
Walmart	What would you like to know about Walmart?	Statistics on the rise of methamphetamine labs in rural America

Open-ended questions encourage users to open up about their topics and explain them in their own words. They elicit user responses that reveal the context of their queries. For example, the Conversions query brings to mind metric conversions, religious conversions, monetary conversions, and scoring points in football. The only way to find out which type of conversion interests the user is to ask her in a way that doesn't predispose or bias her to answer one way or another. The librarian's open-ended question does just that, revealing the user's interest in the religious conversion pertaining to Thomas Merton.

The initial queries for School Lunches, History Books, and The Middle East are broader representations of users' negotiated queries. Such representations are typical of initial queries. The reasons users express their queries in broad terms may be due to their way of summing up their interests at the start of the reference interview, their limited knowledge of the subject, their desire to sample what the library has on a topic before committing to something specific, their way of obfuscating personal interests that they don't want to admit to others, their knee-jerk reaction to a topic imposed by a college instructor or a boss, and so on. The imposed query comes from someone else, typically a teacher, family member, boss, friend, or colleague. Whether users who approach you with imposed queries have negotiated them with the original inquirer, identifying the impetus for the query or what the inquirer really wants is doubtful, so you will have to do the best you can with the information they are able to provide. Imposed queries are the norm at public, academic, and school libraries, accounting for one-quarter to one-half of the queries posed to reference librarians (Gross 2001; Gross and Saxton 2001). Find out whether the user you are interviewing is dealing with an imposed query, and if he is, the "trick . . . is to get him to talk about what he does know, not what he doesn't" (Ross, Nilsen, and Radford 2009, 139–40).

On occasion, you won't understand what a user means. For example, the librarian hears the user say "jackass tails," and maybe that's what she actually said. Rather than repeat what the user says, the librarian tells the user he isn't sure what she means and asks for more clarification. Eventually the user provides enough information so that the librarian understands what the user is saying and responds accordingly.

As a reference librarian, you will encounter just about every topic under the sun. You cannot be an expert on everything, but you can be an expert on how to find information on topics geared for domain novices, experts, and people somewhere in between. Get in the habit of responding to users' initial questions with open-ended questions—it's your key to unlocking what users know about their topics so you can find relevant information for them.

Being Present

In the context of the reference interview, "being present" means actively listening to the user, being interested in the task of answering the user's question, and enlisting both verbal and nonverbal cues to reassure the user that you truly are present and engaged in his or her particular problem.

Active listening is a communications skill that requires the librarian to listen to what the user says and repeat it back, paraphrasing it in his own words so that he can confirm his understanding of the message with the user. Active listening enables librarians to successfully usher user queries from initial to negotiated status. Unfortunately, active listening is hard to do because the rapid pace and constant interruptions of everyday life make it difficult to settle down. The only way to develop your active-listening skills is to practice them, concentrating single-pointedly on the reference interaction to the exclusion of almost everything else.

Interest means your interest in the task of answering the user's question, not in the actual question itself. How you demonstrate your interest in the task is conveyed to the user both nonverbally and verbally. Nonverbal cues are your eye contact with the user, smiling, head nods in response to the user's replies, and an open stance. Resist the temptation to cross your arms, fold your hands, or put your hands in your pockets because these are closed-body gestures that users may interpret as your disinterest, nonapproval, or even outright hostility. Avoid nervous gestures, such as tapping your fingers, playing with your hair, or fidgeting with an object. While assisting one user, resist the temptation to multitask and work on another user's inquiry or your own work.

In person and on the phone, verbal cues are your explanations of the online sources you are accessing and why you are accessing them and, possibly, sentence fragments that are indicative of what you are reading. Your cues need not be a play-by-play account of everything you are experiencing but enough to assure the user that she has your attention and you are working on her problem. Verbal cues are essential when responding to phone calls, chat, and texts because users cannot see you. When the user is talking on the phone, an occasional "uh-huh," "OK," or "I see" substitutes for the head nods that are characteristic of in-person reference interactions. Called encouragers, these utterances function as "noncommittal acknowledgments" that you are actively listening to what the user is saying and "can encourage the user to continue talking" (Smith and Wong 2016, 68).

Somewhat comparable are the simple "searching . . ." and "working . . ." messages that you should send to a user every two or three minutes or so when you are trying to answer a reference question during a chat or text-message reference interview. Such messages give you time to think or work during the interview while reassuring the user that you are busy solving their problem.

When you have answered the same question on numerous past occasions or are close to the end of your shift on the reference desk, demonstrating interest may be difficult. Get in the habit of physically and mentally regrouping between users. Take at least two or three long breaths—not shallow ones—but deep, long, belly breaths that feature longer exhalations than inhalations; relax your shoulders, your jaw, and any other part of your body that tenses when you are under pressure. While checking yourself physically, think about your breaths and not this or that inquiry past, present, or to come. Taking at least twenty seconds to regroup from time to time should refresh you physically and mentally for the next user.

Closed-Ended Questions

When users have in-depth queries in mind that warrant a comprehensive database search, additional negotiation may be necessary to shed more light on user queries and to answer database-specific questions (table 3.3). Closed-ended questions requiring the user's yes, no, or short answers are appropriate for obtaining answers to most of these questions. Knowing the user's discipline or field of study, the kind of information she wants, her level of sophistication with the topic and discipline, and what research she has already done helps the librarian make database selection decisions.

Table 3.3. More Negotiation for In-Depth Queries

What You Want to Know	How to Ask
What discipline or field of study underlies the user's query	Are you looking for answers from a particular perspective or discipline? What is it?
What the user's level of sophistication is with both the topic and discipline	Do you want advanced material or something basic and easy to understand?
What kind of information the user wants	What instructions did your instructor give you about the types of information he or she wants you to use? What kind of information do you want? [Statistics, news stories, lesson plans, scholarly journal articles, etc.]
What research the user has done already	What have you done so far? If you've found something you really like, could you show it to me so we can use it to find more like it?
Whether the search should produce high-recall or high-precision results	Do you want to find everything written about this topic, or do you want a few useful articles?
How the user intends to use the information he or she finds	It would help me to answer your question if you could tell me a little about how you will use the information we find. We have lots of information on [topic]. I could help you better if I knew what you are trying to do.
When the user needs the information	When do you need this information? What's your deadline?

Of all the questions listed in table 3.3, asking users how they intend to use the information may be the most sensitive. Asking this in an academic library might not be problematic because so many uses pertain to coursework and publicly funded research; however, special-library and public-library users might balk at a direct question that asks how they will use the information they find. The rule of thumb is to ask indirectly, explaining to users that knowing how they intend to use the information will help you answer their question. Users who respond with "I'm not sure yet" or "I'm helping a friend" are probably not ready to share their intended uses with you, so back off and do the best you can with the information they *are* willing to share with you.

Resist the temptation to make assumptions about users. If you find yourself sizing them up based on such personal appearance cues as dress, hairstyle, age, and accessories, you run the risk of voicing your assumptions during the interaction or letting your personal reactions affect your assistance to them. The well-known adage "You can't judge a book by its cover" applies here. A user who looks homeless or poor might have interrupted yard work to run errands that includes stopping at the library. A user who looks like an ex-con with body piercings and tattoos may be a highly paid digital artist seeking background information and inspiration for a new project he just took on. Do your best to help each user, treat everyone with respect, respect their privacy, and let them be in control of what they are willing to share about their information needs.

Search Phase

The next phase is the librarian's search for information. Some reference interviews don't involve searches, particularly inquiries categorized as Referrals, Directions, Technical Assistance, and Policy & Procedural Matters. Depending on the circumstances, the librarian may conduct the search himself or guide the user through the searching process while explaining the ongoing search using language that is relatively jargon free and understandable to the user.

Table 3.4 lists the seven steps that make up the search process. Included are each step's objective and the numbers of chapters that cover each step in-depth. In fact, these seven steps of the search process are the framework for *Online Searching*'s chapters 3 through 12. The seven steps of the online searching process function as a road map to tell you where you have been, where you are, where you are going, and what you can expect to accomplish along the way. Initially, you will experience steps 2, 3, and 4 as discrete and separate activities, but as you transition to expert-searcher status, you will perform them almost simultaneously. Iteration and looping might occur during steps 6 and 7, when searchers enter their searches, display retrievals, and assess the relevance of retrieved sources. Should the search fail, you might loop back to step 2 to choose another database and then continue forward. As a last resort, you might loop back to step 1, consulting the user for additional clarification and direction so that you can put subsequent searches on track.

Results-Presentation Phase

The interview's results-presentation phase could involve a simple fact, the answer conveyed verbally on the spot, along with the source of the answer. For in-depth queries, regardless of their being in-person, on the phone, or virtual reference interviews,

Table 3.4.   Seven Steps of the Online Searching Process

Step	Objective	Chapters
1. Conducting the reference interview	To determine what the user really wants	3
2. Selecting a relevant database	To produce useful information that is in sync with the user's knowledge of his topic	4
3. Typecasting the negotiated query as a subject or known-item	To reveal clues about formulating search statements	5
4. Conducting a facet analysis and logical combination	To plan for search statements that address the big ideas, concepts, or themes that make up the negotiated query	5
5. Representing the negotiated query as input to the search system	To formulate search statements that produce relevant retrievals	6 to 10
6. Entering the search and responding strategically	To conceptualize the search overall so that its execution is efficient and effective	11
7. Displaying retrievals, assessing them, and responding tactically	To ensure that the execution of important aspects of the search are done efficiently and effectively	12

this phase will probably involve an email message from you or from the system you searched, bearing links to the ongoing search, search results, and/or attached full-texts. Your email message should invite the user to contact you or your colleagues with additional questions about the search results or anything else and close the interview on a positive note.

Follow-Up Phase

Users who have additional questions set the follow-up phase into motion. Some users might ask you to explain the search results, the terminology you used to conduct the search, or the databases you searched. Other users might tell you that the search results are not relevant, making the follow-up phase loop back to the negotiation and searching phases so that you can further develop your understanding of the user's query and respond with additional searches and relevant retrievals. (Refer back to figure 3.4 on page 45).

Closing Phase

The final phase of the reference interview is the closing, in which you verify that the information satisfies the user's query. Your closing should make users feel good that they sought your assistance and assure them that they can ask follow-up questions on this particular project or on something else. Examples are the simple "Glad to help; come back and see us anytime" or the somewhat longer "Glad I could help; come back if you need help on this or anything else you are working on, and if I'm not here, one of my colleagues will be happy to help."

KNOWING WHEN TO STOP SEARCHING FOR INFORMATION

Knowing when to stop may be easy for Referrals, Directions, Reference, Policies & Procedural Matters, and Technical Assistance. It's not as easy for in-depth Subject queries and hard-to-find Known-Items because there's always more information available in licensed databases and on the open Web. Being an expert intermediary searcher, you know it's there and how to retrieve it. Some users will tell you when they have enough information. Others will emit subtle nonverbal cues—a deep breath, eyes wide open, head tilted backward, crossed arms—that indicate they've reached the saturation point. Let them get started with what you found initially. In your closing, tell users that you know that you can find more information and they are welcome to contact you in the event they need it. Then back off.

Consider the implications of the Berrypicking Model (pages 40 to 41). Your initial assistance produces information for users. They process what you have found, and in the course of doing so, not only does their original query evolve, but they may also generate new and different queries altogether. Their subsequent searches (with or without your assistance) may yield retrievals that they deem more useful than the original ones or build on what they learned from the originals. If users revisit you for additional information, they may express new and entirely different queries due to their exposure to information you helped them find earlier.

When users aim to be comprehensive in their search for information, finding the same sources repeatedly or failing to find sources that say something new and different is an indication that the search is achieving high recall. Yet, there are so many ways to search for information (chapters 6 to 10), different strategies (chapter 11), and tactics (chapter 12) that conducting a comprehensive search for information that retrieves all the relevant information on a topic may be well-nigh impossible.

SOME IMPORTANT DEFINITIONS

That the end user initiates a reference interview thrusts the librarian on the stage, bifurcating the information-seeking process into what the user does and what the two of them accomplish together. This bifurcation is acknowledged in subsequent chapters of *Online Searching*, using separate terms and definitions for concepts that could be considered equivalent but really aren't. The following are a handful of such terms and their definitions. Acquaint yourself with the differences between them so that you can choose the right terms to communicate with your instructor, classmates, and future librarian colleagues.

- Information need. The user's recognition that what she knows is inadequate or incomplete to satisfy an overarching goal.
- Keywords. The words and phrases that end users enter into search systems to express their queries.
- Negotiated query. The librarian's understanding of what the user wants as a result of conducting a reference interview with him or her.
- Query. The user's immediate expression of her information need.
- Search statement. An expression of the negotiated query that the expert intermediary searcher formulates, with reference to the search system's searching language and the database's controlled and free text vocabularies, and enters into the search system, with the expectation that, on its own or in conjunction with other search statements, it will produce relevant retrievals.

QUESTIONS

1. Categorize table 3.2's initial and negotiated queries. Notice how the librarian's negotiation changes the categorization for most queries.
2. Is negotiation always necessary? Scrutinize table 3.2's five initial queries, deciding which you should negotiate and which you should take at face value. When you've

made your decision, jot down the characteristics of initial queries that fit into your "negotiate" and "don't negotiate" categories. Answers are given at the end of the chapter.

a. Good morning! Where would I be able to find really good information on fashion? I tried women's studies but didn't get much.
b. Do you have a current travel guidebook to France?
c. Hi. I need something on etiquette.
d. I'm having trouble using PubMed.
e. Hi. I know about Bob Hope, the comedian who entertained the troops, but how did all that "entertaining the troops" stuff get started in the first place?

SUMMARY

This chapter begins with an examination of several models of the information-seeking process to help you, the reference librarian, bridge the gap between your understanding of this process and being a key participant in it. These models anticipate incongruity between what users say they want and what they really want, placing the burden on you to resolve the incongruity during the reference interview to gain a complete and thorough understanding of what the user wants. This chapter also spotlights the reference interview and categorizes the types of queries you should expect from users. Your interaction with them is divided into these seven steps: (1) greeting the user, (2) eliciting the user's initial query, (3) negotiating the query, (4) searching for relevant information online, (5) presenting search results, (6) following up, and (7) closing the interview in a positive manner that encourages the user to seek the assistance of reference staff in the future. An important goal is making users feel comfortable and at ease during the interview so that they are forthcoming about their information needs and positively inclined to consult you or your colleagues for help with their information needs in the future. Eventually, you'll put your knowledge of the user's information needs to work and conduct online searches that produce relevant information.

BIBLIOGRAPHY

Arnold, Julie, and Neal K. Kaske. 2005. "Evaluating the Quality of a Chat Service." *portal: Libraries and the Academy* 5, no. 2: 177–93.

Bates, Marcia J. 1989. "The Design of Browsing and Berrypicking Techniques for the Online Search Interface." *Online Review* 13, no. 5: 407–24.

Cassell, Kay Ann, and Uma Hiremath. 2018. *Reference and Information Services: An Introduction.* 4th ed. Chicago: ALA Neal-Schuman.

Dewdney, Patricia, and Gillian Michell. 1997. "Asking 'Why' Questions in the Reference Interview: A Theoretical Justification." *Library Quarterly* 67 (Jan.): 50–71.

Durrance, Joan C. 1989. "Reference Success: Does the 55 Percent Rule Tell the Whole Story?" *Library Journal* 114, no. 7: 31–36.

Gross, Melissa. 2001. "Imposed Information Seeking in Public Libraries and School Library Media Centers: A Common Behaviour?" *Information Research* 6, no 2. http://www.infor mationr.net/ ir/6-2/paper100.html.

Gross, Melissa, and Matthew L. Saxton. 2001. "Who Wants to Know? Imposed Queries in the Public Library." *Public Libraries* 40: 170–76.

Harmeyer, Dave. 2014. *The Reference Interview Today: Negotiating and Answering Questions Face to Face, on the Phone, and Virtually.* Lanham, MD: Rowman & Littlefield.

Kirk, Thomas. 1974. "Problems in Library Instruction in Four-Year Colleges." In *Educating the Library User*, edited by John Lubans, Jr., 83–103. New York: R. R. Bowker.

Kracker, Jacqueline, and Peiling Wang. 2002. "Research Anxiety and Students' Perceptions of Research: An Experiment. Part II. Content Analysis of Their Writings on Two Experiences." *Journal of the American Society for Information Science and Technology* 53, no. 4: 295–307.

Kuhlthau, Carol. 2003. *Seeking Meaning: A Process Approach to Library and Information Services.* 2nd ed. Westport, CT: Libraries Unlimited.

———. 2018. "Information Search Process." *Rutgers School of Communication and Information.* Accessed June 17, 2018. http://wp.comminfo.rutgers.edu/ckuhlthau/ information-search-process/.

Magi, Trina J., and Patricia E. Mardeusz. 2013. "Why Some Students Continue to Value Individual, Face-to-Face Research Consultations in a Technology-Rich World." *College & Research Libraries* 74, no. 6 (Nov.): 605–18.

McKewan, Jaclyn, and Scott S. Richmond. 2017. "Needs and Results in Virtual Reference Transactions: A Longitudinal Study." *Reference Librarian* 58, no. 3: 179–89.

Radford, Marie L. 1999. *The Reference Encounter: Interpersonal Communication in the Academic Library.* Chicago: American Library Association.

Radford, Marie L., and Lynn Sillipigni Connaway. 2013. "Not Dead Yet! A Longitudinal Study of Query Type and Ready Reference Accuracy in Live Chat and IM Reference." *Library & Information Science Research* 35, no. 1: 2–13.

Radford, Marie L., et al. 2011. "'Are We Getting Warmer?' Query Clarification in Live Chat Virtual Reference." *Reference & User Services Quarterly* 50, no. 3: 259–79.

Ross, Catherine Sheldrick. 2003. "The Reference Interview: Why It Needs to Be Used in Every (Well, Almost Every) Reference Transaction." *Reference & User Services Quarterly* 43, no. 1: 38–43.

Ross, Catherine Sheldrick, Kirsti Nilsen, and Marie L. Radford. 2009. *Conducting the Reference Interview: A How-to-Do-It Manual for Librarians.* 2nd ed. New York: Neal-Schuman.

RUSA (Reference & User Services Division). 2018. "Guidelines for Behavioral Performance of Reference and Information Services Providers." Accessed June 17, 2018. http://www.ala .org/rusa/resources/guidelines/guidelinesbehavioral.

Shannon, Claude E., and Warren Weaver. 1949. *The Mathematical Model of Communication.* Urbana, IL: University of Illinois Press.

Smith, Linda C., and Melissa A. Wong. 2016. *Reference and Information Services: An Introduction.* 5th ed. Santa Barbara, CA: Libraries Unlimited.

Taylor, Robert S. 1968. "Question-Negotiation and Information Seeking in Libraries." *College & Research Libraries* 29, no. 3 (May): 178–94.

SUGGESTED READING

Ross, Catherine Sheldrick, Kirsti Nilsen, and Marie L. Radford. 2009. *Conducting the Reference Interview: A How-to-Do-It Manual for Librarians.* 2nd ed. New York: Neal-Schuman. Drawing on research findings for its practical guidelines and exercises, this book is *the* go-to source for everything you always wanted to know about the reference interview, and its third edition should be available in 2019.

ANSWERS

1. **Categorize table 3.2's initial and negotiated queries.** Subject (Middle East War) becomes Known-Item (*Three Cups of Tea*). Subject (Conversions) becomes Known-Item (a biography). Subject (School Lunches) becomes more specific Subject (Peanut Allergies). Directions (History Books) becomes a Subject (Sherman's March). Subject (Opera) becomes Reference (Opera Singers). Subject (Cornwall) becomes Reader's Advisory (books like this one). Something not understandable (Jackass Tales) becomes a Known-Item (Jataka Tales). Maybe a Subject or a Known-Item (Walmart) becomes a more specific Subject (Meth Labs).

2. **Is negotiation always necessary?** Of the five initial queries, only two describe exactly what the user wants—the Travel Guidebook query and the Entertaining the Troops query. As a result of negotiation, the three remaining queries on Fashion, Etiquette, and PubMed become these negotiated queries:

   - Successful entrepreneurs in the fashion industry
   - Whether it is ever appropriate to cry in the workplace
   - Antiretroviral therapy for treating HIV

There's nothing special, unique, or distinctive about the former or latter queries that identifies them up front as candidates for negotiation. Sometimes one-faceted queries, such as Fashion or Etiquette, mean that users are stating their interests broadly to get the interview started. Other times, users really are interested in their one-faceted queries. They just need to shop around for ideas to limit their topics, possibly using the clusters that accompany search results in some databases. The PubMed query is especially interesting; the librarian's negotiation with the user transforms what initially appears to be Technical Assistance into a Subject query.

The bottom line on negotiation is to negotiate each and every query. Ross, Nilsen, and Radford (2009) point out, "If it turns out to have been unnecessary then no harm is done" (5).

4

Selecting a Relevant Database

As a result of the negotiation phase in the reference interview, you should have an understanding of what the user wants in the form of a negotiated query. You should also be able to categorize the negotiated query. If it is a Subject, Known-Item, Reference, or Reader's Advisory, you are ready to take the next steps of the online searching process, particularly selecting a relevant database. If it is a Policy & Procedural Matter, Technical Assistance, Directions, or Referral, online searching probably won't be necessary. By the way, categorizing the negotiated query as a Subject, Known-Item, Reference,

Check out what's important about databases in the short video at http://www.onlinesearching.org/p/4-database.html.

or Reader's Advisory doesn't mean that you'll conduct a subject, known-item, reference, or reader's advisory search. (In fact, there really is no such thing as a "reference search" or a "reader's advisory search.") Categorizing helps you think things through, preparing for steps 2 (database selection), 3 (typecasting), and 4 (facet analysis) of the online searching process, which, with experience, will happen almost simultaneously; however, as an aspiring expert searcher right now, you'll tackle them one at a time.

DEFINING DATABASES

A database is a collection of data or information systematically organized to facilitate retrieval. Database publishers build and maintain databases in response to people's needs to access the published literature of a discipline, such as chemistry, education, or psychology; the full encyclopedic array of published literature across the disciplines; or a particular genre or form, such as journal articles, dissertations, government publications, or newspapers. Database publishers formulate selection rules that guide what information they do and don't select for their databases, and they make a concerted effort to collect as much information as they can while remaining faithful to their selection guidelines.

Databases are no longer exclusive to scholarship and academic publishing. Everyday people now contribute citations, media, field observations, tags, biographical information, and much more to social media databases and citizen science databases. In fact, the World Wide Web could be conceived as a database, bearing contributions from just about everyone under the sun. Even individual websites have database-like attributes. For example, such major North American grocers as Publix, Meijer, Loblaws, and Wegmans offer websites where their products and services are summed up in photos, brief descriptions, sizes, and prices.

Database publishers either offer online searching to their databases via their own search systems, or they license access to their databases to one or more database aggregators. The database aggregator indexes the database and makes it (along with many other publishers' databases) accessible to users via its proprietary search system. Some database aggregators are also database publishers, adding their own databases to their supermarket-like search services. Search is pervasive across the World Wide Web, and most websites with database-like attributes feature a search capability. For example, you can search grocer websites to find out whether desired products are in stock locally.

Because Google's search engine is such a prominent aspect of the World Wide Web, it isn't readily apparent that the Web is first and foremost an information space where documents identified by uniform resource locators (URLs) are connected via hyperlinks. Third parties, such as Google, Microsoft, and Yahoo, generate income via advertising to support their Web search engines, which use Web spiders to navigate hypertext links and find and index new Web content.

A CLASSIFICATION OF DATABASES

There are thousands of databases. Even if your library provides access to a small percentage of them, remembering each database's specifics is difficult to do except for the databases you use on a daily basis. To help you conceptualize the universe of databases, figure 4.1 classifies databases based on five dimensions, enlisting an optical illusion that gives equal emphasis to all five. When helping a user, one or more dimensions may pop out at you due to a variety of user-need and information-seeking factors. The five dimensions are:

1. Source type. Whether searching the database results in an actual *source* or in a *surrogate* for this source.
2. Genre. The nature of the source or sources contained in the database—what the source is, such as *text, media, numeric and spatial data,* or a *combination* of these.
3. Selection principle. The underlying principle that governs the database publisher's selection guidelines—*genre- or form-specific* content, *subject-specific* content, or *encyclopedic* content.
4. Form. The database's structure. The database is for *reference*, filled with facts and meant for quick look-ups, or for *research*, filled with information that doesn't provide instant answers but is meant for study, in-depth analysis, and synthesis.
5. Editorial control. Whether domain experts apply *quality control*, mediating database content.

To apply the classification depicted in figure 4.1, select any database from your library's website or the open Web and classify it using one aspect from each of the square-based pyramid's five sides. For example, a classification of the Walmart website is:

- Source type = surrogate. Retrievals are surrogates for actual products or services. You have to visit the store or order online to secure your selected products and services.
- Genre = text (product and service names, sizes, prices) and media (photo).
- Selection principle = Encyclopedic. Walmart covers a vast array of products and services.
- Form = reference. Most users make a quick check of a product's availability, size, and price.
- Editorial control = mediated, Walmart applies quality control to its surrogates so shoppers can find and purchase merchandise that interests them. Its "Terms of Use" suggests that Walmart evaluates shopper-contributed reviews of purchased items and removes problematic reviews that aren't in keeping with these terms.

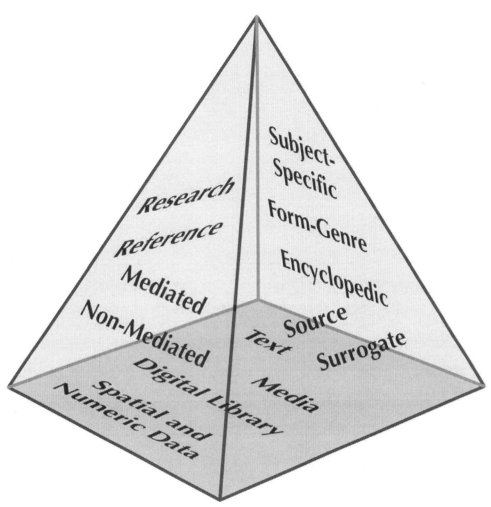

FIGURE 4.1
A Classification of Databases

Your library's website will have tools to help you with database selection, at the very least, assisting you with the *selection principle* attribute (i.e., encyclopedic, subject-specific, or genre- or form-specific). It is difficult to present a perfect classification of databases. Give this classification a chance because knowing databases' source type, genre, selection principle, form, and editorial control will facilitate the selection task, enabling you to pinpoint the one particular database from among the dozens, hundreds, or thousands available at your library's website and on the open Web that has the most promise for satisfying a user's query.

SURROGATE AND SOURCE DATABASES

Whether a database is a source database or a surrogate database must be determined along two dimensions. The first dimension pertains to the document representation that your search statements search. When they search an abbreviated form of the actual source, such as an abstract or summary, it is a *surrogate* database. When they search the actual sources themselves, it is a *source* database. This implies that media cannot be source databases because media are experienced with one's senses, such as hearing, seeing, and touching; however, when text-rich media, such as plays, screenplays, broadsides, and video are transcribed into words and become the representation that queries search, then they are *source* databases.

The second dimension addresses whether the database produces retrievals that are the actual sources themselves or retrievals that are descriptions of actual sources, such as a citation or summary. The former is a source database, and the latter, a surrogate database. Most surrogate databases at the library's website bear resolver links that query other databases for desired sources and, when they find them, display them to users, along with the option to download them to their personal computers. Rarely is it apparent to end users that another database other than the one they are searching supplies their desired sources. To be honest, most users don't care who supplies actual sources, as long as obtaining them is straightforward and effortless; however, one could argue that a database that relies on resolver links for a sizable share of its actual sources isn't a source database on its own.

DATABASES AND THEIR GENRES

Three types of sources are contained in databases: texts, media, and numeric and spatial data. Digital library databases usually excel at two or all three genres.

Texts

Texts are written documents. The most common text-based genres contained in licensed databases are the products of *academic scholarship*, such as journal articles, conference papers, dissertations, theses, research reports, books, and book reviews, and the products of *news reporting*, such as newspaper articles, newswire stories, magazine articles, and blogs. In surrogate databases, search systems index and search the texts of surrogates, usually their citations, index terms, and abstracts. In source databases, search systems index and search the texts of both full-texts and their accompanying surrogates. Whether searching a surrogate or source database, most systems usually give searchers the option to search one particular field (e.g., author, title, journal name, number of pages), a combination of fields, or all fields.

Figure 4.2 shows a surrogate record topped by a downloaded full-text from the America: History and Life (AH&L) database on EBSCOhost. AH&L is a surrogate

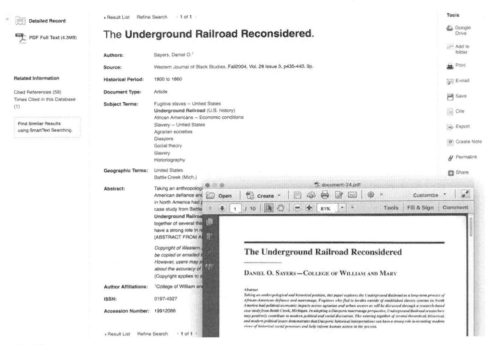

FIGURE 4.2
Surrogate Record and Downloaded Full-Text from the America: History and Life Database on EBSCOhost

Source: Thanks to EBSCO Information Services for granting permission for this and the many screenshots of EBSCO databases that follow.

database that searches surrogates and relies on its database aggregator, EBSCO, and on the library's resolver links to supply the actual sources themselves from journal aggregator databases.

Media

Because most media document what people experience via their visual, auditory, or tactile senses, search systems do not search the media per se; instead, they search surrogates that describe in words what they see, hear, or feel. For example, digitized images in the public domain fill the University of Michigan's Special Collections Image Bank. You don't search the actual images themselves; you search their accompanying surrogate records bearing fields for titles, creators, dates, subjects, and more. Figure 4.3 shows one of several retrievals that the Image Bank produces in response to the search statement `children's literature`, bearing both image and surrogate that illustrate a Victorian-era novel.

Retrievals in the Filmakers Library Online database are streaming documentary films on an encyclopedic array of topics (Alexander Street Press 2018). Figure 4.4

"Capture of Tom and Jacob Doodle-Calf at the school porch," p. 56; Tom Brown's school days, by an old boy

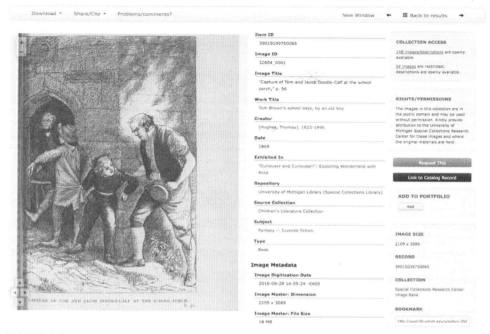

FIGURE 4.3

Photograph and Surrogate from the Special Collections Image Bank

Source: Courtesy of the University of Michigan's Special Collections Image Bank. Screenshots made available under a Creative Commons Attribution license by the University of Michigan Library.

FIGURE 4.4

Clicking on a Retrieved Title in the Filmakers Library Online Database Displays Surrogate and Transcript and Streams the Film to Your PC

Source: Courtesy of Alexander Street Press, a ProQuest Company.

shows the film *Blinky and Me* that the search system retrieves for the search statement `animators`. It displays streaming video on the left and matching terms in the film's transcript and accompanying surrogate on the right.

Numeric and Spatial Data

Numeric data are data expressed in numbers. They reside in a numeric database's tables, graphs, maps, charts, and figures. You don't necessarily query the numbers per se; instead, you query surrogates that describe in words what the numbers mean or the words that accompany the numbers in actual tables, graphs, maps, charts, and figures.

ProQuest's Statistical Insight database indexes publications bearing statistics issued by US federal agencies, state governments, private organizations, intergovernmental organizations, and selected international sources (ProQuest 2018). It might be a productive source for the query "I need statistics on how much Americans walk and bike to work." In fact, a search of Statistical Insight for the search statement `(walk or bicycle) and commuting` produces more than one hundred retrievals, of which one of the first is a US Census Bureau report entitled *Modes Less Traveled: Bicycling and Walking to Work in the U.S., 2008–12*. Figure 4.5 displays the report's surrogate enumerating table captions that describe exactly what the user wants.

Entirely new are databases of numeric and spatial data with built-in data sets and searchable parameters that users choose to find answers to their queries and, in the process, are able to generate their own unique graphs, maps, charts, and/or tables. Choose the SimplyAnalytics database to draw on its business, demographic, and marketing data for creating custom maps (SimplyAnalytics 2018). Three steps get you started: (1) placing your cursor on the "Locations" button and entering a location into the search box, (2) placing your cursor on the "Data" button and choosing a data category listed beneath this button, and (3) choosing a specific data variable from the list. For example, to create the sample map in figure 4.6, the searcher enters the location name `Chicago` into the "Locations" search box, chooses the "Popular Data" data category, and selects the data variable "% Speaks Spanish." Last, the searcher enters the keyword "Library" into the "Business" search box to map locations of libraries in the city.

Browse SimplyAnalytics' thousands of data variables for ones that interest you and map them to counties, states, census tracts, census block groups, congressional districts, or ZIP codes. You also can export high-resolution images of your custom-made maps into written reports, slide-show presentations, and websites and accompany your maps with tables bearing the exact data points that they represent graphically. In addition to maps, use SimplyAnalytics to generate custom reports using data from one or more variables that interest you, or export SimplyAnalytics data into Excel, CSV, or DBF files for follow-up financial and statistical analyses in a software application of your choice.

PQSI

‹ prev Document **2** of 159 next ›

Email Print Add to selected items

Title Info

Title	Modes Less Traveled: Bicycling and Walking to Work in the U.S., 2008-12 : American Community Survey Reports
Summary	(18 p.) Published: May 2014, Source: Bureau of Census, Record Number: 2014 ASI 2316-14.22
Accession No	2316-14.22
Product Year	2014
Durable URL:	https://statistical.proquest.com/statisticalinsight/result/pqpresultpage.previewtitle?docType=PQSI&titleUri=%2Fcontent%2F2014%2F2316-14.22.xml

BIB Data

Report Title: Modes Less Traveled: Bicycling and Walking to Work in the U.S., 2008-12
Series Title: American Community Survey Reports
Date: May 2014
Source: Bureau of Census
Length: 18 p.
Record Number: 2014 ASI 2316-14.22
Available on ASI microfiche

Abstract

Report on commuters bicycling and walking to work, by commute mode, city, region, and selected demographic characteristics, aggregate 2008-12 with some trends from 1980. Data are from ACS and decennial census.

TABLES AND SELECTED CHARTS:

Fig. 2. Percent distribution of workers, by commute mode (car, truck, van; public transportation; work at home; bicycle; walk; other), aggregate 2008-12. (p. 3)
Fig. 3. Percent of workers bicycling and walking to work, decennially 1980-2000 and aggregate 2008-12. (p. 3)
1. Workers walking and bicycling to work, for each of 50 largest cities, 2000 and aggregate 2008-12. (p. 8)
2. Percent of workers walking and bicycling to work, for each of 15 cities with highest walking and bicycle commuting rates, arranged by city size, aggregate 2008-12. (p. 9)
3. Workers aged 16 and older, by age, sex, race/ethnicity, presence of children in household, household income in past year, and educational attainment of workers aged 25 and older; by commute mode, aggregate 2008-12. (p. 12)
4. Workers aged 16 and older, by travel time to work, time of departure, vehicles available for workers in household, and whether workplace is located inside or outside residence; by commute mode, aggregate 2008-12. (p. 15)
A.1. Percent of workers bicycling and walking to work, by region and city size, aggregate 2008-12. (p. 17)
A.2. Workers who did not work at home, by travel time to work, time of departure, vehicles available for workers in household, and whether workplace is located inside or outside residence; by commute mode (bicycle, walking, other), aggregate 2008-12. (p. 18)

Index Term

Bicycles; Commuting; Pedestrians; Time of day; Time use

FIGURE 4.5
Finding Statistics on Commuting to Work on Foot or on Bicycle in ProQuest's Statistical Insight Database

Source: The screenshots and their contents are published with permission of ProQuest LLC. Further reproduction is prohibited without permission. Inquiries may be made to: ProQuest LLC, 789 E. Eisenhower Pkwy, Ann Arbor, MI 48106-1346 USA. Telephone (734) 761–4700; Email: info@proquest.com; Web page: http://www.proquest.com.

FIGURE 4.6
Mapping the Percent of Spanish Speakers in Chicago using the SimplyAnalytics Database
Source: © 2018 SimplyAnalytics, Inc.

Digital Libraries

Digital library databases are libraries in and of themselves. They are focused collections of digital artifacts on a particular subject, practice, or genre. The database's digital artifacts may run the gamut from text and media to numeric and spatial data or specialize in one or two of these. Some digital libraries strive to be one-stop service centers, satisfying users' information needs entirely, while others are more like bus stops, being one of several databases that users search during the course of their research.

An example of the latter is the USC Shoah Foundation's Visual History Archive (VHA), which began as a repository of Holocaust testimony and has expanded to include four more twentieth-century genocides (USC Shoah Foundation 2018). USC Shoah Foundation staff record lengthy interviews with survivors and witnesses, which may include photographs, artifacts, and personal documents that interviewees show them. Processing an interview requires staff to divide it into one-minute segments and assign controlled vocabulary (CV) terms to segments that name the people, geographic locations, time periods, and places that the interviewee mentions; describe the interviewee's specific experiences, emotions, and feelings; and identify the interviewee's role (e.g., Jewish survivor, political prisoner, liberator). Figure 4.7 shows a user searching VHA, choosing the CV terms "schools" and "persecuted group insignia," and combining them in a Boolean AND relationship. VHA responds to the user clicking on the "Next" button by retrieving seventy-four interviews, along with a report

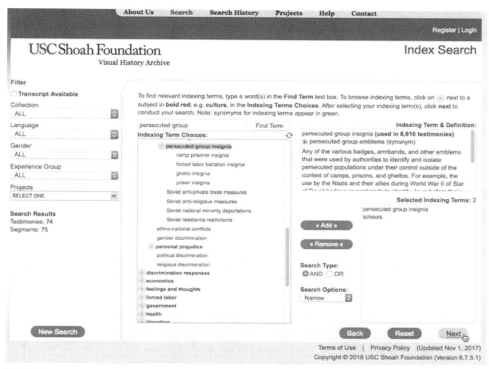

FIGURE 4.7
Index Searching in the USC Shoah Foundation's Visual History Archive
Source: Courtesy of USC Shoah Foundation—The Institute for Visual History and Education.

of the segments where the interviewee describes experiences pertaining to these two terms. Accompanying these interviews are interviewee biographical data, CV terms assigned to individual segments, world maps that pinpoint geographic locations mentioned in interviews, and much more.

SELECTION PRINCIPLE

The selection principle governs the database publisher's decisions about which resources to include and exclude from the database. Databases bear *genre-* or *form-specific* content, *subject-specific* content, and/or *encyclopedic* content. You can see the selection principle in action when you choose a database at your library's website. You can list databases alphabetically and apply qualifiers to limit the list to general (encyclopedic) content, specific subjects, databases by form, databases by genre, or combinations of these. For example, an Easy Search user qualifies databases by subject, choosing "Engineering" from the "Subjects" menu (top left) and is about to qualify by "Genre" (top left center; figure 4.8). Check your library's website to see how the selection principle works for you through list qualification.

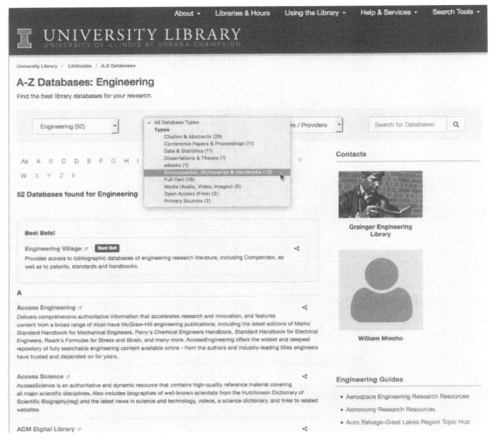

FIGURE 4.8
Qualifying Databases by Subject and Type (or Form) in Easy Search
Source: Screenshots provided under a Creative Commons Attribution license by the University of Illinois at
Urbana–Champaign Library.

FORM

Form is the database's structure. Databases filled with facts and meant for quick look-
ups are *reference* databases. Databases filled with information that doesn't provide
instant answers but are meant for study, in-depth analysis, and synthesis are *research*
databases.

Reference Databases

Reference sources are your destination for facts. A fact is something that exists now
or is something known to have existed in the past, such as an object, event, situation,
or circumstance. In table 3.2, the negotiated query Opera is categorized as reference;
the user wants to know the names of the singers who created the major roles in the

Gershwins' opera, *Porgy and Bess*. For the answer, check the reference sources *Grove Book of Opera Singers* or *Wikipedia*.

The rest of this section analyzes reference databases based on their genre. Understanding the wide variety of reference database genres is the first step to becoming more knowledgeable and experienced with the databases at your library's website so that you quickly and efficiently target the right reference database for the job.

Before reference sources were digitized and their contents configured into databases, they were print-based reference books. No one actually ever read a reference book cover to cover; instead, they consulted its alphabetized entries or special indexes; matched the event, name, phrase, or word that interested them; and read the corresponding entry. This is still true, but the book structure in which digital reference databases have their roots is hardly apparent today because you can search these databases in so many more ways than print-based books.

When indexing programs process reference books, they cut the text into separate entries and index each entry separately. For example, consider a reference database that is a biographical directory of famous people living in America today. The search system cuts the text into separate entries, one biography per famous person, and indexes each biography separately. Your searches of a biographical directory for unique names like "Serena Williams" and "Barack Obama" retrieve one and only one biography, but common names like "Dan Brown" and "Bill Gates" might retrieve several biographies, and you'd have to scan retrievals in search of the particular "Dan Brown" and "Bill Gates" that interests you. Table 4.1 gives definitions of the major reference database genres and specifies whether each genre is a source or surrogate database.

Biographies

Consult a biography for information about a person's life, anything from their accomplishments to such factual data as birthdate, birthplace, names of immediate family members, and education. The licensed Marquis Who's Who database is a biographical database that retrieves entries for well-known modern persons, bearing their birth and death dates, family members, education, career histories, accomplishments, interests and hobbies, contact information (if still living), and much more (Marquis Who's Who 2018). Be prepared for differences between fielded entries; for example, the fields that describe an artist (figure 4.9) will be different from the fields that describe an educator because of differences in the nature of the work and accomplishments.

Not only can you enter people's names into Marquis Who's Who and expect to retrieve their biographies, but you can also search for classes of well-known people; for example, people born in your hometown (or anywhere else), graduates of your alma

Table 4.1. Reference Database Genres

Genre	Definition	Surrogate or Source
Almanac	A collection of facts, statistics, and lists (Smith and Wong 2016, 477).	Source
Biography	Accounts of a person's life, often supplemented with one or more other appropriate genres (e.g., bibliography, catalog, discography, filmography, etc.) to report their accomplishments.	Source
Dictionary, Language	A collection of entries for acronyms, proper nouns, phrases, or words giving definitions, etymology, foreign-language equivalents, grammar, orthography, pronunciations, regionalisms, synonyms, usage, visual imagery, and/or written-out forms.	Source
Dictionary, Discipline Based	A collection of entries for concepts, events, objects, or overarching topics in a discipline, subject, or field of study, along with definitions and short explanations.	Source
Directory	A collection of entries for persons and organizations bearing definitions, explanations, contact information, and other potentially useful information, such as age, gender, and occupation for persons and founding date, number of employees, and contact person for organizations.	Source
Encyclopedia	Same as discipline-based dictionary, but encyclopedia entries have more depth and detail, giving background information, definitions, explanations, current issues and trends, and bibliographical references to seminal sources.	Source
Handbook	"A handy guide to a particular subject, with all of the critical information that one might need" in a single source (Smith and Wong 2016, 478).	Source
Manual	"A convenient guide to a particular procedure, typically with step-by-step instructions" (Smith and Wong 2016, 478).	Source
Yearbook	A review of trends, issues, and events pertaining to a topic, place, or phenomenon in a particular year.	Source

mater, and people who work at certain occupations or enjoy certain hobbies. Such searches are possible because Marquis Who's Who indexes and searches every word in biographical entries.

Biographies may cover living persons, dead persons, or both, and they may be national, regional, or international in scope. Encyclopedias and dictionaries are also excellent sources of biographical information. The open Web is a source of biographical information, but be careful about accepting web-based information at face value. Someone who publishes a website about a famous person, living or dead, may be doing so to promote a personal agenda or one that is consistent with an off-beat group. Verify what you find on the Web in other more-trusted sources. Such social networking sites as Facebook and LinkedIn may also provide the biographical information you are seeking.

Dictionaries

Most people are familiar with language dictionaries, which give definitions, etymology, pronunciations, and usages of words. Less familiar are discipline-based

FIGURE 4.9

Marquis Who's Who Entry (Above the Fold) for John A. Ruthven

Source: Courtesy of Marquis Who's Who LLC.

dictionaries, which give definitions for and explanations of concepts, events, objects, and overarching topics.

The open web-based Acronym Finder is an encyclopedic language dictionary (http://www.acronymfinder.com/). Enter an acronym, and in response, the system lists written-out forms of the acronym. Peruse the list, and you are likely to recognize the one that fits your situation. That's all there is to it.

The most comprehensive and authoritative dictionary of the English language is the Oxford English Dictionary database (Oxford University Press 2018). Enter a word into the quick search box to learn its meaning, history, and pronunciation. Alternatively, launch the advanced interface, choose "Senses" or "Quotation" from the pull-down menu, and enter a word or phrase—breaking wind, an empty space, evanescent—to search for occurrences of your entered word or phrase in the texts of definitions or in quotations, respectively.

Discipline-based dictionaries run the gamut. Some focus narrowly on a specific topic, and others are encyclopedic or cover whole disciplines. Some bear one-line entries, and others feature signed articles that are comparable to encyclopedia entries and rival scholarly journal articles in length and comprehensiveness. Also, be prepared for discipline-based dictionaries that use the terms *encyclopedia*, *companion*, and *reference guide* in place of *dictionary* in their titles, leading you to believe they give encyclopedia-length entries. Only by entering a few search statements and displaying retrieved entries will you know how much depth to expect. For example, netLingo (http://www.netlingo.com) entries describe the meanings of new technology-related words, phrases, and abbreviations in a sentence or two, whereas entries in the Dictionary of Canadian Biography Online (http://www.biographi.ca/en/) are multipage essays bearing bibliographies, author names, and links to author affiliations. Licensed database publishers Gale and Oxford University Press have stuffed hundreds of reference sources into their Gale Virtual Reference Library and Oxford Reference Online databases, respectively. Both databases give users the option to search one reference source, multiple reference sources by subject, or all sources in one fell swoop.

Directories

Consult a directory for contact information for persons and organizations. Online directories are so much more versatile than their print counterparts. For example, print-based white pages and yellow pages limited you to browsing alphabetical lists of names of persons and organizations for the phone numbers you wanted. Now you can search telephone directories on the open Web (the white pages at http://www .whitepages.com and yellow pages at http://www.yellowpages.com) and enter names, categories (for businesses), phone numbers, addresses, or combinations of these. Reference USA is the licensed database equivalent of the print-based white pages and yellow pages.

The licensed Associations Unlimited database covers nonprofit associations and professional societies from around the world. Entries for each association include contact information (e.g., name, street and email addresses, phone number, website URL); contact name; and a brief description of the association's purpose, services, and activities (Gale, a Cengage Company 2018). Association Unlimited's custom search form lets users target their searches to one or more fields or search the entire entry. Figure 4.10 displays an entry for the Women's Professional Rodeo Association, bearing contact information, description, founding date, publications, membership dues, and much more.

PROVIDED BY

LIBRARY

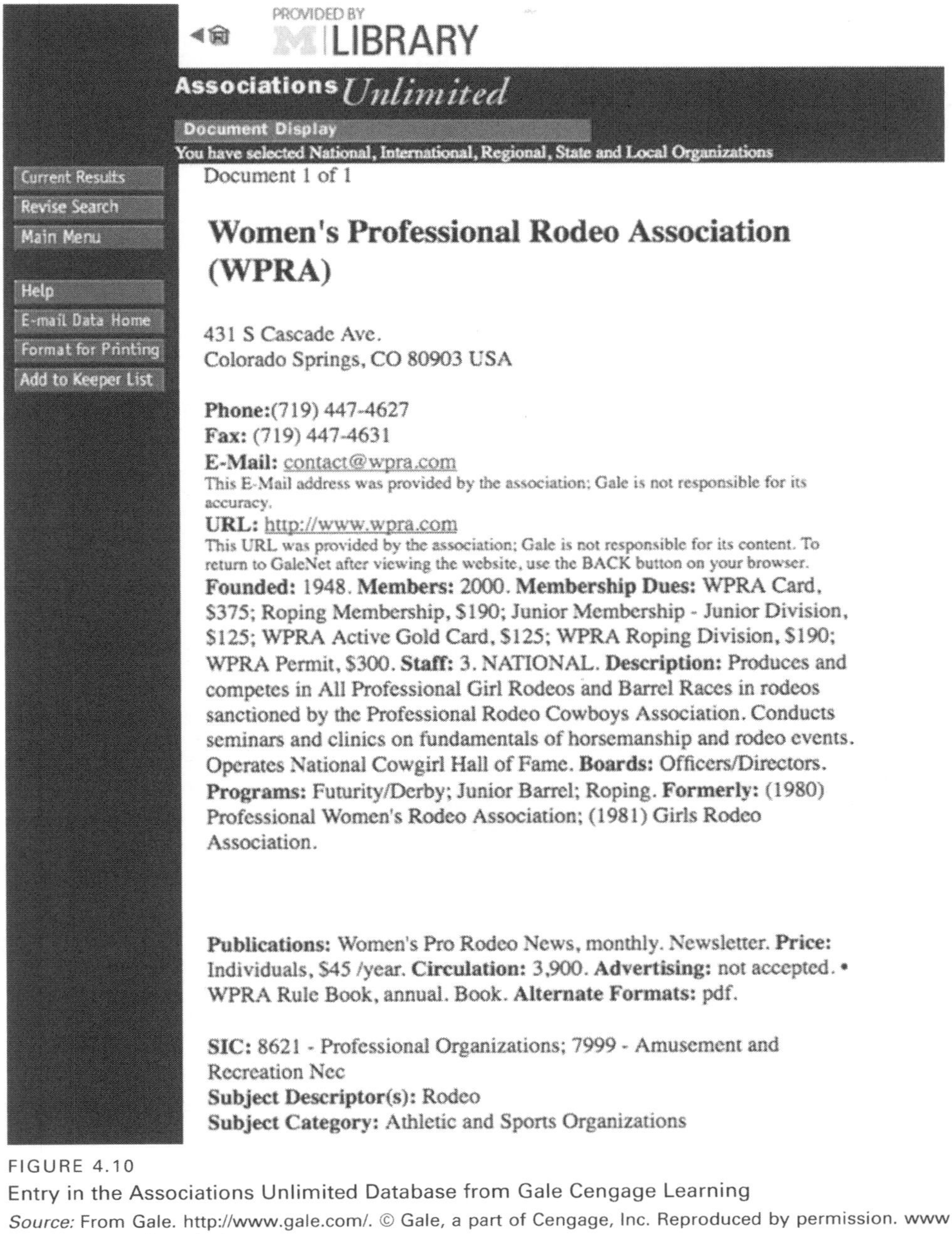

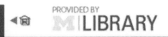

Associations *Unlimited*

Document Display

You have selected National, International, Regional, State and Local Organizations

Current Results

Revise Search

Main Menu

Help

E-mail Data Home

Format for Printing

Add to Keeper List

Document 1 of 1

Women's Professional Rodeo Association (WPRA)

431 S Cascade Ave.
Colorado Springs, CO 80903 USA

Phone:(719) 447-4627
Fax: (719) 447-4631
E-Mail: contact@wpra.com
This E-Mail address was provided by the association; Gale is not responsible for its accuracy.
URL: http://www.wpra.com
This URL was provided by the association; Gale is not responsible for its content. To return to GaleNet after viewing the website, use the BACK button on your browser.
Founded: 1948. **Members:** 2000. **Membership Dues:** WPRA Card, $375; Roping Membership, $190; Junior Membership - Junior Division, $125; WPRA Active Gold Card, $125; WPRA Roping Division, $190; WPRA Permit, $300. **Staff:** 3. NATIONAL. **Description:** Produces and competes in All Professional Girl Rodeos and Barrel Races in rodeos sanctioned by the Professional Rodeo Cowboys Association. Conducts seminars and clinics on fundamentals of horsemanship and rodeo events. Operates National Cowgirl Hall of Fame. **Boards:** Officers/Directors. **Programs:** Futurity/Derby; Junior Barrel; Roping. **Formerly:** (1980) Professional Women's Rodeo Association; (1981) Girls Rodeo Association.

Publications: Women's Pro Rodeo News, monthly. Newsletter. **Price:** Individuals, $45 /year. **Circulation:** 3,900. **Advertising:** not accepted. • WPRA Rule Book, annual. Book. **Alternate Formats:** pdf.

SIC: 8621 - Professional Organizations; 7999 - Amusement and Recreation Nec
Subject Descriptor(s): Rodeo
Subject Category: Athletic and Sports Organizations

FIGURE 4.10

Entry in the Associations Unlimited Database from Gale Cengage Learning

Source: From Gale. http://www.gale.com/. © Gale, a part of Cengage, Inc. Reproduced by permission. www.cengage.com/permissions.

Becoming familiar with the directories available at your library's website will help you answer a host of queries posed by certain classes of people. For example, job seekers researching potential employers and business intelligence specialists researching products, inventions, and competitors benefit from such business directories as Gale Business Insights, Standard and Poor's NetAdvantage, and Mergent Online. Scholars searching for grants, publishing venues, like-minded scholars, and research centers benefit from the Foundations Directory, Europa World of Learning, Cabell's Directory of Publishing Opportunities, American Men and Women of Science, and Scholar Universe.

Encyclopedias

An encyclopedia is a collection of entries for concepts, events, objects, or overarching topics in a discipline or subject that give background information, definitions, detailed explanations, and current issues and trends and include bibliographical references to seminal sources. Consulting encyclopedias for information enables users to develop a working knowledge of the topics that interest them and direct them to relevant sources for more information. Encyclopedias are also satisfactory for finding facts about phenomena to answer simple reference questions, such as "Why isn't Pluto considered a planet anymore?" and "In what years did the Hekla volcano erupt?"

Published by the Cornell Lab of Ornithology (2018), the licensed Birds of North America (BNA) is an encyclopedia bearing illustrated and comprehensive life histories for the more than seven hundred birds on the North American continent. All entries are signed and include range maps, video, audio and photo galleries, and bibliographies. Figure 4.11 displays the beginning of the lengthy introduction to the Golden-Winged Warbler's entry; click on the "Listen" button to hear this warbler's thin and buzzy song.

Almanacs, Handbooks, Manuals, and Yearbooks

This final group of reference sources is a potpourri that yields facts to answer typical reference questions. Much of the information published in almanacs, handbooks, manuals, and yearbooks is available elsewhere, but a number of factors have conspired to give rise to these genres. When a user asks a reference question to which a factual answer is possible, librarians keep these handy reference sources in mind.

Consult almanacs for facts, statistics, and lists (Smith and Wong 2016). An example is the Information Please Almanac (http://www.infoplease.com/almanacs.html) on the open Web that can answer such questions as "What was the cost of a first-class stamp in 1965?" "What day of the week was I born on?" and "What religions have current and former US Supreme Court justices practiced?"

Yearbooks review trends, issues, and events pertaining to a topic, place, or phenomenon in a particular year. Part almanac and part yearbook is the licensed CQ

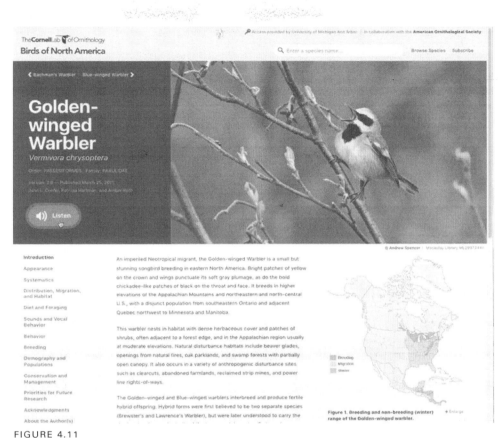

FIGURE 4.11

Online Entry for the Golden-Winged Warbler from Birds of North America
Source: https://birdsna.org, maintained by the Cornell Lab of Ornithology.

Almanac that "organizes, distills, and cross-indexes for permanent reference the full year in Congress and in national politics" (CQ Press 2018).

Handbooks "serve as a handy guide to a particular subject, with all of the critical information that one might need for a particular field" in a single source (Smith and Wong 2016, 478). Manuals do much the same, but they cover procedures. A prime example of a handbook is the Diagnostic and Statistical Manual of Mental Disorders (DSM) that health professionals consult to diagnose mental disorders (American Psychiatric Association 2018).

Research Databases

Especially consult research databases to answer queries that require subject searches. Typically, such searches produce multiple retrievals, none of which answers the user's question entirely. To generate answers, users must synthesize the useful information they extract from retrievals and exercise their judgment, weighing the evidence and taking into account their particular situation and circumstances. In table 3.2, negotiated queries on Peanut Allergies, Sherman's March, and Meth Labs are categorized as subjects; they are definitely candidates for subject searches in research databases. What remains in table 3.2 are these four negotiated queries:

1. A known-item that is a book called *Three Cups of Tea*
2. A known-item that is a biography on William Tecumseh Sherman
3. A reader's advisory that is a book like *Poldark*
4. A known-item called *Jataka Tales*

These queries, too, are candidates for a research database, but knowing which research database is likely to target the one known-item you want and how to search for it requires knowledge of and experience with research databases generally. The rest of this section analyzes research databases based on their genre. Understanding the wide variety of research database genres is the first step to becoming more knowledgeable and experienced with these databases so that you quickly and efficiently target the right research database for the job. Table 4.2 gives definitions of the forms of research databases and specifies whether each genre is likely to be a source or surrogate database.

Table 4.2. Forms of Research Databases

Form	Definition	Surrogate or Source
A&I Database	A special type of index enhanced with abstracts (also called summaries) that describe sources' contents.	Surrogate
Bibliography	A systematic listing of citations, usually organized alphabetically by author name, and restricted in coverage by one or more features, such as subject, publisher, place of publication, or genre.	Surrogate
Catalog	A special type of index bearing surrogate records that describe sources contained in a collection, library, or group of libraries and that are organized according to a formal scheme or plan.	Surrogate
Full-Text Database	A systematic organization of values (e.g., words, phrases, or codes) contained in a database's full-text sources, along with the pointers, references, or addresses that the search system uses to retrieve the full-texts in which the values occur.	Source
Index	A systematic organization of values (e.g., words, phrases, codes) contained in a database's surrogate records, along with the pointers, references, or addresses that the search system uses to retrieve the surrogates in which the values occur.	Surrogate

Bibliographies and Indexes

A bibliography is a systematic listing of citations, usually organized alphabetically by author name, and restricted in coverage by one or more features, such as subject, publisher, place of publication, or genre. An example of an entry in a bibliography is:

Thurman, Robert A. F. 1999. *Inner Revolution: Life, Liberty, and the Pursuit of Real Happiness.* 1st Riverhead Trade Paperback ed. New York: Riverhead Books. 322 pp.

The entry bears just enough identification information so that the user can find the actual source in a source database or physical collection. It is easy to convert the bibliography into an index entry. An editor parses citation data into separate fields:

Title:	Inner Revolution: Life, Liberty, and the Pursuit of Real Happiness
Author:	Thurman, Robert A. F.
Edition:	1st Riverhead Trade Paperback
Place:	New York
Publisher:	Riverhead Books
Date:	1999
Pages:	322

Add the fielded entry into a search system, and the system's indexing program processes field values (words, phrases, codes, or numbers) into separate indexes, one for each field type, and into one big combined index. When you search multiple field entries like this one, the bibliography has become an index. Users want more than just citations, so over the years, publishers of bibliographies have enhanced them with index terms, summaries, even full-texts, and in the process, bibliographies have become indexes, catalogs, A&I databases, and even full-text databases.

If a database's title bears the word *bibliography*, chances are that it has transitioned or it is in the process of transitioning into a different form of research database. Examples are ARTbibliographies Modern, Bibliography of the History of Art, and MLA International Bibliography. The same applies to national bibliographies that contain surrogates for sources written by a country's citizens, published by the country's publishers, in its national language(s), and about the country. Why their publishers have not changed their names to reflect their more-than-a-bibliography status may be due to the many loyal and long-time users of these databases who are so familiar with their names.

Catalogs and Indexes

A catalog is a special type of index. It bears surrogate records that describe sources contained in a collection, library, or group of libraries and that are organized according to a formal scheme or plan. The most familiar catalog is the library's online public

Table 4.3. Catalog Record from an OPAC

Field	Surrogate Data
Call number	D811.5 W486
Title	Green Armor
Author	White, Osmar
Edition	1st
Place of publication	New York
Publisher	W. W. Norton & Co.
Date	1945
Physical description	288 pp., maps, 22 cm
Subject headings	World War, 1939–1945—Personal narratives—New Zealand; World War, 1939–1945—New Guinea; World War, 1939–1945—Solomon Islands
Language	English
Bibliographic level	Monograph/Item

access catalog (OPAC). The plans that organize OPACs are subject headings, a library classification, and the main-entry principle. Most libraries in the English-speaking world choose subject headings from the controlled vocabulary called the Library of Congress Subject Headings (LCSH). A subject heading is a subject word or phrase to which all material that the library has on that subject is entered in the catalog. Table 4.3 shows a catalog record from an OPAC bearing index terms from LCSH. In the absence of subject headings, the user would not know what the book is about because the book's title is not descriptive of its subject contents.

Indexes are almost the same as catalogs, but missing from their definition are emphases on collections and organizational schemes. An example is the Avery Index to Architectural Periodicals database, which indexes journal articles from periodicals in the fields of architecture and architectural design and history (Columbia University Libraries 2018). Figure 4.12 shows an Avery Index record bearing a citation and index terms that describe the subject matter of the indexed article.

Book Review Index Plus (BRIP) is an index that culls book reviews from journals, newspapers, and general interest publications. Search BRIP using names or titles, and you retrieve citations to book reviews. For example, a search for book reviews for the book *Scaredy Squirrel Prepares for Halloween* yields two reviews in issues of *The Horn Book Guide* and *School Library Journal* (figure 4.13). Clicking on the "Download PDF" button unites users with full-text reviews from Gale, BRIP's publisher, or a journal aggregator's database.

A&I (Abstracting and Indexing) Databases

A&I databases are indexes that have been enhanced with an abstract (also called summary) of the source's contents. You'll encounter three types of abstracts in A&I databases. *Informative* abstracts function as a substitute for the source, detailing its quantitative or qualitative substance. *Indicative* abstracts function like tables of

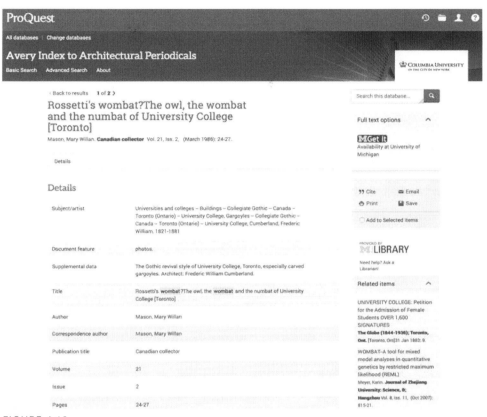

FIGURE 4.12

Index Record from the Avery Index of Architectural Periodicals on ProQuest

Source: The screenshots and their contents are published with permission of ProQuest LLC. Further reproduction is prohibited without permission. Inquiries may be made to: ProQuest LLC, 789 E. Eisenhower Pkwy, Ann Arbor, MI 48106-1346 USA. Telephone (734) 761-4700; Email: info@ proquest.com; Web page: http://www.proquest.com.

contents, describing the source's range and coverage and making general statements about the source. *Indicative-informative* abstracts are part indicative of the source's more significant content and part informative of its less significant content.

Many A&I databases began life as indexes, and as the technology became more powerful and storage space less costly, their publishers added abstracts, transitioning them to A&I databases. Few pure A&I databases exist today because full-texts may be available via the database itself or via journal publishers and journal aggregators through accompanying resolver links. One of the few A&I databases that relies almost entirely on the library's resolver links for full-text fulfillment is Public Affairs Index. Its coverage includes "all aspects of national and global contemporary public policy issues . . . includ[ing] public health, the environment, housing, human and civil rights,

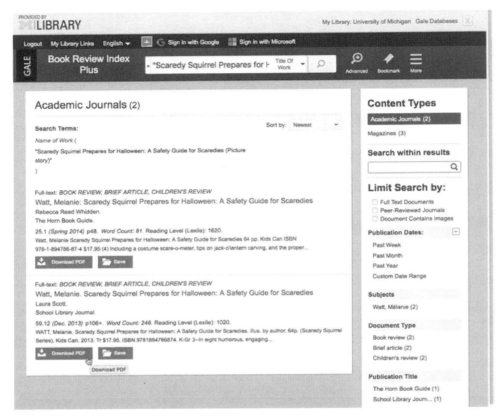

FIGURE 4.13
Citations to Book Reviews in the Book Review Index Plus Database from Gale Cengage Learning
Source: From Gale. http://www.gale.com. © Gale, a part of Cengage, Inc. Reproduced by permission. www
  .cengage.com/permissions.

and international commerce" (EBSCO Industries 2018). Figure 4.14 displays brief surrogate records that a search for `sustainability and clothing` retrieves. Fields for article title and subject do a good job of introducing each source's contents. Clicking on accompanying "Download PDF" resolver links unites the user with a full-text or initiates an interlibrary loan request for the desired source.

Full-Text Databases

Search a full-text database, and the search system matches your search terms with words in full-texts and surrogates. Finding matches, the system displays elements from surrogates, typically titles, index terms, and snippets from abstracts to help you assess relevance. Full-text databases deliver digital full-texts to users in HTML, PDF, and various media formats or give them a choice of format. When users print digital full-texts and their accompanying tables, figures, diagrams, and photographs, they might look

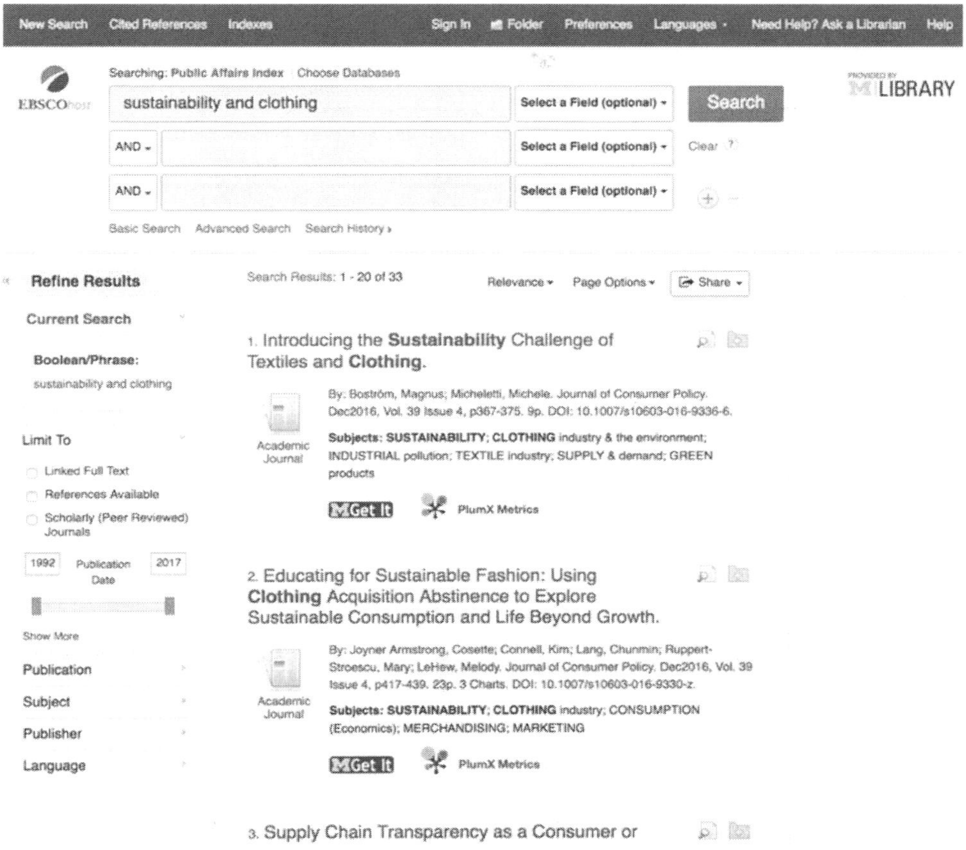

FIGURE 4.14
Surrogate Record from the Public Affairs Index on EBSCOhost

almost exactly like a photocopy of the printed page or—even better—like an original snipped from the pages of the print journal! Examples of full-text databases are Lexis-Nexis, ABI/Inform, and JStor on the licensed Web and arXiv and Google on the open Web. Textbox 4.1 explains in detail the utility of surrogates in full-text databases.

Choosing the Right Research or Reference Database for the Job

Categorizing databases using this chapter's five attributes gives you a surface orientation to the potential of this or that database for answering user queries. Pairing your database categorization with your categorization of the user query as a subject, known-item, reference, or reader's advisory gets you even closer to being able to answer it. You'll conduct subject searches in research databases for many of the negotiated queries you categorize as subjects. Likewise, you'll choose reference databases for queries you categorize as reference.

THE UTILITY OF SURROGATES IN FULL-TEXT DATABASES

Let's take a moment to determine why source databases bear both surrogates and full-texts. You may think that the existence of the latter should contradict the former; that is, surrogates should be superfluous in a full-text database because of the availability of the full-texts. Yet, full-text databases almost always include surrogate records, typically in the form of A&I records bearing citations, index terms, and abstracts. Why do these databases go the extra mile, enhancing full-texts with A&I records?

To answer this question, think about the searches you've conducted in full-text databases. Most likely, they've produced hundreds of retrievals. Retrieving all those sources minus the surrogate records that bear citations and possibly index terms and abstracts would be akin to someone plunking down a stack of three hundred books on your desk in response to their search of the library's book collection for a topic that interests you. How would you respond? After rolling your eyes and taking a deep breath, you'd probably scan through the pile; reading their titles; winnowing the list down to the most promising titles; and then reading their book jackets, forewords, or introductions to determine whether you should put the effort into reading the whole book. That's exactly how surrogates function. You review surrogate contents, scanning their titles and their index terms, and then read their abstracts, all the while looking for evidence that the source is relevant. Convinced of relevance, you are then ready to invest your time reading the full-texts of the most promising ones.

Marcia Bates (1998) reports on the findings of researchers who have studied "levels of access," counting the number of characters that readers encounter as they proceed from a book's title to its table of contents, back-of-the-book index, and full-text. Summarizing their research, she reports that book readers encounter thirty times more characters at each level along the way. It is the same for journal articles—their titles being one-thirtieth the size of their index terms, their index terms being one-thirtieth the size of their abstracts, and their abstracts being one-thirtieth the size of their full-texts. Because this research was conducted long before the Internet and World Wide Web, there are no data for websites, but I bet that website readers encounter thirty times more characters as they proceed from a website's title to the snippets matching their search terms, to the Web page, and finally to the full website. About these research findings, Bates (2003) concludes that the "persistence of these ratios suggests that they represent the end result of a shaking down process, in which, through experience, people became most comfortable when access to information is staged in 30:1 ratios" (27).

These findings are intriguing because they appear to confirm how readers familiarize themselves with retrievals before making the commitment to read full-texts from start to finish. Thus, the utilitarian nature of surrogate records alongside full-texts makes perfect sense. Surrogate records enable readers to decide whether to invest their time and effort in reading full-texts.

Choosing the right research database for the job usually boils down to subject matter; that is, matching the subject of the user's query with a research database's field of study or discipline. However, you could circumvent the subject matter issue altogether, choosing a database that is encyclopedic in coverage. Research databases vary in terms of the amount of subject information available for indexing, searching, and display: catalogs and indexes provide only titles and subject index terms, A&I databases add abstracts, and full-text databases add full-texts. That a research database is bereft of abstracts and full-texts rarely impedes expert searchers because of their knowledge of index terms and experience with Boolean searching for conducting high-precision searches.

Database selection for reference databases is trickier than for research databases, starting with the problem of choosing between the many genres of reference databases. Consider, too, the nature of reference genres themselves, in a state of flux due to their migration from print to online sources; new functionality is transforming online versions of reference sources into different or entirely new genres that defy classification into one of the traditional reference genres, and their publishers are reluctant to update their names with terminology that reflects their different or new forms. When you find yourself consulting a reference source, think about its genre and how the characteristics of the genre team up to make it possible for you to answer the question, so that the next time a user asks a comparable question, you will be prepared to seek out this particular reference source or others of the same genre to answer it.

Ultimately, there is no one-to-one correspondence between query categorization and the choice between reference and research databases. Your search of reference databases might fail for queries you categorize as reference, forcing you to consult research databases, and vice versa. Two important query categorizations—reader's advisory and known-item—have no corresponding database categorization, so you'll have to learn how to extract information from the negotiated query and retrofit it into the searching functionality of reference and research databases.

Initially, you might feel that trial and error best describes how you respond to user queries. Be patient with yourself, and when things don't go as planned, keep in mind that your use of a particular resource might be not be fruitful this time, but by using it, you learned something about the resource on which you can rely in the future. Over time, as you gain more experience using library resources and interacting with library users, you'll find that making choices between reference and research databases will become less deliberate and more reflexive.

EDITORIAL CONTROL

Since the World Wide Web's origins in the early 1990s, publishing has evolved from exclusivity, a private club open to deep-pocketed newspaper, magazine, journal, television, radio, and film moguls, to inclusivity, an open playing field, where *anyone* who has access to the Web through a desktop, laptop, tablet, or mobile device can publish messages that have the potential to reach almost half of the people on earth. This turn of events can be perceived as a boon, putting publishing in the hands of everyday people; a bust, transferring the burden of evaluating messages from such gatekeepers as editors, publishers, peer reviewers, broadcasters, or producers to message recipients, who must judge for themselves whether the messages they read, listen to, watch, or play are accurate and reliable; or a battlefield, where both message issuers and recipients cast aspersions on broadcasters, whose messages aren't in sync with their beliefs and values.

Librarians have long been concerned about authority, choosing quality sources issued by reputable publishers, authors, and editors for print collections, but the World Wide Web really grabbed their attention because of the absence of editorial oversight there. Their initial response to exerting some measure of editorial control over the World Wide Web was to build and maintain such web-based subject directories as Argus Clearinghouse, Infomine, and Librarian's Index, where they showcased quality websites. When their efforts failed due to the explosive growth and dynamic nature of the Web, librarians put their attention into information literacy, advising users to evaluate what they find on the open Web. In the wake of the fake news phenomenon, librarians have redoubled their efforts in this regard, taking advantage of new opportunities to reach end users about the importance of source evaluation. Their intent is not to dissuade people from consulting the Web for information but to encourage them to evaluate what they find and to give them a protocol for conducting an evaluation.

Subject directories may be passé, but librarians still recommend Web databases, doing so through their website's databases checklist or its LibGuides. When librarians evaluate an open Web database, they want to know the nature of editorial control that its creators have exerted over the database's content. Databases that usually pass the test have been issued by national governments; scholarly academies; professional associations; and cultural heritage institutions, such as libraries, museums, colleges, and universities because they enlist professionals with scholarly, scientific, or technical expertise to both author and review content. Databases that don't pass the test have no editorial control in place, or they use social media, where people use consensus to shape their likes and dislikes instead of engaging in a critical evaluation that reveals the currency, accuracy, comprehensiveness, objectivity, and authority of what they read, listen to, watch, or play.

If an academic institution excels in a particular subject or field of study or hosts a special collection, consult its database checklist in case it sponsors an open Web database that may be of interest to your library's users and warrants entry into your library's database checklist. For example, Cornell University's world-renowned Lab of Ornithology publishes the All About Birds database on the open Web, a database that would be especially appropriate for public-library database checklists and for academic libraries in educational institutions where ornithology is taught because of the lab's leadership in bird study, appreciation, and conservation (Cornell Lab of Ornithology 2018). Eventually you'll have responsibilities for choosing databases for your library's website, and should it include open Web databases, ask your colleagues what protocol they use to evaluate such databases so that your chosen databases are in sync with the quality standards they use.

Ultimately, editorial control is relative. That an organization enlists domain experts to make sure its web-based information is accurate and reliable doesn't mean it will be acceptable to everyone. Consider how high feelings run when people discuss global warming, gun control, presidential politics, immigration, Walmart, refugees, creationism, animal experimentation, and so on. You may advise users to check websites that run counter to their personal beliefs so that they may be inclined to include opposing arguments in their deliberations.

QUESTION

In column 1 of the following table are several open Web databases. The first listed database, WordReference, has been classified in columns 2 to 6 according to this chapter's five database attributes. Use it as an example to classify the other databases.

(1) Database Name	(2) Source Type	(3) Genre	(4) Selection Principle	(5) Form	(6) Editorial Control
WordReference (http://www .wordreference .com/)	Source	Reference: Dictionary, language	Subject: Languages	Text; Definitions, pronunciations, usage, etc.	Mediated
AULIMP (http:// www.dtic.mil/dtic/ aulimp/)					
Kelley Blue Book (https://www.kbb .com/)					
Stanford Encyclopedia of Philosophy (https://plato .stanford.edu/)					
YouTube (https:// www.youtube .com/)					

(1) Database Name	(2) Source Type	(3) Genre	(4) Selection Principle	(5) Form	(6) Editorial Control
ArXiv (https://arxiv.org/)					
Amazon (https://www.amazon.com/)					
US Board on Geographic Names (https://geonames.usgs.gov/)					

SUMMARY

During the reference interview, you generate an understanding of what the user wants in the form of a negotiated query. You should also be able to categorize the negotiated query. Now you are prepared to tackle database selection, a daunting task due to the sheer volume of databases at your library's website and on the open Web. Chapter 4 gives you tools to simplify the task, presenting five attributes for classifying databases: (1) source type, (2) genre, (3) selection principle, (4) form, and (5) editorial control. Figure 4.1 presents this classification in the form of a five-sided pyramid.

Classifying databases using these five attributes gives you a surface orientation to the potential of this or that database for answering user queries. Pairing your database classification with your categorization of the user query as subject or known-item gets you even closer to being able to answer it. Because there are no searches dedicated to reader's advisory and reference query categorizations, you'll have to learn how to extract information from the negotiated query and retrofit it into the searching functionality of reference and research databases. Query categorizations and database classifications are tools to help you bridge the gap between the reference interview and conducting a search for the user's query. When searches go awry (and they will), set aside your original interpretation of the query and apply a different categorization so that you can respond with new database classifications that have potential for identifying fruitful databases where relevant retrievals await you.

BIBLIOGRAPHY

Alexander Street Press. 2018. "Filmaker's Library Online: Second Edition." Accessed June 19, 2018. https://alexanderstreet.com/products/filmakers-library-online-second-edition.

American Psychiatric Association. 2018. "Diagnostic and Statistical Manual of Mental Disorders. DSM-5." Accessed June 19, 2018. https://www.psychiatry.org/psychiatrists/practice/dsm.

Bates, Marcia J. 1998. "Indexing and Access for Digital Libraries and the Internet: Human, Database, and Domain Factors." *Journal of the American Society for Information Science* 49 (Nov. 8): 1185–1205.

———. 2003. "Task Force Recommendation 2.3 Research and Design Review: Improving User Access to Library Catalog and Portal Information; Final Report (Version 3). June 1." Accessed June 20, 2018. https://www.loc.gov/catdir/bibcontrol/2.3BatesReport6-03.doc.pdf.

Columbia University Libraries. 2018. "Avery Architectural & Fine Arts Library." Accessed June 19, 2018. http://library.columbia.edu/locations/avery/avery-index.html.

Cornell Lab of Ornithology. 2018. "Explore Birds of North America (BNA)." Accessed June 19, 2018. https://birdsna.org/Species-Account/bna/home.

CQ Press. 2018. "About CQ Almanac Online Edition." Accessed June 19, 2018. https://library.cqpress.com/cqalmanac/static.php?page=about&type=public.

EBSCO Industries. 2018. "Public Affairs Index." Accessed June 19, 2018. https://www.ebsco.com/products/research-databases/public-affairs-index.

Gale, a Cengage Company. 2018. "Associations Unlimited." Accessed June 19, 2018. https://www.gale.com/c/associations-unlimited.

Marquis Who's Who. 2018. "Marquis Who's Who: Our History." Accessed June 19, 2018. https://www.marquiswhoswho.com/pages/about-us/.

Oxford University Press. 2018. "OED, Oxford English Dictionary: About." Accessed June 19, 2018. http://public.oed.com/about/.

ProQuest. 2018. "Statistical Insight Collection." Accessed June 19, 2018. http://www.proquest.com/products-services/Statistical-Insight.html.

SimplyAnalytics. 2018. "Powerful Data Visualization." Accessed June 19, 2018. http://simplyanalytics.com/features/.

Smith, Linda C., and Melissa A. Wong. 2016. *Reference and Information Services: An Introduction*. 5th ed. Santa Barbara, CA: Libraries Unlimited.

USC Shoah Foundation. 2018. "Visual History Archive." Accessed June 20, 2018. https://sfi.usc.edu/.

ANSWER

(1) Database name	(2) Source Type	(3) Genre	(4) Selection principle	(5) Form	(6) Editorial Control
WordReference (http://www.word reference.com)	Source	Reference: Dictionary, language	Subject: Languages	Text; Definitions, pronunciations, usage, etc.	Mediated
AULIMP (http:// www.dtic.mil/ dtic/aulimp/)	Surrogate	Research: Catalog	Subject: Military science	Text: Surrogates for journal articles, interviews, book reviews, and speeches	Mediated
Kelley Blue Book (https://www.kbb .com/)	Source	Reference: Directory	Subject: Motor vehicle shopping	Text and numeric data: Product specifications for motor vehicles	Mediated
Stanford Encyclopedia of Philosophy (https://plato. stanford.edu)	Source	Reference: Encyclopedia and biography	Subject: Philosophy	Text: Encyclopedia articles	Mediated
YouTube (https:// www.youtube. com/)	Source	Research and reference	Encyclopedic	Media: Videos	Non-mediated
ArXiv (https:// arxiv.org/)	Source	Research: Full-text	Subject: Physics	Text: Journal articles, proceedings papers, working papers, etc.	Mediated
Amazon (https:// www.amazon. com/)	Surrogate	Research and reference	Encyclopedic	Text, media	Mediated
US Board on Geographic Names (https:// geonames.usgs. gov/)	Source	Reference: Dictionary	Subject: Geographic nomenclature	Text, numeric and spatial data	Mediated

5

Presearch Preparation

Search systems have had plenty of time to evolve over their fifty-year history. Their developers have listened to both expert searchers and end users, responding to their needs by implementing a wide range of tools in their systems. Yet, successful searches don't start with great system functionality. They start with the expert inter-

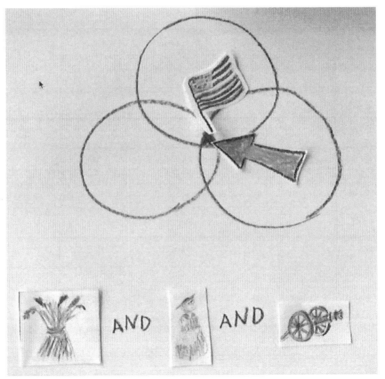

Summing up everything that's important about presearch preparation is this brief video at http://www.onlinesearching.org/p/5-preparation.html.

mediary searcher developing a clear understanding of the user's query and restating this query in the language of the search system so that the system produces relevant retrievals. Chapter 5 covers the presearch preparation that enables you to bridge the gap between your understanding of the user's query and your transformation of it into the system's searching language.

TYPECASTING NEGOTIATED QUERIES

An important milestone in the reference interview is the negotiated query—your understanding of what the user really wants. Here are examples of negotiated queries:

1. The use of humor to treat people who are depressed but not with bipolar disorder.
2. What is the highest temperature ever recorded in Miami, Florida?
3. The user wants to read more novels by the author of *The Lovely Bones*.
4. Will I feel better or worse about myself as a result of using social media, particularly Facebook?
5. Get the complete citation for a source entitled "The Combined Use of Alphavirus Replicons and Pseudoinfectious Particles for the Discovery of Antivirals Derived from Natural Products" by Philip C. Deletka and others.
6. How did President Johnson convince conservative lawmakers to pass his War on Poverty legislation?
7. Eating disorders, possibly with an emphasis on women.
8. Which countries have higher life expectancies than the United States?
9. A recently published biography about the religious protagonist in the movie *Chariots of Fire* that shows a runner on the cover.

Typecasting the negotiated query is a heartbeat away from formulating a search statement and submitting it to your chosen research or reference database. Typecasting boils down to your choice between conducting a subject search or a known-item search for the negotiated query. Here are definitions of each:

- Subject search is a request for information about a topic. To conduct a subject search, enter a search statement made up of words and phrases that describes a topic, idea, object, phenomenon, person, organization, etc., and expect to retrieve several sources, none of which answers the user's query entirely but require greater scrutiny, deliberation, and synthesis on the user's part to arrive at an answer.
- Known-item search is a request for an actual source that you or the user knows exists. To conduct a known-item search, enter a search statement made up of words and phrases that describes an actual source's title, author, publisher, journal title, conference name, genre, date, or other publication-specific attributes. An efficient

known-item search retrieves only the one desired source or puts it atop the ranked retrievals list.

With these definitions in mind, take a moment to typecast the nine earlier negotiated queries as candidates for a subject search or a known-item search. In the course of typecasting them, jot down whether you'd search for them in a research database or a reference database.

Let's examine your typecasting and database selections, starting with subject searches. Queries 1, 4, and 7 are open-ended subject queries with no rock-solid answers. Conduct subject searches for these queries in research databases. Users will have to read relevant retrievals and synthesize what they read to address their topics. The problem with query 7 is the sheer volume of information about eating disorders generally and about women with eating disorders. This user needs to focus on something more specific, and thus, an alternative approach would be to get the user started with a subject search for Eating Disorders in a reference database, such as an encyclopedia that addresses the topic broadly and surveys the various issues, trends, and ideas that occupy the research community studying this topic. Invite her to revisit you when she has targeted a specific interest so that you can help her find information specific to her topic via subject searches in a research database. Query 6 requires a subject search of your library's OPAC, a research database, for biographies of former President Lyndon Johnson; however, you could also conduct a subject search for this president's name in a reference database that is a biography with comprehensive, detailed entries. Conduct subject searches for queries 2 and 8 in a reference database, choosing an almanac or encyclopedia.

Conduct known-item searches for queries 3 and 5. In query 3, the user volunteers the title of a novel, so choosing your library's OPAC would be the right research database to start. A known-item search for this title reveals its author. Then follow up with a known-item search for the author to determine what other books this author has written and are available for borrowing at your library. The user who submits query 5 needs a full citation, and to fulfill his request, you'll conduct a known-item search in a research database using the title and/or author data. Because author names can be difficult to spell correctly, conducting a title search for this query may be advisable before conducting an author search or a combined author-title search.

Query 9 is complicated because it requires two separate searches: first, a known-item search of the title *Chariots of Fire* in a reference database, either a directory or encyclopedia that specializes in films, to learn the protagonist's name and, second, a subject search for this protagonist's name (Eric Liddell) in a research database, such as Amazon or your library's OPAC, where you can browse retrievals for recently published biographies and scan their covers for an image of a runner.

CONDUCTING THE FACET ANALYSIS

Presearch preparation involves not only typecasting and database selection but also a facet analysis of the user's query, expressing it in no more than a handful of big ideas, major concepts, or facets that should or should not be present in retrievals. A facet is a word or very short phrase that describes a single concept or idea.

Despite the passing of forty years since I conducted my first facet analysis, I remember the sample query that the late Ed Terry, expert intermediary searcher at The Johns Hopkins University's Milton S. Eisenhower Library, posed to me: "Does smoking cause lung cancer?" Take a few moments to think about this query's facets. If you are stumped, restate the query:

- Is there a relationship between lung cancer and smoking?
- If I smoke, am I going to get lung cancer?
- Lung cancer may be due to smoking.

To distinguish facets from other online searching conventions, *Online Searching* represents facets in bold type and capitalizes the first letters of facet words. Your facet analysis should produce these two facets:

A. **Smoking**
B. **Lung Cancer**

If it did, then you detected two facets: one facet expressed as the one-word noun *smoking* and the second facet expressed as the two-word adjectival phrase *lung cancer*. Perhaps you analyzed this differently, arriving at these three facets:

A. **Smoking**
B. **Lungs**
C. **Cancer**

If you did, then you divided the facet **Lung Cancer** into two separate and broader facets, **Lungs** and **Cancer**. To determine whether your division is right, wrong, or somewhere in between, a discussion of adjectival phrases is in order. Adjectival phrases are common in the English language. On their own, these phrases convey ideas that are both specific and complex. Examples are:

- *college athletes*
- *role playing*
- *health care reform*

- *academic achievement*
- *opioid addiction*

Torn apart, the individual pieces *colleges* and *athletes*, *role* and *playing*, or *academics* and *achievement* convey ideas that are broader and simpler than their original forms, *college athletes*, *role playing*, or *academic achievement*. The English language uses adjectival phrases to express many specific, complex ideas. Accustomed to the English language, you understand an adjectival phrase as a specific, complex idea but understand it as a single, unitary, and indivisible idea. In fact, if your doctor gave you lung cancer as his diagnosis for the symptoms that you are experiencing, you wouldn't break this adjectival phrase into two separate parts, *lungs* and *cancer*; you'd be blown away by his diagnosis, thinking to yourself, "Oh my! I've got lung cancer!" You have conceptualized the combination of the two words into an adjectival phrase as a single, unitary, and indivisible concept. Using adjectival phrases frequently in everyday speech, English-language speakers have come to think of them as one concept, not two or three concepts or however many words make up the phrase. In library and information science, this phenomenon is called precoordination, the combination of individual concepts into complex subjects before conducting a search for them.

Let's revisit the facet analysis for Ed's query "Does smoking cause lung cancer?" Now, knowing about precoordination, which facet analysis is right—the two facets **Smoking** and **Lung Cancer** or the three facets **Smoking**, **Lungs**, and **Cancer**?

For the time being, both facet analyses are right. You won't know for sure which is correct until you choose a database and represent these facet names with the search terms that the database uses to express these facets; however, the two-facet formulation is probably more correct than the three-facet formulation because of precoordination. Most likely, databases bearing relevant retrievals for this query will use an index term in the form of the precoordinated phrase "Lung Cancer" for the facet **Lung Cancer** and not break up the facet into the two broader facets **Lungs** and **Cancer**, using the index term "Lungs" for the former and the index term "Cancer" or "Neoplasms" for the latter. A discussion of how databases represent these facets in index terms and searchers represent these facets in search terms delves into complicated stuff that can wait until chapters 6, 7, and beyond.

CONDUCTING THE LOGICAL COMBINATION OF FACETS

Your next step is to indicate to the search system how it should combine the query's facets in an online search. Boolean-based search systems use Boolean operators for combining facets. (These operators are named for George Boole, a famous nineteenth-century English mathematician, who invented Boolean logic.) *Online Searching* represents Boolean operators in capital letters so you can distinguish the Boolean operators

AND, OR, and NOT from the English-language conjunctions *and* and *or* and the adverb *not*. Whether you would capitalize Boolean operators when you enter a search statement is dependent on the particular search system you are using—complicated stuff that can wait until chapters 6, 7, and beyond. The most well-known Boolean operators are:

- AND. Inserted between two facets, this operator tells the search system to find sources bearing both facets.
- OR. Inserted between two facets, this operator tells the search system to find sources bearing either facet.
- NOT. Inserted between two facets, A and B, this operator tells the search system to exclude sources bearing the second facet B from the first facet A.

For this query, you want the search system to find sources bearing both facets, and thus, you insert the Boolean AND operator between them:

Smoking AND **Lung Cancer**

Venn diagrams are helpful visual representations of Boolean combinations. In figure 5.1, the rectangle represents all the sources in the database. The light-gray circle on the

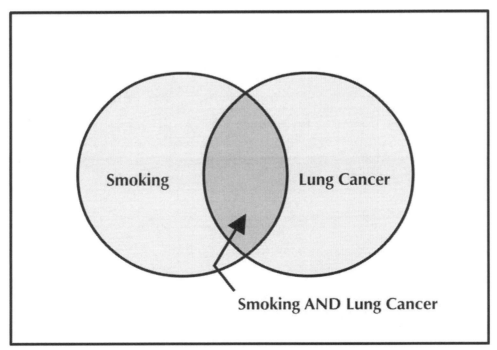

FIGURE 5.1
Venn Diagram Demonstrating the Boolean AND Operator

left represents all sources in the database that discuss the **Smoking** facet. The light-gray circle on the right represents all sources in the database that discuss the **Lung Cancer** facet. Where the two circles overlap reside sources that discuss both concepts, smoking and lung cancer. This is the area of the database that the search system retrieves as the result of a Boolean search for **Smoking** AND **Lung Cancer**. You don't want the search system to retrieve the areas where there is no overlap because those areas discuss only **Smoking** or only **Lung Cancer**, not both facets at the same time. Presumably, sources that discuss both facets **Smoking** and **Lung Cancer** talk about the cause-and-effect relationship between the two; that is, whether smoking causes lung cancer. (By the way, Venn diagrams like the one in figure 5.1 were named for the English logician John Venn, who popularized their usage more than one hundred years ago.)

EXPRESSING RELATIONSHIP FACETS

Some user queries are expressed in ways that anticipate a relationship between one, two, or more conditions, A and B, that tempt the searcher to express a third facet, C, describing a type of relationship between the conditions. The query "Does smoking cause lung cancer?" is definitely a candidate in this regard, inviting the searcher to identify a relationship or a causality facet.

For the time being, omit the relationship facet from your facet analysis. Sometimes you can convince yourself that the relationship facet isn't needed by restating the query. In fact, when you restate this query as "If I smoke, am I going to get lung cancer?" causality disappears—a clue that the causality facet isn't needed in this query's facet analysis and logical combination.

Table 5.1 describes other relationship types that predispose the searcher to establish a relationship facet and add it to the facet analysis and logical combination. Queries like these scream at you to establish an effect, impact, or influence facet. Let the Boolean operator AND establish the relationship for you. Conduct the search minus the relationship facet and invite the user to read retrieved sources to find out what their authors have to say in this regard.

There will be occasions when you add a relationship facet to your facet analysis and logical combination. Those occasions coincide with your decisions about database

Table 5.1. Relationship Types

Relationship Type	Query Example	Description
Effect	I am doing a project on how steroid use affects election into the Baseball Hall of Fame.	Do one, two, or more conditions A, B, etc., affect C?
Impact	What was the impact of the alleged connection between vaccines and autism?	Do one, two, or more conditions A, B, etc., impact C?
Influence	How does religion influence nonmarital sexuality?	Do one, two, or more conditions A, B, etc., influence C?

selection, controlled vocabulary, and searching full-texts—complicated stuff covered in chapters 6, 7, and beyond. When *Online Searching* describes these topics, it will revisit this discussion about the need for relationship facets. For the time being, omit relationship facets from your facet analysis and logical combination.

MORE FACET ANALYSIS AND LOGICAL COMBINATION

Let's work together on a second facet analysis and logical combination. The query is "I really need to know whether switching to flextime or flexible work schedules will improve my employees' morale and motivation." Take a few moments to think about this query's facets. If you are stumped, restate the same query in different ways:

- Is there a relationship between flextime and employees' morale and motivation?
- Does flextime matter when it comes to the morale and motivation of employees?
- Do employees on a flextime work schedule have better morale and motivation?

The facet analysis for this query yields our facets:

A. **Flextime**
B. **Employees**
C. **Morale**
D. **Motivation**

Your next step is to indicate to the search system how it should combine these four facets in an online search. You want the search system to find sources bearing the **Flextime** and **Employees** facets, and thus, insert the Boolean AND operator between them. Then things get tricky. The user is interested in her employees' morale, and she's also interested in her employees' motivation. She probably doesn't care whether retrieved sources discuss both; as long as they discuss one or the other in the context of flextime and employees, she would be satisfied. Thus, insert the Boolean OR operator between the **Morale** and **Motivation** facets. The logical combination for this query is:

Morale OR **Motivation** AND **Flextime** AND **Employees**

Use a Venn diagram to represent the logical combination of this query's facets. In figure 5.2, the rectangle represents all the sources in the database. There are four circles, one each around the sources in the database that discuss the concepts *flextime*, *employees*, *morale*, and *motivation*. Medium- and dark-gray splotches mark the area of the database that you want to retrieve. Notice that you retrieve one area where all four facets intersect and two areas where three of the four facets intersect.

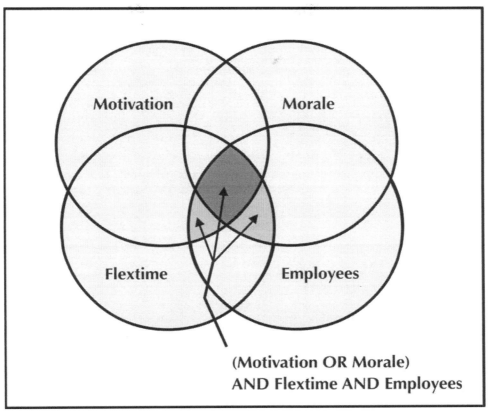

(Motivation OR Morale)
AND Flextime AND Employees

FIGURE 5.2
Venn Diagram Demonstrating the Boolean AND and OR Operators

Your logical combination for this query bears a combination of Boolean operators: one OR operator and two AND operators. Each search system has its own rules for processing queries. Some process them left to right, and others, right to left. Some systems have a rule called the *precedence of operators*; for example, they process ANDs first, then ORs, or vice versa. Memorizing precedence of operator rules for thousands of search systems is a waste of your time and energy. Instead, insert parentheses into your logical combinations to force the system to perform Boolean operations correctly. The use of parentheses is called nested Boolean logic, and it works the same way as the parentheses you used in algebra; for example, $(5 \times 5) + 3 = 28$ or $5 \times (5 + 3) = 40$. That is, the search system *first* performs the Boolean operation(s) *nested in parentheses* and then moves on to operations not in parentheses. When nested Boolean logic is added to the logical combination, the query becomes:

(Morale OR **Motivation)** AND **Flextime** AND **Employees**

The original presentation of this query purposely uses the conjunction *and* between the **Motivation** and **Morale** facets to demonstrate that Boolean operators (i.e., AND, OR, NOT) and English-language parts of speech (i.e., conjunctions *and* and *or* and adverb *not*) are *not* one and the same. When users discuss their queries with you, they will use *English-language parts of speech*. Disregard the parts of speech they use when conducting the facet analysis and logical combination. If you are unsure whether the user would agree with your logical combination, ask her; for example, "Would you be satisfied with sources that discuss whether flextime improves employee morale but fail to mention motivation? Would you also be satisfied with sources that discuss whether flextime improves employee motivation but fail to mention morale, or are you only interested in sources that discuss all four ideas?" How she responds determines your search's logical combination:

(**Morale** OR **Motivation**) AND **Flextime** AND **Employees**

or

Morale AND **Motivation** AND **Flextime** AND **Employees**

Let's conduct a third facet analysis and logical combination together. The user's query is "I am researching the use of humor to treat people who are depressed but not with bipolar disorder." Take a few moments to think about this query's facets. If you are stumped, restate the query in your own words. The facet analysis for this query yields four facets:

A. **Humor**
B. **Depression**
C. **Treatment**
D. **Bipolar Disorder**

Your next step is to indicate to the search system how it should combine these four facets in an online search. You want the search system to find sources bearing the three facets **Humor**, **Depression**, and **Treatment**, so you insert the Boolean AND operator between them:

Humor AND **Depression** AND **Treatment**

The user isn't interested in people with bipolar disorder, so you can add this facet to the logical combination with the Boolean NOT operator. Because you are mixing two types of Boolean operators, you need to add nested Boolean logic (the parentheses) to tell the search system how to process the statement logically. Nesting the facets combined with AND tells the system to process this combination first, then subtract from it retrievals that bear the facet **Bipolar Disorder**:

(**Humor** AND **Depression** AND **Treatment**) NOT **Bipolar Disorder**

Use a Venn diagram to represent the logical combination of this query's facets visually. In figure 5.3, the rectangle represents all the sources in the database. There are four circles, one each around the sources in the database that discuss the concepts humor, depression, treatment, and bipolar disorder. The white area represents all **Bipolar Disorder** retrievals that are excluded by the NOT operator. The dark-gray area marks the area of the database that the searcher wants to retrieve—the intersection of **Humor**, **Depression**, and **Treatment** facets minus the **Bipolar Disorder** facet.

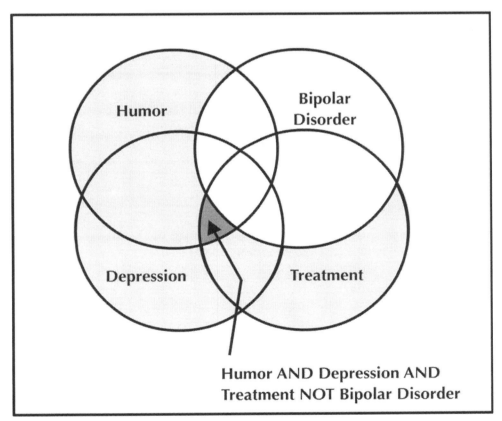

FIGURE 5.3
Venn Diagram Demonstrating the Boolean AND and NOT Operators

There's almost always a hitch when using the NOT operator; that is, this operator is likely to eliminate relevant retrievals. For example, envision a perfectly relevant source that is an experiment comparing the use of humor to treat people who are depressed and who have bipolar disorder with the use of humor to treat people who are depressed but who do not have bipolar disorder. The experiment's results show that humor relieves depression for people generally, whether they have bipolar disorder or not. Such a relevant source would not be retrieved in a search that enlists the Boolean NOT operator. When you build logical combinations bearing the NOT operator, think about the relevant retrievals that the logical combination eliminates. For this query, a logical combination bearing the three facets joined by AND should suffice:

Humor AND **Depression** AND **Treatment**

Eventually you may conduct a subject search for this topic. If the concept bipolar disorder predominates retrievals, then add a **Bipolar Disorder** facet to the search using the NOT operator.

FACET ANALYSIS AND LOGICAL COMBINATION FOR KNOWN-ITEM SEARCHES

The facet analysis for known-item searches isn't much different from subject searches. Scrutinize the negotiated query for facets that are publication-specific attributes of actual sources, such as title, author, contributor, publisher, journal title, conference name, genre, date, etc. Cull these elements directly from the negotiated query. For the logical combination, insert Boolean AND operators between each publication-specific element. For example, query 5 on page 96 deserves a known-item search. The user volunteers two elements: (1) title ("The Combined Use of Alphavirus Replicons . . .") and (2) author (Philip C. Deletka). Culling these **Title** and **Author** elements from this query completes the facet analysis. You want the search system to find sources bearing both **Title** and **Author** facets, and thus, you'd insert the Boolean AND operator between them to complete the logical combination:

[**Title**] AND [**Author**]

Brackets around the publication-specific element names here mean that you'd replace element names with the title and author data you culled from the query. Figure 5.4 is a Venn diagram that represents the logical combination of this query's facets visually. The rectangle represents all the sources in the database. The light-gray circle on the left represents all sources in the database that match the desired source's **Title** words and phrases. The light-gray circle on the right represents all sources in the database that match the desired source's **Author** name elements. Where the two circles overlap

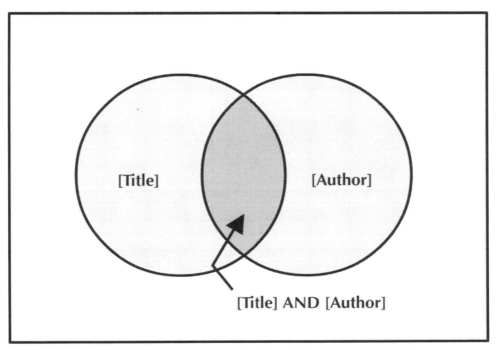

FIGURE 5.4
Venn Diagram Demonstrating a Known-Item Search

reside sources that match both title and author elements, producing retrievals that are most likely to include the one that interests the user.

Eventually you may conduct a known-item search for this negotiated query. Because the desired source has such a long title and bears several unique title words (e.g., *alphavirus, replicons, pseudoinfectious, antivirals*), you might conduct a search for the **Title** facet only, thinking that it should limit retrievals to the one you want. If there are too many retrievals, add the **Author** facet to the search using the AND operator.

PRESEARCH PREPARATION TIPS

Successful searches start with presearch preparation that involves a facet analysis and logical combination. The facet analysis and logical combination are abstract activities that take place at a conceptual level. You are working with concepts and logical relationships between concepts. You are not getting your hands dirty, so to speak, choosing databases and entering search statements into them. If you are thinking about keywords and quotation marks when you conduct the facet analysis and logical combination, then you are working ahead. Resist the temptation to do so, and think instead about identifying the concepts or big ideas that make up user queries for subjects or the publication-specific attributes that make up user queries for known-items, establishing them as facets, naming them, and formalizing relationships between facets using the Boolean AND, OR, and NOT operators.

Eventually you will make the leap from conceptual to concrete modes of operation: selecting relevant databases, identifying the right search terms, formulating them into search statements, and much more. You might have to adjust your facets and their logical combination based on the index terms that your chosen database uses to express big ideas and concepts. The likelihood of future adjustments shouldn't stop you from performing an initial facet analysis and logical combination.

QUESTIONS

First, typecast these negotiated queries as candidates for a subject search or a known-item search. Second, perform a facet analysis and logical combination on these queries. If you are stumped, rephrase the query in your own words, and draw a Venn diagram to represent the logical combination visually. Omit relationship facets. Third, jot down whether you'd search for each query in a research database or a reference database. Answers conclude the chapter.

1. I'm a new school bus driver, and I want to know more about handling discipline problems on school buses.
2. In what year were zebra mussels discovered in the Great Lakes, and how did they get there?
3. Are teens from broken homes likely to develop eating disorders?
4. When adult learners engage in conservation education, does their behavior change? For example, are they more likely to recycle, turn down their home thermostats, purchase energy-efficient vehicles and appliances, and so on?
5. Get a complete citation for a source with the title "Trends in Extreme Apparent Temperatures over the United States, 1949–2010."
6. Who was the speaker preceding Martin Luther King on the day he gave his "I Have a Dream" speech, and what did this speaker have to say?
7. Someone told me that a wandering mind is an unhappy mind. Really? Show me the research!
8. I'm looking for the sequel to Gerda Klein's book *All but My Life.*

SUMMARY

When you develop a working understanding of what the user wants and identify one or more databases that have the potential to provide an answer, your next steps are to typecast the user's query as a subject or known-item search; conduct a facet analysis of the user's query, expressing it in no more than a handful of big ideas, major concepts, or facets that should or should not be present in retrievals; and conduct a logical combination of facets. Although there is no set order for performing these steps, initially you may find yourself being deliberate and circumspect, accomplishing each step in a checklist fashion. With experience and practice, your execution of presearch preparation steps—database selection, facet analysis, logical combination, and type-casting—will take place simultaneously. On occasion, the facet analysis reveals queries that would benefit from a relationship facet. For the time being, restrain yourself from adding such a facet because the Boolean AND operator usually sets it up for you; that is, it produces retrievals with full-texts that elaborate on the relationship for users who bother to read them.

ANSWERS

Answers are given in this order: typecasting (subject or known-item), facet analysis and logical combination, and database (reference or research).

1. Subject. **School Buses** AND **Discipline Problems**. Research.
2. Subject. **Zebra Mussels** AND **Great Lakes**. Reference.
3. Subject. **Eating Disorders** AND **Broken Homes** AND **Adolescents**. Research.
4. Subject. **Conservation Education** AND **Adults** AND **Behavior Change**. Research.
5. Known-item. [**Title**] AND [**Date** (after 2010)]. Research.
6. Subject. **Speakers Before** AND **Martin Luther King** AND **I Have a Dream**. Reference.
7. Subject. **Wandering Mind** AND **Unhappiness**. Research.
8. Known-item. [**Author**]. Research.

Controlled Vocabulary for Precision in Subject Searches of Boolean Systems

Four steps of the online searching process are now behind you. You've conducted the reference interview, selected a database, performed a facet analysis and logical combination, and typecast the negotiated query for a subject or known-item search. Next, you'll represent the search as input to the search system, focusing on subject searches in chapters 6, 7, and 8 and known-item searches in chapter 9.

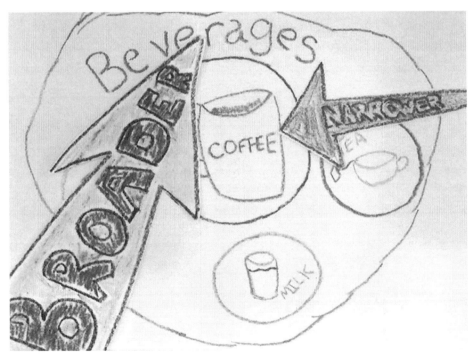

In less than two minutes, the video at http://www.onlinesearching.org/p/6-controlled.html introduces you to the basics of controlled vocabulary.

If your selected database is spot-on, then your subject search should retrieve more than enough information. Expert searchers gravitate toward conducting subject searches with controlled vocabularies (CVs) because they know CVs yield high-precision results; that is, searches with mostly relevant retrievals. Thus, it makes sense to start our analysis of step 5 of the online searching process—representing the negotiated query as input to the search system—with CV searching, an extraordinarily powerful tool for producing relevant retrievals.

DATABASE FIELDS

Databases are made up of surrogate or source records or both. Records use fields to designate information about sources. A field is a set of characters in a database that, when treated as a unit, describes a particular kind of data, like an author, title, or summary. Fields perform a very useful function: They designate the meaning or semantics of fielded data. When search systems index the values in fields, they keep track of the fields from which the values were extracted. Eventually a user comes along, enters his terms into the search system, and designates them for a particular subject or known-item search. For the sake of example, let's say the user conducts a known-item search, entering title words and designating them for a title search. This prompts the system to conduct a title search, comparing the user-entered title words to values it has extracted from title fields and placed in its title index. When there's a matching record, the system reports the match to the user, and hopefully, the match is exactly the title that the user wants.

Eliminate fields from surrogate and source records, and the search system isn't able to identify the meaning of surrogate-record or source-record data. About all the system can do is process all the data into one big index. Searches would be possible, but the results would lack precision. For example, a search for paris would retrieve sources published in Paris or about the city, Greek god, or a celebrity named Paris or written by authors whose first, middle, or last name is Paris or issued by the city government of Paris and much more.

Table 6.1 is a sample database bearing seven surrogate records that Online Searching uses to demonstrate CV searching, Boolean-based free text (FT) searching, extended-Boolean FT searching, and known-item searching in chapters 6, 7, 8, and 9, respectively. To fit this database into *Online Searching*, its records bear much shorter abstracts than their actual counterparts in the ERIC database, and its fields are limited to four known-item fields (author, title, publication, and year) and three subject fields (title, descriptor, and identifier).

Table 6.1. Sample Database Bearing Seven Surrogate Records

1

Title	Squirrels—A Teaching Resource in Your Schoolyard
Author	LaHart, David E.
Publication	Nature Study; v44; n4; pp20–22
Date	1991
Abstract	This lesson plan demonstrates how to use common animals in your backyard or school grounds to study basic ecological principles with students. An example study uses squirrels for observational study.
Descriptor	Ecology; Educational Resources; Environmental Education; Field Studies; Field Trips; Instructional Materials; Intermediate Grades; Learning Activities; Natural Resources; Observational Learning; Outdoor Education; Teaching Methods

2

Title	Woodland Detection
Author	Fischer, Richard B.
Publication	Outdoor Communicator; v20; n1; pp2–7
Date	1988–1989
Abstract	Presents tips on nature observation during a woodland hike in the Adirondacks. Discusses engraver beetles, Dutch elm disease, birds' nests, hornets' nests, caterpillar webs, deer and bear signs, woodpecker holes, red squirrels, porcupine and beaver signs, and galls.
Descriptor	Environmental Education; Naturalistic Observation; Outdoor Education; Wildlife
Identifier	Adirondack Mountains; Hiking; Nature; New York

3

Title	Transforming Campus Life: Reflection on Spirituality and Religious Pluralism
Author	Miller, Vachel W. (editor); Ryan, Merle M. (editor)
Publication	New York; P. Lang
Date	2001
Abstract	This collection explores the religious and spiritual dimensions of college life. It offers innovative approaches for positive change and addresses legal, organizational, and cultural issues involved in making campuses more hospitable to the human spirit.
Descriptor	College Students; Cultural Pluralism; Diversity (Student); Educational Environment; Higher Education; Religion; Religious Differences; Religious Education; Spirituality

4

Title	How to Help Students Confront Life's "Big Questions"
Author	Walvoord, Barbara E.
Publication	Chronicle of Higher Education; v54; n49; pA22
Date	2008
Abstract	Many college students are interested in spirituality and the "big questions" about life's meaning and values, but many professors seem not to know how to respond to that interest.
Descriptor	Critical Thinking; College Students; Higher Education; Religious Factors; College Faculty; Religion Studies; Religious Education; Beliefs

5

Title	The Correlates of Spiritual Struggle during the College Years
Author	Bryant, Alyssa N.; Astin, Helen S.
Publication	Journal of Higher Education; v79; n1; pp1–27
Date	2008
Abstract	This study explores factors associated with students' experiences of spiritual struggles during college. Data indicate that spiritual struggle is associated with experiences in college that challenge and disorient students, affecting psychological well being negatively but increasing students' acceptance of individuals of different faith traditions.
Descriptor	Religion; Spiritual Development; College Students; Student Experience; Well Being; Psychological Patterns; Consciousness Raising; Religious Factors; Hypothesis Testing; Self Esteem

(continued)

Table 6.1. *Continued*

6	
Title	Religiousness, Spirituality, and Social Support: How Are They Related to Underage Drinking among College Students?
Author	Brown, Tamara L.; Salsman, John M.; Brechting, Emily H.; Carlson, Charles R.
Publication	Journal of Child & Adolescent Substance Abuse; v17; n2; pp15–39
Date	2008
Abstract	This study's findings indicate that religiousness and spirituality are differentially associated with alcohol use and that only certain aspects of religiousness (intrinsic but not extrinsic) are related to lower levels of alcohol use.
Descriptor	College Students; Drinking; Religious Factors; Social Support Groups
7	
Title	The Greening of the World's Religions
Author	Tucker, Mary Evelyn; Grim, John
Publication	Chronicle of Higher Education; v53; n23; pB9
Date	2007
Abstract	This article presents what religious leaders and local communities from different countries are doing regarding environmental issues.
Descriptor	Environmental Education; Religion; Conservation (Environment); Environmental Standards; Ethics; World Problems; International Cooperation

Source: Adapted from the ERIC Database.

HOW CONTROLLED VOCABULARY INDEXING AND SEARCHING WORKS

To index Table 6.1's seven surrogate records for CV searching, a search system's indexing program processes each record, extracting descriptors and identifiers from descriptor and identifier fields, placing them in a huge alphabetical index from A to Z, and adding their record numbers and the name of the CV field (descriptor or identifier) from which they were extracted. The correct name is an inverted index because indexed words and phrases are listed along with positional data that can be used to rebuild the original text. Table 6.2 displays our sample database's inverted index for CV searching. Notice that the column to the immediate right of each CV term uses the abbreviated labels "de" and "id" to identify whether the term is extracted from a descriptor or an identifier field.

Search systems impress their own searching language on searchers. Encoding search statements into a system's searching language, searchers are able to control how systems process their search statements. At a minimum, this language tells systems which fields to search, whether to enforce word adjacency or proximity, and whether to stem entered words and phrases. In most search systems, prefacing your search statement with a descriptor (de) field label instructs systems to search for your entered words and phrases only in CV (also called descriptor) fields. Enclosing quotes around your search words and phrases instructs search systems to retrieve the exact phrase inside the quotes. Omitting the quotes gives search systems the authority to truncate words and phrases and be lax about word adjacency, allowing other words or phrases to intervene. Each search system has its own language, so be prepared to memorize

Table 6.2.   Sample Database's Inverted Index for CV Searching

CV Term	Record Number and Field	CV Term	Record Number and Field
adirondack mountains	2 id	international cooperation	7 de
beliefs	4 de	learning activities	1 de
college faculty	4 de	naturalistic observation	2 de
college students	3 de; 4 de; 5 de; 6 de	natural resources	1 de
		nature	2 id
consciousness raising	5 de	new york	2 id
conservation (environment)	7 de	observational learning	1 de
critical thinking	4 de	outdoor education	1 de; 2 de
cultural pluralism	3 de	psychological patterns	5 de
diversity (student)	3 de	religion	3 de; 5 de; 7 de
drinking	6 de	religion studies	4 de
ecology	1 de	religious differences	3 de
educational environment	3 de	religious education	3 de; 4 de
educational resources	1 de	religious factors	4 de; 5 de; 6 de
environmental education	1 de; 2 de; 7 de	self esteem	5 de
environmental standards	7 de	social support groups	6 de
ethics	7 de	spiritual development	5 de
field studies	1 de	spirituality	3 de
field trips	1 de	student experience	5 de
higher education	3 de; 4 de	teaching methods	1 de
hiking	2 id	well being	5 de
hypothesis testing	5 de	wildlife	2 de
instructional materials	1 de	world problems	7 de
intermediate grades	1 de		

the searching languages of systems you search repeatedly so that you can control how they perform retrieval.

The following are ten search statements for retrieving records from the sample seven-record database in table 6.1. Our sample database's search system features a CV searching language that requires the entry of abbreviated field labels (e.g., de and/or id) to limit retrievals to one or both of these CV fields, quotes around CV terms to limit retrievals to the exact phrase, and capitalized Boolean operators between search terms. Keeping this searching language in mind, refer only to our sample database's inverted index (table 6.2) to determine which records these search statements retrieve (answers conclude this section):

```
1. de ("outdoor education")
2. de ("religion studies" OR "religious education")
3. de ("college students" AND "well being")
4. de ("world problems" AND "environmental education")
5. de ("environmental education" OR "outdoor education")
6. de ("religion" OR "spirituality")
```

```
 7. de ("college studnets")
 8. id ("hiking" AND "new york")
 9. de ("self-esteem")
10. de, id ("critical thinking" AND "world problems")
```

Tables 6.1 and 6.2 set you up to perform manually what search systems do automatically, and if you completed the exercise, then you experienced firsthand how CV indexing and searching work!

(Answers: 1. Records 1 and 2; 2. Records 3 and 4; 3. Record 5; 4. Record 7; 5. Records 1, 2, and 7; 6. Records 3, 5, and 7; 7. No records because *students* is misspelled; 8. Record 2; 9. No records because there is no hyphen in this CV term in the inverted index; 10. No records because no record bears both CV terms.)

THE STRUCTURE OF CONTROLLED VOCABULARIES

CVs vary in complexity. Some feature a simple base of authorized subject terms and unused synonyms directing users to authorized terms, and others add subject-term relationships, scope notes, and even more to this simple base.

Simple Controlled Vocabularies

A simple CV is an alphabetical list of authorized subject search terms (also called index terms). For example, a CV for a sports database is likely to include the index term "Sneakers" in the list. Checking the CV for index terms for a query's **Athletic Shoes** facet, you look under "Athletic Shoes," "Running Shoes," and "Racing Shoes." Finding nothing, you finally look under "Sneakers" and hit pay dirt. "Sneakers" is the simple CV's authorized index term for this object in your chosen sports database.

Many simple CVs have one added layer of complexity. They enlist "see references" or "use references" for the unused synonyms "Athletic Shoes," "Running Shoes," and "Racing Shoes." You look under "Athletic Shoes," and instead of arriving at a dead end, the CV says, "Use Sneakers," directing you to the authorized index term for this object. Simple CVs are flat, consisting only of authorized index terms or authorized index terms and unused synonyms.

The Thesaurus: A Controlled Vocabulary with Term Relationships

More sophisticated is the CV called a thesaurus, and its sophistication is expressed in relationships between authorized terms. These relationships are editorially established by lexicographers, the people who build and maintain CVs. The broader term–narrower term (BT-NT) relationship between index terms is hierarchical and one of two types:

- Genus : Species | [example] Apparel : Clothes
- Whole : Part | [example] Shoes : Soles

The related-term (RT) relationship is associative, designating relationships between index terms that are closely related conceptually but not hierarchically.

Our sports thesaurus designates three authorized index terms in **bold** for "Apparel," "Shoes," and "Sneakers." All three have BTs, NTs, or both; two have RTs. On the printed page here, there's only room for "Racing Shoes," one of the CV's six unused synonyms; its entry means "Racing Shoes, Use Sneakers."

Apparel	Racing Shoes	**Shoes**	**Sneakers**
UF Clothing	Use Sneakers	UF Footwear	UF Athletic Shoes
RT Dress Codes		UF Footgear	UF Racing Shoes
NT Shoes		BT Apparel	UF Running Shoes
		NT Sneakers	RT Gymnasiums
			BT Shoes

The UF (used for) designation traces an authorized index term's unused synonyms. For example, the unused synonym "Racing Shoes" is traced under the index term "Sneakers," and it means "'Sneakers' is Used For Racing Shoes."

Most thesauri are limited to common nouns. Although such proper nouns as Michael Jordan, Nike, and Under Armour may be unacceptable in a thesaurus, indexers might assign them to the personal name, corporate body, and identifier fields of surrogate records. Some databases, such as ERIC, feature an identifier field, where indexers assign proper nouns and new subjects. Lexicographers monitor the latter, promoting them to index terms when there is literary warrant; that is, enough domain experts have written about them.

The thesaurus network of index term relationships—BTs, NTs, RTs, and UFs—is called a syndetic structure. Also added to thesauri may be scope notes (i.e., brief statements of the intended usage of an index term or explanations that clarify an ambiguous term or restrict the term's usage); add dates (i.e., the date when the index term was added to the thesaurus); and categories, classification captions, or classification codes (i.e., one or more broad categories or classes that describes this index term).

Searching databases with index terms that come from a thesaurus is easy because the syndetic structure gives you so many ideas for search terms to add to your searches. CVs are especially helpful when you have to search databases in fields of study and disciplines that are unfamiliar to you.

CONDUCTING CONTROLLED VOCABULARY SEARCHES

You are now ready to put your knowledge of facet analysis, Boolean operators, and thesaurus relationships to work at conducting CV searches of Boolean search systems. Each Boolean search system has its own unique CV searching language. You can expect similarities between languages and rely on your browser's graphical user interface instead of searching language to perform some search operations. You will want to learn the searching languages for the search systems that you use all the time so you can search them quickly, effectively, and efficiently.

Conducting subject searches in databases that have an online thesaurus requires very little knowledge of the search system's searching language. The only new searching language feature that you will encounter is *sets*. Sets are temporary storage bins for search results. You enter a query into the Boolean search system, and the system saves your retrievals in set 1. You enter a second query into the system, and it saves your retrievals in set 2, and so on. You can recall your saved sets later in the search and use set numbers and Boolean operators to combine sets.

Facet Analysis and Logical Combination

Demonstrated here is a CV search for the query "The use of humor to treat people who are depressed but not with bipolar disorder." The facet analysis for this query results in the three facets **Humor**, **Depression**, and **Treatment**. The **Bipolar Disorder** facet is disregarded because the NOT operator almost always eliminates relevant retrievals (pages 104 to 106). The logical combination is:

Humor AND **Depression** AND **Treatment**

Database Selection

Facets for **Depression** and **Bipolar Disorder** are big-time hints that a psychology database is best for this query. The go-to psychology database is PsycINFO. Published by the American Psychological Association (APA), PsycINFO began as an abstracting and indexing (A&I) database bearing surrogate records with citations, index terms, and abstracts. Its 4.5 million A&I records describe the scholarly literature of psychology published in journal articles, books, and dissertations back to the field's seventeenth-century origins (American Psychological Association 2018a). PsycINFO's CV for subject index terms is the *Thesaurus of Psychological Index Terms* (American Psychological Association 2018b). It is the real deal, featuring authorized index terms, a syndetic structure, unused synonyms, scope notes, and more. PsycINFO indexers assign up to fifteen index terms per surrogate record. They may designate up to five index terms per surrogate record as major index terms, meaning that the source is really, really about the subjects described by its major index terms. APA has licensed the EBSCO database aggregator to provide PsycINFO's EBSCOhost search system.

Browsing the Online Thesaurus

Browse PsycINFO's online thesaurus, choosing index terms for each facet. Start with the **Depression** facet. Switch to PsycINFO's advanced-search interface, and click on the "Thesaurus" link. EBSCOhost's PsycINFO allows you to find authorized index terms in three ways: (1) browsing for index terms beginning with the entered term `depression`, (2) browsing for index terms bearing the entered term `depression`, or (3) browsing for index terms based on relevance ranking. Become familiar with each approach so you choose the right one for the job. For now, choose "Term Contains," enter `depression` into the search box, and click on the "Browse" button (figure 6.1). PsycINFO responds with a list of authorized index terms and entry vocabulary bearing your entered term `depression` (figure 6.2). No PsycINFO index term is an exact match of your entered term. The closest match is "Major Depression." Select the index term "Major Depression," and the EBSCOhost search system displays these elements in the index term's authority record (figure 6.3):

- The index term "Major Depression."
- The date this index term was added to the PsycINFO Thesaurus.
- The index term's scope note; that is, the index term's definition and/or explanatory information about the index term's proper usage, such as clarifying an ambiguous term or restricting the term's usage.
- The index term's syndetic structure in the form of BTs, NTs, and RTs.
- The index term's entry vocabulary; that is, its unused synonyms designated as used-for (UF) terms in the authority record.

Examine the authority record, first reading the index term's scope note to make sure this term is in sync with your interests. This scope note defines "Major Depression" and suggests the index term "Depression (Emotion)" for PsycINFO content on people with nonclinical depression. "Major Depression" has one BT and several NTs and RTs. Almost all listed NTs are satisfactory for representing the **Depression** facet. You can check the boxes to the left of these index terms to add them to the

FIGURE 6.1
Entering a Term into the PsycINFO Thesaurus on EBSCOhost

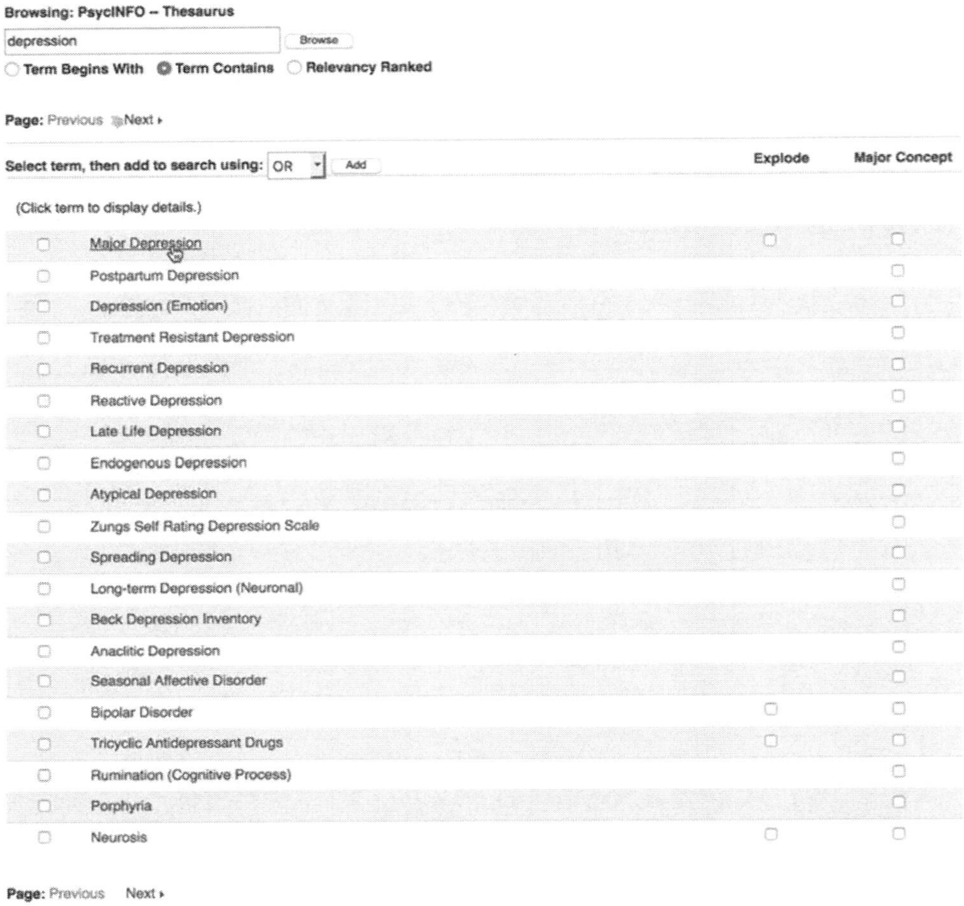

Browsing: PsycINFO -- Thesaurus

| depression | Browse |

○ Term Begins With   ● Term Contains   ○ Relevancy Ranked

Page: Previous Next ▸

Select term, then add to search using: OR ▾ Add	Explode	Major Concept

(Click term to display details.)

		Explode	Major Concept
☐	Major Depression	☐	☐
☐	Postpartum Depression		☐
☐	Depression (Emotion)		☐
☐	Treatment Resistant Depression		☐
☐	Recurrent Depression		☐
☐	Reactive Depression		☐
☐	Late Life Depression		☐
☐	Endogenous Depression		☐
☐	Atypical Depression		☐
☐	Zungs Self Rating Depression Scale		☐
☐	Spreading Depression		☐
☐	Long-term Depression (Neuronal)		☐
☐	Beck Depression Inventory		☐
☐	Anaclitic Depression		☐
☐	Seasonal Affective Disorder		☐
☐	Bipolar Disorder	☐	☐
☐	Tricyclic Antidepressant Drugs	☐	☐
☐	Rumination (Cognitive Process)		☐
☐	Porphyria		☐
☐	Neurosis	☐	☐

Page: Previous Next ▸

FIGURE 6.2
Index Terms and Entry Vocabulary Bearing the Searcher's Entered Term in the PsycINFO The-saurus on EBSCOhost

search. If you deem *all* NTs relevant, check the box to the right of the index term in the "Explode" column. After finishing up here, you can check the authority record for "Depression (Emotion)" for additional index terms.

Always be circumspect about checking "Explode" and "Major Concept" columns in authority records. "Explode" automatically selects *all* listed NTs—make sure this is really what you want because doing so could pollute retrievals with many nonrelevant ones and tracking down the source of nonrelevant retrievals is difficult and time-consuming. (Whether the system also chooses the NTs of selected NTs is database- and system-dependent.) Checking "Major Concept" limits retrievals to major index terms. Use it sparingly, perhaps to reduce very-high-posted searches. In figure 6.3, check marks indicate the index terms selected by the searcher.

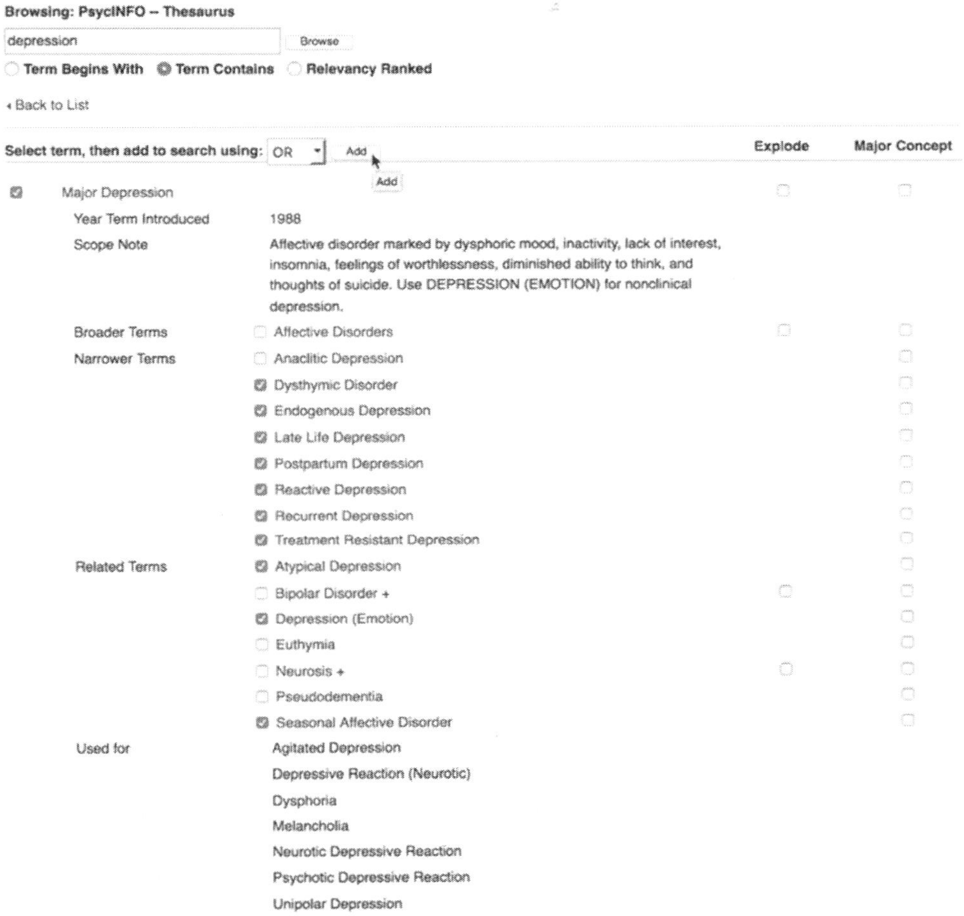

FIGURE 6.3
Authority Record for "Major Depression" in the PsycINFO Thesaurus on EBSCOhost

Next, click on "Depression (Emotion)," scan its syndetic structure for relevant index terms, and check their selection boxes (figure 6.4). When you are done selecting index terms from the "Major Depression" and "Depression (Emotion)" entries, click the "Add" button, and leave the default Boolean operator set to OR (see where the searcher's cursor is positioned in figure 6.4). In response, EBSCOhost encodes your PsycINFO thesaurus selections in its CV searching language and places a search statement into the search box (figure 6.5). Your next step is to click on the "Search" button. EBSCOhost places PsycINFO retrievals into set 1, reports the number of retrievals, and displays the first twenty retrievals.

Search for this query's remaining two facets, **Humor** and **Treatment**, the same way, entering search terms for each facet into the PsycINFO Thesaurus and choosing relevant index terms from authority records. Ultimately, the expert searcher's objective is

FIGURE 6.4
Selected Index Terms in the Authority Record for "Depression (Emotion)" in the PsycINFO Thesaurus on EBSCOhost

FIGURE 6.5
EBSCOhost's Searching Language for Selected PsycINFO Thesaurus Terms

to gather index terms for each query's facet using the online PsycINFO thesaurus, save the results for each facet in sets (e.g., **Depression** index terms in set 1, **Humor** index terms in set 2, and **Treatment** index terms in set 3), and then combine these three sets using the Boolean AND operator.

When you are done creating three separate sets for this query's three facets, click on the "Search History" link under the search box. EBSCOhost lists your search's sets, presumably one for each facet. Combine retrievals using the Boolean AND operator—checkmarking sets 1, 2, and 3 and clicking the "Search with AND" button (figure 6.6). In response, EBSCOhost combines the three separate sets 1, 2, and 3 in a Boolean AND operation, retrieving surrogate records bearing at least one index term per facet. Alternatively, combine sets directly, entering set numbers and Boolean AND operators into the search box:

```
s1 AND s2 AND s3
```

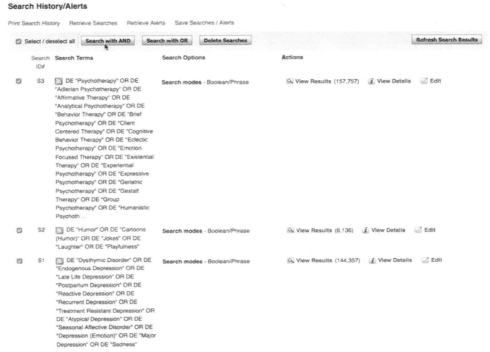

Search History/Alerts

Print Search History   Retrieve Searches   Retrieve Alerts   Save Searches / Alerts

☑ Select / deselect all   Search with AND   Search with OR   Delete Searches   Refresh Search Results

	Search ID#	Search Terms	Search Options	Actions
☑	S3	DE "Psychotherapy" OR DE "Adlerian Psychotherapy" OR DE "Affirmative Therapy" OR DE "Analytical Psychotherapy" OR DE "Behavior Therapy" OR DE "Brief Psychotherapy" OR DE "Client Centered Therapy" OR DE "Cognitive Behavior Therapy" OR DE "Eclectic Psychotherapy" OR DE "Emotion Focused Therapy" OR DE "Existential Therapy" OR DE "Experiential Psychotherapy" OR DE "Expressive Psychotherapy" OR DE "Geriatric Psychotherapy" OR DE "Gestalt Therapy" OR DE "Group Psychotherapy" OR DE "Humanistic Psychoth ...	Search modes - Boolean/Phrase	View Results (157,757) View Details Edit
☑	S2	DE "Humor" OR DE "Cartoons (Humor)" OR DE "Jokes" OR DE "Laughter" OR DE "Playfulness"	Search modes - Boolean/Phrase	View Results (6,136) View Details Edit
☑	S1	DE "Dysthymic Disorder" OR DE "Endogenous Depression" OR DE "Late Life Depression" OR DE "Postpartum Depression" OR DE "Reactive Depression" OR DE "Recurrent Depression" OR DE "Treatment Resistant Depression" OR DE "Atypical Depression" OR DE "Seasonal Affective Disorder" OR DE "Depression (Emotion)" OR DE "Major Depression" OR DE "Sadness"	Search modes - Boolean/Phrase	View Results (144,357) View Details Edit

FIGURE 6.6

Combining Sets 1, 2, and 3 in a Boolean AND Operation in EBSCOhost's PsycINFO Database

The s preceding each number refers to the set number. Omit it, and EBSCOhost searches for the numbers 1, 2, and 3.

EBSCOhost's search of the PsycINFO database yields a dozen retrievals. Figure 6.7 displays these results, along with a few surrogate records, listing the most relevant ones first. Considering how few retrievals this search produces, you don't need to add the **Bipolar Disorder** facet to the search because combining it in a Boolean NOT operation with the three other AND sets would reduce retrievals even more.

Tips for Controlled Vocabulary Searching

Here are important points to keep in mind about CV searching.

Rule of Specific Entry

When you check a database's thesaurus for index terms, you may find several relevant index terms to represent one or more of the query's facets. Choose as many relevant index terms as possible per facet so that you retrieve surrogates bearing these index terms. That there are several relevant index terms per facet has to do with the rule of specific entry (also called specificity). This rule governs indexers' assignment of index terms to surrogate records, requiring them to assign the *most specific* index term

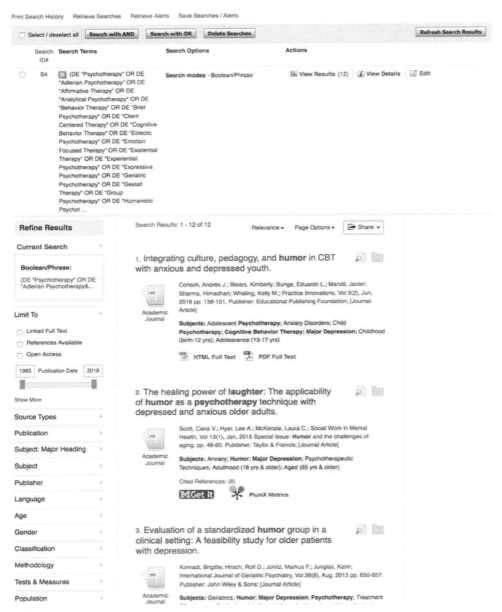

FIGURE 6.7

CV Search Results in EBSCOhost's PsycINFO Database

to the surrogate that describes the subject content of the actual source, not a broader index term that encompasses the specific term. Here are three examples of the rule of specific entry in action:

- If the source is about the use of humor to treat patients diagnosed with recurrent depression in client-centered therapy, the PsycINFO indexer will assign the index term "Recurrent Depression," not the broader term "Major Depression."
- If the source is about the use of humor to treat clinically depressed patients in client-centered therapy, the PsycINFO indexer will assign the index term "Client Centered Therapy," not the broader term "Psychotherapy."
- If the source is about the use of jokes to treat clinically depressed patients in client-centered therapy, the PsycINFO indexer will assign the index term "Jokes," not the broader term "Humor."

Expert searchers have to accommodate the rule of specific entry in their CV searches, choosing the most specific index terms to represent each facet. Strive to be comprehensive, selecting as many relevant index terms as there are for each facet, and avoid going too far afield.

Author-Keywords

PsycINFO and many other research databases include an author-keyword field in their surrogate records. In this field are words and phrases that journal editors ask authors to add to their manuscripts when they submit them to the journal for review. Authors don't choose them from the CV(s) used in the database(s) where their articles will be indexed, nor are authors aware of or given instructions to formulate keywords that are faithful to the rule of specific entry. Authors make up these terms based on their manuscripts' contents and knowledge of their field's jargon. Thus, terms from author-keyword fields are a hodge-podge of specific, broader, and narrower terms.

The Source of Dynamic Term Suggestions

Some search systems respond with dynamic term suggestions while you enter your terms into the database's online thesaurus or enter your search statements into the system's search box. If you don't know where the system is getting these terms, avoid them like the plague! You want suggestions that are the database's CV, but you may get user-entered keywords instead. Keeping track of the source of each system's dynamic-term suggestions requires too much memorization or note-taking on your part, so just keep on typing, ignoring the system's suggestions and responding instead to the CV terms you browse and select from the database's online thesaurus.

Entering Search Statements Singly or in One Fell Swoop

Personally, I prefer entering search statements for facets one at a time, creating separate sets for each facet, and then combining sets with set numbers and the Boolean AND operator. In the case of the **Humor** query, I would create sets 1, 2, and 3 bearing retrievals for the **Humor**, **Depression**, and **Treatment** facets, respectively. Then I would click on "Search History," where EBSCOhost lists my previously created sets and provides me with a search box into which I would enter set numbers combined with the Boolean AND operator: `s1 AND s2 AND s3`. It is easy to make changes to my search with its separate-sets approach to data entry. The one-fell-swoop approach means reentering the entire search to make changes.

Featured in textbox 6.1 are the changes searchers make to ongoing searches. Keep these changes in mind, and if you find yourself repeatedly making one or more of these changes, it might convince you to embrace the separate-sets approach.

Whether NTs Have Fewer Postings than BTs

Don't be fooled into thinking that NTs have fewer postings than BTs. This is *not true*. For example, the index term "Major Depression" produces a whopping 110,000 retrievals, in comparison to only 13,000 for its broader term, "Affective Disorders."

TEXTBOX 6.1

THE CHANGES SEARCHERS MAKE TO ONGOING SEARCHES

1. Correcting misspelled search terms

2. Fixing logic errors due to missing parentheses or incorrect Boolean operators

3. Tightening up or loosening proximity operators

4. Adding relevant search terms to facets that the searcher culls from relevant retrievals

5. Omitting terms from search statements that have an adverse effect on retrievals

6. Eliminating search statements from the final logical combination to increase retrievals

Direct Entry of Index Terms

Choosing index terms from a database's online thesaurus saves time and effort. To enter them manually into the EBSCOhost search system, the searcher has to search the thesaurus, jot down relevant index terms on a piece of paper or digital sticky note, and then clothe them in the system's searching language. In the EBSCOhost search system, this means:

- Prefacing the search statement with the DE field label
- Capitalizing Boolean operators (OR)
- Putting straight quotes around your entered index terms (`"psychotherapy"`)
- Enclosing your entered index terms in parentheses (`"treatment"`)

Here is a search statement that produces the same results as selecting the relevant index terms for the **Depression** facet from the PsycINFO Thesaurus:

```
DE ("anaclitic depression" OR "dysthymic disorder" OR
"endogenous depression" OR "late life depression" OR
"postpartum depression" OR "reactive depression" OR
"recurrent depression" OR "treatment resistant depression"
OR "depression (emotion)" OR "major depression" OR
"sadness")
```

That's a lot of typing. By the way, the searcher can either preface nested index terms with the DE field label or select "DE subjects [exact]" from the "Select a Field" pull-down menu. Doing so restricts the search system's retrieval of these phrases to index term fields of PsycINFO surrogate records. The search system places the results in the next set. The searcher could do the same for the **Humor** and **Treatment** facets, entering each term individually instead of selecting them from the BTs, NTs, and RTs displayed in authority records. The searcher's final statement would combine sets for all three facets, either typing it directly into the search box or using check boxes and prompts at the "Search History" feature.

Direct Entry of Index Term Words

On occasion, there are so many relevant index terms for a facet that entering them directly would not only be time consuming, but it also would require much effort, patience, and attention to detail to collect the index terms, spell them correctly, and type them into the advanced-search interface. Search systems, such as EBSCOhost, offer a shortcut, allowing users to search for the words that occur repeatedly in index terms. Take your sample query's **Treatment** facet as an example. The scope note under "Treatment" advises searchers to use more-specific index terms. Checking several other index terms' authority records reveals that the number of relevant index terms under "Treatment," "Psychotherapy," "Therapy," and "Counseling" may surpass six dozen or so. Keeping in mind the rule of specific entry, the searcher might want to include all of them to be comprehensive about retrievals. Typing them into the system's advanced-search interface or placing check marks in the boxes accompanying these terms in authority records could take a long time. You also know that the CV search for this topic results in few retrievals (see figure 6.7). Populating your CV search with *all* index terms bearing the words "treatment," "psychotherapy," "therapy," and "counseling" may increase the final result set without sacrificing precision because the search is still based on index terms.

Here are your next steps. Enter the four relevant index term words into the advanced-search box, nest these terms inside parentheses, and preface them with the SU field label. Here is a search statement for the **Treatment** facet:

```
SU (treatment OR psychotherapy OR therapy OR counseling)
```

By the way, the searcher can either preface nested index terms with the SU field label or select "SU Subjects" from the "Select a Field" pull-down menu (figure 6.8). EBSCO-host responds by retrieving surrogate records bearing these words in index terms and in author-keyword fields. Putting quotes around each word limits retrieval to the word in quotes, not its plural, singular, and possessive forms. Omitting quotes retrieves the word and its plural, singular, and possessive forms.

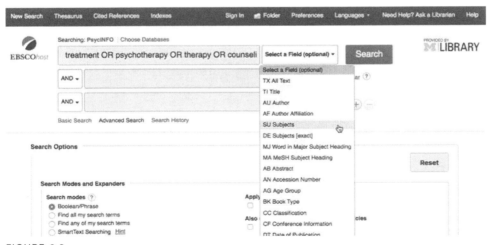

FIGURE 6.8
Direct Entry of Index-Term Words in a Search of EBSCOhost's PsycINFO Database

Substituting a search statement that retrieves index term words for the **Treatment** facet more than doubles the retrievals for the **Humor** query. Examples of additional relevant titles are:

- "Effects of Laughter Therapy on Depression, Cognition, and Sleep among the Community-Dwelling Elderly"
- "Laughter Therapy in a Geriatric Patient with Treatment-Resistant Depression and Comorbid Tardive Dykenesia"
- "Effects of Laughter Therapy on Immune Responses in Postpartum Women"

You can preview the index term words that the search system retrieves by browsing the thesaurus, choosing the "Term contains" option, and entering the index term word you intend to search. If you think that the majority of listed index terms are relevant, then shortcut. If not, select index terms from the display of authority records, or search for index terms directly.

THE BUILDING BLOCK SEARCH STRATEGY'S BUFFET EDITION

The expert searcher's execution of the search for the **Humor** query is planned, deliberate, and systematic—choosing index terms for each facet, combining synonymous index terms for each facet with the Boolean OR operator, creating sets of retrievals for each facet, and combining sets with the Boolean AND operator. The inspiration for search execution is search strategy. Search strategy is defined as a "plan for the whole search" (Bates 1979, 206). The search strategy that you used to conduct the **Humor** query is called the Building Block Search Strategy. Its name refers to the searcher's building block approach to the overall search formulation, developing each facet of the query separately as if it were a subsearch on its own, and then making the final logical assembly of the individual subsearches. Figure 6.9 is a diagram depicting the Building Block Search Strategy, using three separate blocks, one atop the other, to represent separate sets of retrievals for the individual facets and arrows protruding from the three blocks' right sides, all meeting on the left side of a single block representing the final set of search retrievals. Building Block is the strategy that all library and information science (LIS) instructors (present company included) use as the basis for teaching their students how to conduct in-depth searches of research databases (Hawkins and Wagers 1982; Markey and Atherton 1978; Meadow and Cochrane 1981).

Over the years, I have observed certain students struggle with Building Block searches in Boolean search systems. Thinking that this strategy's name and the diagram associated with it fail to capture *how searchers build individual facets*, I have long sought an elaboration of the Building Block Search Strategy that is more illustrative of what goes on during building block construction. Dubbed the "Buffet

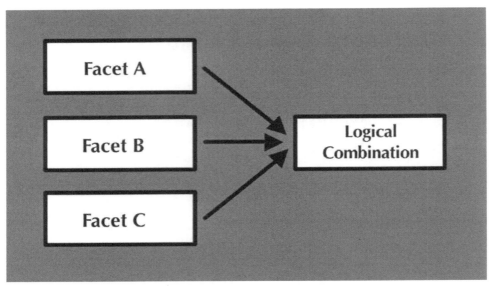

FIGURE 6.9
Building Block Search Strategy

Edition" of the Building Block Search Strategy, this elaboration pertains to searching Boolean search systems.

Let's examine this Buffet Edition up close and personal. A user approaches you with a query, and your negotiation results in a three-faceted query. You search the thesaurus, finding several index terms that are satisfactory for describing the first facet and selecting several of their BTs, NTs, and RTs. You then combine everything with the Boolean OR operator. Done with the first facet's construction, you proceed with the second, repeating the process until you have constructed separate search statements for every facet in the search formulation. Your final step is to combine sets for the separate OR facets using the Boolean AND operator. This is analogous to what happens when you eat from a buffet. You visit separate buffet tables—one each for appetizers, soups and salads, entrees, side dishes, beverages, and desserts. These tables are analogous to your query's facets. You choose several items per buffet table, arrange everything onto your plate, and chow down. Choosing several food items per buffet table is like choosing index terms and their relevant BTs, NTs, and RTs from the database's thesaurus displays to construct separate OR search statements for each of the query's facets. Combining separate OR sets with the Boolean AND operator concludes the search. Figure 6.10 depicts the Buffet Edition of the Building Block Search Strategy visually, bearing several selections on your plate from each buffet table. Taking in the whole scene, you have enjoyed a full meal.

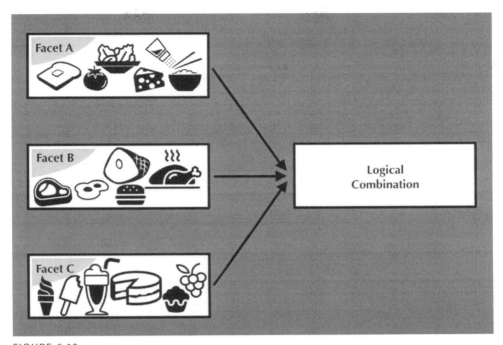

FIGURE 6.10
Buffet Edition of the Building Block Search Strategy

Source: Created using symbols from the Noun Project (http://thenounproject.com): "Toast" symbol by Jacob Halton; "Salad" symbol by Peter Chlebak; "Tomato" symbol by Marco Olgio; "Cheese" symbol by Consuelo Elo Graziola; "Salt Shaker" symbol by Nathan Thomson; "Food" symbol by Mister Pixel; "Steak" symbol by Anuar Zhumaev; "Egg" symbol by Jacob Halton; "Ham" symbol by jon trillana; "Turkey" symbol by Quan Do; "Fast Food" symbol by Saman Bemel-Benrud; "Ice Cream" symbol by Gustav Salomonsson; "Popsicle" symbol by Kristin McPeak; "Cake" symbol by Maurizio Fusillo; "Milkshake" symbol by Diego Naive; "Cupcake" symbol by Alessandro Suraci; "Grapes" symbol by Thomas Hirter.

CONTROLLED VOCABULARY SEARCHING IN OPACS

Searching your library's OPAC will satisfy many user queries, so it is important to master its searching capabilities. Libraries have one or two OPAC interfaces:

1. The classic OPAC that excels at CV searching via alphabetical browsing and authority control. Typically found in but not limited to academic libraries.
2. The next-generation OPAC, called the OPAC's discovery interface or its discovery layer, featuring a Google-like interface, a single search box, and relevance-ranked retrievals. Typically found in both academic and public libraries.

Featured here is the classic OPAC because it excels at CV searching. To conduct successful subject searches in the classic OPAC, you must become familiar with its CV, called the Library of Congress Subject Headings (LCSH). LCSH's origins trace back to the late nineteenth century to the OPAC's precursor: the card catalog. So that library users could find desired resources, librarians recorded their authors, titles, and subjects on cards and filed them in the card catalog. Typing and filing cards are very detailed and time-consuming tasks. To increase efficiency, librarians established strict rules that reduced the numbers of cards (also called entries), such as limiting author cards to a resource's first three authors and developing a subdivision system for LCSH that expressed the subject matter of a book in one complex, lengthy, subdivided LCSH. Flash forward to today, and computerization has enabled librarians to relax most of the rules centered around number of entries, but we still use LCSH, expressing some subjects in *main* LCSHs (e.g., "Women," "Women adventurers," and "Women in computer science") and other subjects in complex, lengthy *subdivided* LCSHs (e.g., "Women—Korea (South)—Economic conditions—Regional disparities" and "Women adventurers—United States—Biography—Juvenile literature").

Except for one-word main LCSHs, most main and subdivided LCSHs are bona fide examples of precoordination—the combination of individual concepts into complex subjects before conducting a search for them. For example, implicit in the one LCSH "Women in computer science—Developing countries" are three facets: **Women**, **Computer Science**, and **Developing Countries**. Surrogate records assigned this heading are likely to be relevant in searches with these facet analyses and logical combinations: **Women** AND **Computer Science**, **Women** AND **Developing Countries**, and **Women** AND **Computer Science** AND **Developing Countries**. When your facet analysis of a user query bears facets that are likely to be expressed in a single LCSH, all you have to do is browse your library's classic OPAC for this LCSH. When you find it, browse forward and backward in search of additional LCSHs. Table 6.3 lists several precoordinated LCSHs. Because these main and subdivided LCSHs are so complex, added to table 6.3 are columns that bear the facets in these LCSHs and their meanings.

The closest thing to a full published list of LCSHs is at the Library of Congress (LC) Authorities website (http://authorities.loc.gov/). Click the "Search Authorities" link, choose "Subject Authority Headings," and enter a word or phrase. LC Authorities responds with an alphabetical list of LCSHs in the alphabetical neighborhood of your entered word or phrase. In fact, you are browsing an alphabetical list of all the authorized LCSHs that LC has assigned to its surrogate records since it automated its cataloging operations in the late 1960s.

When you know the words that make up an LCSH but don't know the order of main and subdivision elements, choose the "Keyword Authorities (All)" search, and enter the words you have in mind. LC Authorities responds with a list of LCSHs bearing your words in individual LCSHs. Because you're searching *all* authorized headings, retrievals include titles, but ignore them, scanning instead for relevant LCSHs. If

Table 6.3.   LCSHs, Their Facets, and Their Meanings

LCSHs	Facets	Meanings
Airline passenger security screening	**Airlines, Passengers, Security Screening**	Airline passenger security screening
Women death row inmates	**Women Prisoners, Death Row**	Women on death row
Serial murderers in motion pictures	**Serial Murderers, Film**	Serial murderers in films
African Americans—Monuments—Conservation and restoration—Georgia—Periodicals	**African Americans, Monuments, Restoration, Georgia, Periodicals**	Periodicals on the conservation and restoration of monuments to African Americans in Georgia
Automobiles—Bodies—Maintenance and repair—Estimates—Examinations—Study guides	**Automobile Bodies, Repair, Estimates, Exams, Study Guides**	Examination study guides for making estimates on the maintenance and repair of automobile bodies
Catholic Church—Italy—Relations—Protestant churches—History—20th century—Congresses	**Catholic Church, Italy, Protestant Churches, Relationships, 20th Century, History, Conferences**	Twentieth-century conferences on the history of the relationship of the Catholic Church in Italy with Protestant churches
Lincoln, Abraham, 1809–1865—Political career before 1861—Press coverage	**Abraham Lincoln, His Political Career Before 1861, Press Coverage**	Press coverage of Abraham Lincoln's political career before 1861
Melanoma—Patients—United States—Biography	**Melanoma Patients, United States, Biography**	Biographies of melanoma patients in the United States
Music—Louisiana—New Orleans—20th century—History and criticism	**Music, New Orleans, 20th Century, History**	History and criticism of music in twentieth-century New Orleans
World War, 1914–1918—Battlefields—France—Verdun—Guidebooks	**World War I, Battlefields, Verdun, Guidebooks**	Guidebooks to World War I battlefields in Verdun, France

you're struggling for the right LCSHs, check out LCSH's syndetic structure for term suggestions, but keep in mind that BTs, RTs, NTs, and entry vocabulary exist for most main LCSHs, not for subdivided LCSHs because subdivided LCSHs are not established editorially. (LCSH is a huge topic, so go overboard preparing yourself and take a cataloging course, where you'll learn how to construct subdivided LCSHs.)

Classic OPACs approach LCSH browsing in the same ways as LC Authorities. They respond with an alphabetical list of LCSHs in the neighborhood of your entered word or phrase. Figure 6.11 shows an alphabetical list of LCSHs triggered by the user's entry of the search statement `african americans monuments` into the U-M's classic OPAC. The first-listed LCSH precedes the entered phrase in the alphabet, the second-listed LCSH matches it, three subdivided forms follow, and the remaining five LCSHs come after the entered phrase in the alphabet. Accompanying LCSHs are the number of surrogate records to which each LCSH has been assigned. Select a listed LCSH, and the classic OPAC displays retrieved surrogate records. You can also browse backward or forward in the list.

FIGURE 6.11
Browsing LCSHs in the Alphabetical Neighborhood of the Entered Term in the University of Michigan's Classic OPAC

Source: Screenshots made available under the Creative Commons Attribution license by the University of Michigan Library.

Alternatively, classic OPACs respond with a keyword search of LCSHs, retrieving LCSHs that bear every word in your search statement. In response to the search statement `pets anecdotes`, the Cleveland Public Library's OPAC retrieves thirty-three LCSHs, lists them alphabetically, and includes the number of retrieved surrogate records per LCSH. Here are examples of retrieved LCSHs, along with their postings:

Gerbils as pets—Anecdotes (1)

Otters as pets—Scotland—Anecdotes (2)

Pets—Anecdotes (53)

Pets—Anecdotes—Juvenile literature (9)

Pets—Behavior—Anecdotes (5)

Pets—Michigan—Lowell—Anecdotes (5)

Pets—Therapeutic use—Anecdotes (1)

Pets—United States—Anecdotes (4)

Pets and travel—British Columbia—Anecdotes (1)

Presidents' pets—United States—Anecdotes (2)

Raccoons as pets—Anecdotes (3)

Snails as pets—Anecdotes (3)

Swine as pets—England—Anecdotes (3)

Wild animals as pets—Anecdotes (1)

Wild birds as pets—Nova Scotia—Anecdotes (1)

Notice that all retrieved LCSHs bear every word in the user's search statement. Search words can start, finish, and/or be embedded in retrieved LCSHs. See for yourself how this CV search works by searching Cleveland's OPAC at https://search.clevnet.org/client/en_US/clevnet. Mouse down on the "All Fields" pull-down menu, choose "Keyword in Subject Headings," enter one or more words from table 6.3's LCSHs into the search box, and click on the "Search" button.

When the meaning of an LCSH covers all of the facets in a user's query, rely on your library's classic OPAC to retrieve this LCSH through its alphabetical browsing capability or its keyword search of LCSHs. Precoordination does all the work for you, making facet analysis and logical combination implicit in your desired LCSH. All you have to do is select this LCSH from alphabetical or keyword displays of LCSHs and assess the relevance of the library materials to which your selected LCSH is assigned.

CONDUCTING CONTROLLED VOCABULARY SEARCHES FOR UNFOCUSED QUERIES

So far, this discussion of CV searching involves very specific queries. Often users aren't sure what they want. They have a vague notion: "Depression interests me." "It has to be something about K–12 students." or "Maybe something about the local food movement, but I don't know much about it." Each one of these queries is vague, unfocused, and bears one facet—**Depression, K–12 Students, Local Food Movement**. CV searches for these one-facet queries are likely to result in thousands of retrievals.

Databases and search systems are able to help users who have unfocused queries, situating them in a search space that addresses their interests but placing the burden on the database to suggest fruitful avenues that they might explore within the search space. One approach enlists clusters of CV terms to characterize salient aspects of retrievals. The Depression query serves as an example. A CV search for this query yields almost 150,000 retrievals in EBSCOhost's PsycINFO database (refer back to figure 6.6, set 1). On the left side of the window, EBSCOhost invites the searcher to "refine results" with clusters (figure 6.12). By the way, clusters vary depending on the number of retrievals—the more retrievals, the more clusters. In high-posted searches, it is useful to conceive of clusters as occupying two camps: *nonsubject clusters* and *subject clusters*. Applying these *nonsubject clusters* will reduce retrievals without affecting their overall subject matter:

- *Peer Reviewed*
- *Excluding Dissertations*
- *Linked Full-Texts*
- *Source Types* (e.g., journals, dissertations, books, encyclopedias)
- *Publication* (e.g., *Dissertation Abstracts International, Journal of Affective Disorders, American Journal of Insanity*)

Applying these *subject clusters* will not only reduce retrievals but, depending on the selected cluster value, also change the overall subject matter of retrievals:

- *Age* (adolescence [13–17 yrs], middle age [40–64 yrs], very old [85 yrs & older])
- *Gender* (female or male)
- *Population* (outpatient, inpatient, male, female, human, or animal)
- *Methodology* (empirical study, interview, clinical case study)
- *Subject: Major Heading* (various PsycINFO index terms, such as "Self Esteem," "Social Support," and "Dementia")
- *Subject* (various PsycINFO index terms, such as "Drug Therapy," "Risk Factors," "Epidemiology," and "Mothers")
- *Classification* (various PsycINFO classification captions, such as "Clinical Psychological Testing," "Military Psychology," and "Childrearing & Child Care")
- *Tests & Measures* (names of specific tests and measurements, such as "Hamilton Rating Scale for Depression," "Beck Depression Inventory," and "Mini Mental State Examination")

Clicking on the arrow adjacent to each facet opens the cluster, revealing its details. For example, open in figure 6.12 is the *Subject: Major Heading* cluster, where major subjects (i.e., PsycINFO index terms that are really, really about this topic) are listed, beginning with the highest-posted ones.

The highest-posted cluster values aren't very useful because they are PsycINFO index terms you searched for. Clicking on the "Show More" link opens a pop-up window bearing more subjects than can be listed along the left side of the page. Scroll

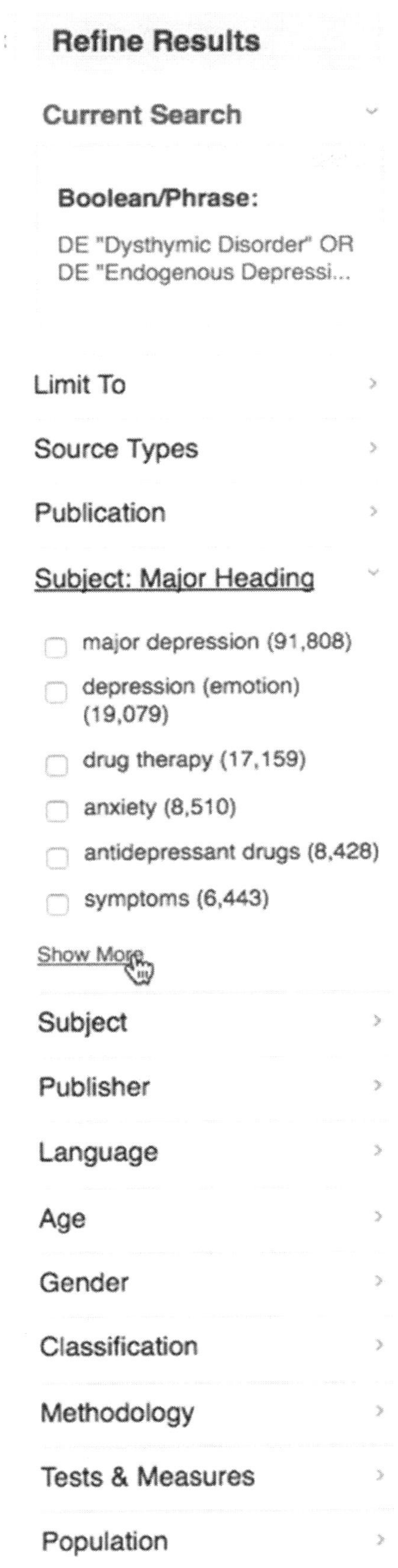

Refine Results

Current Search ⌄

Boolean/Phrase:

DE "Dysthymic Disorder" OR
DE "Endogenous Depressi...

Limit To >

Source Types >

Publication >

Subject: Major Heading ⌄

☐ major depression (91,808)

☐ depression (emotion)
   (19,079)

☐ drug therapy (17,159)

☐ anxiety (8,510)

☐ antidepressant drugs (8,428)

☐ symptoms (6,443)

Show More

Subject >

Publisher >

Language >

Age >

Gender >

Classification >

Methodology >

Tests & Measures >

Population >

FIGURE 6.12
Clusters with the *Subject: Major Heading* Cluster Open in EBSCO-host's PsycINFO Database

down to the medium-posted subjects, and you will see several major subjects that are likely to pique the interests of users researching Depression. Examples are "post-traumatic stress disorder," "aging," and "suicide" (figure 6.13). Selecting one of these subjects reduces this search's retrievals to several hundred.

Not all search systems have a cluster capability. When it is available, put it to work helping users who come to you with ill-defined, diffuse, or unfocused queries. Get the process started by conducting a CV search for the one or two facets that are present in the unfocused query, and then invite users to browse cluster entries, not just the highest-posted entries, but also entries farther down the list. Advise them to choose an

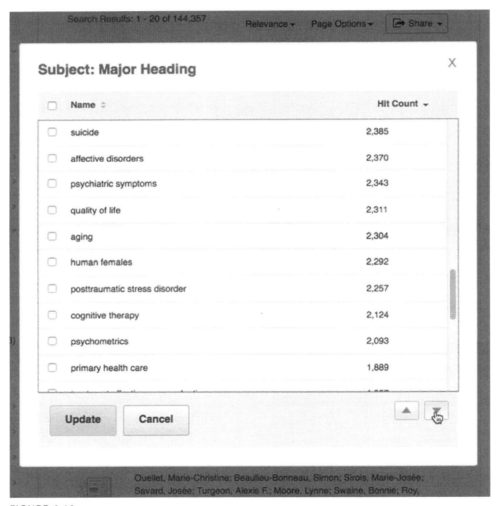

FIGURE 6.13
Pop-Up Window Bearing Medium-Posted *Subject: Major Heading* Cluster Values in EBSCO-host's PsycINFO Database

entry, scan the titles of retrieved sources, read their abstracts, and rethink their topics. This process takes time, concentration, and patience, but reassure users that they are making progress all the while, becoming more familiar with the topic generally and sampling fruitful subtopics that they might want to pursue in greater depth.

Another approach to handling unfocused queries is browsing alphabetical lists of subdivided LCSHs in classic OPACs. Here's an example using the U-M's classic OPAC (http://mirlyn-classic.lib.umich.edu/) for the negotiated query "What was life like for Germany's Jews before Hitler took power?" with the facet analysis and logical combination **Jews** AND **Germany** AND **Life**. Choose this OPAC's "Subject begins with . . ." search from the pull-down menu, and enter the subdivided LCSH jews germany. Browse forward in the alphabetical list of LCSHs in search of subdivided LCSHs that express this query's **Life** facet, such as "—Cultural assimilation," "—Economic conditions," "—Identity," "—Intellectual life," "—Social conditions," and "—Social life and customs." Browsing alphabetical lists of LCSHs takes time, effort, and concentration but eventually pays off with such relevant retrievals as *Jews Welcome Coffee*; *Jewish Life in Germany*; *The German-Jewish Economic Elite, 1920–1935*; and *Constructing Modern Identities: Jewish University Students in Germany, 1815–1914*.

Yet another approach to helping users with ill-defined topics is to seek out a digital library database that is narrowly focused on a particular subject, practice, issue, or genre. Using the database may start the user at an encyclopedia-like article that briefs him on the subject. Then the database invites the user to explore, using predetermined clusters to organize sources on the subject.

Opposing Viewpoints is such a digital library database. It is focused on today's hot topics. Clicking on one of its more than four hundred "Hot Topics" displays the hot topic's home page, where the hot topic is described in a one-page overview (figure 6.14). Opposing Viewpoints invites users to increase their familiarity with the topic, reading featured viewpoint essays, news and magazine stories, and journal articles. A wide range of sources are here, including statistics that pertain to the topic, primary sources, images, and investigative news reports. By the way, Opposing Viewpoints has a hot topic homepage on Depression.

When a user's topic doesn't entirely map onto an Opposing Viewpoints hot topic, users should explore related topics. For example, the user who is vague about K–12 Students could explore these hot topics to concretize his interests: Bullying, Charter Schools, Childhood Obesity, Homeschooling, Peer Pressure, School Violence, or Underage Drinking.

BENEFITS OF CONTROLLED VOCABULARY SEARCHING

When your chosen database has a thesaurus, *use it* to represent the concepts that interest the user. The database publisher has gone to great lengths to develop the thesaurus:

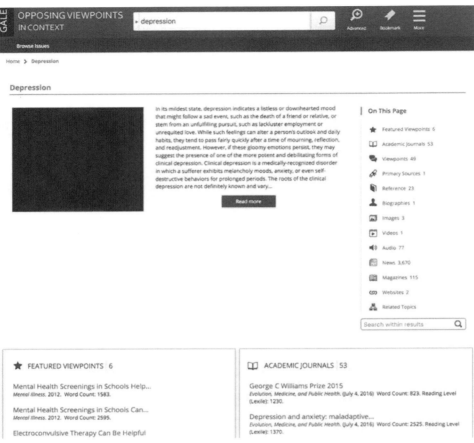

FIGURE 6.14

Depression Homepage (Above the Fold) Featuring a Topic Overview and Clusters in the Opposing Viewpoints Database from Gale Cengage Learning

Source: From Gale. http://www.gale.com/. © Gale, a part of Cengage, Inc. Reproduced by permission. www .cengage.com/permissions.

establishing each authorized term editorially; deciding which of several synonyms should be the authorized term for a concept; linking term variants and synonyms to the authorized term; and characterizing relationships between authorized terms as broader, narrower, or related. Indexers assign CV terms to surrogate records to represent the concepts, big ideas, and themes that sources discuss. CV searching is nothing more than indexing in reverse. Instead of consulting the thesaurus to choose CV terms to *index* sources, the searcher consults the thesaurus to choose CV terms to *search* for sources. Matching CV terms that indexers assign to surrogate records should produce mostly relevant retrievals: high-precision searches.

Controlled vocabulary is like the utensils you use to eat food: forks, knives, and spoons. When you don't have these utensils, you have to use your fingers or put your head into the bowl to eat. All the food gets mixed together, and what you chow down doesn't necessarily come in the proportions that you want. Using eating utensils, you can be precise and on target about choosing exactly what is on your plate to eat and placing it in your mouth. That is exactly how CV searching works, enabling you to conduct high-precision searches bearing mostly relevant retrievals. Whenever there is good reason to believe that you can do a good job of representing the facets of the patron's query in appropriate CV terms, controlled vocabulary searching is the most effective way to search!

CONTROLLED VOCABULARY SEARCHING TIPS

You won't be able to rely entirely on CV searching. First, there are databases that don't have a CV. Second, be on the lookout for database publishers that "fastcat" (fast-catalog) sources into their database. Fastcat databases omit index terms from surrogates for several reasons: (1) They want to put new content into users' hands as fast as possible, (2) they are catching up on backlogs and will add index terms to surrogates in good time, (3) they might have a policy of never adding index terms to certain surrogates, and (4) a combination of these three. When you notice surrogates bereft of index terms, check the database's help, FAQs, and tutorials for its indexing policies and practices. Third, the database's CV doesn't have index terms to express one or more of your query's facets. For all three situations, you'd conduct a free text (FT) search, a topic that chapters 7 and 8 cover in-depth.

Occasionally, you'll search several databases, simultaneously at a database supermarket or successively from different database publishers. When you do, you'll have to be deliberate about selecting index terms from each database's CV because databases use different CVs.

CV searching is not a given across all databases and search systems. You have to scrutinize the database's homepage, advanced search, or expert search pages, looking for links or tabs with names like "Thesaurus," "Thesaurus Search," "Browse," "Subjects," or "Subject Guide Search." CV functionality isn't always obvious, so click on various links and tabs to see whether they reveal index terms. Some CVs have thesaurus relationships; that is, BTs, NTs, and RTs. Other CVs are flat, limited to authorized index terms, maybe UFs. One search system may display the scope notes and history notes in a database's thesaurus, and other systems won't.

Table 6.4 is a cheat sheet that compares CV searching via thesaurus browsing across five search systems. Thesaurus browsing in ProQuest is similar to EBSCOhost, but ProQuest splits up the syndetic structure into two separate displays. Added to thesaurus

Table 6.4. Browsing the Online Thesaurus in Several Search Systems

Search System	Browsing the Thesaurus Online	Displays for Finding Index Terms	Contents of Authority Records	Search Multiple Index Terms	Explode Index Terms
EBSCOhost	Click on "Thesaurus"	Alphabetical, keyword, relevance	Authorized index term, scope note, BTs, NTs, RTs, UFs, and year term added	•	•
ProQuest	Click on "Thesaurus"	Alphabetical, keyword	Two separate displays: (1) authorized index term, BTs, and NTs and (2) RTs, UFs, and scope note	•	•
Engineering Village	Click on "Thesaurus Search"	Alphabetical, keyword, exact term	Authorized index term, BTs, NTs, RTs, UFs, subdivisions	•	
PubMed	Put your cursor on the database pull-down menu and choose "MeSH"	Keyword	Hierarchical displays of BTs, NTs, and RTs in which the authorized index term resides; scope note; UFs; subdivisions; year term added	•	•
Gale's Gen. OneFile and Acad. OneFile databases	Click on "Subject Guide Search"	Keyword with dynamic term suggestions	Listed separately from the authorized index term are its BTs, NTs, RTs, UFs, and subdivisions		

browsing in Engineering Village and PubMed is the selection of subdivided index terms. For an entirely different thesaurus-browsing experience, check out the Subject Guide Search in Gale databases, such as General OneFile and Academic OneFile. As searchers enter their search statements, the Subject Guide Search responds with dynamic term suggestions. Choosing a suggested term enables you to browse its BTs, RTs, NTs, and subdivisions. Subject Guide Searches are limited to searching for one index term at a time. Alternatively, you could browse index terms through Subject Guide Searches, jotting down the relevant index terms you find on a piece of paper or digital sticky note; then formulate a search statement bearing multiple index terms and enter it directly into the search system's advanced interface.

QUESTIONS

Conduct online searches for one or more of these negotiated queries. Choose search terms only from the database's CV, selecting them from the database's online thesaurus or entering them directly using the search system's CV searching language. If you don't have access to some databases, the ERIC database produces relevant retrievals for several queries, so use it. You can search ERIC on EBSCOhost or ProQuest. ERIC is also available on the open Web at http://eric.ed.gov; unfortunately, its online thesaurus selection functionality is limited. Suggested CV search formulations for these queries conclude this chapter.

1. For the ERIC database: I'm a new school bus driver, and I want to know more about handling discipline problems on school buses.
2. For the PsycINFO (or ERIC) database: Are teens from broken homes likely to develop eating disorders?
3. For your library's classic OPAC: I'd like to read about the real-life experiences of American fighter pilots in World War II.
4. For the ERIC database: When adult learners engage in conservation education, does their behavior change? For example, are they more likely to recycle, turn down their home thermostats, purchase energy-efficient vehicles and appliances, and so on?
5. For the PubMed database: New technology devices to help ALS patients communicate with family, friends, and caregivers.

SUMMARY

Into the index-term fields of surrogate records, human indexers assign controlled vocabulary (CV) terms to describe the subject contents of sources indexed in databases. CV terms describe the concepts, big ideas, or themes in these sources, not just topics that they mention in passing. Because CV terms are comparable to the names you give to a query's facets, replacing facet names with relevant CV terms and adding them and their broader, narrower, and related terms to your search statements are the surest ways to retrieve relevant information. Searching a database's online thesaurus, you are able to select index terms and bypass the system's CV searching language almost entirely. To finish off the search, enter each facet's set number combined with the Boolean AND operator. Searchers can also enter CV terms or words in CV terms directly into a system's search box, but to do so, they must learn the system's CV searching language.

Facet analysis and logical combination are implicit in CV searching of the library's classic OPAC because of the precoordination that is built into the OPAC's CV, called the Library of Congress Subject Headings (LCSH). All you have to do is identify an LCSH that covers all of the facets in the user's query, select it using the OPAC's alphabetical or keyword displays of LCSHs, and assess the relevance of the library materials to which the LCSH is assigned.

Search strategies are helpful for giving searchers an overall plan for conducting the search. Executing the Building Block Search Strategy, the searcher develops each facet of the query separately as if it were a subsearch on its own and then makes a final logical assembly of the individual subsearches. Specifically, this is the Buffet Edition of the Building Block Search Strategy, for which the searcher enlists the full range of Boolean search functionality to build individual facets of synonyms and then combines them so that retrievals are guaranteed to address every facet of the query. You could apply this strategy to Boolean searches for every multifaceted query.

Use CV searching to help users with unfocused queries. Search for CV terms that satisfy one or two facets the users are sure about, and then invite them to apply one or more clusters that describe topics that interest them. In classic OPACs, search for main LCSHs, and then invite users to browse subdivided LCSHs, selecting ones that describe the topics that interest them.

BIBLIOGRAPHY

American Psychological Association. 2018a. "PsycINFO: Highlights." Accessed June 22, 2018. http://www.apa.org/pubs/databases/psycinfo/index.aspx.

———. 2018b. "Thesaurus of Psychological Index Terms." Accessed June 22, 2018. http://www.apa.org/pubs/databases/training/thesaurus.aspx.

Bates, Marcia J. 1979. "Information Search Tactics." *Journal of the American Society for Information Science* 30 (July): 205–14.

Hawkins, Donald T., and Robert Wagers. 1982. "Online Bibliographic Search Strategy Development." *Online* 6, no. 3: 12–19.

Markey, Karen, and Pauline Atherton. 1978. *ONTAP: Online Training and Practice for ERIC Database Searchers*. Syracuse, NY: ERIC Information Resources Clearinghouse. ED160109.

Meadow, Charles T., and Pauline A. Cochrane. 1981. *Basics of Online Searching*. New York: Wiley.

SUGGESTED READING

Shiri, Ali. 2012. Powering Search: *The Role of Thesauri in New Information Environments*. Medford, NJ: Information Today. A comprehensive examination of the thesaurus in online search systems.

ANSWERS

1. **I'm a new school bus driver, and I want to know more about handling discipline problems on school buses.** ERIC database

Facets	Choosing Terms for Search Statements (in EBSCOhost)
School Buses	DE ("school buses" OR "busing" OR "bus transportation")
Student Behavior	DE ("student behavior" OR "discipline" OR "discipline problems" OR "aggression" OR "bullying" OR "antisocial behavior" OR "sexual harassment")
To combine sets	Choose "Search History." Checkmark set numbers for these two facets, and click on the "Search with AND" button.
Retrieved titles	"Bullying and Aggression on the School Bus: School Bus Drivers' Observations and Suggestions;" "Managing Student Behavior on the School Bus: A Key to Bus Safety;" "Sexual Harassment on the School Bus: Supporting and Preparing Bus Drivers to Respond Appropriately"

2. **Are teens from broken homes likely to develop eating disorders?** PsycINFO database

Facets	Choosing Terms for Search Statements (in EBSCOhost)
Eating Disorders	Click the "Thesaurus" tab, and enter eating disorders. Checkmark the "Explode" box under "Eating Disorders," forcing PsycINFO to select all NTs. Choose "Select term, then add to search using OR."
Broken Homes	Click the "Thesaurus" tab, and enter divorce. Select relevant index terms, such as "Divorce," "Child Custody," "Divorced Persons," and "Marital Separation." Click on these index terms to browse and select their BTs, NTs, and RTs, such as "Parental Absence," "Mother Absence," and "Father Absence." Choose "Select term, then add to search using OR."
Adolescents	Be prepared to choose a relevant value from the *Age Group* cluster.
To combine sets	Choose "Search History." Checkmark set numbers for the first two facets, and click on the "Search with AND" button. Then choose "adolescence 13–17 yrs" from the *Age Group* cluster.
Retrieved titles	"Incidence of Broken Home Family Background in Bulimia;" "Risk Factors for Bulimia Nervosa: A Controlled Study of Parental Psychiatric Illness and Divorce."

3. **I'd like to read about the real-life experiences of American fighter pilots in World War II.** Classic OPAC

Facets	Relevant LCSH
Fighter Pilots	World War, 1939–1945—Aerial operations, American
Real-Life Experiences	
World War II	
To retrieve this LCSH	Choose the OPAC's alphabetical browsing search, enter this LCSH's initial words, browse forward until the OPAC displays this LCSH, select it, and display retrievals.
Retrieved titles	*The Last Fighter Pilot: The True Story of the Final Combat Mission of World War II*; *In Their Own Words: The Tuskegee Airmen*; *Last of the Randolph Blues: Personal Stories of Ten World War II Pilots*

4. **When adult learners engage in conservation education, does their behavior change?** ERIC database

Facets	Choosing Terms for Search Statements (in ProQuest)
Conservation	`su.exact("conservation education"` OR `"energy education"` OR `"environmental education"` OR `"energy conservation"` OR `"sustainable development"` OR `"recycling")`
Adult Education	`su.exact("adult learning"` OR `"adult students"` OR `"adult programs"` OR `"adult education"` OR `"adult development"` OR `"continuing education")`
Behavior Change	`su.exact("behavior change"` OR `"behavior patterns"` OR `"behavior"` OR `"attitude change"` OR `"attitudes"` OR `"attitude measures"` OR `"community attitudes"` OR `"motivation")`
To combine sets	Choose "Recent searches." Into the search box, enter set numbers for the three facets combined with the Boolean AND operator: `s1 AND s2 AND s3`.
Retrieved titles	"Using Post-Visit Action Resources to Support Family Conservation Learning Following a Wildlife Tourism Experience;" "Learning for a Change: Exploring the Relationship between Education and Sustainable Development"
Notes	Prefacing terms with `su.exact` retrieves them as descriptors and identifiers, and prefacing them with `mainsubject.exact` retrieves them as descriptors.

5. **New technology devices to help ALS patients communicate with family, friends, and caregivers.** PubMed database

Facets	Choosing Terms for Search Statements (in PubMed)
ALS	`"amyotrophic lateral sclerosis"[Mesh]`
New Technology Devices	Select these two unsubdivided MeSH: `"Self-Help Devices"[Mesh:NoExp]` OR `"Communication Aids for Disabled"[Mesh]`. Select also these two MeSH bearing these subdivisions: instrumentation, methods, standards, supply and distribution, therapeutic use, trends, utilization.
To combine sets	Click "Advanced Search." Into the "Builder," enter set numbers for the two facets combined with the Boolean AND operator: `#1 AND #2`.
Retrieved titles	"Assisting Persons with Advanced Amyotrophic Lateral Sclerosis in Their Leisure Engagement and Communication Needs with a Basic Technology-Aided Program;" "An Eye-Tracking Assistive Device Improves the Quality of Life for ALS Patients and Reduces the Caregivers' Burden"

7

Free Text for Recall in Subject Searches of Boolean Systems

Free text (FT) searching allows searchers to use any words and phrases in their search statements, not just those that come from the database's controlled vocabulary (CV). Because it extends searching to the entire surrogate record, even to such entire full-texts as journal articles, encyclopedia entries, conference papers, and whole books, it yields high recall results; that is, searches with as many retrievals as possible. FT searching is an especially fruitful approach for searching queries that explore cutting-

The searching language that powers free-text searching is described in a nutshell in the video at http://www.onlinesearching.org/p/7-free.html.

edge topics for which there is no consensus about the right terminology to apply to the object, event, or phenomenon. For example, when the AIDS virus became front-page headlines in the late 1970s, the disease was entirely new, the medical community did not know how people contracted it, nor did they have a name for it. Eventually, the US Centers for Disease Control and Prevention (CDC) assigned the name Acquired Immune Deficiency Syndrome (AIDS) to the disease, but if you were researching AIDS back then, FT searching was the only way to search for information on the topic. It still is the only way to search for today's cutting-edge topics.

This chapter presents FT searching of surrogate records and full-texts in Boolean systems. You control search and retrieval in these systems, designating which fields you want searched, which words you want searched, how close these words are to one another, and which Boolean operations the system performs.

EXPRESSING IDEAS AND CONCEPTS IN TEXTS

FT searching requires you to think about how people would express ideas and concepts in a written text, and it isn't easy because of the many different ways people use language to communicate. Rarely are you able to predict the exact words that a person will say. Even when greeting a longtime friend, what you say varies greatly:

- Hi, how are you?
- How's it going?
- Wazzup?
- Yo.
- Hey.

Your friend's responses vary even more, ranging from a positive response, such as "Fine, thanks, and you?" to a negative one that includes a list of his or her latest troubles, such as "Not so good. I hate my job, I know my boss is out to get me, I don't get paid enough, and I have a sore throat." Predicting a greeting is probably much easier than a friend's response, but typically, both texts are highly variable. So it is with formal, written text, even text that is highly formalized, compact, and goal-oriented, such as a scholarly text's abstract. Despite the difficulty of predicting text, you must do so to conduct FT searches because CVs don't cover every concept under the sun.

Expert searchers wield FT searching tools that give them the power to search some or all database fields. To make decisions about what to search, it is helpful to think about database fields coming in the following flavors:

- CV fields bearing editorially established words and phrases that designate the big ideas, important concepts, and ideas discussed in full-texts

- Uncontrolled surrogate record fields bearing summary information (usually in the form of a title, abstract and author-keywords) that describes the intellectual contents of full-texts and media
- Citation information, such as journal title, publisher, place, and date of publication, that helps people find full-texts or media in libraries, bookstores, and databases and cite them in their written works
- Full-text; the text of the actual source itself
- Cited references; sources that the source in hand cite
- Citing references; sources that have cited the source in hand since its publication
- A combination of two or more of these flavors

When expert searchers conduct FT searches, they scrutinize the flavors that databases come in and then choose the best FT tools at hand for producing search results bearing as many relevant retrievals as possible while minimizing the retrieval of nonrelevant material.

FREE TEXT SEARCHING TOOLS

Like CV searching, FT searching begins with a facet analysis and logical combination. When you are certain that you understand what the user wants, represent his or her query using facets, and combine these facets using Boolean operators. Some databases don't have CVs, so your searches will be FT exclusively. Other databases will have CVs, but there may be no or not enough CV terms to represent one or more of the query's facets, so you'll use FT instead. Terminology for FT search terms starts with the user's terminology and snowballs outward (textbox 7.1).

Search systems index each and every word in surrogate records and in full-texts (when available) for FT searches. Here's how most search systems define a word: A word is a string of alphabetical, numeric, or alphanumeric characters separated by spaces, tabs, paragraph breaks, or symbols. To avoid memorizing the three different ways systems can index hyphenated words, searchers who strive for high recall search them as hyphenated phrases (`decision-making`), phrases (`"decision making"`), and closed-up phrases (`decisionmaking`). Failure to do so may result in fewer relevant retrievals than you expect.

Here's a topic for a FT search, "The entrepreneurial activities of women whose livelihoods depend on farming." Your facet analysis and logical combination result in two facets combined by the Boolean AND operator:

Entrepreneurship AND **Farm Women**

Checking the database's CV, you can't find suitable index terms for the **Farm Women** facet. Thus, your only recourse is to represent this facet using FT terms.

TEXTBOX 7.1

SOURCES OF FREE-TEXT SEARCH TERMS

- The terminology that the requester uses to express his or her interests during the reference interview
- Use references in the database's CV
- Authorized index terms in this database's CV
- Authorized index terms and use references in other databases' CVs in the same disciplines or fields of study
- Authorized index terms and use references in encyclopedic CVs, such as the Library of Congress Subject Headings, Roget's Thesaurus, or Sears Subject Headings
- A database record for a relevant source that you find online or your client has in hand, especially its abstract and author-keywords
- Your knowledge of how people write, ranging from the vernacular (for sources like popular magazines and newspapers) to serious scholarship (for such sources as journal articles, conference proceedings, and research reports)

Adjacency, Nearby, and Word Order Matters

Starting with the **Farm Women** facet, you want to retrieve an exact match (ignoring capitalization) of the adjectival phrase *farm women* in text. Thus, a retrieval must meet these three conditions:

1. The word *farm* and the word *women* must reside in the same surrogate or full-text
2. The word *farm* must be adjacent to the word *women*
3. The word *farm* must come before the word *women*

The Boolean AND operator is satisfactory for handling condition 1 only. Needed is a more powerful tool than a Boolean operator to make sure the two words are adjacent and word order is preserved, and many search systems provide it in the form of a proximity operator. Be prepared for proximity operator names and syntax to vary from system to system. EBSCOhost's adjacency-and-word-order-matters proximity operator is w0 and ProQuest's is pre/0 or p/0. Here are EBSCOhost and ProQuest search statements that retrieve the phrase "farm women" in text:

EBSCOhost: `farm w0 women`

ProQuest: `farm pre/0 women`

ProQuest: `farm p/0 women`

In both systems, you can substitute quotes for this particular proximity operator:

EBSCOhost or ProQuest: `"farm women"`

For the sake of brevity, *Online Searching* refers to the adjacency-and-word-order-matters proximity operator as the *adjacency* operator.

In text, the idea of "farm women" could be expressed in many different ways. For example, consider these strings of text in which the word *farm* is a few words away from the word *women*, but the string still conveys the idea of farm women:

1. "farm and rural women"
2. *All We Knew Was to Farm: Rural Women in the Upcountry South, 1914–1941*
3. "farm, rural, and country women"
4. "farm-hardened, agrarian women"

Adjacency operators bear a number that searchers can manipulate to designate the maximum number of intervening words between their search words. For example, replace the 0 in EBSCOhost's w0 or the 0 in ProQuest's pre/0 or p/0 adjacency operator with a number to designate how far apart your search words can be. Here are examples:

`farm w1 women` retrieves only example 2 in EBSCOhost

`farm w5 women` retrieves all examples in EBSCOhost

`farm pre/4 women` retrieves all examples in ProQuest

`farm p/1 women` retrieves only example 2 in ProQuest

The farther apart the two words are, the more likely that intervening words will contribute to the source's nonrelevance or steer meaning in one or more undesirable directions. Furthermore, words adjacent or in close proximity to one another do not always express the desired concept. One or more of these search statements would retrieve nonrelevant sources bearing the following sentence fragments:

- "grew up on a farm where women worked hard and moved away"
- "this is not about farm, rural, or country women but about"
- "the historic farm house that women architects designed"

Retrieving nonrelevant retrievals is the chance searchers take when they conduct FT searches. FT searching enlists *postcoordination* to produce retrievals—the searcher's deliberate combination of words into search statements *after* the search system has extracted words from texts into its inverted indexes. There's no guarantee that FT searches will produce relevant retrievals for the ideas searchers have in mind.

Adjacency, Nearby, and Word Order Does Not Matter

The idea of farm women need not be limited to the word *farm* preceding the word *women*. Consider these phrases, in which the words are reversed but still convey the idea of farm women:

1. "women who farm"
2. "women work hard, full-time on the farm"
3. *Characteristics of Women Farm Operators and Their Farms*

Boolean systems enlist the nearby (also called near or neighbor) proximity operator to retrieve search words that are adjacent or close to one another and for which word order does not matter. EBSCOhost's nearby proximity operator is n0, and ProQuest's nearby operator is near/0 or n/0. Replace the zero with a positive number to designate how many intervening words can separate your search words. Search statement examples are:

farm n0 women retrieves example 3 in EBSCOhost

farm near/1 women retrieves examples 1 and 3 in ProQuest

farm n3 women retrieves examples 1 and 3 in EBSCOhost

farm n/6 women retrieves all examples in ProQuest

The nearby proximity operator is handy for FT searches involving names. If you are unsure whether the system indexes names in direct (e.g., Friedman, Thomas) or indirect (e.g., Thomas Friedman) form, use the nearby proximity operator to retrieve multiple forms (thomas near/0 friedman).

Truncation

The concept of farm women comes through despite changes to the forms of the words themselves. Consider these texts:

- "women farmers"
- "The woman took over several farms"
- "farming is for both women and men"
- "These fields, farmed exclusively by women"

Explicit truncation is a FT search tool for retrieving singular and plural forms of words and word variants. It usually involves the insertion of a symbol, such as a question mark (?), pound sign (#), exclamation point (!), or asterisk (*), to the beginning or end of a word stem or embedded somewhere between. Textbox 7.2 covers the wide range of truncation functionality in online systems.

In the absence of truncation symbols or quotes around FT terms, most search systems default to retrieving simple singular, plural, and possessive forms of your search terms (e.g., squirrel and squirrels, party and parties) but not necessarily irregular ones (e.g., goose and geese, child and children). Few systems are comprehensive with respect to explicit truncation, so consult your chosen search system's online help pages under such topics as truncation, wildcards, singular, plural, and possessives to learn about its truncation functionality, and then formulate your search statements accordingly.

CONDUCTING FREE TEXT SEARCHES OF SURROGATE RECORDS

FT searching tools in most Boolean search systems are proximity operators, truncation, and nested Boolean logic. Not all Boolean systems have these tools, and when they do, there may be restrictions on their use, such as allowing one type of proximity operator per search statement or one truncation operator per search term. Demonstrated here is a FT search in EBSCOhost's Women's Studies International (WSI) database, an A&I database that searches surrogates and delivers full-texts (mostly through resolver links).

A major objective of FT searching is high recall, retrieving as many relevant retrievals as possible. Thus, enter several FT search terms per search statement that are synonymous for representing each facet. For example, FT search terms for the **Farm Women** facet are:

THE WIDE RANGE OF TRUNCATION FUNCTIONALITY

How systems perform truncation and the syntax they use vary widely. Variable truncation is especially flexible because you designate the stem and as many characters as you want truncated, and you retrieve the stem and up to as many characters as your truncation symbol specifies. Unfortunately, few systems offer it. Beware of wildcards because you retrieve the stem plus any one character but *not* the stem. These truncation examples come from ProQuest, except for unlimited left-hand truncation, which comes from Engineering Village:

- *Unlimited left-hand truncation.* Preface the truncated stem with a symbol. For example, `*graph` retrieves *holograph*, *mimeograph*, *photograph*, *serigraph*, *telegraph*, and many more words bearing these five letters.

- *Unlimited right-hand truncation.* Enter the truncated stem appending a symbol onto it. For example, `observ*` retrieves *observe*, *observer*, *observes*, *observing*, *observant*, *observation*, and many more words beginning with these six letters.

- *Variable truncation.* Enter the truncated stem to retrieve it and as many characters as your truncation symbol specifies. For left-hand variable truncation, enter the truncated stem followed by an asterisk and the number of characters enclosed in brackets: `observ[*3]` retrieves *observe*, *observer*, *observes*, *observers*, *observant*, and *observing*, and `cat[*1]` retrieves *cat*, *cate*, *cato*, *cats*, *cat's*, *cats'*, and *catv*.

- *Wildcard.* Enter a stem with one or more symbols to retrieve the stem bearing as many characters as there are symbols: `observ???` retrieves words bearing any three trailing characters, such as *observing*, *observers*, and *observant*, and `cat?` retrieves *cate*, *cat's*, *cats*, *cats'*, *catv*, and *cato* but not *cat*.

- *Embedded truncation.* Use embedded truncation to retrieve any characters embedded in a word or word stem. ProQuest has three embedded truncation flavors: (1) one embedded character (e.g., `wom?n` retrieves *woman*, *women*, and *womyn*); (2) multiple embedded characters (e.g., `col*r` retrieves up to any five characters where the asterisk resides, like *collider*, *collar*, *collier*, *color*, or *colour*); and (3) variable embedded characters (e.g., `col[*2]r` retrieves up to as many as two characters where the asterisk resides [note that you can specify numbers from 1 to 20]).

```
farmwom?n

wom?n n5 farm*

female n5 farm*
```

The first- and second-listed terms retrieve one- and two-word variants for the expression "farm women." The second-listed term disregards word order and takes into account phrases bearing the singular and plural variants of the word *woman* within five words of the truncated word *farm*. The third-listed term replaces the truncated word *women* with implicit truncation for the synonym *female*. The expert searcher's next step is to script these FT terms into a FT search statement, inserting the Boolean OR operator between them:

```
farmwom?n OR (wom?n n5 farm*) OR (female n5 farm*)
```

Figure 7.1 shows the entry of this search statement into the WSI database (minus the statement's initial characters due to the search box's small size). The searcher mouses down on the "Select a Field" pull-down menu. The first-listed choice, "Select a field (optional)," is the system's default, an unqualified search to which the system responds with searches of author, subject, keyword, title, and abstract fields. The second-listed choice, "TX All Text," searches these same fields plus such citation data as the titles, authors, and publications that authors cite in their bibliographies. Opt for comprehensive results, and choose TX. If citation data produce many nonrelevant retrievals, you can reenter the statement, choosing the more restrictive default.

This initial FT search statement retrieves about 2,200 retrievals. The statement bears nested Boolean logic (the parentheses) around FT terms that are phrases bearing word proximity operators. Added to this statement is nested Boolean logic because two different operators (i.e., two Boolean OR operators and two nearby proximity operators) reside in it.

FIGURE 7.1
Entering a Free Text Search Statement for the **Farm Women** Facet into EBSCOhost's Women's Studies International (WSI) Database

Boolean search systems are governed by a precedence of operators, telling them which operator to process first, second, third, and so on. To override a system's precedence of operators, expert searchers use nested Boolean logic. This logic uses parentheses in the same way that algebra uses parentheses—to designate which operations should be done first, second, third, and so on. Textbox 7.3 expands on the precedence of operators.

Your objective for this search is high recall, so you would also conduct a FT search for the **Entrepreneurship** facet, searching *all* available database fields, not just CV fields. Here is a FT search statement for this facet bearing WSI's index terms "Entrepreneurship," "Small Business," "Businesspeople," and "Economic Development" expressed as FT search terms:

```
TX (entrepreneur* OR (small w0 business) OR (business
w0 enterprise) OR businesspeople OR (business w0 people)
OR businessperson OR (business w0 person) OR (economic
w0 development))
```

This FT search statement produces almost 14,000 retrievals. It truncates the index term "Entrepreneur," retrieving its singular and plural forms and the words *entrepreneurship* and *entrepreneurial*. Added are irregular singular and plural forms of the word *businesspeople*. Adjacency proximity operators have been inserted into phrase index terms, enabling the search system to retrieve these phrases from every database field. Choosing TX (text) instructs EBSCOhost to search all available database fields, even citation data (i.e., the titles, authors, and publications that authors cite in their bibliographies).

Your final step is to combine intermediate results for the two FT search statements using the AND operator. Click on the "Search History" link, and EBSCOhost lists your search's sets, presumably one for the **Farm Women** facet and a second for the **Entrepreneurship** facet. Combine retrievals using the Boolean AND operator—checkmarking sets 1 and 2 and clicking the "Search with AND" button. In response, EBSCOhost combines the two separate sets in a Boolean AND operation, retrieving surrogate records bearing at least one search term per facet (figure 7.2). Alternatively, combine sets directly, entering their set numbers bound by the Boolean AND operator into the search box:

```
s1 AND s2
```

PRECEDENCE OF OPERATORS

Search systems process search statements in one of several different ways:

1. From left to right.
2. From right to left.
3. By a precedence of operators that says process this operator first, then this one, and so on.
4. By the logic that nested Boolean operators specify.

Consider this search statement: `athletes AND college OR professional`. A search system governed by approach 1 (left to right) would process it as `(athletes AND college) OR professional`; that is, retrieving all sources bearing the word *athletes*, retrieving all sources bearing the word *college*, and combining these results in a Boolean AND operation. The system would then retrieve all sources bearing the word *professional* and combine it in a Boolean OR operation with the AND results. Most likely, such results are *not* what the user wants because all occurrences of the word *professional* are retrieved, regardless of whether the word *athletes* is also present.

A search system governed by approach 2 (right to left) would process the search statement as `athletes AND (college OR professional)`; that is, retrieving all sources bearing the word *college*, retrieving all sources bearing the word *professional*, and combining these results in a Boolean OR operation. The system would then retrieve all sources bearing the word *athletes* and combine it in a Boolean AND operation with the earlier OR results. Most likely, these are the results that the user wants because they bear sources on college athletes and on professional athletes.

Approach 3 applies to search systems that are governed by a precedence of operators—rules that tell the system which operator to process first, which second, and so on. Because there are no standards for the precedence of operators, expect a lot of variation from system to system. Check the system's help to learn its precedence of operators, and if you can't find such a discussion, search the system's help using such words as *precedence*, *order*, or *operators*.

Approach 4, nested Boolean logic, overrides all these approaches. The searcher applies this logic using parentheses in the same way that algebra uses parentheses—to designate which operations should be done first, second, third, and so on. Almost every search system heeds nested Boolean logic, and it is much simpler applying nested Boolean logic to your search statements than it is to learn each system's precedence of operators (if you can find it in the system's help).

Here is the rule of thumb regarding the presence of two or more different types of Boolean and/or proximity operators in your search statements: Use nested Boolean logic, adding parentheses to instruct the system which operation to do first, second, etc. Thus, your nested Boolean for this search statement bearing AND and OR would be: `athletes AND (college OR professional)`.

FIGURE 7.2
Free Text Search Results in EBSCOhost's WSI Database

FREE TEXT SEARCHING IN OPACS

Most classic OPACs offer free text searching capabilities. In the U-M's classic OPAC, free text searching is the default search called "Word(s) anywhere" on the Basic Search's pull-down menu (http://mirlyn-classic.lib.umich.edu/). It's also the default search in the UIUC OPAC called "Any Word Anywhere" on the Quick Search's pull-down menu (https://webvoyage.carli.illinois.edu/uiu/cgi-bin/Pweb recon.cgi?DB=local&PAGE=First). Personally, I prefer conducting FT searches via these catalogs' advanced interface because it gives me three search boxes interspersed with the Boolean AND operator, into which I enter words and phrases for each facet of the query.

Conducting FT searches for subjects in the OPAC is difficult because titles and LCSHs are the major contributors of words to the OPAC's inverted index. Surrogate records rarely bear abstracts, and OPACs aren't set up to handle full-texts. Let's use the U-M's classic OPAC to demonstrate a FT search and this query: "Did feminism gain momentum during China's Cultural Revolution?" This query's facets are **China**, **Cultural Revolution**, and **Feminism**. Under each facet are suggested FT search terms:

China	Cultural revolution	Feminism
china	"cultural revolution"	feminism
chinese	"great proletarian"	feminists
sino		women
		females
		gender

Figure 7.3 shows the OPAC's advanced interface, where search statements for each facet are entered into the three search boxes. By the way, search statements are longer than the search boxes, so only their trailing portion is visible in these boxes. Retrieved are about one hundred surrogate records. Maybe a handful are relevant. Examples are *Finding Women in the State: A Socialist Feminist Revolution in the People's Republic of China, 1949–1964; From Mao towards Full Equality;* and *A Feminist Brave New World: The Cultural Revolution Model Theater Revisited.* Most of these hits are assigned LCSHs bearing the search words *china, cultural revolution, feminism,* and *women;* however, no single LCSH bears all four words, thus the only way to produce relevant retrievals for this query in an OPAC is a FT search.

FIGURE 7.3
Free Text Searching Using the Advanced Interface in the University of Michigan's Classic OPAC
Source: Screenshots made available under a Creative Commons Attribution license by the University of Michigan Library.

HOW FREE TEXT INDEXING AND SEARCHING WORKS

To demonstrate how FT indexing and searching works, *Online Searching* uses our sample database of seven surrogate records in table 6.1. First, the system parses words from *all* fields in our sample seven-record database, defining a word as a string of alphabetical, numeric, or alphanumeric characters separated by spaces, tabs, paragraph breaks, or symbols. If a word bears an apostrophe, then the system deletes it and closes up the trailing letter; for example, *world's* becomes *worlds* and *life's* becomes *lifes.* For hyphenated words, the system deletes the hyphens and closes up the words into one. Second, the system numbers the words parsed from fields. Third, it places each word in its inverted index for FT searching, omitting stopwords (i.e., frequently-occurring articles, conjunctions, prepositions, and single-character words) and registering this information about each indexed word in the index:

- The record number in which the word resides
- The field in which the word resides (using the field labels "ti" for <u>ti</u>tle, "dw" for <u>d</u>e-scriptor <u>w</u>ord, and "iw" for <u>i</u>dentifier <u>w</u>ord)
- The word-position number from the field(s) in which the word occurs

Table 7.1 displays our sample database's inverted index for FT searching. It is limited to indexed words from title, descriptor, and identifier fields because including words from *all* fields would have resulted in a very long list. Our system doesn't index stop-words, such as *the*, *from*, *during*, and *of*, but it retains their word-position number; an alternative approach is to treat stopwords like they don't exist, assigning their word-position number to the word that follows.

When searchers enter their queries, our sample database's search system uses these data to produce retrievals: (1) record number, (2) field name, and (3) word-position number. Let's say you want to retrieve records on "campus life." These search state-ments use the FT searching language of the EBSCOhost search system:

```
campus w0 life
```

First, the system searches the inverted index for FT searching, looking for records bearing the word *campus*, and retrieves record 3. It follows up with a search of the inverted index for records bearing the word *life*. It retrieves record 3. This is hopeful because record 3 bears both words. Second, the system checks whether both words occur in the same field. Yes, they both occur in the title field. Last, the system checks word-position data to see whether the word *campus* occurs before the word *life* and whether these two words are adjacent to one another. The word *campus* is word 2 in record 3's title. The word *life* is word 3 in record 3's title. For word adjacency, the first word in the phrase must have a lower word-position number than the second word in the phrase, and subtracting the word-position number for the first word from the word-position number for the second word must equal 1. That's precisely what hap-pens here. Record 3 is retrieved!

Perhaps you are thinking to yourself that this same idea can be expressed in a dif-ferent way, such as the phrase "life on a college campus." This phrase presents the retrieval situation in which the two words *campus* and *life* are three words apart and the word order is switched, *life* preceding *campus*. To search for the adjacent words *campus* and *life* with *no* intervening word and without regard to word order, enter:

```
campus n0 life
```

Table 7.1.   Sample Database's Inverted Index for Free Text Searching

Word	Rec. no., field, pos. no.	Word	Rec. no., field, pos. no.
activities	1 dw 15	natural	1 dw 16
adirondack	2 iw 1	naturalistic	2 dw 3
are	6 ti 7	nature	2 iw 4
being	5 dw 9	new	2 iw 5
beliefs	4 dw 15	observation	2 dw 4
big	4 ti 7	observational	1 dw 18
campus	3 ti 2	outdoor	1 dw 20; 2 dw 5
college	3 dw 1; 4 dw 3; 4 dw 9; 5 dw 4; 5 ti 8; 6 dw 1; 6 ti 14	patterns	5 dw 11
confront	4 ti 5	pluralism	3 dw 4; 3 ti 9
consciousness	5 dw 12	problems	7 dw 10
conservation	7 dw 4	psychological	5 dw 10
cooperation	7 dw 12	questions	4 ti 8
correlates	5 ti 2	raising	5 dw 13
critical	4 dw 1	reflections	3 ti 4
cultural	3 dw 3	related	6 ti 9
detection	2 ti 2	religion	3 dw 11; 4 dw 11; 5 dw 1; 7 dw 3
development	5 dw 3	religions	7 ti 6
differences	3 dw 13	religious	3 ti 8; 3 dw 12; 3 dw 14; 4 dw 7; 4 dw 13; 5 dw 14; 6 dw 4
diversity	3 dw 5	religiousness	6 ti 1
drinking	6 dw 3; 6 ti 12	resource	1 ti 4
ecology	1 dw 1	resources	1 dw 3; 1 dw 17
education	1 dw 5; 1 dw 21; 2 dw 2; 2 dw 6; 3 dw 10; 3 dw 15; 4 dw 6; 4 dw 14; 7 dw 2	schoolyard	1 ti 7
educational	1 dw 2; 3 dw 7	self	5 dw 18
environment	3 dw 8; 7 dw 5	social	6 dw 6; 6 ti 4
environmental	1 dw 4; 2 dw 1; 7 dw 1; 7 dw 6	spiritual	5 dw 2; 5 ti 4
esteem	5 dw 19	spirituality	3 dw 16; 3 ti 6; 6 ti 2
ethics	7 dw 8	squirrels	1 ti 1
experience	5 dw 7	standards	7 dw 7
factors	4 dw 8; 5 dw 15; 6 dw 5	struggle	5 ti 5
faculty	4 dw 10	student	3 dw 6; 5 dw 6
field	1 dw 6; 1 dw 8	students	3 dw 2; 4 dw 4; 4 ti 4; 5 dw 5; 6 dw 2; 6 ti 15
grades	1 dw 13	studies	1 dw 7; 4 dw 12
greening	7 ti 2	support	6 dw 7; 6 ti 5
groups	6 dw 8	teaching	1 dw 22; 1 ti 3
help	4 ti 3	testing	5 dw 17
higher	3 dw 9; 4 dw 5	they	6 ti 8
hiking	2 iw 3	thinking	4 dw 2
how	4 ti 1; 6 ti 6	transforming	3 ti 1
hypothesis	5 dw 16	trips	1 dw 9
instructional	1 dw 10	underage	6 ti 11
intermediate	1 dw 12	well	5 dw 8
international	7 dw 11	wildlife	2 dw 7
learning	1 dw 14; 1 dw 19	woodland	2 ti 1
life	3 ti 3	world	7 dw 9
lifes	4 ti 6	worlds	7 ti 5
materials	1 dw 11	years	5 ti 9
methods	1 dw 23	york	2 iw 6
mountains	2 iw 2	your	1 ti 6

This next search statement retrieves both phrases "campus life" and "life on a college campus":

```
campus n3 life
```

Of course, you can enter n3, n6, n8, and so on, but eventually so many intervening words between *campus* and *life* will result in a different meaning because the two words may be separated by one or more sentences. When you search free text, you must think of all the possibilities for the way in which the phrases you have in mind could be said and then formulate a search statement using your chosen system's searching language that retrieves all of them.

Let's work on another FT search. Let's say you're interested in the idea of religious education. Think of all the possibilities for how this idea could be phrased in written text:

religious education

religious and moral education

education for religious purposes

education for religious communities

In these phrases, the words *religious* and *education* are adjacent, separated by one or two intervening words, and either precede or follow one another. Here is a search statement that retrieves all four:

```
religious n2 education
```

Let's check this statement in our seven-record database's inverted index for FT searching to determine which records it retrieves. Here are these two words' indexing entries:

education: 1 dw 5; 1 dw 21; 2 dw 2; 2 dw 6; 3 dw 10; 3 dw 15; 4 dw 6; 4 dw 14; 7 dw 2

religious: 3 ti 8; 3 dw 12; 3 dw 14; 4 dw 7; 4 dw 13; 5 dw 14; 6 dw 4

Records 3 and 4 are common to both entries. The system ignores all indexing entries except for those in records 3 and 4, which leaves these entries:

education: 3 dw 10; 3 dw 15; 4 dw 6; 4 dw 14

religious: 3 ti 8; 3 dw 12; 3 dw 14; 4 dw 7; 4 dw 13

Fields common to both entries are dw. The system ignores all indexing entries except for those in the dw fields of records 3 and 4, which leaves these entries:

education: 3 dw 10; 3 dw 15; 4 dw 6; 4 dw 14

religious: 3 dw 12; 3 dw 14; 4 dw 7; 4 dw 13

The search statement calls for nearness; that is, word order doesn't matter, so the subtraction of word-position numbers can be negative or positive, and it cannot exceed +2 or -2. The system compares 3 dw 10, the first record 3 entry for *education*, to 3 dw 12, the first record 3 entry for *religious*. Subtracting 10 from 12 equals 2. Record 3 is retrieved! The system ignores remaining record 3 entries and goes onto record 4 entries. The system compares 4 dw 6, the first record 4 entry for *education*, to 4 dw 7, the first record 4 entry for *religious*. Subtracting 6 from 7 equals 1. Record 4 is retrieved! That's how FT indexing and searching works!

When field labels are absent from search statements, most search systems default to searching *all* fields. Add one or more field labels to your search statement to force the system to search the fields specified. In fact, you can conduct a CV search by adding CV field labels to your search statements (see the second example here). Search statement examples bearing field qualification are:

- `ti (underage w0 drinking)` retrieves *underage* adjacent to and preceding *drinking* in the title field
- `dw,iw (religious w3 education)` retrieves *religious* up to three words away from and preceding *education* in the descriptor field, identifier field, or both
- `dw,ti (teaching n2 resource)` retrieves *teaching* up to two words away from *resource* in the descriptor field, title field, or both

Check table 7.1's inverted index to determine which records these queries retrieved (answers conclude this section):

A. `religious w0 factors`
B. `problems n3 world`
C. `(college n1 student) AND (self w0 esteem)`
D. `(outdoor OR wildlife OR nature) AND (field w1 trips)`
E. `conservation n1 standards`
F. `(environment OR environmental) n3 (education OR standards OR conservation)`

Now that you know how Boolean search systems construct their inverted file indexes, you should be able to search for anything under the sun. Comparing your FT search statements and retrievals, you should start to develop an understanding of why some FT retrievals aren't relevant.

(Answers: A. Records 4, 5, and 6; B. Record 7; C. Record 5; D. Record 1; E. None; F. Records 1, 2, and 7)

CONDUCTING FREE TEXT SEARCHES OF FULL-TEXTS

To search full-texts, online searchers use the search system's FT searching capabilities—proximity operators, truncation, and nested Boolean logic. Thus, FT searching tools suffice for searching full-texts. Some systems have added specialized proximity operators for FT searching of full-texts. Examples are proximity operators for retrieving search words in the same or nearby sentences or paragraphs and allowing searchers to prefix proximity operators with the Boolean NOT operator so that they can eliminate certain words and phrases from retrievals. These specialized proximity operators are not unique to FT searching of full-texts. Expert searchers also use the full range of proximity operators routinely for FT searching of surrogate records, too. Because free text searching and full-text searching are one and the same, *Online Searching* uses the phrase "free text searches of full-texts" or the abbreviated form "FT searches of full-texts." *Online Searching* does not use the phrase "full-text searching."

The Facet Analysis for Free Text Searches of Full-Texts

When conducting FT searches of full-texts, you must keep in mind that full-texts can be lengthy; for example, books, research reports, journal articles, and systematic reviews could range from thirty to hundreds of dense, text-filled pages. Searchers cannot depend on Boolean operators to produce relevant retrievals because their search words may be separated by dozens, even hundreds of pages! If your FT search of full-texts isn't producing relevant retrievals, replace its Boolean AND and NOT operators between facets with the system's nearby, sentence, or paragraph proximity operators.

Conducting FT searches of full-texts involves searching such texts as news stories written by journalists, journal articles and books written by scholars and scientists, blogs written by everyday people, and so on. To generate search terms, put yourself in their shoes, thinking about how they would write about the topics that interest you. A useful exercise might be writing a few sentences that you would like to see in your retrievals. If you retrieve full-texts bearing these sentences, you would expect them to be relevant. Then analyze what you have written, performing a facet analysis and logical combination. Check your sentences, distributing relevant words and phrases into the facets where they belong and doing the same for search terms you find in other sources, such as another database's CV, Roget's Thesaurus, or a relevant source that the user has in hand. In fact, make a practice of asking users to show you a relevant full-text or surrogate record that they found on their own. Then cull its relevant search terms, adding them to your search statements.

Free Text Searches of Full-Texts in the LexisNexis Academic Database

The LexisNexis Academic database excels in up-to-date coverage of news, business, and legal matters (LexisNexis 2018). Retrievals are full-text newspapers, magazines, wire services, broadcast media transcripts, newsletters, blogs, and much more.

Like other Boolean retrieval systems, the LexisNexis system features the usual three Boolean operators but uses AND NOT instead of NOT. Of these operators, OR gets the biggest workout, enabling the searcher to combine synonymous search terms within each facet. LexisNexis has many proximity operators:

- Adjacency is `pre/1` (word order matters) and `w/1` (word order doesn't matter)
- Nearby is `w/N` (word order doesn't matter)
- In the same sentence is `w/s`
- In the same paragraph is `w/p`
- In the same field (LexisNexis calls them segments) is `w/seg`
- Negative versions of these are `not pre/N`, `not w/N`, `not w/s`, `not w/p`, and `not w/seg`

Because you are searching full-texts in LexisNexis, don't use its Boolean AND or AND NOT operators. Instead insert this system's nearby `w/N` proximity operator between facets, loosely setting the N between 9 and 15, a range that roughly approximates the length of a sentence in a newspaper or magazine. Still too many retrievals? Tighten the operator with a number from 5 to 8.

Like EBSCOhost, LexisNexis automatically searches for singular, plural, and possessive forms of all but irregular words (i.e., goose and geese, child and children). The system's unlimited truncation symbol is an exclamation point (!), and its wildcard symbol is an asterisk (*).

Demonstrated here is a FT search for the topic "The impact of screen time on children." This query has three facets: (1) **Impact**, (2) **Screen Time**, and (3) **Children**. The logical combination uses proximity instead of Boolean operators to combine facets:

Impact NEARBY **Screen Time** NEARBY **Children**

Under each facet are suggested FT search terms clothed in tight proximity operators:

Impact	Screen Time	Children
impact	screentime	child
effect	screen pre/1 time	children
affect	screen-time	youngster
negative	electronics pre/1 time	kid
positive	technolog! w/3 addict!	boy
consequence		girl

Notice that this query's facet analysis bears an **Impact** facet. Chapter 6 downplays such a facet in CV searches. The reason is that CV searching is concept searching and the presence of two concepts in a source usually indicates a relationship between them (pages 101 to 102). FT searches of full-texts isn't concept searching. It is the letter-for-letter matching of words and phrases in search statements with the occurrences of words and phrases in texts. That the system is able to effect matches between the words and phrases in search statements and texts does not necessarily mean that retrieved sources are actually *about* the matched terms. Thus, searchers who want to establish relationships between one or more conditions and effects should add relationship facets to their facet analysis and logical combination in their FT searches of full-texts, just like you are doing in the Screen Time search.

The LexisNexis system does not have sets, but it does have an "edit search" capability. The searcher could express the entire search in a single search statement or enter it successively, starting with the first two facets, checking retrievals to see if they are on track, and then entering the third facet using the system's edit capability. This single search statement represents the entire search in one fell swoop:

```
(impact or effect or affect or negative or positive or
consequence) w/10 (screentime or (screen pre/1 time) or
screen-time or (electronics pre/1 time) or (technolog!
w/3 addict!)) w/10 (kid or child or youngster or children
or toddler or boy or girl)
```

LexisNexis sports a single interface. Clicking on the "Advanced Options" link (where the cursor resides in figure 7.4) opens a pop-up box, where the searcher sets up various parameters for the search she's about to perform; for example, limiting retrievals to certain dates, to a certain publication (like *The New York Times* newspaper or *All Things Considered* news program), or to certain content types. For your search, limit retrievals to "Newspapers" only by placing a check mark in its box, removing check marks from the other "Content Type" boxes, and clicking on the "Apply" button. Your next step is to enter your search statement into the search box by clicking on the "Search" button (figure 7.5). The search statement is longer than the search box, so only its trailing portion is visible in this box.

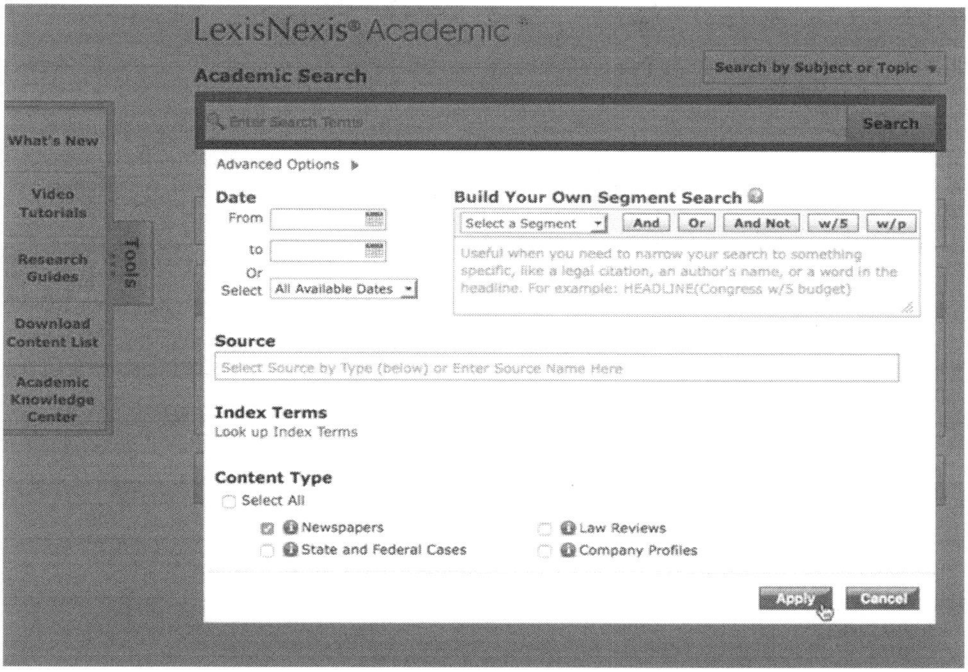

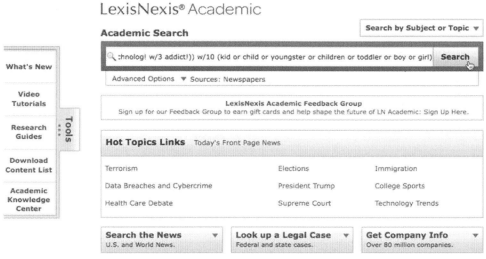

FIGURE 7.4

Clicking on the "Advanced Options" Link and Choosing Parameters for a Free Text Search of the Full-Text LexisNexis Academic Database

Source: LexisNexis, a registered trademark of Elsevier, B.V., image retrieved on 16 July 2018.

FIGURE 7.5

Entering a Free Text Search Statement for All Three Facets into the LexisNexis Academic Database

Source: LexisNexis, a registered trademark of Elsevier, B.V., image retrieved on 16 July 2018.

FIGURE 7.6
Retrievals and Clusters for a Free Text Search in the LexisNexis Academic Database
Source: LexisNexis, a registered trademark of Elsevier, B.V., image retrieved on 16 July 2018.

LexisNexis Academic produces about one thousand retrievals, beginning with the most relevant ones and displaying their titles, dates, number of words, bylines, and publication titles (figure 7.6). You can change LexisNexis's default retrievals display using the "Sort" and "Show" pull-down menus, respectively, on the top-left side of the retrievals. The user has to read full-texts to learn about the various impacts of screen time on children; examples are obesity, heart disease, and disliking one's parents. Along the left side of the page, LexisNexis displays clusters that users can explore and opens the default *Sources by Category* cluster. Choosing the *Subject* cluster and scanning its values yields more hints about excessive screen time consequences, such as "Physical Fitness," "Chronic Diseases," "Cardiovascular Disease," "Mental Health," and "Violence & Society."

FREE TEXT SEARCHING TIPS

This chapter's examination of FT covers basic functionality that you can expect most systems to have. Be prepared for FT search functionality to vary across systems, especially in terms of the syntax systems use for proximity operators and truncation, the ways they perform implicit and explicit truncation, and the abbreviations they use for field labels. Table 7.2 compares FT searching functionality across five search systems.

Table 7.2. Comparing Free Text Searching Functionality

	Boolean Operators		
Search system	Boolean OR operator	Boolean AND operator	Boolean NOT operator
EBSCOhost	OR	AND	NOT
ProQuest	or	and	not
LexisNexis	or	and	and not
JStor	OR	AND	NOT
Engineering Village	OR	AND	NOT

	Proximity Operators			
Search system	Adjacency, word order matters	Nearby, word order matters	Adjacency, word order does not matter	Nearby, word order does not matter
EBSCOhost	w0 or enclose phrase in quotes news w0 media field w0 trips self help	wN drug w2 abuse test w2 bias	n0 dan n0 brown gun n0 control	nN study n2 guide land n3 use
ProQuest	pre/0 p/0 or enclose phrase in quotes news pre/0 media field p/0 trips "self help"	pre/N p/N drug pre/2 abuse test p/3 bias	near/0 n/0 dan near/0 brown gun n/0 control	near/N n/N study n/2 guide land near/3 use
LexisNexis	pre/1 or enclose phrase in quotes news pre/1 media "self help"	pre/N drug pre/3 abuse test pre/4 bias	w/1 dan w/1 brown gun w/1 control	w/N study w/3 guide land w/4 use
JStor	Enclose phrase in quotes "news media" "self help"			land~5 use (Basic Search) land NEAR 5 use (Advanced Search, choose near from menu)
Engineering Village	ONEAR/0 or enclose phrase in quotes or braces news ONEAR/0 media drill bits {neural nets}	ONEAR/N oil ONEAR/2 well vat ONEAR/1 dyes	NEAR/0 dan NEAR/0 brown drill NEAR/0 bit	NEAR/N moon NEAR/2 base land NEAR/3 use

	Truncation				
Search system	Default	Unlimited	Variable	Wildcard	Embedded
EBSCOhost	Simple singulars, plurals, and possessives	observ* rock*		cat? rock??	One character: wom?n Variant spellings: col#r
ProQuest	Simple singulars, plurals, comparatives, and superlatives	observ* rock*	rock[*3] cat[*1] observ[*2]	rock??? cat? observ??	wom?n Mutliple characters: col*r
LexisNexis	Simple singulars, plurals, and possessives	observ! rock!		cat* observ**	One character: wom*n
JStor	(Add & to singular to find simple and irregular plurals)	observ* rock*		cat?	One character: wom?n Multiple characters: col*rful color~
Engineering Village	Turn on autostemming to retrieve the stem plus suffixes	*graph observ*		cat? observ??	One character: wom?n t??th Multiple characters: c*tion t*th

Transitioning from CV searching to FT searching may be daunting, so replace your original CV terms for these queries with FT search terms, and then dress them up in proximity operators, truncation, and nested Boolean operators. Here's how to do it. Start with the original index term "Problem Youth," and make up sentence fragments in which the two words in this index term retain its meaning. Examples are these made-up fragments:

- youths who have problems
- problematic youths
- youths who have serious problems
- problems specific to youth

Then analyze these fragments to choose between the adjacency and nearby proximity operator and to set its N (number of intervening words). In this case, choose the search system's nearby operator, set it to three intervening words, and add variable truncation for these phrases' word endings. Search statements are `youth n4 problem` for EBSCOhost searches and `youth w5 problem` for LexisNexis searches. Need inspiration for more FT terms? Check thesauri in education, sociology, and psychology for UFs, and then apply proximity operators and truncation.

QUESTIONS

Conduct online searches for one or more of these negotiated queries. To generate FT search terms, check your selected database's CV, jotting down descriptors, identifiers, and UFs and then adding proximity operators and truncation to them so that the search system retrieves them from all database fields, not only CV fields. Failure to include relevant CV terms that you enter as FT terms in your search statements will produce many fewer relevant retrievals than the database has to offer. Inspiration for FT search terms starts with the user query. More sources for FT search terms are in textbox 7.1. Suggested FT search formulations for these queries conclude this chapter.

1. For the ERIC database: I'm a new school bus driver, and I want to know more about handling discipline problems on school buses.
2. For the PsycINFO (or ERIC) database: Are teens from broken homes likely to develop eating disorders?
3. For your library's classic OPAC: Do you have anything on the songs and ballads that lumberjacks used to sing?
4. For the ERIC database: How do wilderness survival programs, such as Outward Bound and the Wilderness Encounter Training and Certification Project, help juvenile delinquents?
5. For the Compendex database: Testing ice hockey helmets to make sure they are safe.

SUMMARY

FT searching requires facet analysis and logical combination. Search-term formulation involves consulting the database's thesaurus in search of relevant index terms and UFs, other databases' thesauri, and even a free thesaurus on the open Web. Having identified enough search terms per facet, dress up your search terms in proximity operators, truncation symbols, and nested Boolean operators. Formulate FT search statements for Boolean search systems by inserting the Boolean OR operator between synonymous search terms. When searching surrogates in Boolean systems, combine search statements for facets with the Boolean AND or NOT operators. When searching full-texts in Boolean systems, combine search statements for the query's several facets with the nearby operator. These same guidelines apply to FT searching in classic OPACs.

BIBLIOGRAPHY

LexisNexis. 2018. "What's in Our LexisNexis Database?" Accessed June 27, 2018. https://www.lexisnexis.com/en-us/products/nexis/feature-get-the-story.page.

SUGGESTED READING

Badke, William. 2011. "The Treachery of Keywords." *Online* 35, no. 3: 52–54. This article's keyword searching scenarios are spot-on.

ANSWERS

1. **I'm a new school bus driver, and I want to know more about handling discipline problems on school buses.** ERIC database

Facets	Choosing Terms for Search Statements (in ProQuest)
School Buses **Student Behavior**	"bus" OR "buses" OR "busses" OR "busing" OR "bussing" student[*1] near/behav*) OR disciplin* OR aggressi[*2] OR bully[*3] OR (antisocial pre/0 behavior) OR (sexual[*2] near/2 harass[*4]) OR fight* OR taunt* OR fistfight* or slugfest
To combine sets	Choose "Recent Searches." Checkmark set numbers for these two facets, and click on the "Search with AND" button.
New titles not in CV searches	"Who's Driving This Bus Anyway: Empowering School Bus Drivers;" "Extension of Positive Behavioral Interventions and Supports from the School to the Bus;" "Decreasing Disruptive Behavior among Students on School Buses through Comprehensive School Bus Safety Education"
Notes	Truncating bus retrieves too many nonrelevant hits (e.g., *busy, bush,* and author names beginning with this stem), so enter bus terms with quotes to control what the system searches.

2. **Are teens from broken homes likely to develop eating disorders?** PsycINFO database

Facets	Choosing Terms for Search Statements (in EBSCOhost)
Eating Disorders	(eating n0 disorder*) OR bulimi? OR anorexi? OR (eating n0 binge) OR hyperphagi? OR pica OR (kleine w0 levin w0 syndrome) OR (appetite n2 disorder)
Broken Homes	divorc* OR (broken w0 home*) OR (marital n2 conflict) OR (marital n0 separat*) OR (marriage n2 problem*) OR (child w0 support) OR (joint w0 custody) OR (custody n2 child*) OR (parent n2 absen*) OR (mother n2 absen*) OR (father n2 absen*)
Adolescents	teen* OR youth* OR (high w0 school*) OR (middle w0 school*) OR adolescen*
To combine sets	Choose "Search History." Checkmark set numbers for the three facets, and click on the "Search with AND" button.
New titles not in CV searches	"A Retrospective Exploration of the Childhood and Adolescent Family Mealtime Environment of Women with Binge Eating Disorder;" "The Role of the Father–Daughter Relationship in Eating Disorders"
Notes	Again, so few retrievals for this topic. Chapter 8 shows how to retrieve more.

3. Do you have anything on the songs and ballads that lumberjacks used to sing?
Classic OPAC

Facets	Choosing Terms for Search Statements (in the library's OPAC)
Lumberjacks	lumbermen OR loggers OR lumberjacks OR woodsmen OR "lumber camps" OR "shanty boys" OR shantyboys
Songs	songs OR folksongs OR "folk songs" OR ballads OR music OR anthems OR serenades OR melody or melodies OR "musical instruments"
To combine sets	Choose "Advanced Search." Enter search terms for the two facets into two successive search boxes. Under "Field to search," choose "Word(s) anywhere," and click on the "Search" button.
Retrieved titles	"Ballads and Songs of the Shantyboy;" "Lumbering Songs from the Northern Woods;" "Songs and Ballads of the Maine Lumberjacks"
Notes	Notice two-word and one-word forms of some search terms. If an OPAC's unlimited truncation is unreliable, enter plural forms of search terms because nouns in LCSHs are plural.

4. How do wilderness survival programs help juvenile delinquents? ERIC database

Facets	Choosing Terms for Search Statements (in EBSCOhost)
Surviving in the Wilderness	(surviv* n3 (skill OR education)) OR (outward w0 bound) OR (wilderness n3 (surviv* OR encounter OR skill OR education OR program)) OR (adventure w0 education)
Delinquents	(delinquen* OR (juvenile n2 (offend* OR gang OR justice OR court)) OR (youth n4 (offender OR problem*)) OR recidivism)
To combine sets	Choose "Search History." Checkmark set numbers for these two facets, and click on the "Search with AND" button.
Retrieved titles	"Discovering Potentials of At-Risk Teenagers;" "Practical Partnerships: A Cooperative Life-Skills Program for At-Risk Rural Youth;" "Shouting at the Sky: Troubled Teens and the Promise of the Wild"

5. **Testing ice hockey helmets to make sure they are safe.** Compendex database

Facets	Choosing Terms for Search Statements
Hockey	hockey
Helmets	helmet OR (face near/2 protector) or headgear
Testing	test OR inspect OR safety OR standard
To combine sets	Under "Search," choose "Search History." Checkmark set numbers for these three facets. The system automatically inserts the Boolean AND operator between set numbers in the "Combine searches" search box, and click on the search button.
Retrieved titles	"Protective Capacity of an Ice Hockey Goaltender Helmet for Three Events Associated with Concussion;" "Protective Capacity of Ice Hockey Helmets against Different Impact Events;" "Angular Acceleration Responses of American Football, Lacrosse and Ice Hockey Helmets Subject to Low-Energy Impacts"
Notes	By default, Engineering Village's autostemming feature is on, so truncation isn't needed.

Free-Text for Recall in Subject Searches of Extended-Boolean Systems

This chapter focuses on free-text (FT) searching of extended-Boolean search systems. Mostly, these are Web search engines, such as Google, Bing, and Yahoo, that index and search the full-texts of Web pages; Google Scholar and Microsoft Academic search engines that index and search academic full-texts and surrogates; web-scale discovery (WSD) systems, the library's Google-like interface that indexes and searches the full-texts of licensed digital resources and gives users the illusion that they are searching everything; and the OPAC's discovery interface, the library's Google-like interface that indexes and searches surrogate records for sources in the physical collection. You can still check controlled vocabularies (CVs) for ideas for search terms, but search-statement formulation is simple and straightforward in extended-Boolean systems. There's no need for the complicated proximity operators and truncation functionality that Boolean search systems expect. In fact, extended-Boolean systems have few FT searching tools because their indexing, searching, and ranking algorithms do automatically what searchers of Boolean systems must do deliberately with FT searching tools. Extended-Boolean systems free you up to focus on facet analysis, search-term selection, and search strategy, providing these systems with the essential information they need to produce relevant retrievals.

HOW EXTENDED-BOOLEAN SEARCHING WORKS

To demonstrate how extended-Boolean retrieval works, *Online Searching* uses our sample database of seven surrogate records in table 6.1. Dominating retrieval in extended-Boolean search systems is the Boolean OR operator. In response to a user query, the system conducts a Boolean OR operation, retrieving sources bearing any one or more words in the search statement. Enter the query `is spirituality on the increase on college campuses?` into our sample database, and its extended-Boolean search system eliminates punctuation and stopwords, parses the query into separate words, and stems them. Then it retrieves surrogate records bearing one or more of these four word stems using this Boolean search statement:

```
spiritual OR increase OR college OR campus
```

Checking our database's inverted index (table 7.1) for these word stems results in the retrieval of records 3, 4, 5, and 6. Retrieval in our seven-record database is simple because there are so few surrogate records. Search Google for this query, and it retrieves more than 2.5 million Web pages! Google doesn't display retrievals randomly; it displays the most relevant retrievals first so that users quickly find Web pages that interest them. How extended-Boolean systems like Google determine which sources to rank first, second, and so on is governed by weights that increase and decrease based on how well a source performs relative to criteria, such as these (Liddy 2001):

1. Occurrence of search terms in texts. Matching search terms in a full-text's title or lead paragraph receives higher weights than in other paragraphs and/or fields.
2. Frequency of search terms in each source. The more frequently search terms occur in a source, the higher the weight given to the source.
3. The frequency of search terms across all sources in the database. Search terms that occur infrequently in sources receive higher weights than frequently occurring search words.
4. Occurrence of search terms in retrieved sources. Sources bearing all search terms in queries receive higher weights than sources bearing fewer than all search terms.
5. Proximity of search terms. Sources bearing search terms adjacent to or near one another receive more weight than sources in which search terms are separated by a sentence, paragraph, or more.
6. Order of search terms in search statements. The initial search term in a search statement receives higher weights than the trailing search terms.
7. Search terms occurring in frequently cited sources. Matching terms in frequently cited sources cited by other frequently cited sources receive higher weights than less-frequently cited sources.

Extended-Boolean systems don't publish their indexing, ranking, or vocabulary-assistance algorithms. They are proprietary. Not long after giving birth to Google, its founders published a technical report describing the system's PageRank algorithm that gives higher weights to frequently cited sources cited by other frequently cited sources (Page et al. 1999). Even though anyone can read the report to find out how PageRank works, it is now one of "over 200 factors" that Google uses to rank order retrievals (Google 2018), making it almost impossible for anyone to replicate Google's ranking algorithm. Working with more than two hundred factors to demonstrate how extended-Boolean retrieval works would be a herculean task. It can be demonstrated using the earlier factors 1 to 3, so let's do it!

Once again, we'll use our sample seven-record database (table 6.1) and its inverted index for FT searching (table 7.1). Omitted from the latter are entries for abstract words because their inclusion would have made the table too long and unwieldy; however, their postings are needed to demonstrate weights in this discussion, so you'll have to imagine that abstract words are listed in table 7.1. If you need to verify something about abstracts, you can do it manually by eyeballing abstracts in the sample seven-record database (table 6.1). Before we get started, please rank records 3, 4, 5, and 6 vis-à-vis their relevance for the Spirituality query. Later, you can compare your ranks with our sample system's ranks.

Our sample extended-Boolean system needs more information about the words in individual records to determine how these records fare with respect to ranking criteria 1 to 3. The system accomplishes this by generating an inverted index of word stem weights for every record in the database. Table 8.1 is an example of an inverted index of word stem weights for record 5. The system uses data in columns 2 to 5 to generate the word stem weight in column 6. Here is an explanation of the data in columns 1 to 6:

1. Word stem. The system uses word stems to represent variant forms of indexed words.
2. Field weights. The system awards one point for the word stem's occurrence in the abstract, two points for the descriptor or identifier field, and three points for the title field.
3. The number of occurrences of the word stem in the record.
4. The number of occurrences of the word stem in the ERIC database (in early 2018).
5. The inverse of the number of the stem's occurrences in the ERIC database. (Table 8.1 multiplies this number by one thousand so that inverse numbers aren't so small that they are hard to understand.) Frequently occurring word stems have low inverse numbers, and infrequently occurring word stems have high inverse numbers. Thus, weighting favors the latter.
6. Word stem weight. Sum of the field weights (column 2) × number of the stem's occurrences in the record (column 3) × inverse (column 5).

Table 8.1. Inverted Index of Word Stem Weights for Record 5

1 Word Stem	2 Field Weights	3 No. of Record Occurrences	4 No. of Database Occurrences	5 Inverse of Database Occurrences	6 Word Stem Weight
accept	1	1	35,480	0.028184	0.028184
affect	1	1	88,941	0.011243	0.011243
associat	1 + 1	2	188,094	0.005316	0.021264
being	1 + 2	2	91,192	0.010965	0.065795
challeng	1	1	93,846	0.010655	0.010655
college	1 + 1 + 2 + 3	4	334,324	0.002991	0.083751
consciousness	2	1	8,628	0.115901	0.231803
correlate	3	1	69,137	0.014464	0.043392
data	1	1	282,737	0.003536	0.003536
develop	2	1	645,188	0.001549	0.003099
different	1	1	159,376	0.006274	0.006274
disorient	1	1	360	2.777777	2.777777
esteem	2	1	17,238	0.058011	0.116022
experienc	1 + 1 + 2	3	231,037	0.004328	0.051939
explor	1	1	155,649	0.006424	0.006424
factor	1 + 2	2	164,134	0.006092	0.036555
faith	1	1	4,326	0.231160	0.231160
hypothes	2	1	38,414	0.026032	0.052064
increas	1	1	175,332	0.005703	0.005703
indicat	1	1	186,900	0.005350	0.005350
individual	1	1	231,246	0.004324	0.004324
negativ	1	1	43,318	0.023085	0.023085
pattern	2	1	109,067	0.009168	0.018337
psycholog	1 + 2	2	163,538	0.006114	0.036688
rais	2	1	37,900	0.026385	0.052770
religio	2 + 2	2	24,286	0.041175	0.329407
self	2	1	153,652	0.006508	0.013016
spiritual	1 + 1 + 2 + 3	4	5,456	0.183284	5.131964
struggl	1 + 1 + 3	3	15,855	0.063071	0.946073
student	1 + 1 + 1 + 2 + 2	5	767,613	0.001302	0.045595
study	1	1	659,858	0.001515	0.001515
test	2	1	242,215	0.004128	0.008257
tradition	1	1	75,496	0.013245	0.013245
well	1 + 2	2	157,812	0.006336	0.038019
year	3	1	282,936	0.003534	0.010603

Let's use the word stem `college` to see how our sample system uses data from a record's inverted index to determine a stem's weight:

A. Calculate the stem's inverse by dividing 1 by the number of its occurrences in column 4. Record the results in column 5. For the word stem `college`, the system divides 1 by 334,324 in column 4 (the number of occurrences of this stem in the ERIC database), multiplies it by 1,000, and records the result (0.002991), in column 5.

B. Add the field weights for `college` in column 2, and multiply the sum by the number of stem occurrences in column 3. For `college`, the sum of the weights in column 2 is 7, which is multiplied by the 4 stem occurrences in column 3, resulting in 28.

C. Multiply the result of step B by the stem's inverse in column 5 to produce the weight that is registered in column 6. For `college`, the system multiplies the inverse 0.002991 by 28 and registers 0.083751 in column 6. By the way, `college` is a frequently-occurring word in the ERIC database, so its weight stays low even after applying field weights and record occurrence data.

Imagine such an inverted index for *every record* in our sample database. The user enters a query, and the system eliminates punctuation and stopwords, parses the query into separate words, stems them, inserts the Boolean OR operator between stemmed words, and retrieves records. It checks each record's inverted index of word stem weights for matched word stems, extracts their word stem weights, adds them, and ranks retrieved records based on word stem weight sums. Table 8.2 does exactly this, listing the four retrieved records, word stem weights, and sums for those weights. On the basis of these sums, our extended-Boolean system ranks the four records as follows: 5, 3, 6, and 4. Is this the same as your ranking?

Let's work with one more query, "Teaching students about backyard animals and wildlife." Our sample extended-Boolean system parses this query into five words, stems them, and retrieves records based on this Boolean search statement:

```
teach OR student OR backyard OR animal OR wildlife
```

Table 8.2. Summing Word Stem Weights for the Spirituality Query

Rec. No.	Word Stem	Word Stem Weights and Sums
3	campus	0.223632
	college	0.017946
	spiritual	3.299120
Sum of Record 3's Weights:		**3.540698**
4	college	0.044866
	spiritual	0.183284
Sum of Record 4's Weights:		**0.228150**
5	college	0.083751
	increas	0.005703
	spiritual	5.131964
Sum of Record 5's Weights:		**5.221418**
6	college	0.002999
	spiritual	1.466275
Sum of Record 6's Weights:		**1.469274**

The system checks the inverted index for FT searching to retrieve records from the sample seven-record database (table 7.1). Again, you'll have to imagine that abstract words are listed in table 7.1. Retrieved are all records, except for record 7. Please rank records 1, 2, 3, 4, 5, and 6 vis-à-vis their relevance for the Teaching query. Later, you can compare your ranks with our sample system's ranks.

The system's next step is to check each record's inverted index of word stem weights for matched word stems, extract their word stem weights, add them, and rank retrieved records based on word stem weight sums. Table 8.3 does exactly that, listing the six retrieved records, word stem weights, and sums for those weights. On the basis of these sums, our extended-Boolean system ranks the six records as follows: 1, 2, 5, 4, 6, and 3. Is this the same as your ranking? By the way, summed weights for all but records 1 and 2 are very low. At the very least, you should have two heaps of records, ranking records 1 and 2 high and all other records low. If this happens, not only do you sense content differences between the two sets of records, but our sample extended-Boolean system does, too. Some systems might disregard records whose summed weights fail to reach a particular threshold vis-à-vis the summed weights for the top-ranked retrievals. In fact, everything about ranking algorithms is subject to fine-tuning by systems staff who constantly study their system's retrievals and adjust ranking algorithms to effect better results.

Table 8.3. Summing Word Stem Weights for the Teaching Query

Rec. No.	Word Stem	Word Stem Weights and Sums
1	animal	0.098048
	backyard	4.065040
	student	0.001302
	teach	0.016450
Sum of Record 1's Weights		**4.180840**
2	wildlife	1.013684
Sum of Record 2's Weights		**1.013684**
3	college	0.010421
Sum of Record 3's Weights		**0.010421**
4	college	0.023449
Sum of Record 4's Weights		**0.023449**
5	college	0.026040
Sum of Record 5's Weights		**0.026040**
6	college	0.013020
Sum of Record 6's Weights		**0.013020**

SEARCHING EXTENDED-BOOLEAN SEARCH SYSTEMS

Let's formulate search statements for real extended-Boolean search systems. Here are three sample queries:

- Is spirituality on the increase on college campuses?
- Teaching students about backyard animals and wildlife.
- How do child soldiers adjust to normal life?

Enter these queries directly into your favorite Web search engine, and expect top-ranked retrievals to be relevant. Eventually relevant retrievals taper off. Most likely, the users who asked you to help them find information on these topics have done the same thing, so they are expecting more from you than simply retracing their footsteps.

The facet analysis for searching an extended-Boolean search system is just as important as it is for searching a Boolean-based system. Especially with respect to searching extended-Boolean systems, the facet analysis will supply you with multiple approaches to expressing search statements so that you can keep the flow of relevant retrievals coming.

Demonstrated here is the presearch preparation for a Google search of the Child Soldiers query. Start with a facet analysis that includes generating search terms for each facet. If you have difficulty finding the right words, check a relevant database's thesaurus—you probably won't search this database, but you can swipe its CV and entry vocabulary for a search of the topic at hand. Sometimes consulting Roget's Thesaurus or an online equivalent is enough to spark your creative juices.

The Child Soldiers query has three facets and these salient search terms:

Child Soldiers	Adjustment	Normal Life
child soldiers	adjust	normal life
child combatants	readjust	everyday life
child conscripts	settle	daily life
	resettle	civilian life
	reintegration	live normally
	struggle	
	maladjustment	

Your next step is to choose one search term per facet, putting the most important search term first. Here are examples of search statements for this query. Enter them into your library's WSD system, its "everything" search, the OPAC's discovery interface, or your favorite Web search engine. See for yourself whether they produce relevant retrievals:

```
child soldiers adjust normal life

child combatants reintegration civilian life

child soldiers struggle normal life
```

Missing from the presearch preparation for searching extended-Boolean systems is the logical combination and the conversion of search statements into the system's searching language. You don't have to engage in these tasks because the extended-Boolean system does them for you. You could enclose the search words `child soldiers` in quotes, indicating to the search engine that it is a phrase. Extended-Boolean systems give higher weights to search words occurring close together, so you can expect systems to retrieve sources with these two words and all the others occurring in text as close to each other as possible. Thus, enclosing these search words in quotes may be unnecessary. Try it with and without quotes around phrases.

By the way, search statements for extended-Boolean systems bear only one search term per facet because these systems don't perform automatic facet recognition; that is, they cannot recognize which search terms belong to which facet. Thus, if you entered all six search terms earlier for the **Adjustment** facet along with one search term for the **Child Soldiers** facet and one search term for the **Normal Life** facet, extended-Boolean systems might rank sources bearing the six **Adjustment** synonyms atop the retrievals list, even though their texts don't bear search terms for the other two facets, leaving you with a heap of nonrelevant retrievals.

Figure 8.1 shows Google Scholar's first-listed retrievals for the query `child combatants reintegration civilian life`. Most retrievals here are relevant. Sign onto Google Scholar through your library's search tools, and free full-texts are a click away.

For more practice searching extended-Boolean search systems, revisit the facet analyses you've performed for *Online Searching*'s many sample queries. Compose search statements bearing one salient search term per facet, and enter them into your favorite Web search engine, your library's WSD system, and/or the OPAC's discovery interface. To get you started, here are sample search statements for the Farm Women, Cultural Revolution, and Wilderness Survival queries:

```
farm women entrepreneurship

china cultural revolution feminism

delinquents wilderness survival
```

If a search statement produces lackluster results, experiment with alternate word orders. For example, the Cultural Revolution search statement does all right, fulfilling the **China** and **Cultural Revolution** facets, but it ignores the **Feminism** facet. Reorder search statement elements, putting `feminism` first, and search results are likely to address the **Feminism** facet because most ranking algorithms give greater weights to

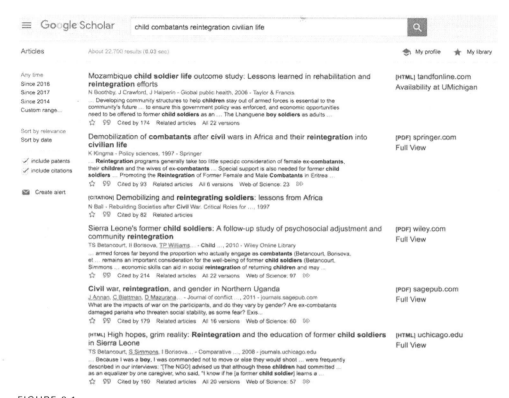

FIGURE 8.1
Extended-Boolean Searching in Google Scholar
Source: Google and the Google logo are registered trademarks of Google LLC, used with permission.

initial words in search statements. If reordering search terms fails to produce any or enough retrievals, substitute synonymous words and phrases held in reserve. Here are follow-up search statements for the same three queries:

```
women farmers entrepreneurs

women great proletarian china

juvenile probationers wilderness survival
```

If lackluster results persist, check your chosen database's CV to make sure your search statements are composed of words and phrases from CV terms. This is especially important for OPAC searches that depend so heavily on LCSH to describe the subject matter of library materials. Ultimately, the problem may be database failure; that is, the database you are searching has no information on the topic you are searching.

THE BUILDING BLOCK SEARCH STRATEGY'S À LA CARTE EDITION

Underlying the search statements you enter into extended-Boolean search systems is the Building Block Search Strategy. Let's use the Child Soldiers query as an example. You conceive the three facets **Child Soldiers**, **Adjustment**, and **Normal Life** and limit your search statement to only one salient search term per facet. This is the À la Carte Edition of the Building Block Search Strategy, and it features *one* search term per facet. You use the most salient search term per facet, and for most queries, this means entering the names of the query's facets. Figure 8.2 depicts the À la Carte Edition visually, bearing one selection per course from the menu.

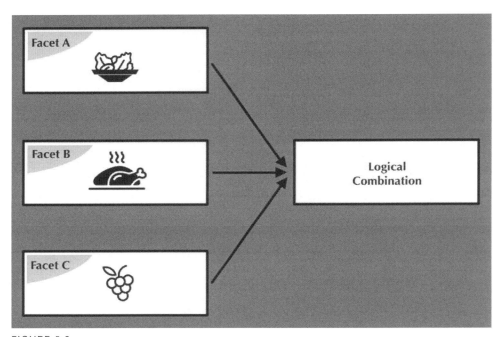

FIGURE 8.2
À la Carte Edition of the Building Block Search Strategy
Source: Created using symbols from the Noun Project (http://thenounproject.com): "Salad" symbol by Peter Chlebak; "Turkey" symbol by jon trillana; "Grapes" symbol by Thomas Hirter.

Here's another sample query: "How did President Johnson convince conservative lawmakers to pass his War on Poverty legislation?" Its facets are **Lyndon Johnson**, **Leadership**, and **War on Poverty**. Put the À la Carte Edition of the Building Block Search Strategy to work at searching an extended-Boolean search system, such as Google, for this query, and start searching using a search statement bearing this query's three facet names:

```
lyndon johnson leadership war on poverty
```

Ranked high on Google's listed retrievals is an essay entitled "Lyndon B. Johnson and the War on Poverty" that accompanies audio recordings from the Johnson White House recordings pertaining to the War on Poverty and other aspects of his domestic policy. The essayist writes, "Through these recorded conversations, listeners gain a sense of Johnson's famous skill as a legislative tactician and of his ability as a deal maker and a flatterer who understood the ways of Washington, and especially of Congress, at an intimate level" (McKee 2014), and this is exactly the type of analysis that the user is seeking.

The reason you use only one search term per facet is the inability of extended-Boolean search systems to perform automatic facet recognition on your entered search terms. If they did, they could parse synonymous terms in your search statements into facets and give higher weights to sources matching one or more search terms *per facet* than to sources matching search terms from fewer than all facets. Because they can't, your only option is to formulate queries bearing one search term per facet, forcing the system to rank sources matching all search terms higher than sources matching fewer than all search terms. To find more retrievals, enter multiple search statements into the system, substituting synonyms for each facet, as demonstrated in these search statements, and experimenting with and without quotes around phrases:

```
lyndon johnson "negotiation skills" "war on poverty"

lyndon johnson "horse trading" "war on poverty"

lyndon johnson strategy "war on poverty"
```

Entering multiple search statements into extended-Boolean search systems is inefficient. Until extended-Boolean search systems can perform automatic facet recognition, the burden will be on the searcher to bear the inefficiency of searching in this regard. Using the À la Carte Edition of the Building Block Search Strategy to represent your search should lighten the load.

RELEVANCE FEEDBACK FOR FURTHERING SEARCHES

Retrieving additional relevant retrievals based on your search results is accomplished by special system functionality that system designers have put in place for this very purpose. The technical name for this is *relevance feedback*. Here are three relevance feedback searches called find-like, bibliography scanning (also called backward chaining), and cited-reference (also called forward chaining) searches.

Find-Like Searches

One or more of these events are likely to trigger the searcher's desire to conduct a find-like search—a low-posted search, the retrieval of an exceptionally relevant source, and the availability of a find-like search in the system you are searching. The search statement for the find-like search is the terminology in a retrieved source. The command for triggering a system's find-like search accompanies brief or full surrogate record displays and has many different names, such as "Find Similar Results," "Find Like," and "Related Articles."

EBSCOhost is most forthcoming about how its find-like search works. Start with a relevant retrieval. Click on the "Find Similar Results using SmartText Searching" link accompanying the retrieval's full surrogate record display. EBSCOhost pastes the source's title, abstract, and index terms into the search box. Click on the "Search" button, and EBSCOhost's SmartText searching responds with an extended-Boolean search and ranks retrievals. By the way, if you don't like one or more of the search words EBSCOhost pastes into the search box, delete them before clicking the "Search" button. You can even edit the original abstract, writing the *perfect abstract* for the sources you want to retrieve.

To demonstrate EBSCOhost's find-like search, let's revisit the Eating Disorders query. Both CV and FT searches fail to produce more than a few dozen retrievals, and less than half are relevant. This query is the perfect candidate for a find-like search. A FT search for this topic produces the relevant title "Connections between Marital Conflict and Adolescent Girls' Disordered Eating." After reading the title's abstract, the searcher clicks on the nearby "Find Similar Results" link. EBSCOhost's response is to fill the search box with the record's title, abstract, and index terms. Figure 8.3 displays this search box. Note that *Online Searching*'s author has edited the search box's contents, limiting its text to the title, the abstract's initial sentences and conclusion, and relevant index terms. Clicking on the "Search" button dispatches the lengthy search statement to EBSCOhost, which performs an extended-Boolean search, reporting more than three million retrievals and ranking these new and potentially relevant titles at the top of the heap: "The Mediating Role of Self-Control and Coping in the Relationship between Family Functioning and Eating Attitudes and Behaviors in At-Risk, Early Adolescent Girls"; "The Unique and Additive Associations of Family Functioning and Parenting Practices with Disordered Eating Behaviors in Diverse Adolescents"; and "Family Environment of Eating Disordered and Depressed Adolescents." It pays to examine these records' index terms and abstracts in search of relevant terms missing from your CV and FT search scripts for this query. In this case, the culprit is the index term "Family Relations," a rather bland and neutral phrase that doesn't convey whether the relations are good or bad; however, subsequent searches for this topic, particularly search alerts (pages 313 to 314), should include it.

In addition to EBSCOhost, Google Scholar, Web of Science, LexisNexis, and Academic Onefile sport this feature. Check your favorite search systems for a find-like search.

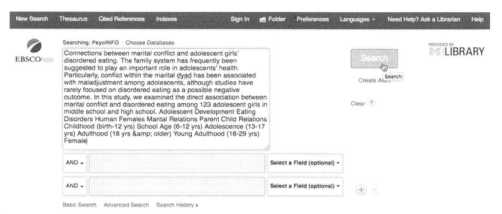

FIGURE 8.3
Relevance Feedback Using a Relevant Retrieval in EBSCOhost's PsycINFO Database

Bibliography Scanning Searches (Backward Chaining)

Bibliography scanning is simple. Find one relevant source, display or download its full-text, and then scan the sources its author cites in the footnotes or bibliography for additional relevant titles. Bibliography scanning yields additional relevant retrievals because authors cite sources that lay the groundwork for their research, support their hypotheses or arguments, and/or supplement their work. Thus, the sources an author cites may be as relevant as the relevant source you have in hand. Bibliography scanning goes *back in time*, finding sources on the desired topic that were published *before* the one in hand.

Web of Science (WOS) and Scopus are two go-to databases for backward chaining, automating bibliography scanning for a relevant source you retrieve in a subject search. When you display a retrieved WOS record's title and abstract, refer to the record's "Citation Network" on the right side, clicking the number above "Cited References." In response, WOS displays the source's bibliography, and when a cited source has promise, click on its title to view its abstract and on its accompanying resolver links to display its full-text. Scopus reacts similarly. In both databases, you'll see some cited references that aren't linked to abstracts or accompanied by resolver links. To retrieve their surrogates or full-texts, you'll have to undertake a known-item search called a full-text fulfillment search (see pages 209 to 212). For the most part, WOS and Scopus provide push-button bibliography scanning!

Typically, you find a relevant source in a database that doesn't have push-button bibliography scanning. An example is the PsycINFO database that we've been searching for the low-posted Eating Disorders topic (pages 145, and 171 to 172). To find more relevant sources, set aside relevant sources from your subject searches for this topic, and then follow up with WOS searches for these sources' bibliographies. (By the

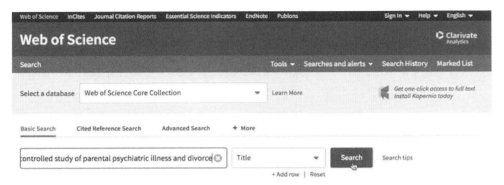

FIGURE 8.4
Conducting a Title Search in the Web of Science Database
Source: Data Reproduced from *Web of Science*® (Clarivate Analytics, 2018).

way, WOS is limited to journal articles so books, reports, and conference proceedings papers won't work.) A relevant journal article title from PyscINFO is "Risk Factors for Bulimia Nervosa: A Controlled Study of Parental Psychiatric Illness and Divorce." In figure 8.4, the searcher searches WOS, entering this title into the search box, choosing "Title" from the fields pull-down menu, and clicking the "Search" button. (The search statement is longer than the search box, so only its trailing portion is visible in this box.)

WOS retrieves the one title that interests the user. Clicking on its title displays the source's abstract in the left and center and its thirty-five cited sources below the fold. Alternatively, click the number above "Cited References" to display the source's bibliography. When a cited source has promise, click on its title to view its abstract and on its accompanying resolver links to display its full-text (figure 8.5). You can get lost in the citation network maze, so be systematic about your review of relevant sources' bibliographies.

When WOS or Scopus searches for your desired titles fail, bibliography scanning becomes a mostly manual process, culling author names and titles from sources and performing known-item searches for them, a topic that chapter 9 explores in detail.

Cited-Reference Searches (Forward Chaining)

Cited-reference searching goes *forward in time*, finding sources on the desired topic published *after* the one in hand. Find one relevant source, and search this source in databases that support cited-reference searching to find authors who have cited it. Don't expect the most recently published sources to have cited references because it takes several years for researchers to build on the work of their peers and cite them in their publications.

Cited-reference searches are a push-button operation in databases and systems that support them. For example, perform cited-reference searches in WOS exactly

FIGURE 8.5
Clicking on a Source's "Cited References" Link for Backward Chaining or Its "Times Cited" Link for Forward Chaining in the Web of Science Database
Source: Data Reproduced from *Web of Science*® (Clarivate Analytics, 2018).

like bibliography scanning searches, entering the title of the relevant source into the WOS search box, choosing "Title" from the fields pull-down menu, and clicking the "Search" button (figure 8.4). WOS responds with retrieved titles. Click on the one that interests you, and WOS displays the source's abstract in the left and center window areas. Under "Citation Network" on the right, click the number above "Times Cited" to display sources that cite the displayed title (the number 9 in figure 8.5). When a cited source has promise, click on its title to view its abstract and on its accompanying resolver links to display its full-text.

Cited-reference searching is subject searching, but it requires known-item search-ing skills to search for and verify the relevant source that interests you so that you can follow up with cited-reference searches. To avoid this, pay attention to retrievals in the database you are searching, looking for links to cited references. EBSCOhost's Psyc-INFO does this with the "Times Cited in this Database" link. When your PsycINFO subject searches produce a relevant retrieval bearing this link, click on it to see a list of sources that have cited the original source (figure 8.6). Scan them, and when one interests you, click on it to display its surrogate and download its full-text.

19. **Risk factors** for **bulimia nervosa**: A controlled
study of parental psychiatric illness and divorce.

Boumann, Christine E.; Yates, William R.; Addictive Behaviors, Vol 19(6), Nov-
Dec, 1994 pp. 667-675. Publisher: Elsevier Science; [Journal Article]

Academic
Journal

25 women with normal-weight **bulimia nervosa** (BN) were compared with 25
age- and weight-matched women without BN on measures of parental
psychiatric illness. All Ss, as well as their parents, comp...

Subjects: Bulimia; Divorce; Mental Disorders; Parental Characteristics;
Adulthood (18 yrs & older)

Times Cited in this Database: (7)

FIGURE 8.6
Clicking on a Retrieval's "Times Cited in this Database" Link in EBSCOhost's PsycINFO Database

The PsycINFO database is limited to psychology, and so, too, are its cited references. Google Scholar and the licensed WOS and Scopus databases feature cited-
reference searches, and their databases are encyclopedic. When your Google Scholar,
WOS, and Scopus subject searches produce a relevant retrieval, click on the retrieval's
accompanying "Cited by N," "N Times Cited," and "Cited by N" links, respectively,
and the database responds with a list of sources that have cited the original source. (*N*
refers to the number of citing references.)

Few users are systematic about checking cited-reference links while conducting
subject searches. They realize some time afterward that they have too few relevant
retrievals and come to you needing more. When they do, ask them for a list of their
relevant retrievals. Then conduct title searches in Google Scholar, WOS, or Scopus
for them, and click on their cited-reference links. For example, a CV search for the
Eating Disorders query retrieves "Characteristics of Family Background in Bulimia."
Launch Google Scholar through your library's search tools, and type this title verbatim
into Google's search box (figure 8.7). Clicking on its "Cited by N" link produces two
promising cited references: "Early Family Experiences of Women with Bulimia and
Depression" and "Parental Variables Associated with Bulimia Nervosa."

**BENEFITS OF FREE TEXT SEARCHING IN BOOLEAN
AND EXTENDED-BOOLEAN SYSTEMS**

The benefits of FT searching center on using terminology that is not represented in
a database's thesaurus and producing comprehensive search results. Of course, some
databases have no CV, so FT searching is your only recourse. You can check any da-

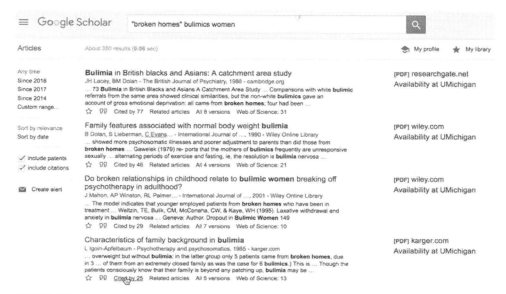

FIGURE 8.7

Clicking on a Source's "Cited by N" Link to Display Sources Citing It in Google Scholar

Source: Google and the Google logo are registered trademarks of Google LLC, used with permission.

tabase's CVs for search term ideas, but in a Boolean system, you will have to search the terms you find using the system's FT searching language—proximity operators, truncation, and nested Boolean logic. In Boolean databases with CVs, searchers can supplement CV terms, adding FT words and phrases to one or more facets of the search using the end user's terminology or the words and phrases that experts writing in the discipline or field of study use to describe the idea.

Lexicographers don't add new index terms for new phenomena immediately to their CVs. They wait until experts in the field have published enough information about the phenomenon. The waiting period between the time a new phenomenon arises and when a new index term is established in a CV is called *literary warrant.* During the waiting period and for a period of time after the CV bears an authorized index term for the phenomenon, searchers must represent their searches for it using FT to retrieve all relevant information.

FT searching yields comprehensive results, also known as high recall. When you help end users, high recall results are usually the exception rather than the rule. Doctoral students researching their dissertation's literature review, attorneys preparing a case for a lawsuit, researchers writing a systematic review, and inventors preparing a patent application are examples of information seekers concerned with high recall results. If you are in doubt about a user's search objectives, ask him whether and why full recall is desired. By the way, high recall is impossible to accomplish in practice. There are so many different ways authors write about phenomena, and formulating FT searches to retrieve them produces so much nonrelevant information that sorting through all of it would be too time-consuming. Plus, in the meantime, new information is being published, including new developments that are expressed in subtly different ways that the original search failed to retrieve. At best, searchers may strive for comprehensive search results, covering all the issues and representative reactions to the issues.

Extended-Boolean searching is a boon for both end users and intermediary searchers. No longer burdened by this or that searching language, they can enter natural-language queries into search systems. Finding a relevant source can also lead to additional retrievals using the search system's find-like functionality, which uses the source's terminology as a search statement to query the database.

QUESTIONS

Here are negotiated queries for you to practice searching extended-Boolean systems. Conduct a facet analysis, generate search terms for each facet using terms from the query and consulting sources of FT search terms (textbox 7.1), and formulate search statements bearing one salient search term per facet. Conduct online searches for these negotiated queries in such extended-Boolean search systems as Google Scholar or Microsoft Academic, your OPAC's discovery interface, your library's WSD system, or your favorite Web search engine. Consider choosing one query, searching all four systems for it, and comparing retrievals across systems with respect to their depth, tone, and insight. As you search, click on accompanying cited-reference links (when available) to find additional relevant retrievals.

1. Should college athletes be paid?
2. Why do Vietnam veterans return to Vietnam?
3. How do wilderness survival programs, such as Outward Bound and the Wilderness Encounter Training and Certification Project, help juvenile delinquents?
4. Is there scientific evidence that global warming affects the departure and arrival dates of migrating birds?
5. What draws people to cults and new religious movements generally?

SUMMARY

Extended-Boolean searching is characteristic of Web search engines, web-scale discovery (WSD) systems, the library's "everything" search, and the OPAC's discovery interface. The Boolean OR operator dominates retrieval in extended-Boolean search systems. In response to a user query, the system conducts a Boolean OR operation, retrieving sources bearing any one or more words in the search statement, and relies on relevance ranking to put the most promising retrievals at the top of the retrievals heap. Start your search of extended-Boolean systems like you approach all other searches: Conduct a facet analysis of the query in hand, give especially salient names to the query's facets, and generate additional search terms for each facet. To formulate a search statement for an extended-Boolean search engine, simply enter the names of the facets, putting the most important facet name first. For additional retrievals, replace facet names with other words and phrases you generated for each facet. When you search extended-Boolean systems, free text (FT) searching tools aren't needed because these systems rank retrievals according to the relative usage of search terms across the database, accomplishing implicitly what expert searchers do explicitly in Boolean systems.

Associated with high recall, FT searching is embraced by expert searchers who aim to retrieve as much relevant material on a topic as they can. FT searching is the only way to retrieve information on new phenomena. Even after literary warrant kicks in and index terms are established for phenomena, searchers will want to search for older sources, and FT is the only way to do it. When FT searches fail to retrieve enough sources, use relevant retrievals to find more, performing find-like searches and backward- and forward-chaining searches in the databases where you originally found these retrievals. If their databases don't support these searches, Google Scholar, Web of Science, and/or Scopus will help you out in this regard.

BIBLIOGRAPHY

Google. 2018. "How Google Search Works." Accessed January 7, 2018. https://support.google .com/webmasters/answer/70897?hl=en.

Liddy, Elizabeth. 2001. "How a Search Engine Works." *Searcher* 9, no. 5: 38–45.

McKee, Guian. 2014. "Lyndon B. Johnson and the War on Poverty." Accessed June 28, 2018. http://prde.upress.virginia.edu/content/WarOnPoverty.

Page, Lawrence, Sergey Brin, Rajeev Motwani, and Terry Winograd. 1999. "The PageRank Citation Ranking: Bringing Order to the Web." Accessed June 28, 2018. http://ilpubs.stan ford.edu:8090/422/1/1999-66.pdf.

ANSWERS

1. Should college athletes be paid?

Facets	Search Terms and Search Statements
College Athletes	college athletes, college football players, college basketball players, college athletics
Payments	payments, paying, exploiting, exploitation, salaries, unionization

Sample search statements	`payments college athletes`
	`unionization college football players`
	`salaries college athletes`
	`exploitation college athletics`

2. **Why do Vietnam veterans return to Vietnam?**

Facets	Search Terms and Search Statements
Vietnam Veterans	vietnam veterans, vietnam vets
Return	return, revisit, visit, go back, vacation
Vietnam	vietnam

Sample search
   statements
	`"vietnam veterans" return vietnam`
	`"vietnam veterans" revisit vietnam`
	`"vietnam vets" go back vietnam`

3. **How do wilderness survival programs, such as Outward Bound and the Wilderness Encounter Training and Certification Project, help juvenile delinquents?**

Facets	Search Terms and Search Statements
Wilderness	wilderness survival, outdoor survival, wilderness education, outward bound, wilderness programs, wilderness therapy
Delinquents	delinquents, at risk youth, youthful offenders, problem youth, juvenile gangs, troubled teens

Sample search
   statements
	`wilderness survival delinquents`
	`outward bound delinquents`
	`outdoor survival at risk youth`
	`wilderness programs problem youth`
	`wilderness education youthful offenders`
	`wilderness survival troubled teens`

4. **Is there scientific evidence that global warming affects the departure and arrival dates of migrating birds?**

Facets	Search Terms and Search Statements
Birds	birds
Global Warming	global warming, climate change, climate warming
Migration Dates	arrival, departure, migration patterns, migration dates

Sample search
   statements
	`birds global warming arrival`
	`birds migration patterns climate change`
	`birds departure climate warming`
	`birds climate warming migration dates`

5. **What draws people to cults and new religious movements generally?**

Facets	Search Terms and Search Statements
Cults	cults, new religious movements, nrms

**Sociological
   Aspects**
	sociology, psychology, social aspects, psychological aspects,
	   understanding, attraction

Sample search
   statements
	`sociology cults`
	`psychology new religious movements`
	`understanding cults`
	`social aspects new religious movements`
	`attraction cults`

Known-Item Searching

A known-item search is a request for a specific source that you know exists—it is a particular journal article, book, conference paper, blog, person, organization, film, magazine or journal, author, advertisement, or television program. Basically, known-item searching boils down to finding one source among all the billions of sources in the vast and varied information universe. Known-item searching stands in sharp contrast to subject searching and its emphasis on casting a broad net.

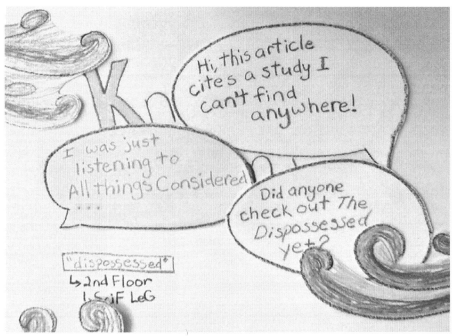

Discover how to search the vast information universe to find the one known-item that interests the user in the video at http://www.onlinesearching.org/p/9-known.html.

Your decision to conduct a subject or known-item search is the result of typecasting the user's query and choosing a database, steps 3 and 4 of the online searching process (pages 96 to 97). Both steps inch you closer to your ultimate search objective—representing the search as input to the retrieval system so that the search system produces relevant retrievals.

This chapter provides an in-depth examination of the two most common types of known-item searches—authors and titles. Because authors are names, you can generalize this chapter's discussion of author searches to searches for the many types of names, such as organizations, places, and brands. Citation verification and full-text fulfillment searches are specialized known-item searches. Knowing how to perform them will enable you to help users complete a citation for a known-item, get their hands on its full-text, or find a source someone recommended to them. Known-item searches also pave the way for the journal run. Get past its funny name because it is the subject search of last resort, producing relevant retrievals when all other subject searches fail. Database detective work is all about searching databases using a combination of subject and known-item searches to answer the offbeat questions users ask.

TITLE SEARCHES

Title searches come in two basic flavors:

1. Users want to read, scan, listen to, look at, or watch the source.
2. Users want to scan a source's contents because they know that it has published, issued, or broadcast information in the past on their topic of interest. They think that, by browsing the source's contents, they might find more like it. Ultimately, this is a subject search in which the user browses the source's content to find more like a piece he read, scanned, listened to, looked at, or watched in the past. Its formal name is the *journal run*, and you'll initiate it with a title search.

Impetus for the Title Search and Journal Run

The impetus for the title search is an exact or not-quite-exact title that the user knows exists. Here are sample scenarios that describe how the source's existence came to the user's attention:

- Someone else, such as a colleague, instructor, friend, or relative, recommended the title.
- The user culled the title from the footnotes or bibliography of a book, a journal article, an encyclopedia entry, or credits from a film or television program.

- Several times the user has noticed this title in bibliographies, suggested readings, or retrieved sources, which are clues that it merits closer scrutiny.
- The user conducted a search; found one or more relevant sources; and, wanting to read the full-text, clicked on resolver links that didn't work.

In all four scenarios, the exact title may not make the trip intact from its point of origin to your interaction with the user: Maybe the person who suggested the title got it wrong; the citation was incorrect; the user omitted, added, or transposed title words; or the user was relying on his or her memory of a search conducted one day, one week, one month, or even one year ago! As a result, always be skeptical about the titles users give to you.

To find the known-item that the user wants, you must get its title and more information from the user. Be attuned to:

- The user's confidence in the title's correctness or how it might be incorrect so that you can experiment with various titles and title searches.
- The title's genre so you know which database to search.
- For a journal or magazine, whether the user intends to browse individual issues so that you can set him or her up with a journal run.
- The discipline that characterizes this article title to give you direction for choosing a database in this same discipline or an encyclopedic database that is likely to index it.
- Where the user got the title so you can retrace the user's steps to find it

Here's a reference interview from a chat transcript in which the user describes her desire for a particular title:

User	15:09	Hi . . . I contacted you last week and someone gave me an online ebbok name to help me write a practicum report. I am looking for guideleines in writing practicum rpeorts. I did another search and coldn't find anytihng. Do you happen to know of the online book I can access?
Librarian	15:10	Hi. Searching now. Are you an Ed[ucation] student?
User	15:12	yes Im getting my MSED in FACS to be a teacher.
Librarian	15:15	. . . Still searching . . .
User	15:16	I am still going to look as well. The funny thing is the title didnt have the word practicum in it (I think) thats why I cant find it. thanks anyway for any help you can give me.
Librarian	15:20	Still looking. Checking with the Education Librarian . . .

The user's uncertainty about the title makes this an exceedingly difficult search. Conduct a known-item search for this title, but you'll find that it eventually morphs into a subject search because the user provides so little information about the title, even though she had the electronic book "in hand" a week earlier.

Selecting Relevant Databases

Find out what the user knows about his desired title, and put it to work selecting a database. Search your library's OPAC to find titles of monographs, journal titles, annual conference proceedings, films, musical compositions, and maps. If you still can't find it, follow up with searches of the Open WorldCat database, which accesses the holdings of libraries worldwide. If the title is a journal article, conference paper, or unpublished working paper, search your library's WSD system, "Everything," or Google Scholar (launching Google Scholar through your library's database hub to avoid the paywall). If you come up empty-handed, follow up with searches in such database aggregators as EBSCOhost, Gale, and ProQuest and then in such journal aggregator databases as ProQuest Research Library, SpringerLink, and Science-Direct. If title searches in encyclopedic databases, such as JStor, Scopus, or Web of Science, fail, then your last resort may be to search databases in the same discipline as the desired title.

Facet Analysis

The facet analysis for the title search is simple, consisting of one facet for the desired title. No logical combination of facets is necessary in a one-faceted search.

Representing the Search as Input to the Search System

Search systems feature one or more types of title searches: (1) alphabetical browsing of the search system's inverted-title index, (2) free text (FT) searches of words in titles producing unranked retrievals, and/or (3) FT searches of words in titles producing ranked retrievals. Confident in the title's initial words, choose alphabetical browsing because you are likely to quickly spot the desired title in the alphabetical neighborhood of retrieved titles. Alphabetical browsing is a standard feature of classic OPACs, but it has become a threatened species in most other systems due to the popularity of FT searches with relevance-ranked retrievals (Badke 2015).

To perform alphabetical browsing, choose this option from the classic OPAC's fields pull-down menu, and enter the title's first few words. What OPACs call this search varies considerably:

- Indexes (Mouse down on the accompanying pull-down menu, and choose the title index.)
- Title-begins-with
- Title-index
- Browse titles
- Look up titles
- Title phrase

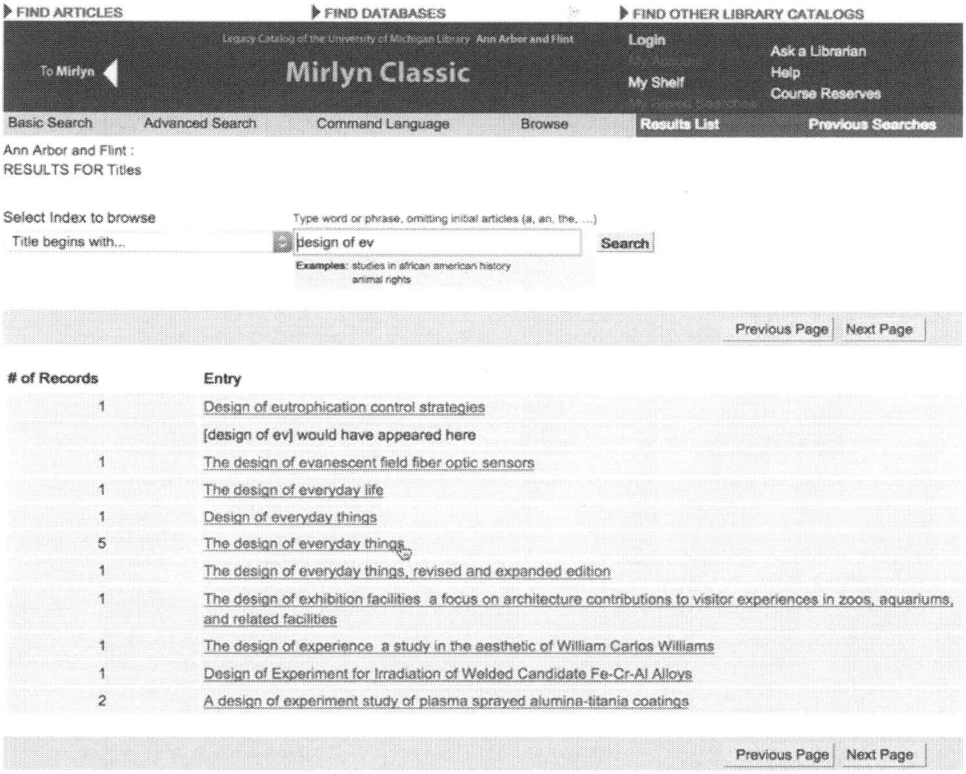

FIGURE 9.1

Alphabetical Browsing for a Title in the University of Michigan's Classic OPAC

Source: Screenshots made available under the Creative Commons Attribution license by the University of Michigan Library.

To browse the title index of the U-M's classic OPAC, the searcher chooses the "Title begins with . . ." search and enters the initial title words `design of everyday` into the search box. In response, the OPAC lists titles in the alphabetical neighborhood of this title fragment, giving the searcher buttons for paging forward and backward to find the desired title *The Design of Everyday Things* (figure 9.1). Personally, I find the title-begins-with search almost effortless because it requires a minimal amount of data entry, and finding the title on the first page of listed titles is a recognition task that takes a few seconds.

You do *not* want to conduct FT searches of titles in the classic OPAC because it doesn't rank retrievals. Its retrievals list for lengthy titles or titles bearing uncommon words might be manageable, but very short titles or titles bearing common words may retrieve hundreds of records, making it difficult and time-consuming for you to find the title you want. Opt instead for the OPAC's discovery interface, which conducts FT searches with relevance ranking. The discovery OPAC displays exact matches first,

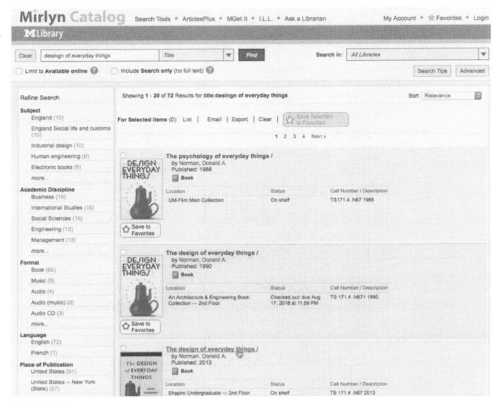

FIGURE 9.2

Free Text Title Search with Ranked Retrievals in the University of Michigan's Discovery OPAC

Source: Screenshots made available under a Creative Commons Attribution license by the University of Michigan Library.

titles with your entered words in close proximity second, and titles bearing one or more of your entered words last. In figure 9.2, the user selects "Title" from the discovery OPAC's pull-down menu and enters `design of everyday things` into the search box. In response, the discovery OPAC ranks and displays brief records for various editions of the desired title atop the list.

In the course of conducting the citation verification search, full-text fulfillment search, or journal run, you'll need to find the title of a journal or magazine. Check your library's classic and discovery OPACs to see if they have a title search specifically for journals and magazines. If they do, proceed with the classic OPAC's alphabetical browsing of the journal-title index. Alternatively, conduct a FT search of journal titles in the discovery OPAC, relying on its relevance ranking to put the desired journal title at the top of the retrievals.

Research databases are likely to have one FT search for the titles of the journals they index and a second FT search for the titles of individual journal articles. For the former, choose "publication," "publication title," "publication name," or "source" from the fields pull-down menu, and enter title words into the search box. For the latter, choose "document title," "article title," or "title" from the fields pull-down menu, and enter title words into the search box. Few research databases have alphabetical browsing, and when they do, it's usually limited to the titles of journals, not the individual articles in journals. *Online Searching*'s discussion of citation verification searches revisits searching for journal titles (pages 209 to 212).

AUTHOR SEARCHES

Author searches come in two basic flavors:

1. Users want to read, scan, listen to, look at, or watch a particular source that a person wrote, edited, illustrated, photographed, scripted, painted, performed, sculpted, produced, and so on. This is an author search.
2. Users want to scan a list of sources that a particular person wrote, edited, illustrated, etc. because they like what the person writes about, and they want to find more like it. Calling it an author-bibliography search here distinguishes it from the author search. Truth be told, this is a subject search, but an author search fulfills it.

Impetus for the Author and Author-Bibliography Searches

The impetus for author and author-bibliography searches is an author name that is known to the user from past experience or others' recommendations. Sample scenarios that describe how the author's name came to the user's attention and possible inaccuracies are the same as for titles (pages 196 to 197). Thus, always be skeptical about the names users give to you.

To find one or more works connected with the name that interests the user, you must get the name and more information about it from the user. Be attuned to:

- Whether the user seeks a particular *title* written, edited, illustrated, etc., by this person. By the way, this is the *first* information you should get from the user. If the user knows the title, then several avenues are open to you for finding the source: title, author, or a combination of the two. Because research demonstrates that people are *more successful* searching for *titles* than for authors when both are known (Kilgour 2004; Lipetz 1972; Wildemuth and O'Neill 1995), conduct a *title* search first.
- The user's confidence that the name is correct or clues about how it might be incorrect so that you can experiment with various names in your author searches.
- Who is the person behind the name so you know which database(s) to search.
- Where the user got the name so you retrace the user's steps to find the name.

Problems Searching for Author Names and for Proper Nouns Generally

Because authors are proper nouns, this discussion of author searches can be generalized to searches for proper nouns generally, such as names of persons, organizations, places, programs, and projects. People's names change due to marriage, divorce, remarriage, Anglicization, stage names, pseudonyms, sex changes, and deliberate changes of name (legal or otherwise). Some publishers apply strict editorial rules about the names on their title pages; for example, representing them as the first and middle initials followed by a single or hyphenated surname. Names of organizations change due to mergers, acquisitions, buy-outs, Anglicization, image campaigns, acronyms, splits, and the decisions publishers make about how organization names appear on their title pages. Family names and names of places change. Names of projects, programs, legislation, roads, buildings, monuments, brand names, governments, and other proper nouns change and are known by nicknames, shortened forms, and/or acronyms. They also adopt one-word names that are words used in common everyday language (e.g., CASTLE, DESIGN, LEADER, MIRACLE, PEAK, SMART, SNAP). Names also bear numbers that could be written out or represented as Roman numerals or Arabic numbers. Because proper nouns also figure prominently in subject searches, all this name-changing business applies to your subject searches for them, too.

Authority control is the editorial process used to maintain consistency in the establishment of authorized index terms. When library catalogers and database publishers practice name-authority control, they assume the burden of establishing authorized names for persons, corporate bodies, and families; linking all the unused, synonymous names to the authorized names; and building a syndetic structure into their databases to refer searchers from unused names to authorized names. For example, in an OPAC governed by authority control, you can expect it to respond to your entry of the name `babe didrikson` with a reference to the database's authorized name: "Use Zaharias, Babe, Didrikson, 1911–1956."

The library catalogers who build OPACs maintain a record of their authority-control decisions in the Library of Congress Name Authority File (LCNAF). When you think a name may be problematic, search LCNAF for alternate names (https://authorities .loc.gov). If you aren't familiar with the MARC (Machine-Readable Cataloging) format, LCNAF records may be difficult to understand, so display authority records using LCNAF's "Labeled Display." Figure 9.3 shows the top half of a labeled display of Babe Didrikson's authority record. Use the names you find in the "Personal name heading," "Corporate name heading," "See also," and "Variants" fields to formulate the search statements you enter into relevant databases.

LCNAF includes names of organizations, places, projects, programs, titles, and proper nouns generally. Other name authority files are the Getty Thesaurus of Geographic Names (TGN) at http://www.getty.edu/research/tools/vocabularies/tgn/ and

LC control no.: n 50062017
LCCN Permalink: https://lccn.loc.gov/n50062017
Descriptive conventions: rda
Personal name heading: Zaharias, Babe Didrikson, 1911-1956
    Variant(s): Zaharias, Mildred Babe Didrikson, 1911-1956
          Didrikson, Babe, 1911-1956
    Birth date: 1911
    Death date: 1956
    Found in: Her Championship golf, 1948
          Title nine iron, 2015: leaf 1 (Mildred Ella "Babe" Didrikson Zaharias; woman athlete; 1911-1956)

FIGURE 9.3
Library of Congress Name Authority File's Labeled Display of a Name Authority Record
Source: Courtesy of the Library of Congress.

the Union List of Artist Names (ULAN) at http://www.getty.edu/research/tools/vocabularies/ulan/. Biographies, such as Marquis Who's Who and American National Biography Online, may trace the many names a person is known by (pages 75 to 77).

Except for OPACs, authority control is the exception rather than the rule. Don't expect authority control in most databases. By the way, the problem of multiple names is not limited to women's name changes due to marriage, divorce, or both. Check LCNAF for these men whose authority records list multiple names: John Creasey, Pope Francis I, Prince, Barack Obama, and Stephen King.

Authority control solves the problem of multiple names for an author. It doesn't help with misspelled author names or variants. To be comprehensive about retrieval, formulate search statements bearing as many variant forms of the name as you can think of. Consider initials, initials only, missing name elements, punctuation, symbols, and so on. Whether you are conducting a known-item search for works by an author or a subject search for works about the author, consider all the possibilities, and then formulate your search statements accordingly.

If you suspect a misspelled name, enter it into Google, Bing, or Yahoo because these Web search engines suggest corrections that you can cut and paste into another search system. Google even detects users' misspelled author names embedded in phrases:

- `books by rosamund smith`: Google suggests `books by Rosamond Smith`
- `ruth rendle's last mystery`: Google suggests `Ruth Rendell's last mystery`
- `writings of harald robens made into movies`: Google suggests `writings of Harold Robbins made into movies`
- `stephen jobs helath`: Google suggests `Steve Jobs health`

The ORCID identifier (also called Open Researcher and Contributor ID) has promise for improving the accuracy of manual and automatic approaches to authority control as well as streamlining academic publishing generally. ORCID is a nonprofit organization, describing its work as "open, transparent, and non-proprietary" (ORCID 2018). Participating academic, research, and professional institutions encourage anyone involved in scholarship to register free for an ORCID identifier that persists throughout one's professional career. To be successful, ORCID must achieve worldwide adoption. Indications that ORCID is gaining momentum are such early adopters as Web of Science, which has added the "author identifier" to its fields pull-down menu so that searchers can enter an ORCID identifier to retrieve journal articles written by the person assigned this identifier (Vieira 2015), and academic institutions, which automatically assign ORCID identifiers to their faculty and doctoral students (Thomas, Chen, and Clement 2015).

Selecting Relevant Databases

As soon as you establish the user's interest in a particular name, ask her for clarification. For a person, ask who this person is, in which discipline he is active, or what he is known for. For an organization, ask what kind of organization or business it is, what type of work or business it does or did, or what it is known for. In a pinch, consult an encyclopedia article to learn more about the proper nouns that figure into user queries.

If the user wants everything written by the person, she may be conducting an author-bibliography search—a subject search in disguise. Such searches may be for names of modern-day researchers connected with academic institutions or not-for-profit laboratories, research centers, and think tanks or for names of writers whose literary works interest the user.

Search for researchers on the Web using your favorite Web search engine to find the researcher's Web page where his or her curriculum vitae is posted and provides you with a comprehensive list of his or her publications. Follow up with author searches of such encyclopedic databases as Google Scholar, your library's WSD system, Scopus, and Web of Science and then one or more discipline-based databases.

Search for authors of literary works in your library's OPAC. For a comprehensive list of monographs, search the Open WorldCat, which accesses the holdings of libraries worldwide, and suggest that the user request relevant WorldCat retrievals that your library doesn't own through interlibrary loan (ILL). Alternatively, inquire about the writer's genre, and recommend writers in the same genre.

Facet Analysis

The facet analysis for both author and author-bibliography searches is simple, consisting of one facet for the author's name. No logical combination of facets is necessary in a one-faceted search.

Representing the Search as Input to the Search System

Formulating search statements for both author and author-bibliography searches is the same. Differences between the two pertain to the user's handling of retrievals. For the former, users are searching for one particular title. For the latter, users want all or selected works by this author.

Search systems feature one or more types of author searches: (1) alphabetical browsing of the search system's inverted-author index, (2) FT searches of words in author fields producing unranked retrievals, and (3) FT searches of words in author fields producing ranked retrievals. These types of searches are comparable to their title counterparts on pages 198 to 201.

If you remember how to look up a person in an old-fashioned telephone directory, that's exactly how alphabetical browsing of author names works in classic OPACs. You scan the first element of the string for the desired author surname and then check first and middle names. Scanning is quick and almost effortless because you are likely to quickly spot the name you want in the neighborhood of alphabetized author names. Alphabetical browsing has several different names:

- Author index
- Author (last name first)
- Author (last name, first name)
- Browse authors
- Look up authors

In figure 9.4, the searcher browses the U-M's classic OPAC for an author's name. She mouses down on the fields pull-down menu, chooses the "Author (last name first)" option, and enters the inverted name brown, dan. Because this is a common name, she enters both surname and given name. It might take her a half-minute to browse forward and backward in the alphabetical list, selecting this and that Dan Brown entry to find the Dan Brown that interests her (i.e., the author of *The Da Vinci Code*) among the half-dozen Dan Browns listed (figure 9.4).

You do *not* want to conduct FT searches for author names in the classic OPAC because it doesn't rank retrievals. Its retrievals list for unique author names might be manageable, but common names will retrieve hundreds of records, making it difficult and time-consuming for you to find the known-item you want. Opt instead for the OPAC's discovery interface, which conducts a FT search and ranks retrievals. In response to your entered author words, the discovery OPAC displays records bearing exact matches of author names first, records bearing your entered author words in close proximity second, and records bearing one or more of your entered author words last. In figure 9.5, the user selects "Author" from the discovery OPAC's pull-

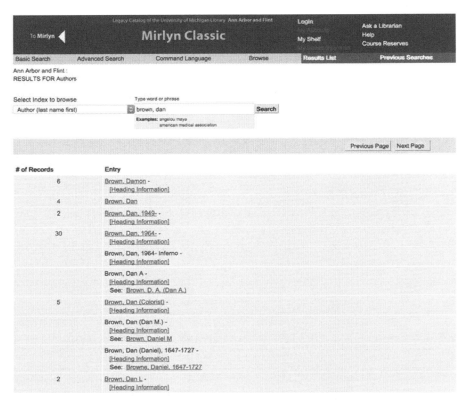

FIGURE 9.4

Alphabetical Browsing for an Author in the University of Michigan's Classic OPAC

Source: Screenshots made available under the Creative Commons Attribution license by the University of Michigan Library.

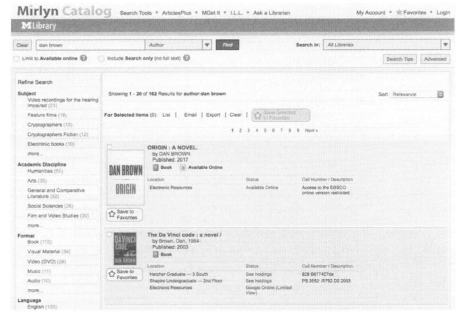

FIGURE 9.5

Free Text Author Search with Ranked Retrievals in the University of Michigan's Discovery OPAC

Source: Screenshots made available under the Creative Commons Attribution license by the University of Michigan Library.

down menu and enters dan brown into the search box. Displayed first are retrievals by authors with this exact name.

Most research databases feature one of the two FT searches for author names. From the searcher's perspective, FT searches with ranked retrievals is preferred because first-listed retrievals keep name elements in close proximity. Less likely in research databases is the alphabetical search of the database's inverted-author index. If it is available, it might not be designated on the fields pull-down menu, showing up as a link elsewhere on the interface and leading you through a multiple-step entry and selection process. In EBSCOhost databases, click on the "Indexes" link on the top center left of the interface, choose "Author" from the "Browse an Index" link, enter the inverted form of name, and choose the listed name(s). In ProQuest databases, choose "Author – AU" from the fields pull-down menu, which exposes the "Look up Authors" link under this menu. Click on this link, enter the inverted form of name into the pop-up search box, enable the "Begins with" radio box, and hit the "Find" button. By the way, limit the names you search via alphabetical browsing to surnames and the initial of the given name so that ProQuest displays forms of names that are fuller than your entered elements. That's what the searcher does in figure 9.6, entering lancaster, f only, and in response, ProQuest's ERIC database shows fuller forms of this name: (1) surname and initials of given and middle names and (2) surname and written-out given and middle names. You'll want to select both to continue this search.

Searches for names confuse users. They aren't always sure whether the person figures into their search as an author or a subject. Consider this problematic chat:

USER	18:55	How do I find a journal on a specific person? The title is Philosophical Studies, the person is Aristotle.
LIBRARIAN	18:57	Under the first box type in Aristotle and then in the second box type in Philosophical Studies.

Unfortunately, this chat is doomed from the start because the librarian doesn't bother to find out what the user really wants. Consider the negotiation that is needed to help this user. You have to determine whether the user actually has a citation in hand for a journal article about Aristotle published in the journal named *Philosophical Studies*. If so, conduct a citation verification search. If not, search the Ulrichsweb database to see if there really is a journal named *Philosophical Studies* and which databases index its articles, and then proceed accordingly. Most likely, the user's instructor gave her and other students in the class a directive to use sources from scholarly journals. The user is unsure what to do, so she posits her question to the librarian in a way that elicits a response that remains faithful to her professor's directive about using sources from scholarly journals. If this is the case, I'd advise the user to search a database that specializes in philosophy, choose "Subject" from the fields pull-down menu, enter

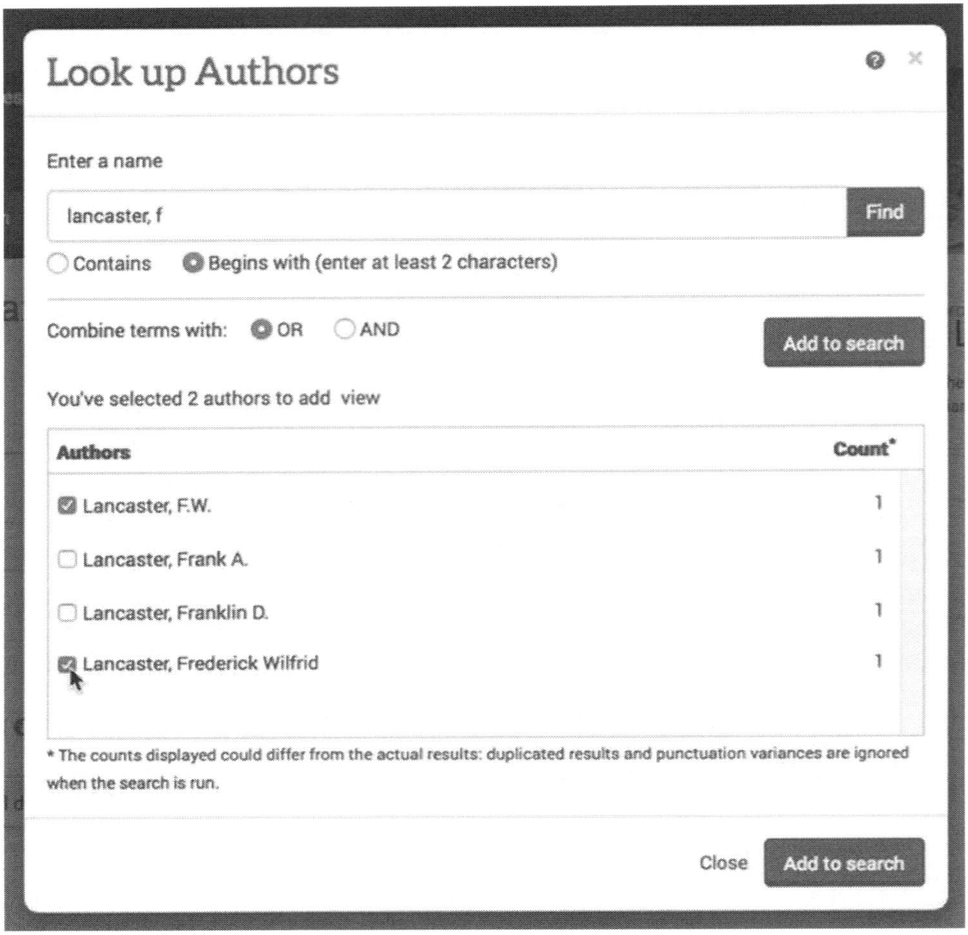

FIGURE 9.6
Alphabetical Browsing for an Author in ProQuest's ERIC Database

Source: The screenshots and their contents are published with permission of ProQuest LLC. Further reproduction is prohibited without permission. Inquiries may be made to: ProQuest LLC, 789 E. Eisenhower
Pkwy, Ann Arbor, MI 48106-1346 USA. Telephone (734) 761–4700; Email: info@proquest.com; Web page:
www.proquest.com.

`aristotle` into the search box, and review clusters for a particular aspect about
Aristotle that interests her.

THE DIGITAL OBJECT IDENTIFIER (DOI): AN ALTERNATIVE APPROACH
TO KNOWN-ITEM SEARCHES

The Digital Object Identifier (DOI) uniquely identifies "physical, digital, or abstract
entities" (Paskin 2010, 1). DOIs usually appear in the margins of journal articles,

book chapters, tables, and figures. Also look for DOIs in footnotes and bibliographies. You're looking for a string of numeric and alphabetic characters separated by a slash and preceded by the acronym DOI. Here are three sample DOIs for journal articles cited in this chapter:

10.1081/E-ELIS3-120044418

10.1080/00987913.2015.1099399

10.1080/0361526X.2015.1017713

Since 2000, the DOI system has been "implemented through a federation of registration agencies, under policies and common infrastructure provided by the International DOI Foundation which developed and controls the system" (Paskin 2010, 1). If you have a source's DOI, you are a few heartbeats away from finding the actual source, so make it a point of asking users whose queries involve known-items whether they have one or more pages from the actual source or the original source that references the source they want. If they do, check it for a DOI. With the DOI of the desired source in hand, navigate to DOI at http://www.doi.org/index.html or to Google at http://www.google.com, and enter the DOI into the search box. Alternatively, preface the DOI with `http://dx.doi.org/`, and enter it into your favorite Web browser; an example is:

`http://dx.doi.org/10.1080/0361526X.2015.1017713`

DOI, Google, and your Web browser should display the source's surrogate and provide enough information so that you can find a full-text provider through your library's search tools or order full-text from interlibrary loan.

CITATION VERIFICATION AND FULL-TEXT FULFILLMENT SEARCHES

A citation verification search is a known-item search that verifies the citation data the user has in hand for a source or completes it for citation purposes. Which style the user follows for citing sources depends on the disposition of the piece she is writing, so be prepared not only to verify the citation but also to help the user formulate a citation that is faithful to a particular style's conventions.

Very similar to the citation verification search is the full-text fulfillment search, a user's request for assistance in finding a full-text for a desired source. Because you must have in hand a source's citation to find its full-text, it makes sense to lump the two searches together here.

Impetus for Citation Verification and Full-Text Fulfillment Searches

Initiating the citation verification or full-text fulfillment search is the information users have in hand about a known source that they need verified to complete a citation and/or to obtain the source's full-text. Find out exactly what the user wants because verifying citation data is usually quick and straightforward, whereas obtaining full-texts requires the added steps of finding and downloading the source from a database. Users who are under time constraints might not wait for interlibrary loan (ILL) to supply the source, so you end up helping them find something like the source they originally wanted.

Don't expect the citation data users have in hand to be correct. Even if they copied and pasted it from a digital source, such as a full-text's bibliography, a Web page's text, or a database's surrogate record, inaccuracies are typical in original citations, everything from misspelled titles or author names to an incorrect year of publication, volume, or issue number.

Users who verify citations are usually missing or uncertain about one or more citation elements; that's why they're asking for your help. Users wanting full-texts often have in hand full citations. Although you can verify citations and retrieve full-texts with a few elements in hand, the more elements that you have in hand to experiment with, the more likely it is that your search will succeed.

Selecting Relevant Databases

Database selection recommendations for citation verification and full-text fulfillment searches are the same as for title searches (page 198).

Facet Analysis

The facet analysis for the citation verification or full text-fulfillment search depends on the citation information that the user provides. If the user only has a title or author name in hand, then the facet analysis involves one element. No logical combination of facets is necessary for a one-faceted search, and your only course of action is to conduct a title search (pages 198 to 201) or an author search (pages 201 to 208).

The user might have multiple elements or is just missing one element that would complete the citation. For the most part, citations can be boiled down to a title, author name, journal title or publisher, and date elements, and thus, search statements for most verification queries could be represented by a maximum of four facets—one each for each of these elements; however, enter as few facets as possible because errors or inaccuracies may prevent you from retrieving the citation the user wants. Deciding how to proceed depends on your assessment of the situation:

- How sure the user is about the correctness of her citation's elements
- How unique each citation element is
- Whether the database(s) you plan to search responds with Boolean or extended-Boolean searching

Representing the Search as Input to the Search System

When searching an extended-Boolean system, you can copy and paste all available citation elements into the system's search box and let the system do the heavy lifting, so to speak, producing retrievals and ranking them so that retrievals matching all or almost all search terms are ranked higher than retrievals matching one or a couple of search terms. If the desired citation isn't popping onto page 1 of the retrievals list, limit elements to titles and publishers (for books) or to titles and journal titles and possibly the author's surname (for journal articles). Extended-Boolean systems simplify citation verification and full-text fulfillment searches considerably because they have a certain "forgiveness" factor that allows one or more search terms in search statements to fail without torpedoing the entire search.

When searching Boolean systems, you have to do the heavy lifting, deciding which elements are likely to quickly and efficiently produce the desired citation. Consider starting with one or two elements and adding more until you have a manageable number of retrievals. If you are stumped about how to get started, remember research findings demonstrate that the title element alone is usually effective for retrieving the desired citation.

Searches may fail because of the ways in which citation data are represented in the surrogate record and indexed in the database. For example, databases might represent journal titles, conference proceedings, and book and anthology titles in full, acronym, and/or abbreviated forms. For example, here are PsycINFO's indexed forms for the journal *Psychiatric Quarterly*:

psychiat. quart

psychiat. quart.

psychiatric quarterly

psychiatric quarterly supplement

These forms deviate due to abbreviations, punctuation, and written-out title elements. Much the same happens to indexed forms for the *Journal of the American Helicopter Society* in the Compendex database:

j am helicopter soc

j amer helicopter soc

journal of the american helicopter society

If a citation verification or full-text fulfillment search fails, the problem may be that your search statement fails to accommodate for the variant forms of a journal's title. You need to perform alphabetical browsing of the database's journal-title index, scan for variant forms of the desired journal title, select them, and combine their retrievals into one combined set using the Boolean OR operator. Unfortunately, not all search systems offer alphabetical browsing of journal-title indexes, so you might have to guess at variant forms, enter them directly, and/or use truncation to get the job done. Journals change their titles. Search their authority records in the Ulrichsweb Global Serials Directory database, and open the database's "Title History Details" tab for a list of previous names.

Personally, I am partial to alphabetical index browsing, especially when book titles, journal titles, and names of persons are involved (figures 9.1, 9.4, and 9.6). It is much easier to recognize desired titles or names in an alphabetical list than it is to guess at variant forms and dress them up in truncation symbols to retrieve all the possibilities. When a citation verification or full-text fulfillment search leaves you stumped, activate alphabetical browsing, and scan the alphabetical list to find what you are looking for.

DATABASE DETECTIVE WORK

Databases are able to answer questions that are different from the subject and known-item queries that they were originally designed for because database fields document a wide range of information, such as author affiliations, publisher names, grant names and numbers, methodologies, target audiences, study locations, and types of illustrations. Choose these fields from the database's fields pull-down menu to search them. Alternatively, conduct a subject or known-item search, and you retrieve not only sources that have potential for answering the query but also clusters that characterize interesting aspects of your retrieved sources.

To develop your detective skills, scrutinize the databases you search on a daily basis, and become familiar with the purpose and content of each and every field. Think about the questions that users might ask that could be answered by searching these fields, alone or in combination with other fields, presearch qualifiers, and postsearch clusters. This type of searching requires searchers to excel in investigation, data collection, ingenuity, and deductive reasoning, so it is called "database detective work." Here are a couple of sample searches.

Sample Search 1: Hot or Not Topics

You conduct a reference interview with an upperclassman who is contemplating her senior thesis and wants to write about the effect of television violence. She asks for your help to determine whether her topic is passé. In response, you formulate a FT search in the ERIC database and generate FT search terms from ERIC descriptors so your search is as comprehensive as possible. Retrieving almost one thousand retrievals, you show her ProQuest's "Publication Date" cluster results, where research peaks in the 1970s, slows down in the 1980s, peaks again in the 1990s, and slows down through the present day (figure 9.7). You suggest she examine the "Subjects" cluster

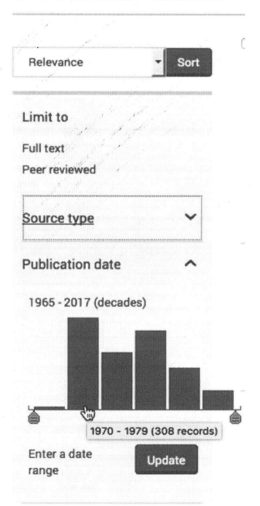

FIGURE 9.7

Scrutinizing Clusters for Insight into a Mature Topic in ProQuest's ERIC Database

Source: The screenshots and their contents are published with permission of ProQuest LLC. Further reproduction is prohibited without permission. Inquiries may be made to: ProQuest LLC, 789 E. Eisenhower Pkwy, Ann Arbor, MI 48106-1346 USA. Telephone (734) 761–4700; Email: info@proquest.com; Web page: http://www.proquest.com.

in search of unique descriptors assigned to newer retrievals that might give her ideas for a fresh examination of this topic. Additionally, she could limit retrievals to the "Encyclopedias and Reference Works" source type to learn how domain experts talk about this topic's research questions, findings, and trends.

Sample Search 2: Research Funding

You conduct a reference interview with a new and enterprising faculty member wanting to see research papers published as a result of funding from the Bill & Melinda Gates Foundation. In response, you search Scopus, using this foundation's name qualified by the FUND-SPONSOR field label:

```
FUND-SPONSOR("bill and melinda gates foundation")
```

In response, Scopus reports more than 8,500 retrievals, displaying the most recent ones and using clusters to characterize retrievals (figure 9.8). You suggest that the faculty member scrutinize cluster results to determine subject areas receiving funding, most active researchers, highest-funded research institutions, and so on, and then limit retrievals by his subject area to see how cluster values change. Clicking on "Analyze Search Results" presents graphical views of cluster data, and clicking on "Export Refine" exports cluster data into a spreadsheet for manipulation.

Few beginning searchers are naturals at database detective work. It takes time and experience to familiarize yourself with your library's databases. Develop a sixth sense of the usefulness of database fields and their content, and apply your knowledge, searching skills, and ingenuity to answer the question at hand. Answer this chapter's questions to get started (page 217).

THE JOURNAL RUN

The journal run has a funny name until you realize what it is all about. By whatever means, the user identifies a relevant journal and then retrieves the journal with the intention of scanning one or more issues to find relevant sources. Clusters make it easier than ever to identify journals that publish articles repeatedly on certain topics. Yet, high-posted searches aren't the right candidates for follow-up journal runs because users are overwhelmed with relevant retrievals and have little incentive to conduct journal runs to find even more. Instead, low-posted searches are the best candidates for follow-up journal runs.

It's quicker to perform the journal run when the results of a subject search are at hand, clicking on accompanying resolver links to navigate to journal publisher and journal aggregator databases, where full runs of journals reside. Unfortunately, you don't know how little is written on a topic until you've run the gamut, conducted subject

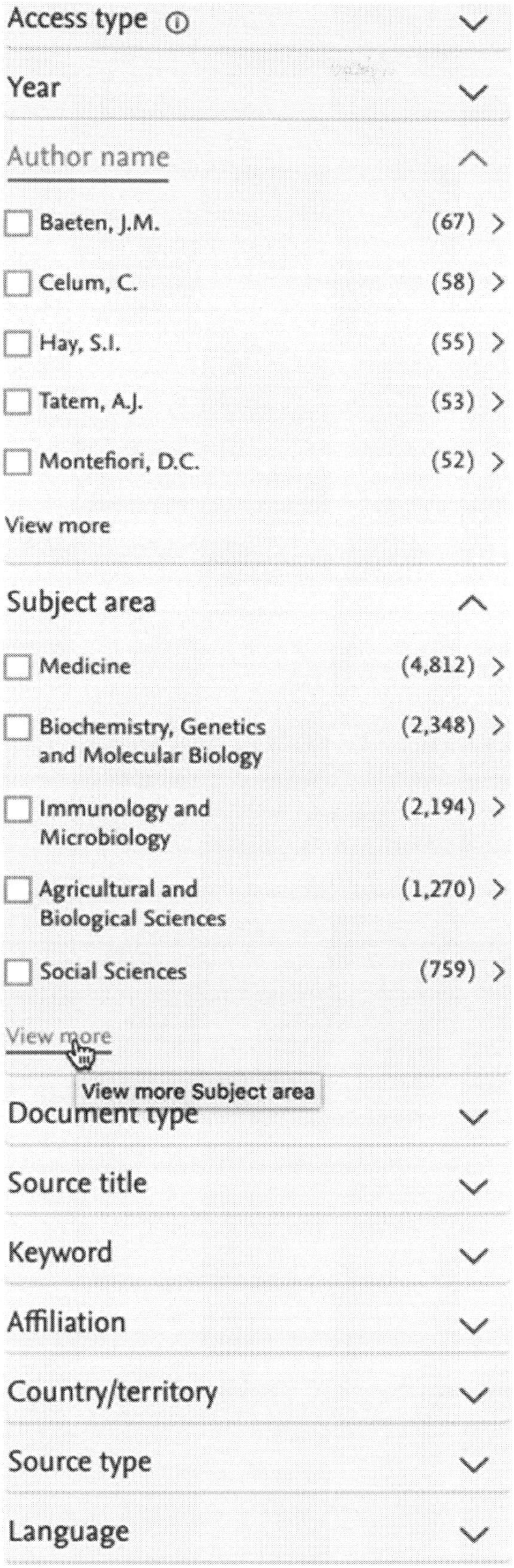

FIGURE 9.8
Scrutinizing Clusters for Insight into Research Funding in the Scopus Database

Source: Scopus, a registered trademark of Elsevier, B.V., image retrieved on 17 July 2018.

searches in several discipline-based databases and encyclopedic databases, followed up with relevance feedback searches, and came up with little to show for your efforts. Now it's time to initiate the journal run, and it's a search that you'll have to perform manually.

Navigate to your library's website, and scan it for a link to online journals. The link may be hidden under a pull-down menu, and the terminology used for the link will vary from library to library. Examples are:

- Digital journals list
- E-Journals
- eJournals A–Z
- Electronic journals list
- Journal titles
- Journals
- Online journals

Clicking on the "Online Journals" link produces a search box, into which you type the journal's name. The system might give you a choice between alphabetical browsing of the database's inverted-title index or a FT search of words in journal titles. Although I'm partial to the alphabetical browsing search, choose the search type that you prefer. Scan retrieved journal titles, and in response to your selection of the desired title, the system displays links for one or more full-text providers. Some providers supply full runs that go back to the journal's first volume and issue many years ago, and others are limited to volumes in a specific range of years. When conducting the journal run, most users want to start with the most recent issue and go backward in time, so make sure the provider supplies the desired journal for the years and volumes that interest the user.

An alternate approach to finding online journals is a search of the library's OPAC. On the OPAC's fields pull-down menu, choose the journal title search. If there's no such menu, switch to the OPAC's advanced search, and look for it there. Again, maybe the OPAC will automatically respond to your entered journal title with an alphabetical browsing search or a FT search or give you a choice between the two. When you find yourself scanning retrieved journal titles for the desired one, finishing up is the same as above; that is, choose the desired title from the retrieved-titles list, and choose from the providers list a full-text provider that is able to supply the volumes and years that interest the user.

Because browsing individual issues takes time, effort, concentration, and perseverance, the journal run is for serious, motivated researchers whose interests are on the cutting edge and who may have trouble finding relevant information. It is not for the casual inquirer who needs a handful of refereed journal articles to write a paper that is due tomorrow afternoon. If neither approach—searching the library website's journal-titles index or the OPAC—yields the desired journal title, your library probably does not subscribe to it. This ends your journal-run search because an interlibrary loan requires known-items, not entire runs of journals.

SEARCHING FOR A JOURNAL ARTICLE IN A JOURNAL FROM SCRATCH

When full-text fulfillment searches for journal articles fail or you need to verify a citation, you can search for a journal from scratch. The process is the same as the journal run, choosing "Journals" from the library's website or searching for a journal in the library's OPAC. If you can't find the journal listed in the journal-titles index or in the OPAC, your library doesn't have access to the journal. The user will have to order the desired article from interlibrary loan. Should you find the journal, make sure the full-text provider supplies the desired year, volume, and issue. Then select the provider, and drill down to the year, volume, and issue in which the article is published. Become familiar with the various ways to find online journals on your library's website because you will help many users find journals, issues of journals, and journal articles on a daily basis.

QUESTIONS

Keep a record of the steps that you took to find answers to these questions, and then compare your steps with those described in the answers.

1. A user needs help finding the full citation for the article "Tibet's Primeval Ice" from *Science* magazine.
2. A user tells you he has read all the library's books by Dan Chernenko and wants to know whether the library has more recent books by this author.
3. A user wants to watch an old television commercial. She remembers that a college student comes home for Christmas, surprises a sibling who yells "Peter!" and it advertises Folger's coffee.
4. A user needs the full citation for a source entitled "Competitive Sports Activities for Men." She can't remember the database where she found the source. She doesn't know its author. She had trouble downloading the source, so she copied and pasted the source's text into a three-page Word document. She tells you that the article talks about sports for elderly men suffering from memory problems.
5. A user wants to compile a complete bibliography of items written by the late, great Jerry Salton from Cornell, who taught in its computer science department.
6. A user wants to read as much as possible on Salton's SMART search system, which was the precursor to today's Web search engines, including Google.

SUMMARY

When you conduct a search for a known-item, you expect to retrieve a source that you know exists. Examples are a journal article, book, conference paper, blog, organization, film, television commercial, journal, or author. This chapter spotlights the two most common known-item searches—title searches and author searches. These may be subject searches in disguise. In the case of authors, the user wants to scan an author's works in case the author has produced more works like those the user knows about. In the case of titles, the user wants to scan a particular title's contents because it has published relevant information in the past and he thinks that, by browsing what else the source has published, he might find more like it. The latter is the journal run, and it is usually the search of last resort for low-posted subject queries.

Known-item searching can be problematic because of the original citing source's published inaccuracies, the faulty memories of the persons recommending known-items to users, and the incomplete information users provide. Database publishers could ameliorate the situation by performing authority control, but it is expensive to implement and maintain. Except for the OPAC, few databases perform authority control. The burden is on you, the searcher, to overcome the limitations of databases bereft of authority control to find what the user wants.

BIBLIOGRAPHY

Badke, William. 2015. "What Happened to Browse?" *Online Searcher* 39, no. 2 (Mar./Apr.): 71–73.

Kilgour, Frederick G. 2004. "An Experiment Using Coordinate Title Word Searches." *Journal of the American Society for Information Science & Technology* 51, no. 1: 74–80.

Lipetz, Ben-Ami. 1972. "Catalog Use in a Large Research Library." *Library Quarterly* 41, no. 1: 129–39.

ORCID. 2018. "ORCID: Our Values." Accessed June 29, 2018. https://orcid.org/node/8.

Paskin, Norman. 2010. "Digital Object Identifier (DOI) System." In *Encyclopedia of Library and Information Sciences*. 3rd ed., pp. 1586–92. Boca Raton, FL: CRC Press.

Thomas, William Joseph, Barbara Chen, and Gail Clement. 2015. "ORCID Identifiers: Planned and Potential Uses by Associations, Publishers, and Librarians." *The Serials Librarian* 68, nos. 1–4: 332–41.

Vieira, Scott. 2015. "Disambiguating Author Names: Part Two." *Serials Review* 42, no. 2: 135–41.

Wildemuth, Barbara M., and Ann L. O'Neill. 1995. "The 'Known' in Known-Item Searches: Empirical Support for User-Centered Design." *College & Research Libraries* 56, no. 3 (May): 265–81.

SUGGESTED READINGS

Badke, William. 2015. "What Happened to Browse?" *Online Searcher* 39, no. 2 (Mar./Apr.): 71–73. When the searcher knows an author name or initial title words, alphabetical browsing delivers you quickly and efficiently to the known-item you seek.

Sprague, Evan R. 2017. "ORCID." *Journal of the Medical Library Association* 105, no. 2 (Apr.): 207–8. DOI: 10.5195/jmla.2017.89. An overview of ORCID, its purpose, its services to researchers, its competitors, searching ORCID numbers, and registering for an ORCID identifier and an assessment of its potential for authority control.

ANSWERS

1. **Finding the full citation for the article "Tibet's Primeval Ice" from *Science* magazine.** Navigate to Google Scholar. Into its search box, enter `"tibet's primeval ice" science` (with or without parentheses). Click on the matching title that links directly to *Science*, which displays these bibliographic data: Qiu, Jane. 2016. "Tibet's Primeval Ice." *Science* 351, 6272 (29 January): 436–39. DOI:10.1126/science.351.6272.436.

2. **Find more recent books by Dan Chernenko.** Check LCNAF for this author's authority record (http://authorities.loc.gov/). Dan Chernenko is a pseudonym for Harry Turtledove, an author who writes under several names: Dan Chernenko, Mark Gordian, Eric G. Iverson, and H. N. Turteltaub. Follow up in your library's OPAC with author searches for each name, possibly limiting by date; show the user your library's holdings for each; and suggest he pursue those that interest him.

3. **A user wants to watch an old television commercial. A college student comes home for Christmas, surprises a sibling who yells "Peter!" and it advertises Folger's coffee.** Although this television commercial is a known-item, commercials rarely have titles, so conduct a subject search in Google using these clues: `peter christmas folgers`.

4. **A user needs the full citation for a source entitled "Competitive Sports Activities for Men."** Based on what the user tells you about the source, you should establish a pecking order with respect to searching databases likely to provide a citation. This appears to be a journal article, so search your library's WSD system first, then Google and Google Scholar (launching the latter through your library's website). If your searches fail, continue searching, choosing such database aggregators as EBSCOhost, Gale, and ProQuest and then such journal aggregator databases as ProQuest Research Library, ScienceDirect, or SpringerLink. Consider also such current newspaper databases as LexisNexis, InfoTrac Newsstand, ProQuest News & Current Events, and Access World News.

A title search of all EBSCOhost databases and a Google search of the title words enclosed in quotes `"competitive sports activities for men"` retrieves the full citation: Tolle, Ellen. 2008. "Competitive Sports Activities for Men." *Activities Directors' Quarterly for Alzheimer's and Other Dementia Patients* 9, no. 3: 9–13.

5. **Compile a complete bibliography of items written by Jerry Salton from Cornell, who taught in its computer science department.** If you don't know who Salton is, search him on Google, and take note of his various names: Gerard Salton, Jerry Salton, Gerry Salton, and Gerald Salton. Check LCNAF also. Identify computer science databases in your library's search tools, and search all of them using all forms of this author's name. Search your library's OPAC for Salton's books also.

6. **A user wants to read as much as possible on Salton's SMART search system.** This is a difficult query because the search term `smart` is used in so many different contexts. If you enter `smart`, you must add subject terms as a hedge to give it context. Search the Inspec database using its "Quick Search." Enter `smart` into the search box. Retrieved are one hundred thousand retrievals! Choose the "Thesaurus" tab, and enter information retrieval into the search box. This phrase is a CV term, so click on it to display its syndetic structure. Choose such relevant index terms as "Information Retrieval," "Information Retrieval Systems," "Information Retrieval System Evaluation," "Bibliographic Systems," "Relevance Feedback," "Query Processing," and "Query Formulation," and limit results to the years 1957 (one year before Salton received his PhD) to 1997 (two years after his death). Combine sets using the Boolean AND operator for the `smart` free text term and the **Information Retrieval** facet; that is, #1 AND #2. This reduces retrievals to about one hundred, and you can quickly scan their titles to distinguish relevant sources(e.g., "Implementation of the SMART Retrieval System") from nonrelevant ones (e.g., "Smart Catalogs and Virtual Catalogs"). Eventually you'll encounter a source that reveals SMART's full name—Salton's Magical Automated Retriever of Texts—so you can follow up with known-item searches in Inspec and other databases using the name's most salient terms, `magical automated retriever`.

Assessing Research Impact

This chapter focuses on publication-level and article-level metrics that are used to assess research impact. These metrics come from the well-entrenched library and information science (LIS) area of study called bibliometrics and the fledgling enterprise called altmetrics. Because these metrics pertain to known authors and titles, it makes sense to discuss them here, following on the heels of the known-item searching

Find out how to assess the research impact of a particular journal, journal article, or researcher's publication record in the video at http://www.onlinesearching.org/p/10-impact.html.

chapter. Interested in research impact are college and university faculty, who use these metrics to decide where to publish their research; administrators at research centers, laboratories, think tanks, and academic institutions, who use these metrics to inform employment, tenure, and promotion decisions; and representatives of professional associations, learned societies, national academies, and funding agencies, who use these metrics to aid in decision making for committee selection, editorial boards, elected boards and positions, awards, nominations, grants, and much more.

Because tenure and promotion committees emphasize quantitative indicators of research productivity, research professionals are attracted to social-networking sites, both sites that specialize in the research enterprise and mainstream sites, where they have opportunities to showcase their expertise and accomplishments. Ultimately, their intention is to increase the visibility of their research among their peers, and in the course of doing so, they share news, content, and ideas that you can search to help others answer their questions.

BIBLIOMETRICS

Bibliometrics is the quantitative analysis of the written products of academic inquiry, scholarship, and research to determine the research productivity and impact of their authors and, by extension, the quality and impact of individual products. At the heart of bibliometrics are the citations in scholarly sources. One of the primary reasons scholars cite other scholars is to strengthen their research questions, claims, and arguments with citations to previous knowledge and empirical evidence. The late Eugene Garfield (1955), one of the founders of bibliometrics, designed and published the first citation index called Science Citation Index (SCI) in the mid-1960s. Converted from print into an online database in the 1970s, SCI enabled users who had a known-item in hand to find published sources that cited it in subsequent years. Over the years, Garfield and his colleagues introduced new citation indexes for the arts, humanities, and social sciences. These citation indexes are now combined into the Web of Science (WOS) database (Crotty 2014b). While remaining focused on citation searching, WOS evolved into an A&I database with encyclopedic coverage.

Cited-reference searches in WOS produce citation counts for individuals and for journal articles. The citation count is the number of times a person's publications have been cited in other publications or the number of times a specific publication has been cited. Researchers aim for high citation counts to prove to their colleagues that their research is important.

Assembling an Author's Citation Count in the Web of Science Database

Determining a researcher's citation count is procedural in WOS, compared to the more straightforward and direct process in Scopus and Google Scholar (GS). When you help users conduct cited-reference searches, ask them about the person they are searching—the author's discipline and their specific research interests—because what you learn will help you search WOS and other citation databases and distinguish between persons with the same or similar names. Working with people's names, you must take name changes into account. Check for multiple names for the same person in authority files and in published biographies (pages 75 to 77), and then use what you find to assemble all WOS citation entries for the person.

Search WOS using Cliff Lampe, one of my University of Michigan colleagues who teaches computer–human interaction (CHI), and who has conducted research on social media, online communities, and civic communities since the beginning of the new millennium (Lampe 2018). Launch the WOS database, and click on "Cited Reference Search" to the right of the default "Basic Search" (figure 10.1).

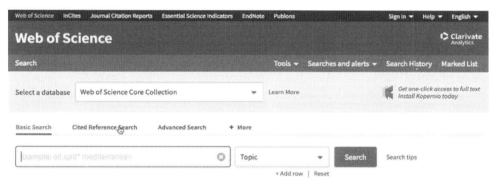

FIGURE 10.1
Choosing the Cited-Reference Search in the Basic Search Interface of the Web of Science Database
Source: Data Reproduced from *Web of Science*® (Clarivate Analytics, 2018).

The cited-reference search interface opens. Stop! Don't enter Cliff's name into the search box yet because of the problems of multiple names and variant forms of author names (pages 202 to 204). Instead, click on the "Select from Index" link underneath the "Cited Author" pull-down menu (figure 10.2) to browse names in the alphabetical neighborhood of Cliff's name. WOS responds by opening its "Cited Author Index," where you enter the surname lampe and first initial c into the search box and click on the "Move To" button (figure 10.3).

In response, WOS displays names from its cited author index in the alphabetical neighborhood of this author's name. Scroll through the full list, and choose listed names, even if you're unsure about them; you'll get a second chance to eliminate their postings from this author's citation count. Knowing Cliff's middle name(s) and initial(s) is essential at this point in the search process so that you select all variant forms from

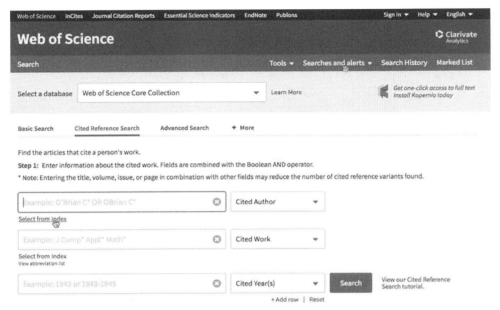

FIGURE 10.2
Choosing the "Select from Index" Link in the Web of Science Database
Source: Data Reproduced from *Web of Science®* (Clarivate Analytics, 2018).

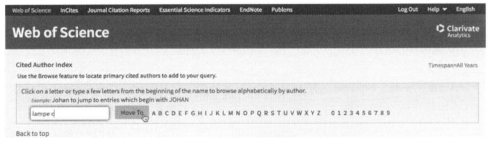

FIGURE 10.3
Entering an Author's Surname and First Initial into Web of Science's Cited Author Index
Source: Data Reproduced from *Web of Science®* (Clarivate Analytics, 2018).

the list. In figure 10.4, the searcher chooses twelve names for Cliff, five bearing various initials for his first and middle names, four bearing shortened or whole forms of his first name and with or without his middle initials, and three bearing possible misspellings of his given name (i.e., *Ciff*, *Cliffe*, and *Cliffobar*). WOS lists these names at the bottom of the page. By the way, WOS extracts these names and citation data generally from footnotes and bibliographies in published sources and, thus, depends on authors for correct cited sources. Click on the "OK" button, and WOS pops the names into its "Cited Reference Search" box (figure 10.5). Click on the "Search" button, and WOS goes to work, retrieving sources that cite authors bearing these names.

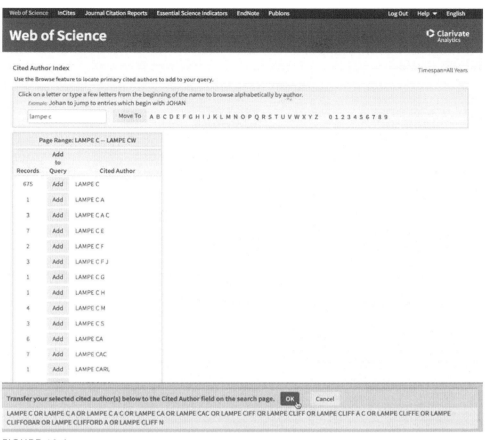

FIGURE 10.4

Selecting Alphabetized Names from Web of Science's Cited Author Index

Source: Data Reproduced from *Web of Science*® (Clarivate Analytics, 2018).

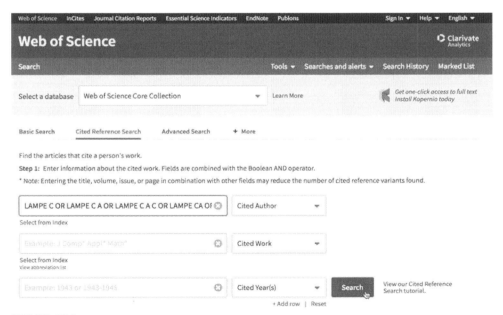

FIGURE 10.5

Searching for Selected Names in Web of Science's Cited-Reference Search Box

Source: Data Reproduced from *Web of Science*® (Clarivate Analytics, 2018).

WOS reports cited-reference search results in a huge "Cited Reference Index" spanning eleven Web pages, with seventy-five results per page. Figure 10.6 shows a very small portion from one page of this big index. Each row of the index records one or more cited references to one of this author's sources. The cited-reference index's columns from left to right are:

1. Select. Review the data in this row, and if you think the author whose cited references you seek wrote this source, check this box.
2. Cited Author. This cited author's name along with his coauthors.
3. Cited Work. An abbreviated form of the publication (usually a journal name but not always) in which the cited source was published.
4. Title. The title of the cited source.
5. Year. The cited source's year of publication.
6. Volume. The cited source's volume number.
7. Issue. The cited source's issue number.
8. Page. The page that is cited. Expect multiple entries for the same source because WOS indexes cited references right down to the *page number*.
9. Identifier. The cited source's unique document identifier, such as a DOI.
10. Citing Articles. Number of times the source is cited.

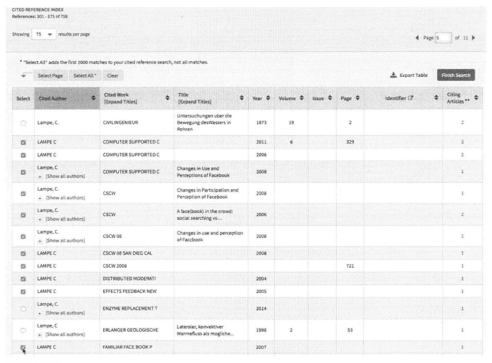

FIGURE 10.6
Cleaning Up Your Author's Cited-Reference Index in Web of Science
Source: Data Reproduced from *Web of Science*® (Clarivate Analytics, 2018)

Your job is to "clean up" this eleven-page index, reducing it to entries that Cliff wrote on his own and with his coauthors. To do so, scan each entry, and check its "Select" check box in column 1 for entries that Cliff and his coauthors wrote. Usually the abbreviated names of cited works in column 3 give you enough information to make a decision; for example, entries in figure 10.6 bearing the words and phrases "CIVILINGENIEUR," "ENZYME REPLACEMENT T," and "ERLANGER GEOLOGISCHE" are ones you'd leave unchecked in this ongoing search because they don't represent the disciplines where Cliff publishes his scholarship. If you are unsure, click on the "[Show all authors]" link in column 2 to see this source's coauthors, or click on titles in column 4 to see the source's abstract and keywords.

Cliff's cited-reference index bears more than 750 entries and takes 11 pages to display, at 75 entries per page, so don't jump the gun, selecting entries on page 1 only and clicking the "Finish Search" button. Additionally, WOS limits checked entries to 500 so you'll have to generate a systematic strategy for building Cliff's complete citation count. Personally, I'd be inclined to create three separate sets, set 1 for pages 1 to 4, set 2 for pages 5 to 8, and set 3 for pages 9 to 11. Then I'd click on "Search History" and combine these three sets using the Boolean OR operator (figure 10.7). It takes time, patience, and attention to detail to build a complete citation count for a prolific author, but after checking entries on a few pages, you'll get used to his coauthors and the abbreviated titles of publications that publish Cliff's research.

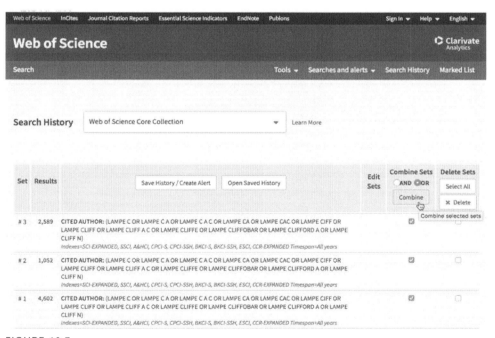

FIGURE 10.7
Combining Three Sets of Cited References for an Author's Cited-Reference Count in Web of Science

Source: Data Reproduced from *Web of Science*® (Clarivate Analytics, 2018).

At long last, your cleanup effort results in a single combined set bearing thousands of cited references to Cliff's works (figure 10.8). In summer 2018, Cliff's WOS citation count was 6,889, and it increases every few days or so. Sorting retrievals by "Times Cited" reveals one work ("Social Network Sites: Definition, History, and Scholarship"), which accounts for 47 percent of Cliff's cited references. WOS accompanies the single combined set with sixteen clusters giving the big picture of Cliff's publication record; for example, which disciplines Cliff's research spans (*Web of Science Categories* cluster), who cites him the most (*Authors* cluster), which journals cite him the most (*Source Titles* cluster), whether citations to Cliff's works are increasing or decreasing over time (*Publication Years* cluster), and more. Figure 10.8 displays names of seven of

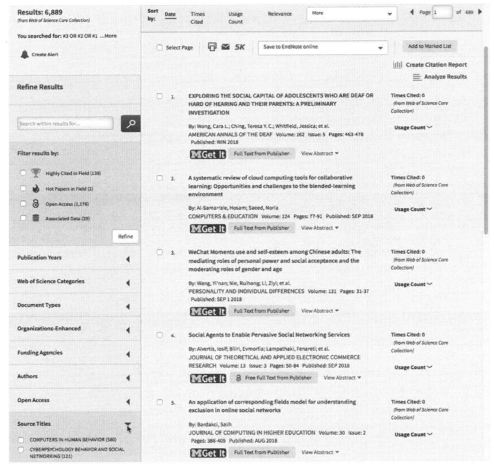

FIGURE 10.8
Your Author's Citation Count with Accompanying Web of Science Clusters
Source: Data Reproduced from *Web of Science*® (Clarivate Analytics, 2018).

the database's sixteen clusters. The eighth cluster is *Source Titles*, and it is open, revealing the top journals citing Cliff's works. Click on the "Analyze Results" link trailing the sixteenth cluster (not shown in figure 10.8 due to the page's long length) for ways to further refine cluster values.

Searching for an Author's Citation Count in the Scopus Database

To search for Cliff's citation count in Scopus, switch from Scopus's default "Document search" to its "Authors" search by clicking on the "Authors" link. Then, enter `lampe` into the "Author Last Name" search box and `cliff` into the "Author First Name" search box, and click the magnifying-glass search icon (figure 10.9).

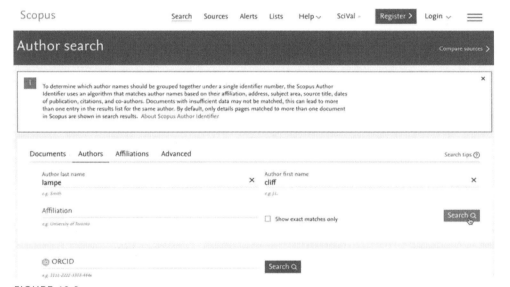

FIGURE 10.9

Entering an Author's Name to Initiate a Citation Count Search in the Scopus Database

Source: Scopus, a registered trademark of Elsevier, B.V., image retrieved on 17 July 2018.

Scopus responds with a list of names. Scan this list using its accompanying author affiliation and disciplinary information to distinguish between people with the same name. In figure 10.10, Scopus responds to Cliff's name with several entries (Scopus calls them profiles). Click on the highest-posted profile to display his Scopus-based bibliometrics (figure 10.11).

By July 17, 2018, Cliff's seventy-four sources had spawned 8,505 cited references in 6,228 journal articles (figure 10.11). Scopus performs authority control on author-name variants, so your retrievals won't be dogged by the many first- and middle-name variants you found in WOS, such as Lampe, C; Lampe, C A; and Lampe, C A C; however, its authority control is limited, and prolific authors (like Cliff) and authors with

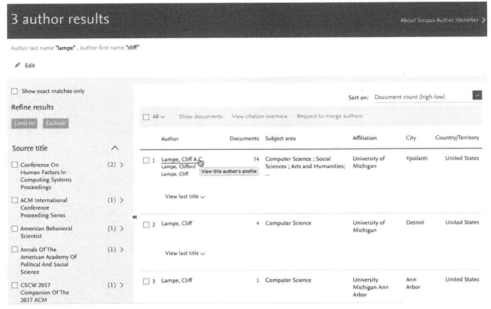

FIGURE 10.10

Retrieved Author Name(s) in the Course of a Citation Count Search in the Scopus Database

Source: Scopus, a registered trademark of Elsevier, B.V., image retrieved on 17 July 2018.

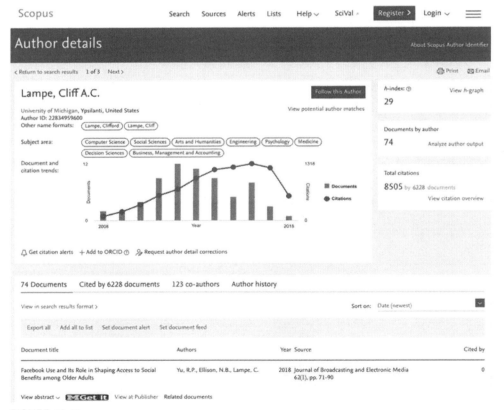

FIGURE 10.11

An Author Profile in the Scopus Database

Source: Scopus, a registered trademark of Elsevier, B.V., image retrieved on 17 July 2018.

name changes (like *Online Searching*'s author) have to contact Scopus directly and ask this database publisher to combine citations for multiple profiles under one preferred profile. If authors don't contact Scopus, they'll have multiple profiles, citation counts, and h-indexes. Thus, users who search for such authors will have to combine multiple profiles manually.

Searching for an Author's Citation Count in the Google Scholar Database

Finally, there is Cliff's citation count in GS. Enter `cliff lampe` into GS's search box, and click on the magnifying-glass icon. GS responds with a retrievals list and the link "User Profiles for Cliff Lampe." Clicking on the link produces this author's GS user profile (figure 10.12). Topping this profile is his citation count—24,293—more than three and a half times as many citations as WOS (figure 10.8) and three times as many citations as Scopus (figure 10.11).

The main reason for disparities between the three citation counts is that each database uses a different set of sources from which to generate cited references (Bar-Ilan 2008; Harzing and van der Wal 2008; Meho and Yang 2007). WOS limits its core set to

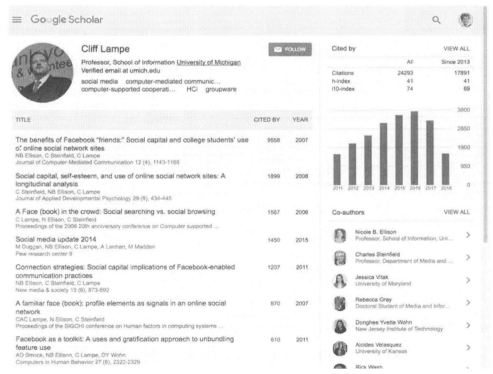

FIGURE 10.12
An Author's User Profile in Google Scholar
Source: Google and the Google logo are registered trademarks of Google LLC, used with permission.

journals, book-based proceedings, and selected books and anthologies. Scopus is less stringent, indexing such serial publications as scholarly journals, trade journals, book series, and conference publications bearing an International Standard Serial Number (ISSN). Google is the least stringent, indexing the full range of academic publications. Boosting Cliff's GS citation count is this database's comprehensiveness covering the many conference proceedings where Cliff publishes his research. Because researchers in his field of study communicate their findings primarily through conference proceedings, GS may be the best source for Cliff's citation count. When you assist users with queries that involve citation counts, suggest that they search all three databases and choose results from the one that best represents how scholars in the particular field of study communicate their research to their peers.

Like Scopus, GS performs authority control on author-name variants, not on name changes. If you are searching an author (like me) who has written under more than one name over the years, be prepared to search Google under all of the person's names, combine retrievals, and calculate bibliometrics manually.

Don't expect to find user profiles for every author you search in GS. Not all authors proactively create a Google account, set up a profile, and make it public. If there is no GS user profile, it means that the searcher has to calculate an author's citation count manually.

JOURNAL-LEVEL METRICS

A byproduct of WOS is Journal Citation Reports (JCR), a database that uses its proprietary impact-factor metric to rate the twelve thousand journals that WOS indexes. JCR calculates this metric by determining the number of times that articles in a journal are cited by other journals over a two-year period, divided by the total number of citable pieces in the journal. You can use the impact factor to evaluate *Computers in Human Behavior* (CHB), the journal that WOS reports as having the most cited references to Cliff Lampe's works (figure 10.8). Choose JCR from your library's search tools. At JCR's opening page, choose "Browse by Journal." JCR responds with a journals list ranked by JCR's proprietary Journal Impact Factor (JIF). [JCR calculates JIF as follows: (1) In this year, count how many times citable sources published in the journal that were cited in the two previous years, and (2) divide by the number of citable sources were published in those two years.] Earning the highest JIFs at 40 and above are the journals *New England Journal of Medicine*, *Nature*, *Lancet*, *Journal of the American Medical Association*, and *Science*. Because these top-ranked journals publish research on important scientific discoveries, researchers generally monitor them, incorporate their findings into their research, and hope that they'll make a discovery that merits publication in one of them. Even the news media monitor the top-ranked journals and broadcast new scientific discoveries to their viewers, making these journals familiar, household names.

Let's search for the impact factor for *Computers in Human Behavior*. Into the "Master Search" box under "Go to Journal Profile," enter `computers in human behavior`, and click on the magnifying glass. Figure 10.13 shows JCR's response—CHB's journal profile page, where CHB's JIF of 3.536 dominates the page above the fold.

JCR places journals into discipline-specific categories so that you can get a sense of how a journal that interests you stacks up to other journals in the discipline. CHB belongs to the "Multidisciplinary Psychology" and "Experimental Psychology" categories.

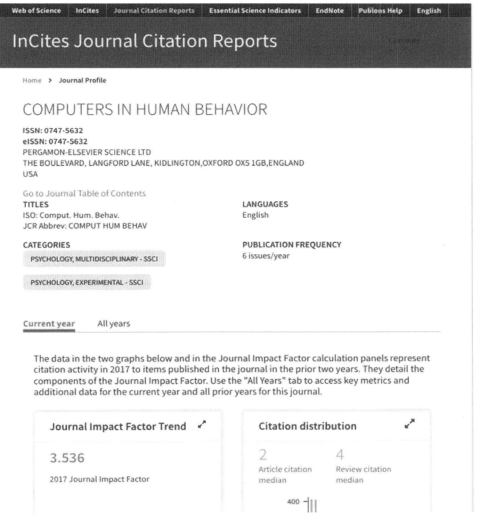

FIGURE 10.13

Journal Profile Page (Above the Fold) Featuring the Journal Impact Factor in the Journal Citation Reports Database

Source: Data Reproduced from *Journal Citation Reports®* (Clarivate Analytics, 2018).

(This is designated on the top right of CHB's journal profile page under the "Categories" heading.) Click on the "Multidisciplinary Psychology" category. In response, JCR uses JIF to rank the list of this category's 135 journals (figure 10.14). CHB's JIF of 3.536 puts it at the sixteenth rank in the "Multidisciplinary Psychology" category, smack dab in the middle of this category's first quartile. Sort "Multidisciplinary Psychology" journals by Eigenfactor score, and CHB jumps up to 3. Click on the "Customize Indicators" link to choose other metrics, such as "5 Year Impact Factor," "Article Influence Score," or "Immediacy Index," for ranking CHB. (For definitions of JCR's many metrics, click on JCR's "Help" link, where there's a link to JCR's glossary; click on the "Glossary" link, and then click on the letter of the alphabet for the metric that interests you.) This introduces you to JCR's journal-level metrics. JCR has many more features.

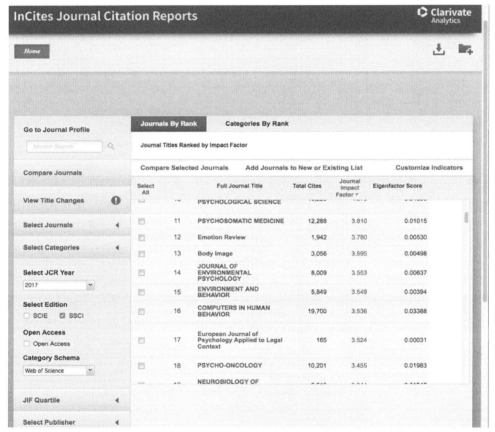

FIGURE 10.14
JIF-Ranked Journals in the Journal Citation Reports Database's "Multidisciplinary Psychology" Category
Source: Data Reproduced from *Journal Citation Reports®* (Clarivate Analytics, 2018).

For example, you can download data into spreadsheets, compare two or more journals, and customize journal profile displays with the metrics that interest you, but for some features, you have to register for and sign onto your account. If you're stumped, click on "Help" to navigate to JCR's glossary and training videos.

By the way, Scopus and GS publish journal-level metrics on the open Web in their Journal Metrics (https://www.scopus.com/sources) and Metrics (http://scholar.google.com/citations?view_op=top_venues) databases, respectively. To rank journals, Scopus uses its proprietary CiteScore metric (Elsevier 2018), and Google uses the h5-index (Google 2018).

Academics do and should use journal-level metrics to decide where to publish their research, but when they use them for peer review, problems arise because these metrics rate journals. They do not rate individual journal articles or the scholars who publish in these journals (Seglen 1997). Professionals who publish in academic journals receive unsolicited email messages asking them to publish in this or that journal. Some requests may be legitimate attempts for a journal to increase submissions or to publicize a new direction for the journal, but others may come from predatory journals that charge authors fees to publish and pocket most of the cash instead of using it to add value to manuscripts, such as submitting them to peer review, correcting spelling and grammatical errors, and using a style sheet that standardizes the look and feel of the articles in the journal's issues. You can help your institution's professionals by making them aware of the problem of predatory journals and checking trusted resources, such as the Directory of Open Access Journals and Beall's List for positive and negative indicators of a journal's legitimacy, respectively (Craft 2016).

USING ARTICLE-LEVEL METRICS TO COMPARE TWO AUTHORS' PUBLICATION RECORDS

The h-index is an article-level metric that Scopus and GS report for cited authors. For example, Cliff's Scopus h-index is 29 (figure 10.11). This means that, of the total sources that Scopus considered to calculate Cliff's h-index, twenty-nine were cited twenty-nine times or more. Cliff's GS h-index is 41 (figure 10.12), thus, of the total sources that GS considered, forty-one sources were cited forty-one or more times. GS adds the i10-index to its metrics for cited authors (figure 10.12). Cliff's i10-index is 74, the number of sources he has written that have been cited ten or more times.

The usefulness of article-level metrics becomes apparent when they are used to compare two authors' publication records. When Cliff was evaluated for promotion to full professor in 2018, perhaps his promotion committee was tempted to compare his citation counts, h-index, and i10-index with those of a recently tenured colleague at a peer institution. I asked Cliff for suggestions, and he told me he is usually compared with Professor Darren Gergle at Northwestern University, who received promotion to

Table 10.1. Comparing Two Academics' Publication Records Using Article-Level Metrics

Data Type	Cliff		Darren	
	Scopus	GS	Scopus	GS
Number of publications	74	158	73	130
Citation count	8,505	24,293	2,126	5,147
h-index	29	41	23	34
i10-index	N/A	74	N/A	56
Number of coauthors	123	28	96	53
Year awarded PhD (from vita)	2006		2006	
Year promoted to associate professor	2013		2011	

full professor in 2015. Table 10.1 compares their publication records using Scopus's and GS's article-level metrics.

Both researchers received their PhDs in 2006. Cited references to Cliff's publications are about four to four-and-a-half times higher than to Darren's publications; however, a large percentage (43.56 percent in Scopus and 39.4 percent in GS) of them come from a paper Cliff coauthored with first author Nicole Ellison on the hot topic "Facebook Friends." According to GS, Cliff and Darren have written 158 and 130 sources, respectively. Coauthor numbers are confusing: Cliff surpasses Darren in Scopus, and Darren surpasses Cliff in GS. All things considered, Cliff's metrics exceed Darren's, but both academics have very high impact factors.

If promotion committees consider research impact data at all, these data are but one small piece of a much bigger puzzle that they assemble to inform decision makers about a scholar's research, teaching, and service contributions. (By the way, Cliff received tenure and promotion to full professor at the University of Michigan in fall 2018.)

ALTMETRICS

Article-level bibliometrics are based on researchers citing the sources of other researchers. At a minimum, this takes two years to happen; that is, researcher A becomes aware of researcher B's article, cites it in a manuscript, submits the manuscript to a journal for review, receives an acceptance, and submits a revised version to the editor, who posts the final version on the journal's online website. Thus, article-level bibliometrics are not very useful for evaluating researchers in the short term. More immediate are altmetrics: quantitative indicators of people's interactions with the written products of academic inquiry, scholarship, and research. These indicators are varied, ranging from one end user's split-second display of a journal article's abstract to another user's tweet that references something substantive in the article. Fueling altmetrics are transactional, content, and usage data pertaining to the written products of academic inquiry, scholarship, and research and generated by users of social-networking services, search systems, and online reference managers. Data science companies, such as Altmetrics.com and Plum Analytics, market almetrics services to database publishers and database aggregators. Their services involve mining data for references to academic sources, matching references to a database's indexed sources, categorizing references according to the types of interactions users have with them, and scoring sources based on both interaction types and volume of interaction types.

A database that is enhanced with altmetrics from Plum Analytics (2018) has the potential to produce an altmetrics report for a retrieved source bearing these data:

1. Usage. Number of clicks, downloads, views, library holdings, and video plays, which signal people are reading the source.
2. Captures. Number of bookmarks, code forks, favorites, readers, or watchers, which indicate people want to come back to the source.
3. Mentions. Number of and links to blog posts, comments, reviews, Wikipedia articles, or news media reports, which demonstrate people are truly engaging with the source.
4. Social media. Number of and links to likes, shares, tweets, or +1s, which measure the "buzz," attention, or promotion of a source.
5. Citations. Number of bibliographic citations, patent citations, clinical citations, or policy citations, which are traditional indicators of a source's societal impact.

When you display a source's surrogate in a database enhanced with one of these companies' altmetrics data, you get a sense of the "buzz" that the source has generated—whether people have noticed the source, what they are saying about it, and how much they notice the source relative to its peers. Figure 10.15 shows a Scopus and PlumX metrics for the journal article "Global Warming and Recurrent Mass Bleaching of Corals" published in *Nature* on March 15, 2017.

Scopus reports this journal article's citation count and two metrics, field-weighted citation count and citation benchmarking, which compare this article's citation count to the citation counts of journal articles in the same field or discipline. Clicking on the "See details" link under the "PlumX Metrics" heading reveals that the article has been referenced in about 150 news reports, a dozen and a half blogs, and 1,700 tweets; it has received well over 1,100 likes, comments, or shares from Facebook users; almost 800 people have displayed its abstract, saved its PDF, or sought a full-text via link resolvers in EBSCOhost databases; and almost 900 people have added its full-text to the Mendeley reference manager. Altmetrics scores and reports do *not* specify whether the attention is good, bad, or indifferent. Such an assessment is the user's job based on reading comments enumerated in the altmetrics report. In fact, click on links for "Blogs," "News," or "Tweets" in PlumX Metrics Report to read what people are actually saying about this article.

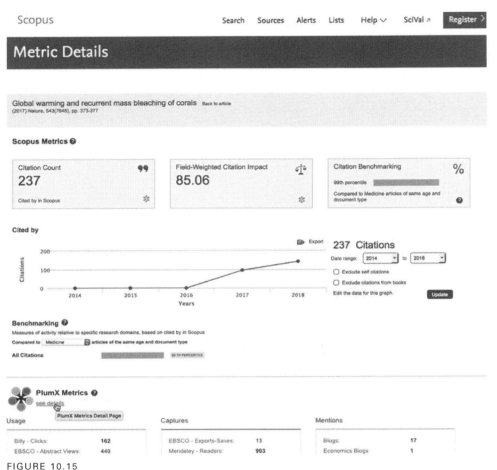

FIGURE 10.15

Scopus and PlumX Metrics for a Source Retrieved in the Scopus Database

Source: Scopus, a registered trademark of Elsevier, B.V., image retrieved on 17 July 2018.

Display altmetrics reports for sources retrieved in the Scopus, Taylor & Francis Online Journals, and PLoS databases and the reports bear different measures. This lack of standardization is due to differences between altmetrics providers—Plum Analytics powering Scopus, Altmetric.com powering Taylor & Francis Online Journals, and PLoS generating its own altmetrics reports. Altmetrics faces other challenges: its susceptibility to gaming (Roemer and Borchardt 2015; Vinyard 2016; Williams 2017); its reliance on the social Web, which rewards sources on trendy topics (Vinyard 2016); and its failure to speak for the vast majority of academic sources. In fact, researchers estimate altmetrics are available for only 15 percent of a database's sources (Costas, Zahedi, and Wouters 2015). Because studies have been unable to establish a strong correlation between altmetrics and bibliometrics

(Costas, Zahedi, and Wouters 2015), researchers suggest that altmetrics are less likely to measure research impact and more likely to measure attention and popularity (Crotty 2014a; Sugimoto 2015; Vinyard 2016).

To date, researchers have overlooked the potential usefulness of altmetrics for helping nondomain experts identify credible and accurate research. A few years ago, I led a research team that interviewed undergraduate students searching for quality information on advanced topics (Markey, Leeder, and Rieh 2014, 151). Undergraduates said this about assessing retrievals:

- "I just really had no idea how to assess credibility at all. . . . Being naïve, you figure, 'If it's published, it's true.' But you don't really know."
- "On the accuracy question, I figured a lot of times like I personally didn't know because I don't know if this information is accurate and that's why I'm looking it up. But at the same time, I didn't know if it was accurate or not because I'm going to them to find out the information. So I'm going to assume it's accurate but you don't know."
- "If I saw that it was from like a university, I automatically [assumed it was credible] . . . but I just felt like I had no idea how credible actually that person was. . . . It was just hard for me to tell what was credible and what wasn't."

Unlike bibliometrics, which are exclusive to domain experts, altmetrics are generated by people from all walks of life and thus have the potential to interpret, clarify, or articulate advanced topics in ways that make them accessible to a wider audience. According to William H. Mischo, director of the University of Illinois at Urbana–Champaign's Engineering Library, who conducts usability studies of UIUC's Easy Search in his role as Easy Search's creator, end users are starting to notice altmetrics. The time is right to study the usefulness of altmetrics for end users because positive findings could give a new direction to this fledgling enterprise. For the time being, expect altmetrics to continue on its present research and development course, which may be followed by a shaking-down period in which altmetrics providers, methods, and metrics expand and consolidate, giving way to the establishment of best practices and standards across the information industry.

SOCIAL-NETWORKING WEBSITES FOR RESEARCH PROFESSIONALS

Both bibliometrics and altmetrics have put pressure on academics to increase the visibility of their research, teaching, and service activities. To connect with like-minded scholars, research professionals are drawn to social-networking websites that specialize in the research enterprise and provide features for showcasing their research, sharing bibliographies with links to full-texts, searching, and building their research reputations.

Academia.edu and ResearchGate (RG) are the two major social-networking websites for research professionals, and they function in similar ways.

Let's examine ResearchGate. Because RG is aimed at research professionals, it performs automatic checks on new members to make sure they are researchers or in a position where research is expected. RG encourages members to add profiles, and when they do, RG harvests their bibliographies, both sources they have written and their full-texts when available, and calculates several publication-based metrics, such as number of sources, number of citations to sources, number of reads or views, h-index, and its proprietary RG Score. RG encourages members to be active, to add full-texts when it can't find them automatically, to ask and answer questions, to search its database for sources of interest, to follow like-minded researchers, and to accumulate followers. RG makes it easy to find like-minded researchers and sends email messages in response to all sorts of RG events—when researchers cite you, when they read your sources, when they upload a full-text that cites you, and so on. You can turn off RG's email notifications, but on occasion, an event brings a relevant source or researcher to your attention that you wouldn't have known about otherwise, so keeping notifications on has its benefits. You can participate in the website's question-and-answer capability to boost your RG score; however, this aspect, as well as the proprietary nature of the RG Score, is controversial (Nicholas, Clark, and Herman 2016). RG also has a jobs component, displaying job openings that match member profiles and linking you to application information.

Consider becoming a member of RG or a comparable network, not only to promote your research, teaching, and service activities, but also to familiarize yourself with its features. Then build on your knowledge of the network to help others. You could alert people involved in research at your institution—graduate students, faculty, postdocs, clinicians, research scientists—about social-networking websites for professional researchers, including demonstrating a website's features using your profile or well-known researchers in their field who are active website users. You could connect with the network's active scholars to stay on top of the field's new developments, even forwarding useful information to colleagues who are reluctant to dip into the social-networking scene. When your database searches leave you empty-handed, consider searching the network's database. At the very least, RG conducts non-Boolean searches, stemming your input words and phrases and possibly using cited references to automatically add to retrievals. For example, enter `games AND information literacy`, and RG disregards the Boolean AND operator, ranking sources bearing all three words in the title higher than RG sources bearing some words in the title and others in the abstract; it also retrieves sources bearing the stem `gam`, such as gaming, gamification, and gamify. Thus, use the Building Block Search Strategy's À la Carte Edition to search the RG database. RG applies fuzzy matching to name searches, so expect retrievals with jumbled syllables; keep in mind that it doesn't use aliases, so searches for `jim jansen` or `chris borgman` won't retrieve James Jansen or Christine Borgman, respectively.

Bookmarking websites and citation management systems, such as CiteULike, Mendeley, and Zotero, encourage users to share their source collections with a class, research project collaborators, coauthors, and like-minded colleagues. Mendeley is a double-duty performer, giving members functionality for social networking and citation sharing. When you interact with users engaged in projects that involve literature searching, turn them onto reference-sharing sites for managing sources; simplifying the production of bibliographies in written works; and sharing sources with students, colleagues, coauthors, and research teams.

Register at social-networking websites and reference-sharing websites to avail yourself of their content and services. In fact, the more members are proactive about disseminating their published research through these vehicles, the bigger they will become, making them go-to destinations for finding the latest research and making connections with like-minded researchers.

GENERAL-PURPOSE SOCIAL-NETWORKING WEBSITES

Familiar to most everyday people are the LinkedIn, Twitter, and Facebook social-networking websites because they figure prominently in politics, popular culture, and entertainment.

LinkedIn

Of the three, academics are most likely to gravitate to LinkedIn, the go-to social network for jobs, professional networking, and business contacts generally. LinkedIn's profile feature is comparable to RG's, requesting members to share information about themselves that would make up an academic's curriculum vita, such as current and previous employment, education, contact information, professional interests, awards and honors, and publications (with links to full-texts when available). In addition, LinkedIn enables you to see what members are talking about. Register for a free LinkedIn account to search for people's names and display their profiles.

LinkedIn's built-in message system asks you to connect to a person before it allows you to message him or her. To work around this, use your knowledge of what you learned about people at LinkedIn to search their organization's online directory on the Web, or drill down from the top of their institution's home page to the department or division where they work in search of more information about them.

Your free LinkedIn account enables you to search for content. LinkedIn conducts extended-Boolean searches in response to your search statements, so use the Building Block Search Strategy's À la Carte Edition to search this system, but be prepared to scroll through lots of retrievals due to the system's lackluster ranking algorithm. For example, LinkedIn responds to the extended-Boolean search statements `robot builds homes`, `trust autonomous vehicles`, and `design ethics conference` with retrievals that address some but not all of these topics. LinkedIn's strength is its ability to connect you with like-minded business professionals, so don't expect it to respond to your searches of the full-texts that members post in their profiles or share in their discussions with retrievals that hit on all cylinders.

Twitter

Underlining both personal and research-professional uses of the Twitter social-networking tool is its tagline "follow your interests, hear what people are talking about, and join the conversation." Twitter encourages all users, regardless of their usage type, to maximize on following and followers, but to do so, you have to tweet content that stimulates people to follow you, and this could cut into the time you've set aside for your research. Less time-consuming is identifying and following domain experts in your field who regularly tweet about new trends, tough issues, breaking news, and cutting-edge developments in advance of traditional channels of communication. You can also search Twitter because it is a massive database of breaking news on an encyclopedic array of topics; in fact, you might want to follow up tweets that pique your interest with searches of the World Wide Web to find more information about the topic. For example, let's say that one of the experts you follow tweets about a new University of Michigan information literacy course on fake news. This interests you, and you want to find other universities offering such a course so you can learn more, including contacting instructors for their syllabi and any other information they're willing to share.

In response to your search statements, Twitter conducts Boolean searches, inserting an implicit Boolean AND operator between single words and phrases enclosed in quotes. Here are Boolean search statements that retrieve tweets discussing information literacy courses on fake news that are offered at the University of Washington, University of Haifa, Loyola University Chicago, and Elgin Community College:

```
university AND course AND "fake news"

college AND course AND "fake news"

university AND class AND "fake news"

college AND class AND "fake news"

university AND class AND "alternative facts"
```

Unfortunately, Twitter can't parse such complex Boolean search statements as (uni-versity or college) AND (course OR class) AND ("fake news" or "alternative facts"), so enter search statements that are faithful to the Building Block Search Strategy's À la Carte Edition. Twitter doesn't stem or truncate words or bound phrases, so you'll have to generate more search statements for plural and grammatical variants.

Table 10.2 summarizes Twitter's search functionality with sample search statements and explanations. When Twitter displays results, you can open Twitter's "Advanced Search" page by clicking on its "Advanced Search" link under "Search Filters." Fill in one or more boxes here to conduct Boolean searches, to limit retrievals to tweets to and/or from accounts bearing the name you enter, and to restrict retrievals by date or date range.

Table 10.2.   Twitter's Search Functionality with Sample Search Statements and Explanations

Search Statement	Explanation
alternate facts	This is Twitter's default search. It performs an implicit Boolean AND operation, retrieving tweets bearing both words but not necessarily these two words adjacent to one another.
alternate AND facts	This is an explicit representation of Twitter's default search. It performs an explicit Boolean AND operation, retrieving tweets bearing both words but not necessarily these two words adjacent to one another. (Same as the search statement above.)
"alternate facts"	Twitter retrieves tweets bearing this exact, bound phrase, with the word *alternate* preceding the word *facts*.
"alternate facts" OR "fake news"	Twitter performs the Boolean OR operation, retrieving tweets bearing either phrase.
fake -news	Twitter performs the Boolean NOT operation, retrieving tweets bearing the word *fake* but not the word *news*.
fake but not news	Twitter performs the Boolean NOT operation, retrieving tweets bearing the word *fake* but not the word *news*. (Same as the search statement above.)
#fakenews	Twitter retrieves tweets bearing the hashtag *fakenews*. Hashtags describe themes or topics. Click on a tweet's hashtags to retrieve the latest tweets bearing the hashtag.
to:librarianA	Tweets sent to the tweeter with the account named librarianA.
from:librarianA	Tweets sent from the tweeter with the account named librarianA.
@librarianA	Tweets sent to or sent from the tweeter with the account named librarianA.
university AND class AND "fake news" since:2017-02-01 until:2017-3-31	Tweets on this topic issued from February 1, 2017 to March 31, 2017.
"fake news" near:"ann arbor"	Tweets on this topic sent near Ann Arbor.

Facebook

If researchers are active on Facebook, they most likely use this social-networking tool to connect with personal friends and family; however, Facebook is rich in information about corporate bodies, "organizations or group of persons that are identified by a particular name and that acts or may act as an entity" (Chan and Salaba 2016, 745). Facebook responds to the entry of a corporate body's name with a type-ahead search, listing names that are likely to match what you have in mind. Finding multiple retrievals, Facebook displays them, along with their categories and a brief blurb. Click on the name that interests you to visit its Facebook page. Berkman (2015) suggests five ways that researchers benefit from searching Facebook:

> Bottom-up, experiential, and anecdotal observations and reports, particularly from activists and passionate advocates for a cause or issue; insights into emerging trends via insider group members' conversations, not reported in the wider media or elsewhere online; strong statements of particular viewpoints on contentious public issues, especially in Facebook groups; clues for finding and reaching hard-to-locate people; [and] possible job search leads. (150)

His observations suggest that what you read on Facebook may be biased, exaggerated, or less than objective or breaking news that changes when facts emerge or journalists learn more. Whether you are putting the information you find on Facebook to work for yourself or helping others, you should get confirmation from other-than-Facebook sources before taking your next steps, especially when your next steps involve making important decisions about a person's health, well-being, or livelihood.

QUESTIONS

These questions give you practice searching WOS, Scopus, and GS to help library users find relevant sources and assess the research impact of individual sources and publication records.

1. Help a user who wants to search WOS for cited references to James Paul Gee's book *What Video Games Have to Teach Us about Learning and Literacy*.
2. Now this same user wants you to show him how to use the Scopus database to find cited references to this book (i.e., James Paul Gee's book *What Video Games Have to Teach Us about Learning and Literacy*).
3. Help a user who wants to search the Scopus database for cited references to Joseph LeDoux's article "Emotion, Memory, and the Brain" published in *Scientific American*.
4. Help a user find cited references to Chris Borgman's book *Scholarship in the Digital Age*. What do Google Scholar's clusters tell you about cited references to this book?
5. You have written an awesome manuscript that is in keeping with the content that the journals *portal: Libraries and the Academy, Journal of Academic Librarianship* (*JAL*), and *College & Research Libraries* (*C&RL*) publish. Which is the most prestigious journal and why?

SUMMARY

Search the three encyclopedic citation databases—Web of Science (WOS), Scopus, and Google Scholar (GS)—to assess the research impact of a particular journal, a particular journal article, or a particular researcher's publication record. Searching them is complicated due to variant forms of author names and cited references in the professional literature.

Academics use journal-level metrics to decide where to publish their research and to determine whether the colleagues they review for employment, promotion, and tenure are publishing in the best journals. Journal Citation Reports (JCR) is the go-to licensed database for journal-level metrics, and there are open access alternatives from Scopus and GS.

When it comes to research impact metrics, altmetrics is the new kid on the block, quantifying the "buzz" that accompanies the publication of new scholarly sources. Generated from journal-aggregator logs, recommender systems, social-networking services, and much more, altmetrics provides immediate feedback about journal articles compared to the half-decade or so that it takes for citation data to accumulate.

Attracting research professionals to social-networking websites that specialize in the research enterprise is their ability to showcase professional accomplishments, connect with like-minded individuals, and increase their visibility among their peers. A byproduct of their participation in both specialized and mainstream social-networking websites is the content, news, and ideas they share at these websites, which you can search to help others satisfy their information needs.

BIBLIOGRAPHY

Bar-Ilan, Judit. 2008. "Which H-Index? A Comparison of WoS, Scopus and Google Scholar." *Scientometrics* 74, no. 2: 257–71.

Berkman, Robert I. 2015. *Find It Fast: Extracting Expert Information from Social Networks, Big Data, Tweets, and More.* Medford, NJ: Information Today.

Chan, Lois Mai, and Athena Salaba. 2016. *Cataloging and Classification: An Introduction.* 4th ed. Lanham, MD: Rowman & Littlefield.

Costas, Rodrigo, Zohreh Zahedi, and Paul Wouters. 2015. "Do 'Altmetrics' Correlate with Citations? Extensive Comparison of Altmetric Indicators with Citations from a Multidisciplinary Perspective." *Journal of the Association for Information Science & Technology* 66, no. 10: 2003–19.

Craft, Anna R. 2016. "Is This a Quality Journal to Publish In? How Can You Tell?" *Serials Review* 42, no. 3: 237–39.

Crotty, David. 2014a. "Altmetrics: Finding Meaningful Needles in the Data Haystack." *Serials Review* 40, no. 3: 141–46. http://doi.org/10.1080/00987913.2014.947839.

———. 2014b. "Happy Anniversary: 50 Years of the Science Citation Index." *The Scholarly Kitchen* (blog) Society for Scholarly Publishing. May 16. https://scholarlykitchen.sspnet .org/2014/05/16/happy-anniversary-50-years-of-the-science-citation-index/.

Elsevier. 2018. "Research Metrics." Accessed June 30, 2018. https://www.elsevier.com/solu tions/scopus/features/metrics.

Garfield, Eugene. 1955. "Citation Indexes for Science: A New Dimension in Documentation through Association of Ideas." *Science* 122: 108–11.

Google. 2018. "Google Scholar: Metrics." Accessed June 30, 2018. https://scholar.google.com/ intl/en/scholar/metrics.html.

Harzing, Anne-Wil K., and Ron van der Wal. 2008. "Google Scholar: A New Source for Citation Analysis." *Ethics in Science and Environmental Politics* 8: 61–73.

Lampe, Cliff. 2018. "Social Computing Research." Accessed June 30, 2018. http://clifflampe.org/.

Markey, Karen, Chris Leeder, and Soo Young Rieh. 2014. *Designing Online Information Literacy Games Students Want to Play.* Lanham, MD: Rowman & Littlefield.

Meho, Lokman I., and Kiduk Yang. 2007. "Impact of Data Sources on Citation Counts and Rankings of LIS Faculty: Web of Science versus Scopus and Google Scholar." *Journal of the American Society for Information Science and Technology* 58, no. 13: 2105–25.

Nicholas, David, David Clark, and Eti Herman. 2016. "ResearchGate: Reputation Uncovered." *Learned Publishing* 29: 173–82.

Plum Analytics. 2018. "PlumX Metrics." Accessed June 30, 2018. https://plumanalytics.com/ learn/about-metrics/.

Roemer, Robin Chin, and Rachel Borchardt. 2015. "Altmetrics." *Library Technology Reports* 51, no. 5.

Seglen, Per O. 1997. "Why the Impact Factor of Journals Should Not Be Used for Evaluating Research." *BMJ: British Medical Journal* 314, no. 7079: 498–502.

Sugimoto, Cassidy. 2015. "'Attention Is Not Impact' and Other Challenges of Altmetrics." *Discover the Future of Research* (blog) John Wiley & Sons, June 24. https://hub.wiley.com/ community/exchanges/discover/blog/2015/06/23/attention-is-not-impact-and-other -challenges-for-altmetrics.

Vinyard, Marc. 2016. "Altmetrics: An Overhyped Fad or an Important Evaluating Tool for Evaluating Scholarly Output?" *Computers in Libraries* 36, no. 10: 26–29.

Williams, Ann E. 2017. "Altmetrics: An Overview and Evaluation." *Online Information Review* 41, no. 3: 311–17.

SUGGESTED READINGS

Herther, Nancy K. 2015. "Advanced Citation Searching." *Online Searcher* 39, no. 3: 44–48. A critical analysis of citations, impact factors, and citation searching in search systems.

Mering, Margaret. 2017. "Bibliometrics: Understanding Author-, Article-, and Journal-Level Metrics." *Serials Review* 43, no. 1: 41–45. A quick read that details bibliometrics for authors, articles, and journals.

Roemer, Robin Chin, and Rachel Borchardt. 2015. "Altmetrics." *Library Technology Reports* 51, no. 5. A comprehensive examination of altmetrics.

ANSWERS

1. **Search WOS for cited references to James Paul Gee's book** *What Video Games Have to Teach Us about Learning and Literacy.* Search your library's OPAC for a correct bibliographic citation for the book (Gee, James Paul. 2003. *What Video Games Have to Teach Us about Learning and Literacy.* New York: Palgrave Macmillan). Launch the WOS database, and choose "Cited Reference Search." Choose "Cited Work" from the fields pull-down menu, enter this book's title into the search box, and click on the "Search" button. WOS displays the Cited Reference Index. Clean up this index so that your selected entries refer only to Gee's book. Don't be surprised if your selected entries only vaguely resemble the book's title (e.g., *Video Games Have Tea*, *What Video Games Hav*, and *Palgrave Macmillan*). To be comprehensive, conduct a second cited-reference search. Click on the "Select from Index" link, enter the surname gee and first initial j in the search box, and click on the "Move To" button. Choose names with Gee's first and middle names written out and in initials. WOS lists your selected names at the bottom of the page. Click on the "OK" button, and WOS returns you to the "Cited Reference Search" page. Enter the book's date of publication (2003) and a few more years to accommodate errors (e.g., 2004, 2005, and 2013) into the "Cited Year(s)" search box, and click on the "Search" button." Clean up WOS's Cited Reference Index so that your selected entries refer only to Gee's book. Again, be prepared to select entries that vaguely resemble the book's title (e.g., *Ffhat Video Games Ha*, *What Vid Gam Hav*, and *What Gaines Have Tea*). Last, click on "Search History," and combine your two sets, one for a title search and a second for an author search, using the Boolean OR operator.

   WOS retrieves more than 2,500 cited references for this book and lists them by most recent date first. When assisting users, show them how clusters reveal authors, publications, and document types that cite this book repeatedly and how to use WOS's "Create Citation Report" to produce a graphical report of cited references over time.

2. **Use the Scopus database to find cited references to this book (i.e., *What Video Games Have to Teach Us about Learning and Literacy*).** Scopus is limited to journal articles. Find cited references to books in WOS and Google.

3. **Search the Scopus database for cited references to the article "Emotion, Memory, and the Brain."** Use the Scopus default "Documents" search, enter the source's title enclosed in quotes into the search box, choose "Article title, Abstract, and Keywords" from the fields pull-down menu, and click on the magnifying-glass search icon. Scopus reports more than four hundred cited references. Click on the number of cited references to retrieve them and to display clusters for authors, subject areas, source titles, and document types that cite this article repeatedly. Click on "Analyze Search Results" for a graphical report of cited references over time.

4. **Find cited references to the book *Scholarship in the Digital Age*.** Search your library's OPAC for a correct bibliographic citation for the book (Borgman, Christine L. 2007. *Scholarship in the Digital Age: Information, Infrastructure, and the Internet.* Cambridge, MA: MIT Press). Launch Google Scholar through your library's search tools. Enter the name `christine borgman`, and choose this author's profile. Browsing her publications list takes a split second because it is ordered by number of cited references, and this book tops the list. Clicking on this title demonstrates that Google Scholar displays no clusters, but it gives a graphical display of cited references, which are plentiful and steady for this book.

5. **Which is the most prestigious journal and why?** Choose Journal Citation Reports (JCR) from your library's search tools. Into the search box, enter one of the three journals' titles. When JCR displays the journal's profile, click on the accompanying "Information Science & Library Science" (IS&LS) button. JCR responds with "Journals by Rank," a list of IS&LS journals ranked by the Journal Impact Factor (JIF). Listed thirty-fourth, thirty-eighth, and fortieth are *C&RL*, *portal*, and *JAL*, respectively. Click on "Customize Indicators" to choose other metrics that might change these journals' rankings. You could base your decision on one, two, or more JCR metrics. If you don't know what these metrics measure, click on "Help," and search its Glossary for these metrics. Finally, which journal would you choose and why?

Search Strategies

The definition of *search strategy* is a "plan for the whole search" (Bates 1979, 206). This chapter presents five search strategies that should suffice for almost all online searches that you conduct in Boolean and extended-Boolean search systems. When choosing a search strategy, there are several factors to take into account. Some are straightforward, such as whether the user's query is single- or multifaceted and whether the

The video at http://www.onlinesearching.org/p/11-strategies.html emphasizes that choosing the right search strategy for the user's query enables you to increase your efficiency and effectiveness as an expert intermediary online searcher.

search system has this or that functionality, and others are more complex, requiring your judgment about the importance of the query's facets relative to one another and the user's overall grasp of his topic. At the end of the chapter is a search-strategy-selection flowchart that will help you choose the right search strategy for the job.

BUILDING BLOCK SEARCH STRATEGY

The Building Block Search Strategy is for multifaceted subject queries. It requires the searcher to develop each facet of the query separately as if it were a subsearch on its own and then make the final logical assembly of the individual subsearches. Figure 6.9 diagrams this strategy using three separate blocks, one atop the other, to represent sets of retrievals for the individual facets and arrows protruding from the three blocks' right sides, all meeting at a single block, representing the final set of retrievals.

The Building Block Search Strategy comes in two editions: (1) the Buffet Edition for Boolean search systems (figure 6.10) and (2) the À la Carte Edition for extended-Boolean systems (figure 8.2). These names are analogies for the ways in which searchers represent search terms in their search statements. The Buffet Edition is reserved for Boolean systems, equating the buffet to the database, the buffet tables to the query's facets, and the various foods that you choose from the buffet tables to the several search terms that make up your search statements for each facet. You choose several items per buffet table, arrange everything on your plate, and chow down. Choosing several food items per buffet table is like choosing an index term and its relevant BTs, NTs, and RTs from the database's thesaurus displays to construct search statements for each of the query's facets. Demonstrating the Buffet Edition is the search for the Humor query on pages 118 to 123.

The À la Carte Edition is meant for searching extended-Boolean systems. These systems aren't yet capable of distinguishing which search terms belong to which facets. They choke over queries that are suited to the Buffet Edition; that is, when they are unable to produce retrievals for all entered search terms, they rank retrievals bearing as many search terms as possible. As a result, your retrievals may address fewer than all of your query's facets. To effect better results in extended-Boolean systems, use the À la Carte Edition of the Building Block Strategy, and enter search statements composed of one search term per facet. Use the most salient search term per facet, and for most queries, this means entering the names of the query's facets. Demonstrating the À la Carte Edition are searches for the Child Soldiers, Farm Women, Feminism, Wilderness Survival, and Lyndon Johnson queries on pages 181 to 185. The benefits of the Building Block Search Strategy are:

- It produces a clear search history that is easy to follow while you are conducting the search, to review and understand later, and to explain to the user; in fact, its search history should read like the actual negotiated query.

- Its retrievals address all aspects of the topic that interest the user.
- Once the searcher scripts a search that conforms to the Building Block Search Strategy, executing it requires less judgment on the part of the searcher, and thus, this strategy appeals to aspiring intermediary searchers who are less confident about their ability to make spur-of-the-moment adjustments online.

The drawbacks of the Building Block Search Strategy are:

- The searcher enters and combines search statements for all facets of the query, when, in fact, fewer facets may be needed to produce relevant retrievals.
- The searcher has no idea how many retrievals she will retrieve until the search's final moment, when she combines sets for each facet using Boolean AND or NOT operators.

The Building Block Search Strategy deserves emphasis as a satisfactory strategy for multifaceted subject searches generally. You could apply this strategy to all multifaceted queries, but you will encounter queries for which there are better strategies, and they deserve your consideration.

CAN'T LIVE WITHOUT THIS FACET FIRST SEARCH STRATEGY

The Can't Live Without This Facet First Search Strategy is also for multifaceted subject queries. Over the years, it has been known by other names—Most Specific Facet First, Lowest-Posted Facet First, Successive Fractions, or Big Bite Strategy (Meadow and Cochrane 1981). It requires the searcher to assess the facet analysis for a query and determine which facet *must* be represented in the retrievals for the user to consider them even marginally relevant.

The Can't Live Without This Facet First name is particularly vivid, and it has caught on with my students more readily than this strategy's other names. The most specific facet is one that is not likely to suffer from any vagueness of indexing. It may be a proper noun, such as a piece of legislation or a person's name, or a concept that is limited in the ways in which you can express it using free text (FT) or controlled vocabulary (CV). The lowest-posted facet is the one that is posted lowest of the query's several facets. You'll have to draw on your online searching experience to determine which facet is likely to be the lowest posted in the database you've chosen. The Can't Live Without This Facet First Search Strategy works in the same way no matter which name is used.

Figure 11.1 depicts the Can't Live Without This Facet First Search Strategy. At first glance, it looks like a carbon copy of the Building Block Search Strategy, but it has important differences. A query's facet analysis may yield several facets, but the searcher has identified one that the user can't live without; that is, the user would be dissatisfied

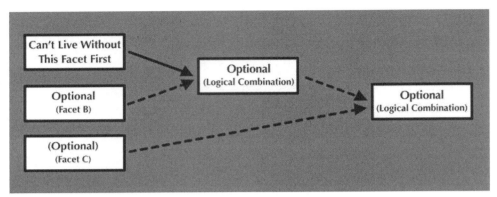

FIGURE 11.1
Can't Live Without This Facet First Search Strategy

with every retrieval in the final result set if this facet's retrievals were not represented. (Alternatively, this facet may be exceptionally specific, or the searcher expects it to be posted low.) The searcher builds a set of retrievals for this facet *first*. If he is searching an extended-Boolean system, then he enters the one search term that represents this facet *first* in the search statement, followed by as many other search terms as there are facets in the query. Extended-Boolean systems usually place more weight on the first search term, so make it the one that the user can't live without.

In a Boolean search system, the searcher builds a set of retrievals for the can't-live-without-this facet, using several synonymous terms combined with the OR operator. The searcher also assesses the number of retrievals and, if few are retrieved, ponders whether more facets are necessary. Making the decision to continue, the searcher builds a set of retrievals for one of the optional facets, using several synonymous terms combined with the OR operator, and then combines its retrievals using the Boolean AND or NOT operator with retrievals for the can't-live-without-this facet. The searcher's choice between which of the two or more optional facets to search second should not be willy-nilly. Instead, it should be guided by which facet the searcher thinks will be more important in terms of producing relevant retrievals. The searcher combines sets for the can't-live-without-this facet and the optional facet using Boolean AND or NOT operators and again assesses the number of retrievals, deciding whether more facets are necessary or whether the results can stand on their own.

Taking into account postings for the can't-live-without-this facet and subsequent one(s) may compel the searcher to end the search before all facets have been incorporated into the search. Here's an example using the negotiated query "What effect does video game violence have on adolescents?" The query's facets are:

Video Games AND **Violence** AND **Adolescents**

Which facet is this query's can't-live-without-this facet? If you choose **Video Games**, you are right! Build a set of retrievals for the **Video Games** facet first. Having done so in a Boolean system, such as ProQuest's ERIC, you find out that the maximum number of retrievals that your search will produce for this topic is no more than 1,500. This number is still too many to review manually, so continue the search, building a set of retrievals for one of the optional facets. Which facet would you tackle next—**Violence** or **Adolescents**? If you are unsure, think about the retrievals that will be produced by the Boolean AND combination of this query's can't-live-without-this facet and optional facets:

- **Video Games** AND **Violence**
- **Video Games** AND **Adolescents**

If this were your query, which combination's retrievals would you rather have? You have to use your judgment here, weighing which combination to search based on what the user wants. Personally, I would be inclined toward the combination bearing the **Violence** facet because its retrievals would more likely address the topic that interests me. Even though the **Adolescents** facet isn't introduced into the combination, reviewing retrievals to determine whether they are or aren't about adolescents would be an easy and straightforward task. The combination bearing the **Adolescents** facet could go in so many nonrelevant directions; for example, which video games adolescents like, prospects for educational video games for adolescents, the impact of excessive video-game playing on adolescents' academic performance, and much more. Definitely prefer the **Video Games** AND **Violence** combination over the **Video Games** AND **Adolescents** combination.

Combining the **Video Games** and optional **Violence** facets reduces ERIC retrievals to about 150. When searching Boolean systems, keep a running total of your retrievals each time you combine search statements using the Boolean AND or NOT operators, just in case a combination drops retrievals precipitously. In fact, keep a running total in Boolean searches regardless of the search strategy that governs the search.

Knowing that the two facets **Video Games** and **Violence** result in about 150 retrievals should make the searcher pause and ponder whether the third facet, **Adolescents**, is necessary. Scanning the first page of twenty retrievals reveals several titles bearing the words *youth* or *adolescents* in article titles or journal titles. Does it make sense to stop here, casting a wide net and advising the user to scrutinize retrievals for evidence that study adolescents? Should the searcher continue searching, entering terms for the **Adolescents** facet? What information could the user provide to help you make this decision?

When searching reference databases, the Can't Live Without This Facet First Strategy is the way to go. Let's examine the two queries from chapter 5 that we'd search in a reference database. Question 2 asks in what year zebra mussels were discovered in the Great Lakes and answers with the facets and logical combination **Zebra Mussels** AND **Great Lakes**. Choose a subject-oriented encyclopedia or dictionary to answer this query, starting with a single word or phrase to represent its can't-live-without-this **Zebra Mussels** facet. In fact, entering the search statement zebra mussels into the McGraw-Hill Encyclopedia of Science and Technology retrieves a three-page entry entitled "Bivalvia." Scanning it for a discussion of zebra mussels yields this sentence: "In 1985, zebra mussels (genus *Dreissena*) native to the Caspian Sea area in Eurasia were discovered in Lake St. Clair between Ontario and Michigan [and] . . . were probably transported from Europe in the ballast water of a freighter entering the Great Lakes" (*McGraw-Hill Encyclopedia of Science & Technology* 2007, 144). A follow-up search in Wikipedia using this same strategy puts the date at 1988 and confirms the theory about ballast water. Question 6 asks who the speaker was preceding Martin Luther King on the day he gave his "I Have a Dream" speech and what the speaker had to say and answers with the facets and logical combination **Speakers Before** AND **Martin Luther King** AND **I Have a Dream**. Because we've got Wikipedia open, let's search for this query's can't-live-without-this **I Have a Dream** facet. Wikipedia's entry exactly matches this facet's name. The entry doesn't mention the speaker preceding Dr. King, but it names and provides a link to the event at which the speeches were given. Clicking on the event's link, "March on Washington for Jobs and Freedom," lists the speakers and displays the program, revealing Rabbi Joachim Prinz as the speaker preceding Dr. King. The entry bears a link to external audio files, and clicking on it produces a listening guide that summarizes each speech's content, including Rabbi Prinz's speech.

Except for lengthy encyclopedia articles, entries in reference sources are usually brief, so using the Can't Live Without This Facet First Strategy is especially efficient for targeting an entry where the information resides in a reference source. You just have to put time into reading the entry or following its links to entries you wouldn't have thought about. Often, the key to answering reference questions is identifying a fruitful source for answering the question. For example, a user wants to know where African American circus performers wintered during the early twentieth century. Instead of representing this query's **20th Century** and **African Americans** facets in search terms, you can cover them by selecting the Black Historical Newspapers and the African American Newspapers databases and by limiting retrievals to early-twentieth-century dates. All that's left is searching for the **Circus** facet, using this facet name and names of famous African American circus performers and troupes as search terms, and studying retrievals for clues about where they spent the off-season.

The benefits of the Can't Live Without This Facet First Search Strategy are:

- It requires less time and effort on the part of the searcher.
- It permits the search to be completed at an earlier point in time than the Building Block Search Strategy.

- It retrieves relevant sources that may be missed when all of the query's facets are represented in the search.

The drawbacks of the Can't Live Without This Facet First Search Strategy are:

- Sometimes the query has no obvious can't-live-without-this, most specific, or lowest-posted facets that make this strategy possible.
- Determining the lowest-posted facet may be difficult in the absence of such search aids as print thesauri, postings notes, and the searcher's experience with a database.
- Failing to represent all facets in the search may result in many postings that the user must scan to find relevant ones.

PEARL GROWING SEARCH STRATEGY

The Pearl Growing Search Strategy is a series of searches that the searcher conducts to find relevant search terms and incorporates them into follow-up searches. It is the most interactive of all the search strategies, requiring your full attention scanning retrievals for relevant terms, distributing them into the facets to which they belong, making on-the-spot decisions about representing them as CV or FT, formulating search statements, and combining these statements to produce relevant results. Fit for both Boolean and extended-Boolean systems, the Pearl Growing Search Strategy is a very effective strategy when you have little time to prepare for the search in advance.

Not only is the Pearl Growing Search Strategy a *series of searches*, but it is also a *series of search strategies*. You may start with the Can't Live Without This Facet First Search Strategy, transition to the Pearl Growing Search Strategy to find more retrievals, and conclude with the Building Block Search Strategy as a result of finding several relevant search terms per facet through Pearl Growing.

To initiate the Pearl Growing Search Strategy, enter a search that is faithful to the À la Carte Edition of the Building Block Search Strategy. Do so regardless of the Boolean or extended-Boolean nature of your chosen search system. Enter *one* search term per facet, using the most salient search term per facet, and for many queries, this means the names of the query's facets. Review retrievals; identify relevant terms in the title, CV, author-keywords, and abstract fields of surrogate records; distribute them into their respective facets; and formulate everything into search statements. If you fall short on relevant terms, cull them from full-texts, too. Then follow up with a search using the Building Block or Can't Live Without This Facet First Strategy and the search terms you gathered from surrogates and full-text retrievals. Figure 11.2 depicts the Pearl Growing Search Strategy—an arrow that expands outward in a circular motion and becomes wider as it gathers additional relevant retrievals from the series of searches you conduct.

FIGURE 11.2
Pearl Growing Search Strategy

Let's walk through an online search that enlists the Pearl Growing Search Strategy. The negotiated query is "Is religious practice a necessary ingredient to prevent alcoholics from relapsing?" This query has three facets: (1) **Religion**, (2) **Alcoholism**, and (3) **Prevention**. Its logical combination is:

Religion AND **Alcoholism** AND **Prevention**

Choose EBSCOhost's PsycINFO database, and conduct a FT search using this query's three facet names. Such a search enlists the À la Carte Edition of the Building Block Search Strategy. The EBSCOhost system gives you several ways to gather search terms from this search's ninety retrievals:

- Clicking on the accompanying *Major Subjects* and *Subjects* clusters' links to display frequently-occurring PsycINFO index terms
- Clicking on the accompanying *Classification* cluster's link to display frequently-occurring PsycINFO classification captions
- Scanning titles, PsycINFO index terms, and abstracts in surrogate record displays
- Searching PsycINFO index terms from relevant retrievals in the thesaurus; gathering relevant BTs, NTs, and RTs; and adding them to the search

Table 11.1 shows relevant search terms collected from the *Major Subjects*, *Subjects*, and *Classification* clusters. It distributes them into facets and identifies them as index terms (IT) or classification captions (CC).

There are so many relevant PsycINFO index terms and classification captions for each facet that it seems pointless to bolster table 11.1's list with FT terms. Other queries might present more of a challenge, requiring the searcher to cull search terms from titles, author-keywords, abstracts, and possibly full-texts.

With the experience of the initial À la Carte search under your belt, you know that there is plenty of information on this topic and follow up with a full-fledged Boolean search using table 11.1's index terms and the Buffet Edition of the Building Block

Table 11.1.   **PsycINFO Index Terms Extracted from Retrievals Using the Pearl Growing Search Strategy**

Facet	Search Term	CV or FT
Religion	religion	IT and CC
	spirituality	IT
	religious beliefs	IT
Alcoholism	drug & alcohol usage (legal)	CC
	alcoholism	IT
	alcohol intoxication	IT
	alcohol abuse	IT
	alcohol drinking patterns	IT
Prevention	health & mental health treatment & prevention	CC
	drug & alcohol rehabilitation	CC
	prevention	IT
	sobriety	IT
	drug rehabilitation	IT
	drug abuse prevention	IT
	alcohol rehabilitation	IT
	alcoholics anonymous	IT

Search Strategy. Figure 11.3 shows the search history for the follow-up search. It produces more than 200 retrievals, with such relevant titles as "The Role of Spirituality in Treatment Outcomes Following a Residential 12-Step Program," "Spirituality during Alcoholism Treatment and Continuous Abstinence for One Year," and "Alcoholics Anonymous: Cult or Cure?" (By the way, you could limit your search statements to table 11.1's classification captions and get equally good results.)

The Pearl Growing Search Strategy is often used as a follow-up to low-posted searches. A perfect example is the Eating Disorder query, a search topic that consistently produces few relevant retrievals for CV and FT searches (pages 145 and 171 to 172). You should be able to double this query's relevant retrievals using the Pearl Growing Search Strategy, and then put your new relevant retrievals to work at finding even more relevant retrievals using follow-up backward-chaining, forward-chaining, author-bibliography, and find-like searches. By the way, the extensive searching that you have done across several chapters for the Eating Disorders query is unusual, more characteristic of the type of assistance given to a doctoral student, faculty member, or researcher who is investigating a new topic for which there is little in the published literature or conducting a comprehensive search for a literature or systematic review.

The benefits of the Pearl Growing Search Strategy are:

- It has the potential to find additional relevant retrievals for searches conducted in both Boolean and extended-Boolean systems.
- It can stand on its own two feet for finding relevant sources, or it can be one or more follow-up searches to increase the results of low-posted searches governed by the Building Block Search Strategy or Can't Live Without This Facet First Strategy.
- When conducting a Pearl Growing search from scratch, little presearch preparation is needed, beyond entering facet names using FT search terms.

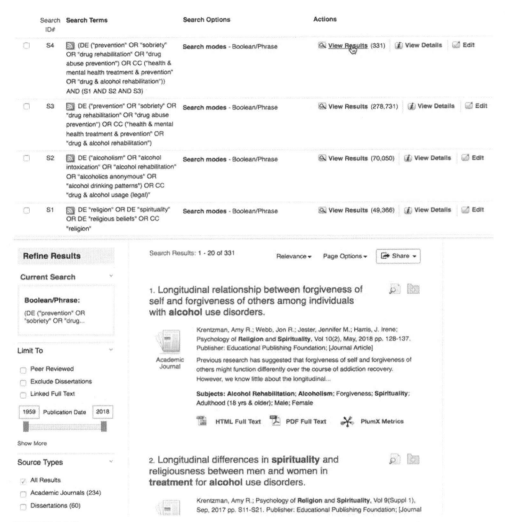

FIGURE 11.3
Follow-Up Controlled Vocabulary Search in EBSCOhost's PsycINFO Database Using Index Terms Culled from the Retrievals of a Pearl Growing Search

The drawbacks of the Pearl Growing Search Strategy are:

- You must be a confident searcher, knowledgeable about online searching, and thoroughly familiar with the search system's capabilities to accomplish the on-the-spot thinking and search formulation that the Pearl Growing Search Strategy requires.
- Following fruitless paths could result in greater use of the search system and more time spent online than you or the end user had expected. For example, if you head down a blind alley, you might have to save results, ponder them offline, and then return to the search.

- Using relevant retrievals to find additional ones can get complicated, requiring the full spectrum of the searcher's experience and knowledge of the search system and database at hand and online searching generally.
- Experience, patience, and perseverance are required for conducting effective Pearl Growing searches.

SHOT IN THE DARK SEARCH STRATEGY

The Shot in the Dark Strategy is for one-faceted queries. Figure 11.4 depicts this strategy using rifle sight that takes aim in the dark. The Free Dictionary gives two definitions for the phrase "shot in the dark": (1) "a wild unsubstantiated guess" and (2) "an attempt that has little chance at succeeding." Let's examine one-faceted queries to

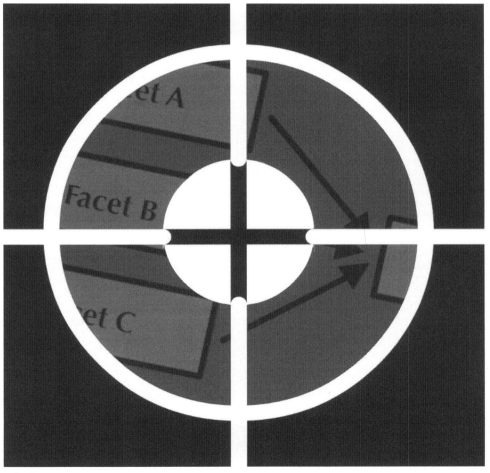

FIGURE 11.4
Shot in the Dark Search Strategy

determine what is going on with this strategy's name. Some queries that are candidates for the Shot in the Dark Search Strategy consist of one word:

- Norway
- Fashion
- ADHD
- Subway
- Madonna
- Oracle

Others are expressed in several words that form a phrase so familiar and common-place that it has come to represent a single big idea, concept, or theme. Examples are:

- Acid Rain
- Capital Punishment
- A Cut Above
- Nevil Shute Norway
- Cerebral Palsy
- Panera Bread

Scanning these queries should leave you puzzled, wondering what it is about Norway, Fashion, Acid Rain, and so on that interests the user. You might even say to yourself that these queries are impossible, that even if you searched for Norway, there would be so much information that the user couldn't possibly read it all, that the reference librarian didn't do his job of conducting a thorough interview to find out which aspects of these topics interest users.

Let me share an experience with you regarding an end user's one-faceted query that happened about forty years ago, just as online searching began. In the academic library where I worked, my late colleague, Ed Terry, was in charge of the online searching service. Because online searching was so expensive, only librarians with special training were allowed to do it. Costs associated with the search, such as connect time and royalties for displaying and printing surrogate records, were usually charged to a grant or departmental account (there were no full-texts back then, and retrieved surrogate records were printed on computer paper and given to users). Members of the general public paid out of pocket for the costs associated with the search. One day, Ed interviewed a user who wanted a search performed on Norway. Ed probed, "What is it about Norway that interests you?" The person assured Ed that he wanted information on Norway. Ed persisted, asking, "What do you want to know about Norway—its climate, trees, mountains, culture, rats?" The user replied, "Everything on Norway." When Ed advised him that the search would be very expensive, the user was unperturbed. Ed conducted the search in whatever database made sense back then (there were hardly more than two dozen available). The user returned a few days later, Ed gave him the printout in the form of a stack of computer paper about twelve inches high, and he paid out of pocket. Ed never saw the user again. Perhaps he is still reading the sources cited on the printout!

I told this story to emphasize that one-faceted *subject* queries *are* impossible to answer. Forty years ago, they retrieved thousands of citations; they would retrieve so many more today; in fact, the stack of computer paper would probably start at your home and reach to faraway Norway! Thus, when you detect a one-faceted *subject* query, negotiate the query, and if the user insists on sticking with his one-faceted query, transition to the Getting a Little Help from Your Friends Strategy (pages 262 to 265).

One-faceted *known-item* queries can be answered; however, before proceeding with them, you have to continue the negotiation and find out exactly what the user wants. Doing so helps you determine which database has potential for providing answers. Examine the queries listed earlier, starting with the name Nevil Shute Norway. Ask the user what interests her about Norway: his novels, one particular novel, films based on his novels, his published works in engineering, his life generally? You would consult your library's OPAC for his novels and films, engineering-specific databases for his engineering works, and biographical dictionaries for his biography.

If the user's interest in Cerebral Palsy involves the major charitable association for this disease, then this is a known-item search, sending you to the Associations Unlimited database; alternately, if he wants to know about this disease, then this is a subject search for the Friends Strategy (pages 262 to 265).

The Oracle query is vague. In the reference interview, find out whether it means Oracle, Inc., or the oracle that past and present cultures consult for advice or prophetic opinions. If the latter, then Oracle is a subject query for the Friends Strategy. If the former, then ask the user to tell you more about her interest in Oracle. Perhaps she wants to learn about Oracle database products, trade news about Oracle in the business electronics industry, how to get a job at Oracle, or something else. When you enter names or proper nouns into Google, it responds very accurately, ranking the official websites of well-known people, organizations, jurisdictions (places), programs, and projects at or close to the top of the list. For example, Google searches for `oracle`, `madonna`, `subway`, and `panera bread` rank the official websites of Oracle, Inc. (the company); Madonna (the popular entertainer); Subway (the fast-food chain); and Panera Bread (the casual restaurant) at the top of the heap of millions of websites. Search the Mergent Online database for names of companies, and its name-authority control functionality helps you match company names with those indexed in the database so that you can retrieve their entries, along with financial information and trade and industry news for companies of interest.

Adding a facet to provide context for a one-faceted query that is a proper noun may be the only way to find relevant information when the noun is a common word or phrase. The query A Cut Above applies to beauticians, clothing, landscaping, meats, trees, video production, and more. Adding a facet that describes the service performed by a business bearing this name and/or the geographical area it serves is almost absolutely necessary to target the business that interests you, and in this case, it is a cut above denver.

Maybe Cerebral Palsy, Madonna, Oracle, and Subway but definitely Norway, Fashion, ADHD, Acid Rain, and Capital Punishment are *subject* queries. All are candidates for the Friends Strategy.

The benefits of the Shot in the Dark Search Strategy are:

- Its criteria for predicting which queries are likely to succeed as one-faceted searches are simple to apply.
- It acknowledges that this strategy is most successful when applied to known-item queries bearing one facet.
- It diverts one-faceted subject queries to the Friends Search Strategy, where they have a greater chance of success as a result of this strategy's tools to help users further develop their queries.

The drawbacks of the Shot in the Dark Search Strategy are:

- It is not appropriate for one-faceted *subject* queries.
- One-faceted queries for known-items that are one-word titles or common author names might be high-posted, requiring searchers to introduce a second facet to reduce retrievals to a manageable size.

GETTING A LITTLE HELP FROM YOUR FRIENDS SEARCH STRATEGY

When the reference interview reveals a one-faceted *subject* query, this is a sign that more negotiation is necessary to find out exactly what the user wants. If the user is still clueless, call on your "friends" to help the user out. Friends refers to system features or specialized reference databases that have been designed with this very purpose in mind—helping users whose interests are undefined, unsettled, or vague. Figure 11.5 depicts the Friends Strategy—a central figure locking the two figures on either side of him in a friendly embrace, all three poised to solve difficult searching problems.

Which friend you recommend to the user depends on your assessment of the situation and your library's available sources. Consider how queries for ADHD, Norway, Cerebral Palsy, Acid Rain, Capital Punishment, Subway, and Fashion would benefit from the Friends that follow.

FIGURE 11.5
Getting a Little Help from Your Friends Search Strategy
Source: Friends symbol by Moriah Rich from the Noun Project (http://thenounproject.com).

Dictionaries and Encyclopedias

If users cannot get a foothold on their topics, it may be because they don't know much about them. Recommend a dictionary or encyclopedia that discusses broad-based topics at a basic level, defines topics, summarizes state-of-the-art knowledge, and cites sources for more in-depth information (pages 76 to 78 and 80). These sources may be encyclopedic or disciplinary, depending on which treatment you think matches your user's understanding and technical expertise with the topic.

Clusters

When users are having trouble finding a focus, get them started with a CV search for their one-faceted query, and then invite them to review the clusters accompanying the results. Review the several searches in which clusters are used to help users add specificity to their broad topics (pages 135 to 139). Clusters are a new feature of databases and search systems, so don't expect them all the time.

Classifications

Incorporated into a minority of discipline-based databases is a classification system, used to represent the discipline's knowledge and provide subject access points for searchers. With regard to the latter, selecting a classification caption, code, or number enables searchers to retrieve and display sources assigned to the particular class. Examples of databases enhanced with classifications are ACM Digital Library, Biosis, Embase, and PsycINFO. Users can browse the classification, select relevant classes, and combine them with Boolean operators and/or accompanying clusters. On its own or in conjunction with clusters, the classification is a means for users to conduct a subject search almost entirely on the basis of recognition, so it may appeal to users who know what they want but cannot express it in words.

Digital Library Databases

Digital library databases are typically narrowly focused on a particular subject, practice, issue, genre, etc. Such databases may invite users to read an encyclopedia-like article that provides an overview of the subject and orients the user to the database's content and organization. Then the database invites the user to explore, using predetermined clusters to organize the database's content. Examples of digital library databases and their focus are CQ Researcher for today's hot topics, Opposing Viewpoints in Context also for today's hot topics, and Oxford Islamic Studies Online for the Islamic world.

Web Subject Directories

Web subject directories classify websites according to subject. These directories consolidate all indexed websites under a dozen or so broad topics. Clicking on a broad subject leads to lists of subtopics that become increasingly narrower in scope. Browsing topics and subtopics is helpful for users who can't quite put their particular interest in words but will know it when they see it. The following are the most well-known directories, along with some notes to help you select the right one. The list of directories has shrunken considerably over the years because directory services rely on human editors to classify websites and keep their directories up to date, and support for editorial staff is expensive over the long term:

Best of the Web at http://botw.org. Navigate from an encyclopedic array of topics to
   increasingly more specific ones. Listed websites are accompanied by one-line descriptions.

Jasmine Directory at http://www.jasminedirectory.com. Jasmine uses a two-layered hierarchy
   to link you with products and services offered by a wide range of businesses. Listed
   websites are accompanied by one- to two-sentence blurbs.

Martindale's The Reference Desk at http://www.martindalecenter.com. Once you get used to this website's clunky interface, you'll find a treasure trove of links to an encyclopedic selection of references with an emphasis on the sciences.

The benefits of the Getting a Little Help from Your Friends Search Strategy are:

- It acknowledges that users might not be able to articulate their queries and provides them with tools to further develop their queries.
- Its tools organize knowledge in systematic ways that users can explore to further develop their queries.

The drawbacks of the Getting a Little Help from Your Friends Search Strategy are:

- Not all search systems and databases are equipped with Friends-like tools, such as clusters and classifications.
- Because Friends tools require time, know-how, effort, and perseverance on the part of users, some users might not want to use them, preferring more direct and immediately gratifying approaches to finding information.
- Friends tools are costly to develop, maintain, and apply to newly published sources because they require human intervention. So many Web subject directories have passed on. To succeed, new and continuing directories eventually take on a business mission, uniting people with commercial products and services.

CHOOSING A SEARCH STRATEGY

When you choose a search strategy, five external factors help you make the decision:

1. If the user's query bears one facet, this is a query for the Shot in the Dark Search Strategy, where you determine whether the user wants a known-item or subject. In the case of a subject, divert to the Getting a Little Help from Your Friends Strategy, which enables the user to further develop his topic. Remaining one-facet queries should be for known-items that involve searches of citation fields of surrogate records, such as author, title, publication year, or publication title fields.
2. If one facet must be present for retrievals to be even marginally relevant, choose the Can't Live Without This Facet First Strategy. In a Boolean system, this means first building a set of retrievals for the can't-live-without-this facet, evaluating search results, and entering one or more remaining facets if needed. In an extended-Boolean system, this means formulating search statements in which terms for the can't-live-without-this facet come first. Keep the Can't Live Without This Facet First Strategy

in mind when consulting reference sources. Their entries are usually so short that reading them may be quicker than populating your search statement with search terms representing multiple facets. Plus, the more requirements in your search statements, the less likely reference sources will produce any retrievals.

3. If you are searching a Boolean system, choose the Building Block Search Strategy's Buffet Edition, and if it is an extended-Boolean system, choose this strategy's À la Carte Edition.

4. If searches from your Building Block Search Strategy or Can't Live Without This Facet First Strategy are low-posted, extract relevant search terms from retrievals, and enhance your search statements with them. This is the Pearl Growing Search Strategy.

5. If you have little time to prepare in advance, conduct a subject search using the Building Block's À la Carte Edition. Then extract relevant search terms from retrievals, and enhance your search statements with them, following up with a search using the Can't Live Without This Facet First Strategy or one of the two Building Block editions for more relevant retrievals. Again, this is the Pearl Growing Search Strategy.

Figure 11.6 is a flowchart to help you choose a search strategy. Strategies for some searches morph into others; for example, a low-posted search from a Building Block Search Strategy becomes a candidate for a Pearl Growing Search Strategy, and a subject search for a Shot in the Dark Strategy becomes a candidate for the Friends Strategy. Right now, search-strategy selection might look complicated, but in time, you will find yourself moving between strategies with the ease of an Olympic figure skater practicing her routine with all its required moves and jumps.

QUESTIONS

The following are negotiated queries. You've encountered some in previous chapters, and others are new. Conduct a facet analysis and logical combination for each query (or reuse your presearch preparation from previous chapters), taking into consideration the suggested databases. Then choose one or more search strategies, and provide a rationale that describes why you chose it.

1. Compendex database: Testing ice hockey helmets to make sure they are safe.
2. ERIC database: A teacher who teaches social studies at the high school level wants instructional materials to help him teach a unit on cultural awareness to his students.
3. Agricultural and Environmental Sciences database: Agent Orange.
4. ProQuest Research Library: How should high school coaches and trainers, parents, and the players themselves respond to possible incidences of sports-related concussions?

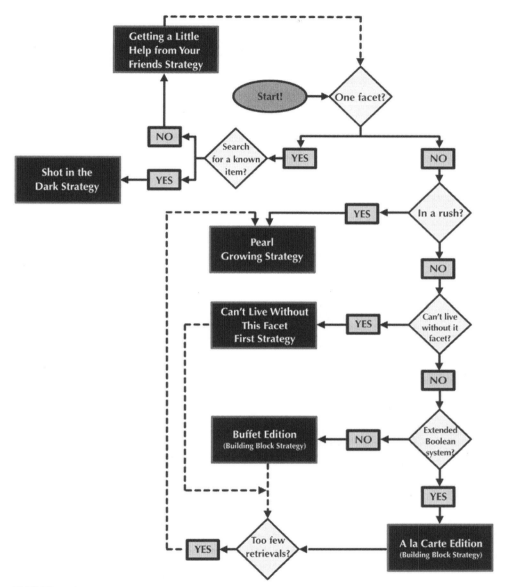

FIGURE 11.6
Search Strategy Selection Flowchart

5. LexisNexis: Recent press about and sources written by Phyllis Chesler so that the user can assess her suitability as a guest speaker for a local celebratory event.

6. Infoplease (http://www.infoplease.com): How many vice presidents have come from Texas?

7. Google: Making money as a travel blogger.

8. PsycINFO: Are college students who get enough sleep more successful academically than students who don't?
9. PubMed: Does mindfulness meditation reduce the stress of pregnancy?

SUMMARY

This chapter presents five search strategies that should suffice for almost all online
searches that you conduct in Boolean and extended-Boolean search systems. Defined
as a "plan for the whole search" (Bates 1979, 206), search strategy requires the searcher
to take stock of the number of facets in the query, the importance of these facets relative to the user's interests, the closeness of these facets with respect to the database's
discipline, the system's Boolean or extended-Boolean nature, and the user's knowledge and understanding of both his topic and its underlying discipline. Search strategy
deployment demands "all the knowledge one can gain about online searching systems
and all one can learn about indexing vocabularies and the conventions practiced in
. . . data base construction" (Meadow and Cochrane 1981, 133).

For the foreseeable future, you might feel comfortable sticking with the Building
Block Search Strategy for the majority of subject queries. When you've got the Building Block Search Strategy down pat, entertain other strategies using this chapter's
search strategy selection flowchart, which boils search-strategy selection down to the
number of facets in negotiated queries. As your confidence grows, experiment with
other strategies, particularly the Can't Live Without This Facet First and Pearl Growing Search Strategies, because they will enable you to increase your efficiency and effectiveness as an expert intermediary online searcher.

BIBLIOGRAPHY

Bates, Marcia J. 1979. "Information Search Tactics." *Journal of the American Society for
   Information Science* 30 (July): 205–14.

McGraw-Hill Encyclopedia of Science & Technology. 2007. 10th ed., s.v. "Bivalvia," by Michael
   A. Rice. New York: McGraw-Hill.

Meadow, Charles T., and Pauline A. Cochrane. 1981. *Basics of Online Searching.* New York:
   Wiley.

ANSWERS

1. **Testing ice hockey helmets to make sure they are safe.** Compendix database.
   Facets: A. **Hockey**, B. **Helmets**, C. **Testing**
   Logical combination: **A** AND **B** AND **C**

   Can't Live Without This Facet First Strategy: Start with the **Hockey** facet because it is key to the user's interests. Then add **Helmets** in a Boolean AND combi-

nation with **Hockey** to focus retrievals on that aspect of the sport. If there are too many retrievals, then proceed with facet C.

Pearl Growing Search Strategy: All searches stand to benefit from this strategy. Initially, get the search started with an À la Carte Edition: Enter one FT term per facet, scan relevant retrievals' index terms, and use them to populate the search statements you enter in the follow-up searches using the Can't Live Without This Facet First Strategy.

2. **Find instructional materials on cultural awareness for high school social studies.** ERIC database.
   Facets: A. **High School**, B. **Social Studies**, C. **Cultural Awareness**, D. **Instructional Materials**
   Logical combination: **A** AND **B** AND **C** AND **D**

   Buffet Edition of the Building Block Search Strategy: This query requires all four facets for retrievals to be relevant. In the ERIC thesaurus are at least a handful of descriptors for representing each facet. Too few retrievals means following up with the Pearl Growing Search Strategy.

3. **Agent Orange.** Agricultural and Environmental Sciences database
   Facets: A. **Agent Orange**
   Logical combination: **A**

   Shot in the Dark Strategy: The user's query bears one facet for a subject search. One-faceted *subject* queries *are* impossible to answer because there is so much information available for them. Divert to the Friends Strategy.

   Getting a Little Help from Your Friends Strategy: Search this database's thesaurus for an index term to represent this query's lone facet, and then show the user this database's clusters for focusing his query on a more manageable subtopic.

4. **Responding to possible incidences of sports-related concussions.** ProQuest Research Library
   Facets: A. **Concussions**, B. **Athletics**, C. **High School**, D. **Reporting**
   Logical combination: **A** AND **B** AND **C** AND **D**

   Can't Live Without This Facet First Strategy: Start with the **Concussions** facet because it must be present for retrievals to be even marginally relevant. If there are too many retrievals, then combine it with the **High School** facet to provide context. Assess retrievals in case the **Reporting** and **Athletics** facets are not necessary. Too few retrievals for all four facets means following up with the Pearl Growing Search Strategy.

5. **Recent press about and sources written by Phyllis Chesler assess her suitability as a guest speaker.** LexisNexis database
   Facets: A. **Phyllis Chesler**

Logical combination: **A**

Shot in the Dark Strategy: The user's query bears one facet for a known-item search. Search for newspaper articles by Chesler.

Getting a Little Help from Your Friends Strategy: Search for newspaper articles about Chesler, and then apply one or more clusters to reveal themes that may shed light on her suitability.

6. **How many vice presidents have come from Texas?** InfoPlease
Facets: A. **Vice Presidents**, B. **Birthplace**
Logical Combination: **A** AND **B**

Can't Live Without This Facet First Strategy: Because you've chosen Infoplease, a reference database, this strategy is the way to go, starting with the **Vice Presidents** facet. Infoplease responds with a list of annotated retrievals, including one referencing "state of birth."

7. **Making money as a travel blogger.** Google
Facets: A. **Travel**, B. **Blogging**, C. **Money**
Logical combination: **A** AND **B** AND **C**

À la Carte Edition of the Building Block Search Strategy: Successively enter search statements bearing one term per facet (e.g., `travel blogging money`, `travel blogger money`, `travel blogging monetization`, `travel blogger revenue`, `travel website make money`, `travel blogging income`).

8. **Are college students who get enough sleep more successful academically than students who don't?** PsycINFO database
Facets: A. **College Students**, B. **Sleep**, C. **Academic Performance**
Logical combination: **B** AND **C** AND **A**

Can't Live Without This Facet First Strategy. Start with the **Sleep** facet first because it must be present for the user to consider retrievals even marginally relevant. Then proceed with **Academic Performance**. Add facet **A** to the mix only if retrievals produced by facets **B** and **C** are not relevant or too many in number. Too few retrievals means following up with the Pearl Growing Search Strategy.

9. **Does mindfulness meditation reduce the stress of pregnancy?** PubMed database
Facets: A. **Mindfulness Meditation**, B. **Stress**, C. **Pregnancy**
Logical combination: **A** AND **B** AND **C**

Buffet Edition of the Building Block Search Strategy: This query requires all three facets for retrievals to be relevant. MeSH features several main and subdivided index terms for representing each facet. Too few retrievals means following up with the Pearl Growing Search Strategy.

Displaying and Assessing Retrievals and Responding Tactically to the Search System

This chapter discusses the seventh and final step of the online searching process—displaying and assessing retrievals and responding tactically to the system throughout the course of the search. Displaying retrievals may sound simple and straightforward, but in recent years, search systems have become more sophisticated about displaying the most relevant ones first. Thus, users have come to expect relevant sources in response to their queries, rarely venturing beyond the first or second page of retrievals.

Search tactics come to the fore the moment the reference interview begins and continue until the search ends. A search tactic is a "move to further the search" (Bates 1979, 206). Search-tactic deployment depends on the judgment of the searcher who is engaged in an ongoing search. While monitoring what is happening, the searcher recognizes that an adjustment is needed to keep the search on track and responds with the use of one or more system features to make the adjustment. There is seldom a one-to-one correspondence between making adjustments and the use of the system's features. Adjustments almost always require a series of deliberate moves on the part of the searcher involving the manipulation of several features. Like search strategies, successful search-tactic deployment requires thorough knowledge of online searching concepts and mastery of online searching skills.

DISPLAYING RETRIEVALS

Most databases give users several options for displaying retrievals:

- Relevance. Displaying the most relevant retrievals first, based on the system's relevance-ranking algorithm.
- Publication date, descending or ascending. Displaying the most recently published or oldest sources first.
- Main entry or author. Displaying retrievals alphabetically by author or by title when authorship is diffuse or anonymous.

- Title. Displaying retrievals alphabetically by title.
- Classified. Displaying retrievals by subject using a classification scheme.
- Times cited. Ordering the retrievals display by the most to the least cited or vice versa. This option is limited to databases with cited-reference searching.

Users have become so accustomed to the relevance-ranked retrieval displays of Web search engines, which are quite accurate at listing relevant sources at the top of the list, that many licensed search systems are now using relevance as their default display mode.

The phenomenon of users limiting their review of retrieved sources to only the first one or two pages is well documented (Jansen and Spink 2006; Pan et al. 2007; Spink at al. 2001; Unkel 2017). When users don't find what they want there, they enter new keywords, reenter their original keywords, or project relevance onto the first-listed retrievals.

When you help users get their searches started, mouse down on the retrievals-display pull-down menu, show them which display options are available, and suggest that they be thorough in their retrievals review because other options may serve up relevant retrievals that relevance ranking misses. Additionally, point out the clusters that accompany retrievals, liken them to an outline or table of contents to retrievals, and suggest that they apply this and that cluster to filter retrievals.

The propensity of users to focus almost exclusively on the highest-ranking retrievals is particularly problematic when they search the open Web. At least Google is up front, telling you that it uses personalized information about you to order for retrievals display (Google 2018a). With other systems, you just don't know.

Ads and sponsored content accompany retrieval displays from Web search systems and coexist alongside the content that was the impetus for your visit to a website. To distinguish between what you do and don't want on the Web, you have to pay attention to such labels as "ads," "sponsored advertising," or "paid advertisement" and/ or such visual cues as borders, background colors, and three-dimensional beveling. Distinguishing between the two is difficult because websites personalize the retrievals they want you to see. For example, Web search engines monitor such factors as your geographic location, previous search statements, bookmarks, cookies, and retrievals you've selected in the past to generate retrievals for the search at hand; consequently, there really is no set of "legitimate" (also called "organic," "natural," or "earned") results for a particular query. Together with friends, family, or classmates, search your favorite Web search engine, and compare your retrievals for various topics to determine whether your earned content is the same as theirs. Extend your analysis to the ads and paid content that accompany your earned retrievals. Then discuss among yourselves whether there really is one set of earned Web retrievals. In class, share your observations with your fellow classmates. Choose your own topics, or use these extended-Boolean search statements:

- Academic: `television violence children`, `alcoholism spiritu-ality relapse`, `windmills birds`
- Consumer health: `diabetes obesity`, `knee injuries women`, `peanut allergies`, `psoriasis treatment`, `life coach`
- For news, sports, and popular culture, enter a search statement naming the latest blockbuster movie, an upcoming big sports event, an approaching holiday, a celebrity experiencing a major life event, a favorite athlete, or a tragedy of epic proportions
- shopping: `ag jeans`, `new car`, `modest clothes`, `golf clubs`

Thinly disguised as substantive content are the Web pages that content farms publish, bearing easy-to-read essays on popular topics and advertising for which the farms receive revenue every time a Web user lands on the page or clicks on an accompanying ad. Clickbait—provocative content that piques your curiosity to the extent that you *have to* click on it—is another less-than-upstanding approach in the race to capture your eyeballs and has been blamed for ushering in the post-truth era (pages 346 to 351).

Search engine optimization (SEO) is the deliberate process of effecting a higher ranking for a website. Acceptable to search engines are "white hat" SEO techniques that bring a website's content to the attention of like-minded users. Google encourages webmasters to use its guide to SEO best practices so that they improve their websites' findability (Google 2018b). Google and Web search engine developers generally do not tolerate "black hat" (deceptive) SEO techniques; in response, they are constantly tweaking their systems' ranking algorithms so that retrievals are not adversely affected by deceptive techniques (Sweeny 2012).

Critics of white-hat SEO, personalized search results, and retrievals ranking generally argue that their long-term effect will stifle our experience of the world, putting content that complements our interests, opinions, and personal viewpoints in front of our eyeballs while distancing us from opposing views. Pariser (2011) explains, "Ultimately, the proponents of personalization offer a vision of a custom-tailored world, every facet of which fits us perfectly. It's a cozy place, populated by our favorite people and things and ideas" (12). Because library users rely on the Web's information for serious and less-than-serious pursuits, your interaction with them should underline the importance of evaluating web-based information and seeking a wide range of different views on the same issue. The latter especially will prepare library users to defend their positions and increase their tolerance for opposing views, able to loosen up on the strength of their convictions in the course of seeing why others embrace views that clash with their own.

What about the search systems that access licensed databases? No one knows how their retrieval-ranking algorithms work because they are trade secrets. What is stopping these systems from programming their algorithms to give greater weights to:

- sources written by higher-cited researchers
- the highest-cited sources
- sources with higher altmetrics
- sources published in journals with higher journal-level metrics
- the most popular sources in terms of numbers of views or downloads

On the one hand, one could argue that it makes good sense for the search system to apply such weights using the logic that sources that garner greater interest among researchers deserve greater exposure to others active in the field, particularly to students who are new to a field and express difficulty assessing credibility and accuracy without assistance from domain experts. On the other hand, one could point out the chilling effect this could have on research generally. Important research that receives little attention could get swept under the rug because no one notices it buried deep in the middle- or tail-end of high-posted retrievals. This could put undue pressure on researchers, especially brand-new, never-cited researchers, to abandon research not likely to pay off in the long term in favor of pursuing research that they know will have an immediate payoff.

An academic researcher retweeted an email message he'd received from a product director at the academic-oriented social-media site Academia.edu, asking him whether he'd consider paying a "small fee" for Academia.edu to boost downloads and readerships of his works (Ruff 2016). The story went viral, and academics, including Academia.edu members, unleashed a hailstorm of criticism on the company running the site. To date, Academia.edu has not followed through on its plan, nor is there any indication it will in view of the outrage heaped upon it.

Wanting to nip comparable problems in the bud before they spiral out of control, librarians have been especially proactive with regard to the newest technology in libraries—web-scale discovery (WSD) systems. They participate side by side publishers and WSD-system providers in the National Information Standard Organization's (NISO) Open Discovery Initiative (ODI), which "address[es] perceptions regarding bias and concern about the possibility of bias in [web-scale] discovery services" (NISO 2014, 2). The NISO report that publishes best practices for WSD systems speaks directly to fair linking, recommending that "discovery services should not discriminate, based on business relationships, among content providers or products (especially their own) in the methods that are used to generate results, relevance rankings, or link order" (25). That WSD-system providers agree to these best practices is expected in the form of their voluntary conformance statements. NISO (2014) continues, "In the absence of [such] voluntary statements, libraries can use the presence or absence of these factors to infer conformance" (vi).

At the present time, search systems that access licensed databases appear to be straightforward, weighting retrievals algorithmically based on Boolean or extended-Boolean criteria. To have a hand in determining whether these systems remain faithful to these criteria, scrutinize Boolean retrievals where you have total control of retrievals based on the CV; FT; and truncation, proximity, and Boolean operators you enter. Telltale signs that a Boolean system is straying from its focus are retrievals that exceed the constraints of your search criteria, new genres that you haven't seen before, or the same publications appearing atop retrievals lists for different topics. Extended-Boolean retrievals may be more difficult to assess because searches produce huge numbers of retrievals. When you find retrievals that don't make sense, save the search, and discuss the situation with a vendor representative.

To save searches and retrievals in licensed databases, users must establish search-system accounts so systems can serve up their saved data in the future. Systems that ask registrants for more personal information than username and password should raise a red flag that prompts you to check licenses and privacy policies to see why such information is collected, how it is used, and with whom it is shared. If clauses in these documents are unacceptable, discuss them with your institution's legal counsel, who might need to negotiate with the vendor so that modifications achieve consensus between parties.

ASSESSING RETRIEVALS

Assessing retrievals for relevance and credibility might seem like a straightforward task, but it really isn't, especially for users who are unsure of their topics. In addition to recommending such users start with an encyclopedia, get them started with the right search terms, facets, and search logic, pointing out relevant sources that are appropriate for their basic level of understanding. While you are at it, ask them which guidelines their instructor gave the class regarding cited sources. If users must cite a quota of scholarly (also called research or refereed) sources, then recommend a database with a "scholarly" presearch qualifier, and demonstrate the feature to them. If their instructor gave them no such guidelines, then recommend a database that would be too basic for a domain expert but appropriate for someone new to the topic or the discipline.

Assessing retrievals is an important component of many academic institutions' information-literacy training. Such training is beyond *Online Searching*'s scope. Plenty of books address information literacy generally, and you should consult them for more information (Broussard 2017; Buchanan and McDonough 2016; Grassian and Kaplowitz 2009; Ragains 2013). Taking a master's-level information-literacy course should be in your academic plans. You'll want to prepare now for your new job, where your information-literacy duties may range from plugging into an existing information-literacy instruction program to helping your colleagues revamp and deploy a redesigned program.

Assessing Relevance

High-posted searches may be overwhelming to users, especially international students for whom English is a second language. Encourage them to be systematic about retrievals, to read each retrieval's abstract, and to save promising ones using the database's save functionality (pages 312 to 316). By the way, some users think that abstracts are the actual articles themselves, so make sure they know that abstracts are summaries and that they will have to follow up and download full-texts for their most promising retrievals (Cull 2011). Finding full-texts isn't always straightforward (pages 209 to 212 and 217), so encourage users to ask you for help when they have full-text fulfillment difficulties.

Because users are likely to experience shifts in their topic as they review surrogate records, their second pass through retrieved sources should be more decisive, eliminating saved surrogates that they deem no longer promising and downloading full-texts for the rest. Suggest that users save downloaded full-texts in a folder on their personal computers named for their project so they will be able to find them later. Alternatively, introduce users to citation management software, where they can store everything about their retrievals—citations, abstracts, keywords, downloaded full-texts, and notes (pages 314 to 316).

Reading full-texts may be a daunting task for users. Compounding the situation may be the quota their instructor imposed on them, requiring them to cite so many scholarly articles. Recommend a database with a scholarly presearch qualifier, and show how the feature works. For users unfamiliar with the research genre, they will be doubly in the dark about how to proceed. Advise users that they don't have to read every source they find from start to finish. Instead, they can perform a technical reading that limits reading to those portions of sources that are the most important for understanding overall content. For research sources, this means scanning these sections:

- Title and abstract to get an overall sense of the source's content
- Introduction for the researcher's objectives and why the research is important
- Methods section to find out how the researcher conducted the experiment
- Conclusions, where the researcher states his most important findings

Nonresearch articles are more varied, making it difficult to give hard and fast rules about which sections to read. At the very least, users should scan the source for this information:

- Title, abstract, and introduction to get an overall sense of its content
- Headings and subheadings, treating them like a table of contents that orients them to the source as a whole
- Discussion, where the author puts his most important points in a real-world context
- Summary or conclusion, which spotlights the most important content

Often users are seeking sources that map entirely onto their interests, perhaps even writing their papers for them. Impress on them that it is rare to find such sources. Instead, they have to read promising sources to determine whether and how the sources' content addresses their interests and synthesize what they learn into a piece that fulfills the requirements of an academic assignment, an answer that addresses their questions, or a decision that enables them to take their next steps. Suggest to users that their chosen topics and the relevance assessments they make for retrieved sources are moving targets as a result of their exposure to new information, which continually shifts their points of view, right up to the moment they complete a project and even beyond.

Assessing Credibility

With relevant Web sources in hand, users know that they should assess their credibility, but few actually do it, and when they do, they have little desire to take a rigorous approach to credibility assessment (page 13 to 14). Research findings that enlist experimental online systems to elicit credibility ratings and assessments from users have been promising. These systems shadow users while they search for information, prompting them to rate a source's credibility and relevance and describe the reasons for their ratings. Their evidence for their credibility ratings usually pertains to authors, author credentials, or the source's genre, and their evidence for their relevance ratings usually pertains to the source's content or its closeness to their chosen or assigned topic (Leeder 2014; Markey, Leeder, and Rieh 2014).

The operational NoodleTools platform supports students while they work through the academic research process (NoodleTools 2018). It just may be the type of online system that is needed to motivate students to think deeply about the sources they use for their papers, getting them in the habit of taking notes from sources, outlining their written reports, staging their notes from sources in their outlines, and citing their sources using a well-known style sheet. For example, NoodleTools transforms the very process of a student entering citation data for retrieved sources into a preliminary evaluation of source credibility. Specifically, it connects the various elements of a citation (i.e., date, the user's annotation about relevance, author, the user's annotation about accuracy, and publisher) with the elements of the CRAAP credibility checklist (i.e., currency, relevance, authority, accuracy, and purpose), respectively.

Your institution's information-literacy training should include source credibility evaluation. Of the various information-literacy venues, stand-alone courses and course-integrated instruction may give librarians ample time to cover credibility in depth. For example, encourage students to perform a taste test, so to speak, retrieving sources on a topic of their own choosing from the open Web and licensed databases. Then let them compare these sources side by side using a CRAAP-like credibility checklist that elicits their credibility assessments and rates the two sources (University of California, Chico 2010). Debrief students by consolidating the results for the whole class to see whether students give higher ratings to sources from open Web or licensed databases. It doesn't matter which source type wins. What is important is that students are exposed to and get experience answering the types of questions they should ask about a source's credibility. Alternatively, invite your students to play CRAP! so that they gain experience applying evaluation criteria to a sample source (Information Literacy Group 2016).

Information-literacy instruction may be more important in public libraries than in academic libraries because public-library users search for information to make decisions about health, finance, retirement planning, job seeking, and much more; that is, decisions that affect not only their lives but the well-being of family members also. On-the-spot reference interviews may be the only opportunity for librarians to impress on such users the importance of source evaluation; however, they may heed what you have to say in this regard because their decision making affects loved ones.

SEARCH TACTICS

Search tactics are the strategic moves searchers make to further the ongoing search (Bates 1979). To execute a search tactic, the searcher may wield one or more system features to get the job done. Not necessarily co-occurring with one or two particular steps of the online searching process or a particular search strategy, search tactics are cross-cutting—searchers execute them when it is appropriate to do so during the course of the online search.

Table 12.1 classifies search tactics into five types, defines them, and lists steps of the search process where the searcher is most likely to perform these tactics. The list is intended to be comprehensive to inform today's intermediary searchers who operate in an exceptionally complex information-retrieval environment where they must be prepared to search both Boolean and extended-Boolean search systems and a wide array of databases that handle form, genre, subject matter, and vocabulary control in all different ways. The list features most of Bates's (1979; 1987) original information search tactics and some of Smith's (2012) Internet search tactics. Drawing on my searching experience and teaching graduate students how to search, I've added more search tactics to the list, eliminated or merged tactics, reclassified tactics from one type to another, and updated tactic names and definitions.

Table 12.1. Search Tactics

Tactic	Definition
Search Monitoring: Tactics to keep the search on track and efficient	
Check	Check your search to make sure it reflects the negotiated topic. (B)
Correct	Correct logical and strategic errors. (B)
History	Keep track of where the search has been, where it is now, and where it is going. (B: Record)
Pattern	Alert to familiar patterns so you can respond in ways that were successful in the past or by improving on them in the present. (B)
Weigh	Weigh current and anticipated actions with respect to costs, benefits, effort, and/or efficiency. (B)
File Structure: Tactics for navigating from the search system's file structure for the database to individual sources and information in those sources	
Find	Use the browser's find feature in search of information in a source. (S)
Hubspoke	Navigate from links in a source to additional sources, including from a source's cited references to these actual sources. (S) (B: Bibble)
Snatch	Search using a noncontent search term that retrieves only what the user wants. (S: URL)
Stretch	Use a database, its sources, or information in the sources for other than their intended purposes. (B)
Search Formulation: Tactics to aid in conceptualizing, assembling, and revising the search formulation	
Block	Block one or more facets and/or search terms. (B)
Broaden	Broaden one or more facets and/or their search terms.
Exhaust	Search all of the query's facets and/or search terms. (B)
Field	Restrict searches to occurrences of search terms in one or more fields.
Precision	Retrieve only relevant retrievals.
Rearrange	Alter the order of terms or search statements. (B)
Recall	Retrieve all relevant retrievals.
Reduce	Search for some, not all, of the query's facets and/or search terms. (B: Cut)
Specify	Enlist search terms that are as specific as the desired information. (B)
Search Term: Tactics to aid in the selection of search terms for the query's facets	
Anticiterm	Search for a wildcard term in a phrase. (S)
Auto–Term Add	Toggle on the system's automatic addition of statistically co-occurring terms to the search.
Citing	Search for sources citing an older source (i.e., forward chaining).
Cluster	Search using one or more co-occurring values from accompanying clusters.
Contrary	Search using terms or facets that are opposite in meaning. (B)
Fix	Apply truncation to search terms, or let the system to do it automatically. (B)
Neighbor	Search for terms in the same alphabetical neighborhood. (B)
Nickname	Search for a term's acronyms, initialed, or nicknamed variants.
Pearl Growing	Search using relevant values from retrievals. (B & S: Trace; S: Backlink)
Proximate	Designate how close together search terms should be. (S: Phrase)
Pseudonym	Search using pseudonyms for names.
Relate	Search using terms that are not in a hierarchical relationship but are related to the facet. (B)
Space & Symbol	Search using one- or two-word variants of the term and/or taking hyphens, slashes, and other symbols into consideration. (B)
Spell	Search using a term's variant spellings. (B)
Sub	Search using terms that are hierarchically subordinate to the facet. (B)
Subdivide	Search using one or more subdivisions appended to a term.
Super	Search using terms that are hierarchically superordinate to the facet. (B)
Evaluation: Tactics to aid in the evaluation of retrievals	
Audition	Cite page elements, such as graphics, layout, spelling and grammatical errors, etc. (S)
Authorship	Use criteria that refer to author credentials, reputation, affiliations with named or unnamed organizations, sponsors, publishers, etc.
Content	Use criteria that refers to the source's subject content.
External Noncontent	Use criteria that describe noncontent of external characteristics of sources (e.g., altmetrics, citing references, format, genre, personal experience, recommendations from other people, reviews).
Impetus	Refer to the impetus that gave rise to the search.
Internal Noncontent	Use criteria that describe noncontent of internal characteristics of sources (e.g., currency, cited references, detail, features, length).

Source: Adapted from Bates (1979; 1987) and Smith (2012)

Search Monitoring Tactics

Search Monitoring Tactics keep the search on track and efficient. Except for HISTORY, these tactics are technology independent. CHECK invites you to make sure you haven't strayed from the negotiated topic. Whereas most reference interactions are one-time events, interactions with professional researchers may be repeat events, focusing on the same topic over a long period of time, so CHECK to make sure your follow-up searches match the user's interests. When you CORRECT, you are looking at both big-picture aspects of the search (e.g., facets, Boolean operators, search strategies, vocabulary control, and feedback mechanisms) and minor aspects of the search (e.g., spelling, truncation types, choice of and settings on proximity operators) to make sure everything is in order, and you correct it if it isn't. To help you CORRECT is HISTORY, the system's record of previous search statements and retrievals. For systems that don't have HISTORY, jot down your search statements or cut and paste them into a sticky note so that you can keep track of what you've done. The WEIGH tactic forces you to think about the ongoing search, what's happening right now, and what you plan on doing in the light of costs, benefits, effort, and/or efficiency. For example, you might want to search several relevant databases for a user's topic, but you WEIGH, considering the time and effort involved in searching each database's CV versus conducting a search in the one database with the most trusted CV. PATTERN is the list's déjà vu tactic, wanting you to be on alert for familiar patterns. Detecting a pattern, you either go on autopilot because of your many successful responses to the pattern in the past, or because of your dissatisfaction with your previous responses to the pattern, you are now circumspect about your response, invoking the WEIGH tactic to determine the best way to respond. For example, you recall that being comprehensive about collecting CV terms with a particular database's thesaurus yields too many nonrelevant results, so the next time, you limit your selections to hardly a handful of CV terms per facet.

File Structure Tactics

File Structure Tactics enable searchers to navigate from the search system's file structure for the database to individual sources and information in those sources. Navigating from a source's links to additional sources powers the HUBSPOKE tactic. On the Web, HUBSPOKE manifests as the links that authors activate on their Web pages to connect you to related content on other Web pages. On a journal article's PDF, these could be links from a reference in a footnote or bibliography linking you to the full-text. There's no doubt that you're familiar with the FIND tactic; that is, retrieving a source and using the browser's "Find" capability to see whether the source bears a word or phrase and how it is used. SNATCH enlists a noncontent search term, such as a DOI, URL, ISBN, ISSN, call number, or accession number, to retrieve the one source that interests the user. For example, you enter the accession number EJ1162017 into the ERIC database to retrieve its assigned source. STRETCH acknowledges that search systems, databases, sources, and their information can be used for other than their intended purposes. I recall wanting to retrieve literature reviews on a subject, but the database didn't have a CV, nor did FT searches for a **Literature Review** facet produce retrievals. To STRETCH the database, I searched for lengthy journal articles (twenty-five or more pages) with lengthy bibliographies (fifty or more cited references) and achieved my objective: finding literature reviews.

Search Formulation Tactics

In previous chapters, you have already wielded certain Search Formulation Tactics to conceptualize, assemble, and maybe even revise a search formulation. EXHAUST and REDUCE should immediately bring to mind Building Block and Can't Live Without This Facet First Strategies, respectively. When you leave an EXHAUST, you conduct a search for all of the query's facets, which is characteristic of the Building Block Search Strategy. When you REDUCE, you start searching with one or two facets that must be present in retrievals to be acceptable to the user, and that is characteristic of the Can't Live Without This Facet First Search Strategy. BLOCK is a tactic that enlists the Boolean NOT operator or the Web search system's minus (-) operator to force the system to eliminate search terms or facets from search results. Several blocking proximity operators are available in LexisNexis. They eliminate words in close proximity and retrieve them farther apart; for example, `market NOT W/5 share` eliminates phrases like "market share" and "share of the market" and retrieves these words when separated by more than five words.

SPECIFY brings to mind the Rule of Specific Entry (pages 123 to 125) that governs the indexer's choice of assigning CV terms to surrogates that are as specific as the topic under consideration. Executing the SPECIFY tactic means populating your search statements with CV and/or FT terms that are as specific as the topic they describe. In contrast, BROADEN fills your search statements with CV and/or FT terms that are broader than the topic under consideration. An example is the Eating Disorders query, in which find-like searches reveal the assignment of the descriptor "Family Relations" to relevant retrievals (page 186). This descriptor is a broader term, being rather bland and neutral about conveying whether the relations are good or bad. Adding "Family Relations" to the search formulation, you might be inclined to double-check the Psyc-INFO thesaurus for more such terms beginning with the words *family* or *parent*, and should you add them into the ongoing search, you've executed the BROADEN tactic.

On occasion, your interaction with users reveals they want high recall (i.e., as much relevant information as is written on the topic) or high precision (i.e., only relevant retrievals). One way to put the RECALL tactic to work is to choose FT terms for high recall, adding truncation or stemming symbols to them and extending retrieval to all fields or all subject-rich fields of surrogates and full-texts. Putting the PRECISION tactic to work is just as complicated, choosing index terms from the database's CV and limiting their retrievals to the database's CV fields. Because today's search systems feature no push-button RECALL and PRECISION tactics, you have to become familiar with a system's functionality to achieve high-recall or high-precision results. If you conduct a CV search, you are automatically invoking the FIELD tactic to limit retrievals only to the database's CV fields. To produce high-precision results in a database that doesn't have a CV, you can limit subject searches to the subject-rich fields in a database's surrogates—title, abstract, and author-keywords—so that the system doesn't produce false drops from searches of other surrogate-record fields, such as author, note, publisher, journal name, publication type, audience, etc. Last but not least is the REARRANGE tactic. Remember it when you conduct subject searches in extended-Boolean systems, double-checking your search statement to make sure the most important search term is first and, if it isn't, putting it first so that the search system gives it higher weights.

Search Term Tactics

Search Term Tactics aid in the selection of search terms for the query's facets. When you consult a database's thesaurus, it gives you functionality to search, display, and select a term's narrower terms (SUB tactic), broader terms (SUPER tactic), and related terms (RELATE tactic). Another approach to selecting search terms is to display the database's alphabetical index (NEIGHBOR tactic), and such a display is particularly useful for finding variant forms of author names, corporate bodies, titles, and identifiers. Some databases subdivide index terms (SUBDIVIDE tactic), providing you with yet another source for finding search terms. To represent an idea, sometimes using search terms that are the opposite in meaning target what you want (CONTRARY tactic). This is an approach typical of free text searches; for example, representing the **Adjustment** facet in the Child Soldiers query are such positive terms as *adjust*, *settle*, and *reintegration*, and negative terms such as *maladjustment* and *struggle* (page 181). Relieving searchers from consulting a thesaurus is the automatic vocabulary assistance feature in some extended-Boolean systems (AUTO-TERM ADD tactic); to activate it, look for a toggle on the search interface or sign on to your account, open preferences, and activate it there.

Several Search Term Tactics affect the representation of words in search statements. The SPELL tactic is a reminder to accommodate multiple spellings for a term, as well as to make sure spelling is correct. When entering phrases, you have to execute the PROXIMATE tactic, making decisions about how close two or more words will be and whether order matters. The decisions you make will govern your choice of proximity operators and their settings. PROXIMATE also applies to bound phrases, the quotes designating to the search system that it must retrieve this exact string of alphabetic and/or numeric characters. The SPACE & SYMBOL tactic is a reminder that spaces, hyphens, slashes, and other symbols must be considered during data entry. At the very least, enter all three forms of hyphenated words so you don't have to remember how each system handles them (e.g., `coffeehouses`, `coffee-houses`, and `coffee w0 houses`—inserting the system's adjacency operator between). The NICKNAME and PSEUDONYM tactics are reminders to use the search system's FT functionality to represent alternate forms of names that are pseudonyms, acronyms, initials, or nicknames. The FIX tactic refers to stemming or truncation; consult textbox 7.2 for the wide variety of explicit approaches to truncation, and be prepared for implicit truncation in extended-Boolean systems.

The PEARL GROWING tactic was on the first search tactics list published forty years ago. Named TRACE by Bates (1979) and BACKLINK by Smith (2012), it has evolved into the find-like capability of extended-Boolean systems that is PEARL GROWING at the push of a button (pages 185 to 187). Also available to searches at the push of a button are the CITING and CLUSTER tactics. In databases bearing citing references, searchers merely click on the "Citing" link accompanying retrievals to retrieve more recently published sources citing the retrieved one (pages 188 to 191). CITING gets complicated when the impetus for CITING is a relevant source recommended by someone else because you have to conduct a known-item search for the source in Google Scholar, Scopus, or a subject-specific database and then click on its accompanying CITING links. Execute the CLUSTER tactic prior to the search to qualify retrievals by certain aspects (e.g., language, refereed sources, date, audience), or apply CLUSTER to search results to tighten up unfocused queries. The CLUSTER tactic is a trusted friend from the Getting a Little Help from Your Friends Strategy (pages 262 to 265). The ANTICITERM tactic is an oddball—searching a database for a wildcard term in a phrase. Put it to work when you struggle to find just the right word to plug into a sentence you are writing. ANTICITERM could be considered a STRETCH, but Google and other search systems provide a symbol for a wildcard word, so it belongs among the Search Term Tactics.

Evaluation Tactics

Evaluation Tactics are Smith's addition, a deliberate reminder that web-based information requires careful scrutiny on the part of searchers. In table 12.1, all Evaluation Tactics except for AUDITION come from an empirical study of the criteria searchers use to evaluate information from the Web and from licensed databases (Markey, Leeder, and Rieh 2014). AUDITION describes such page elements as graphics, layout, spelling, and grammatical errors that give searchers clues about a source's credibility. Searchers typically enlist the AUTHORSHIP tactic to judge a source's credibility, referring to any number of things about authors and their credentials, reputation, affiliations with named or unnamed organizations, sponsors, publishers, and so on. When searchers execute the two tactics INTERNAL NONCONTENT and EXTERNAL NONCONTENT, they rely on noncontent features of sources, such as currency, cited references, altmetrics, and format, to help them assess relevance and/ or credibility. Searchers enlist CONTENT and IMPETUS tactics to judge a source's relevance. CONTENT refers to the source's subject contents, and IMPETUS refers to the impetus that gave rise to the search.

WIELDING SEARCH TACTICS

All these search tactics may leave you feeling confused and overwhelmed. That's to be expected. In fact, you are probably already confusing tactics with search strategies and the many features of this and that search system. Search-tactic deployment demands all the knowledge you have accumulated about online searching. In time, you'll find yourself at an impasse while conducting an online search, wanting to accomplish something. Reviewing these tactics might help you determine what to do next. This chapter's questions and answers challenge you to break the impasse with search tactics.

For the time being, orient yourself to online searching through the seven steps of the process. Initially, rely on the Building Block Search Strategy, making the choice between Buffet and À la Carte Editions contingent on whether you are searching a Boolean or extended-Boolean system. As your confidence increases, ask yourself whether the Can't Live Without This Facet First Search Strategy makes sense for the query in hand over the Building Block Search Strategy. When a low-posted search sparks your interest in search tactics, review the search tactics list, realize you've been there all along, wielding search system functionality to monitor the ongoing search, navigate the system's file structure, formulate the search, select search terms, and evaluate retrievals.

QUESTIONS

1. With a laptop in hand, sit beside a friend, and search Google (http://www.google .com) for shopping, consumer health, popular culture, or academic topics that interest you (see page 273 for examples). Compare retrievals. If retrievals differ, discuss between yourselves how they differ. What do you think Google is factoring into its personalization algorithm for you that differs from your friend and vice versa? Is it a fair assessment of you? Of your friend? When and why would you want to turn off Google's personalization algorithm?

2. Search Google, Bing (http://www.bing.com), and Ask (http://www.ask.com). Where do these Web search engines place ads, and what visual and verbal cues do they add to help you distinguish ads from retrieved content?

3. Search ABI/Inform, Public Library of Science (PLoS), and your library's WSD system. Which presearch qualifiers and postsearch clusters do they give you to limit retrievals to the most credible, scholarly, and trustworthy ones?

4. Conduct a high-precision search in a discipline-based A&I or full-text database for a topic that is very familiar to you, perhaps one that you researched for a course last semester or even more recently. Review the first two pages of retrievals, assessing relevance on a 0-1-2 scale for not relevant, possibly relevant, and relevant, respectively. Exchange your laptop with a friend, describe your search topic to him, and ask him to assess these same retrievals. Compare your results. Whose relevance assessments are higher? Which one of you is a more positive judge of relevance and why? Switch roles and repeat the exercise. Then debrief with the whole class.

5. You conduct a search of the ERIC database on children's safety using social-networking sites and the Internet generally and retrieve two sources, ED558604 ("Cyberbulling among Children and Teens: A Pervasive Global Issue") and ED573956 ("Young People and E-Safety: The Results of the 2015 London Grid for Learning E-Safety Survey"). Enter these two accession numbers into the ERIC database, and download their full-texts. Perform a technical reading of each source, and based on this reading, decide which is the more high-quality source. Then submit each source to the CRAAP test, rating each source using these questions:

   - **Currency:** Does this topic require current information, and if it does, is the source's information current? (Rate: 0 = not current, 1 = somewhat current, 2 = very current)
   - **Relevance:** Does the information relate to the query? (Rate: 0 = not relevant, 1 = possibly relevant, and 2 = relevant)
   - **Authority:** Who wrote the source? What are the author's credentials, and do they qualify the author to write on this topic? (Rate: 0 = not qualified, 1 = somewhat qualified, 2 = qualified)
   - **Accuracy:** What claims does the author make? Does he support his claims with evidence? (Rate: 0 = no evidence, 1 = some but not enough evidence, 2 = enough evidence)
   - **Purpose:** Is the author's purpose to inform, teach, entertain, sell, or persuade? (Rate: 0 = entertain or sell, 1 = persuade, 2 = inform or teach)

   Calculate CRAAP scores for each source. Which source achieves a higher CRAAP score? Does your initial assessment agree with your CRAAP score? If it doesn't, why doesn't it? Is the CRAAP test a more rigorous way to assess quality than your initial assessment? Why or why not? If you were teaching an information-literacy course, would you recommend the CRAAP test to students? Why or why not?

6. Finding yourself at an impasse while conducting a search is not unusual. The following are examples of typical impasses. Consider each, and then select one or more search tactics that you would exercise to break the impasse. Tell why you chose the tactic(s):

- My retrievals address the topic, but they seem really broad.
- This person wrote much more than I'm retrieving here.
- Why does this nonrelevant topic constantly pop up in my retrievals?
- I know I've chosen the right database, so why can't I find anything on this topic?
- Why aren't my retrievals expressing the _____ facet?
- I'm working with a four-faceted search, and I didn't expect it to produce thousands of relevant retrievals.
- Despite plenty of CV terms for this facet, it seems so underposted in this database.
- This legislation was pivotal. Why am I finding so little about it?

SUMMARY

This chapter covers the seventh and final step of the online searching process: displaying and assessing retrievals and responding tactically to system responses throughout the course of the search. Users expect systems to display the most relevant sources first, so they rarely display more than the first or second page of retrievals. Encourage users to reorder the retrievals display because it's much simpler than what they usually do: enter a new keyword, reenter their original keyword, or project relevance onto the first-listed retrievals.

Searching the Web for free and reading retrieved content actually comes with a price: putting advertising in front of your eyeballs that's tailor-made to your interests. It's your job to impress this on users so they evaluate the information they glean from the Web. To date, licensed search systems have been aboveboard with respect to the search and the display of retrievals. Keep it that way, studying vendor licenses and privacy policies and scrutinizing retrievals to make sure they correspond to your search statements.

Search tactics describe the many ways online searchers can maneuver during the ongoing search. There are five tactic types for monitoring, file structure, search formulation, search terms, and evaluation. Initially, you may be overwhelmed by the many search tactics available to you and confuse them with the seven steps of the online searching process and five search strategies. Start simple, orienting yourself to the online searching process through its seven steps and relying on the Building Block Search Strategy for most searches. Should you find yourself at an impasse with respect to finding relevant retrievals, review search tactics (table 12.1) so they become salient and second nature.

BIBLIOGRAPHY

Bates, Marcia J. 1979. "Information Search Tactics." *Journal of the American Society for Information Science* 30, no. 4: 205–14. Accessed February 18, 2018. http://pages.gseis .ucla.edu/faculty/bates/articles/Information Search Tactics.html.

———. 1987. "How to Use Information Search Tactics Online." *Online* 11, no. 3 (May): 47–54.

Blakeslee, Sarah. 2004. "The CRAAP Test." *LOEX Quarterly* 31. Accessed February 25, 2018. http://commons.emich.edu/cgi/viewcontent.cgi?article=1009&context=loexquarterly.

Broussard, Mary Snyder. 2017. *Reading, Research, and Writing: Teaching Information Literacy with Process-Based Research Assignments.* Chicago: American Library Association.

Buchanan, Heidi E., and Beth A. McDonough 2016. *The One-Shot Library Instruction Survival Guide.* 2nd ed. Chicago: ALA Editions.

Cull, Barry W. 2011. "Reading Revolutions: Online Digital Text and Implications for Reading in Academe." *First Monday* 16, no. 6. Accessed July 1, 2018. http://firstmonday.org/ojs/ index.php/fm/article/view/3340/2985.

Google. 2018a. "How Google Search Works." Accessed July 1, 2018. https://support.google .com/webmasters/answer/70897?hl=en.

———. 2018b. "Search Engine Optimization (SEO) Starter Guide." Accessed July 2, 2018. https://support.google.com/webmasters/answer/7451184?hl=en.

Grassian, Esther S., and Joan R. Kaplowitz. 2009. *Information Literacy Instruction.* 2nd ed. New York: Neal-Schuman.

Information Literacy Group. 2016. "The CRAP! Game: A Lagadothon 2016 Case Study." *Information Literacy* (blog), CILIP Information Literacy Group, September 22. https:// infolit.org.uk/the-crap-game-a-lagadothon-2016-case-study.

Jansen, Bernard J., and Amanda Spink. 2006. "How Are We Searching the World Wide Web? A Comparison of Nine Search Engine Transaction Logs." *Information Processing & Management* 42, no. 1: 248–63.

Leeder, Christopher Alan. 2014. "Scaffolding Students' Information Literacy Skills with an Online Credibility Evaluation Learning Tool." PhD diss., University of Michigan.

Markey, Karen, Chris Leeder, and Soo Young Rieh. 2014. *Designing Online Information Literacy Games Students Want to Play.* Lanham, MD: Rowman & Littlefield.

NISO (National Information Standard Organization). 2014. *Open Discovery Initiative: Promoting Transparency in Discovery.* Baltimore, MD: NISO.

NoodleTools. 2018. "NoodleTools: A Research Platform, An Educational Mindset." Accessed July 1, 2018. https://www.noodletools.com/.

Pan, Bing, Helene Hembrooke, Thorsten Joachims, Lori Lorigo, Gery Gay, and Laura Granka. 2007. "In Google We Trust: Users' Decisions on Rank, Position, and Relevance." *Journal of Computer-Mediated Communication* 12, no. 3: 801–23.

Pariser, Elliot. 2011. *The Filter Bubble: What the Internet Is Hiding from You.* New York: Penguin.

Ragains, Patrick. 2013. *Information Literacy Instruction That Works.* 2nd ed. Chicago: ALA Neal-Schuman.

Ruff, Corinne. 2016. "Scholars Criticize Academia.edu Proposal to Charge Authors for Recommendations." *Chronicle of Higher Education.* Accessed February 19, 2018. https://www.chronicle.com/article/Scholars-Criticize/235102.

Smith, Alistair. 2012. "Internet Search Tactics." *Online* 36, no. 1: 7–20.

Spink, Amanda, Dietmar Wolfram, Bernard J. Jansen, and Tefko Saracevic. 2001. "Searching the Web: The Public and Their Queries." *Journal of the American Society for Information Science and Technology* 52, no. 3: 226–34.

Sweeny, Marianne. 2012. "Optimizing Websites in the Post Panda World." *Bulletin of the American Society for Information Science and Technology* 39, no. 1 (Oct. 1): 17–19.

University of California, Chico. 2010. "Evaluating Information: Applying the CRAAP Test." Accessed July 1, 2018. https://www.csuchico.edu/lins/handouts/eval_websites.pdf.

Unkel, Julian. 2017. "The Effects of Credibility Cues on the Selection of Search Engine Results." *Journal of the Association for Information Science & Technology* 68, no. 8 (Aug.): 1850–62.

SUGGESTED READING

Pariser, Elliot. 2011. *The Filter Bubble: What the Internet Is Hiding from You.* New York: Penguin. Even if we want to be exposed to information from different perspectives, we are thwarted by the very tools we use to find it. Read it also for a thought-provoking analysis of contemporary media in the digital age.

ANSWERS

1. **With a friend, search Google for topics that interest you. Compare retrievals.** Discuss your findings with your friend. When students discuss their experiences in class, we tally results for the whole class with respect to personalization, producing different retrievals for searches on shopping, consumer health, popular culture, and academic topics; whether students think that Google's personalization algorithm represents them fairly; and whether, when, and why they want to turn off Google's personalization algorithm.

2. **Where do Web search engines place ads, and what visual and verbal cues do they add to help you distinguish ads from retrieved content?** Search engines change these cues all the time. Here are some things to look for:

   - Sandwiching retrievals between ads, placing ads above the fold and organic content below them, placing ads on the left (where your vision falls naturally) and organic content on the right.
   - Thin horizontal lines separating ads from organic content, ads spread atop pale-grayish backgrounds or the same-colored background as organic retrievals, boxed image displays of merchandise with clickable links.
   - Headings named "Ad," "Shopping," "Shop for," "Sponsored," or "Ads related to [insert your search statement]" or individual ads looking like organic retrievals bearing title, blue-colored URL, and snippet but accompanied by an "ad" label.

3. **What presearch qualifiers and postsearch clusters do ABI/Inform, PLoS, and your library's WSD system give you to limit retrievals to the most credible, scholarly, and trustworthy ones?**

   - *ABI/Inform:* Toggle the *Peer Reviewed* cluster on. Choose the "Scholarly Journals" from the *Source Type* cluster. Also *Source Types*, such as "Trade Journals," "Dissertations and Theses," "Books," and "Conference Papers and Proceedings," may undergo peer review and editorial scrutiny.
   - *PLoS:* PLoS has no postsearch clusters, but its seven journals are controlled by an editorial board, whose members engage in peer review and the journal's future direction.
   - *WSD system:* Check your library's WSD system for clusters similar to ABI/Inform's.

4. **Conduct a high-precision search and review the first two pages of retrievals, assessing relevance.** When students discuss their experiences in class, we tally results for the whole class with respect to who is the more positive judge of relevance. We find that friends are more positive than query originators but not always. We've hypothesized that the originators know exactly what is and isn't relevant because of their experience using retrievals to complete the assignment connected with the query. In contrast, friends are more positive because they don't have these constraints and prefer to leave things wide open so query originators can use retrieval results as they see fit.

5. **Perform a technical reading of each source, and based on this reading, decide which is the more high-quality source.** Debrief in a class discussion. The CRAAP test you administered is my abridgement of a longer version (Blakeslee 2004). If

you wouldn't recommend the CRAAP test to students in an information-literacy class, what is a comparable alternative?

6. **Select one or more search tactics that you would exercise to break the impasse. Tell why you chose the tactic(s).**

   - *My retrievals address the topic, but they seem really broad.* SUB tactic, adding narrower search terms to one or more facets. SUBDIVIDE tactic, adding subdivided forms of CV terms that express aspects of the unsubdivided main heading to one or more facets.

   - *This person wrote much more than I'm retrieving here.* NEIGHBOR tactic, browsing the database's alphabetical author index and choosing variant forms of this person's name. PSEUDONYM tactic, checking LCNAF and biographical databases for pseudonyms.

   - *Why does this nonrelevant topic constantly pop up in my retrievals?* BLOCK tactic, using the NOT operator to eliminate specific search terms or entire facets of search terms.

   - *I know I've chosen the right database. Why can't I find anything on this topic?* Increase retrievals by adding more search terms to the formulation. Tactics for adding synonymous search terms are SPECIFY, RELATE, SPACE & SYMBOL, and PSEUDONYM; narrower is SUB; and broader is SUPER. Alternatively, let the system choose terms by turning on its automatic vocabulary assistance (AUTO TERM ADD tactic). Consider the NEIGHBOR or CONTRARY tactics to increase search terms. Execute the PROXIMATE and FIX tactics to loosen up word-proximity operators and truncation. If you've identified at least one relevant retrieval, use its CV and FT terms to PEARL GROWING, click on the retrieval's find-like link or click on its citing reference link (CITING tactic).

   - *Why aren't my retrievals expressing the _____ facet?* Execute the HISTORY tactic, reviewing the terminology of your previous search statements and the Boolean logic that connects them. Look for search logic errors, and CORRECT them. If your search terms aren't faithful to the rule of specific entry, then engage the SPECIFICITY tactic, substituting search terms that are as specific as the desired information. Check the form of your search terms, executing the SPELL tactic to correct spelling errors and enter variant forms, NEIGHBOR tactic to browse alphabetically for these forms, SPACE & SYMBOL tactic to enter space and symbol variants, NICKNAME tactic to enter acronyms, initialed, or nicknamed variants, and PSEUDONYM tactic to enter pseudonyms for names.

   - *I'm working with a four-faceted search, and I didn't expect it to produce thousands of relevant retrievals.* Execute the HISTORY tactic, reviewing previous search statements and logic. Check the search logic to make sure it is COR-

RECT; make sure the search statements that combine sets for each facet use the Boolean AND or NOT operators. If they do, execute the CLUSTER tactic, limiting retrievals by one or more nonsubject clusters, such as language, publication date, or peer-reviewed.

- *Despite plenty of CV terms for this facet, it seems so underposted in this database.* Consider the CONTRARY tactic for adding CV terms that are the opposite in meaning. Consider also one or more of the FIELD, PROXIMATE, and FIX tactics for adding free text terms to the formulation.

- *This legislation was pivotal. Why am I finding so little about it?* Consider the NICKNAME, NEIGHBOR, SPELL, or SPACE & SYMBOL tactics for representing variant forms of this legislation's name. (This is an impasse you might experience when searching any type of proper noun, such as a company, organization, place, event, or test.)

13

Performing a Technical Reading of a Database's Search System

This chapter's systematic approach to familiarizing yourself with a database is called performing a technical reading of the database's search system. When you put this technical reading into action, you determine whether the search system is equipped with this or that important information-retrieval feature. When it is so equipped, you are able to make informed decisions about putting each feature to work at achieving your aims. None of these features will be new to you. You've already met them one or more times in chapters 6, 7, 8, and 9. Because their implementation varies across the wide array of available search systems, you might have to take the system for a test drive to figure out how to operate certain features to achieve your aims.

The technical reading requires you to answer questions about the availability and implementation of nine important features in a database's search system. If nine seems like a lot, it is, especially when you take into consideration that you will almost always be pressed for time at the reference desk, making it impossible for you to be thorough in testing how each and every feature works. Thus, this chapter includes recommendations about being selective in your technical reading based on whether you are fact finding in a reference database or searching for a subject or a known-item in a research database.

IS THIS DATABASE RELEVANT? (DATABASE RELEVANCE)

Database relevance isn't an actual feature that the searcher is able to wield or manipulate like setting the intervening-words number on a proximity operator or applying the language qualifier on retrievals. It's more like a quality of the database that the searcher takes into consideration vis-à-vis the user's information need. Get it wrong, and no amount of search functionality will produce relevant retrievals; consequently, database relevance is essential for every user query you undertake.

To select a relevant database, you classify promising databases according to these five attributes: (1) source type (source or surrogate); (2) genre (text, media, numeric and spatial data, or a combination of these); (3) selection principle (subject-specific, encyclopedic, genre- or form-specific); (4) form (reference or research); and (5) editorial control (mediated or non-mediated). Chapter 4 is devoted to this classification, so reread it for details or glance at figure 4.1's graphical depiction of the classification to refresh your memory.

At the very least, you want to match the database's subject coverage with the user's topic of interest. In an academic setting, this can be easy: Just ask the user for more information about the class he is taking or the name of the academic department that offers the class. In a public-library setting, this may be more difficult. You might have to probe, asking the user to clarify the impetus for her query. For example, if a user's query addresses abortion, ask her whether she is interested in the biological, ethical, religious, medical, political, or psychological aspects of the topic, and then choose a database that addresses this topic from the desired perspective.

Consider also the database's intended audience. Recommend databases to users that are in keeping with their levels of sophistication vis-à-vis their topics of interest. For example, if the user is a surgeon looking for a source on a new surgical procedure, recommending that he search a database that specializes in consumer health information isn't going to cut it.

DOES THIS DATABASE'S SEARCH SYSTEM RESPOND TO SEARCH STATEMENTS WITH BOOLEAN OR EXTENDED-BOOLEAN SEARCHES? (BOOLEAN)

Knowing whether a search system responds to your entered search statements with Boolean searching, extended-Boolean searching, or a choice between the two drives how you represent the search as input into the search system and which search strategies are available to you. To determine a search system's Boolean status, a quick visual check may be all that is necessary. This usually involves examining the system's default and advanced interfaces and looking for evidence of these Boolean searching conventions:

1. Two to three separate search boxes
2. Pull-down menus between the search boxes, one listing Boolean operators and possibly a second listing database fields
3. Tips that show sample searches with Boolean operators

For example, a quick visual check of the General Reference Center Gold (GRCG) database reveals an advanced search with all the Boolean trimmings: three separate search boxes, one pull-down menu listing Boolean operators, and a second listing database fields. To double-check, follow up with a search of a sample query. A versatile query is "Ethics for research in [insert a commonplace discipline, field, or profession]"; use these three separate search statements, and enter them successively in this order:

```
ethics

ethics AND research

ethics AND research AND [insert discipline]
```

Compare their retrievals. A Boolean search system would produce fewer retrievals for successive search statements, and an extended-Boolean system would produce more retrievals for successive search statements. Entering these three statements into GRCG, with the search term `medicine` added to the third, produces about 91,000, about 21,000, and about 3,400 retrievals. This is almost proof positive that GRCG is a Boolean system. A final check is dropping the Boolean AND operators from these search statements. Here are the results:

```
ethics ~ about 91,000 retrievals

ethics research ~ about 1,000 retrievals

ethics research medicine ~ exactly 5 retrievals
```

Again, GRCG produces fewer retrievals for successive search statements. Without a doubt, GRCG is a Boolean search system; however, statements bereft of Boolean AND operators retrieve far fewer retrievals than statements bearing Boolean AND operators. Evidently, excluding the Boolean AND operator puts into effect a more stringent retrieval condition, possibly the occurrence of all three search words in a single field or paragraph. It's hard to tell in the absence of details from GRCG about its proprietary retrieval and ranking algorithms.

On rare occasions, you'll find a search system that offers both Boolean and extended-Boolean searching. EBSCOhost is such a system. A visual check reveals four options available to searchers on both its basic and advanced-search interfaces:

1. Boolean/phrase
2. Find all my search terms
3. Find any of my search terms
4. SmartText searching

Clearly, the first option is a Boolean search because it is labeled as such. So is the second because, to retrieve sources bearing all your search terms, the system has to perform the Boolean AND operation. EBSCOhost's third option is an extended-Boolean search; the system inserts an implicit Boolean OR operator between each

search term and then conducts the search. For example, entering the search statement ethics research history into EBSCOhost's America: History and
Life database produces more than 520,000 retrievals. That the user is able to find
relevant retrievals is due to EBSCOhost's retrievals-relevance ranking that puts
relevant retrievals at the top of the list. By the way, entering this same query via
EBSCOhost's first option (i.e., ethics OR research OR history) retrieves the same 520,000 retrievals. The fourth option is called SmartText searching,
EBSCOhost's brand name for its extended-Boolean search. By the way, no matter
which of the four search options you choose, EBSCOhost's relevance-ranking algorithm kicks in, placing the most relevant retrievals atop the list.

Here's how you put your knowledge about a search system's Boolean or extended-
Boolean nature to work. In Boolean systems, you choose the Building Block Search
Strategy's Buffet Edition, entering search statements with multiple synonymous
terms for each facet. In extended-Boolean systems, you choose the Building Block
Search Strategy's À la Carte Edition, entering search statements with one search
term per facet, and if your initial search statement fails to produce enough relevant
retrievals, you can follow up with subsequent search statements, substituting a synonym for one or more facets.

WHAT DOCUMENT REPRESENTATION DO MY SEARCH STATEMENTS SEARCH?
(DOC REP)

When you enter a search statement, systems default to searching surrogates, full-texts,
a combination of the two, or "something else." The quickest way to check what document representation they search is to mouse down on the database's fields pull-down
menu accompanying the search box. (Such a menu is almost always present in a
system's advanced-search interface.) See if there is a field label named something like
"Full-Text," "Document Text," "All Text Fields," or "Entire Document," and if there is,
it's a good (but not a sure) sign that your search statements extend to full-texts. To be
sure, you'll have to enter a sample query, preferably one that produces a handful of retrievals, and then display these retrievals, looking for matches of your input words and
phrases in both surrogates and full-texts. Unfortunately, all this takes time and effort.
Less time-consuming is your gut reaction to retrievals. If your searches of this database
consistently produce larger numbers of retrievals than you'd expect, there's a good
chance that your search statements are retrieving from both surrogates and full-texts.

Here's how you put your knowledge about your selected database's default document representation to work. If precision is important, populate your search statements with CV terms and an occasional FT term; retrievals will be fewer and almost
exclusively due to matches in surrogates because CV terms come from surrogate
fields. If recall is important, free-text searching is the way to go, but check retrievals to

make sure top-listed ones are relevant. If they aren't or you think the database could do a better job, then rethink your search statements. Here's how to do it. In a Boolean search system, replace the Boolean operators that combine facets with proximity operators and tighten up the proximity operators that bind words into phrases. In an extended-Boolean search system, you can add a relationship facet (if the query calls for one) or reorder your search terms, making sure the most important one comes first.

If you are conducting a known-item search, switch to the system's advanced interface, mouse down on the pull-down menu, and match your field selection(s) with your available data. For example, if you have publisher, author, or title data in hand, choose the publisher, author, or title field, respectively. If there are no fields corresponding to your data, limit the search to surrogate fields generally. If you've got a passage from the text in hand, limit the search to the full-text; even better would be searching for this text in a database that an extended-Boolean system searches, just in case the passage isn't an exact representation of the text you have in hand.

Now for the "something else." Search systems default to searching document representations that they expect will be effective for the vast majority of incoming queries. For example, a business directory and a substances dictionary might default to searches of company names and chemical names, respectively. Although this "something else" is typical of specialized databases, on occasion, a mainstream database expects subject queries and limits retrievals to subject-rich fields (also called basic index), such as titles, index terms, abstracts, and full-texts (when available), and omits nonsubject fields, such as publisher, author, author affiliation, and place of publication. If your retrievals aren't on the mark, double-check your selected database's default document representation, and if it doesn't have potential for producing relevant retrievals, change it by making selections from the database's fields pull-down menu.

WHICH FIELDS CAN I BROWSE? (BROWSE)

Browsing the indexed values in a database's fields enables you to determine the exact values used to express ideas, concepts, objects, events, and names. Index browsing is mandatory in databases devoid of authority control to gather all variant forms, particularly in the case of authors, journal titles, publisher names, and author affiliations. The OPAC is one of the few remaining database types in which authority control is the rule rather than the exception. For all other databases, compensate by browsing indexes. Unfortunately, browsing is not always available, or when it is, it hasn't been applied to the field that interests you.

To determine whether a search system offers browsing, switch to its advanced interface, and look for a link called "Indexes," "Browsing," "Browse Indexes," or "[insert field name] begins with." Another implementation type is your selection of a field where the system displays a prompt, such as "Look up [insert field name]," "Start of [insert field name]," or "[insert field name] begins with," to which you respond by entering a title, author name, publisher, or other information. Enter as much text as you think is necessary for the system to open its alphabetical display of your selected index at a location where your desired entry is filed. For example, entering three or four letters might suffice for finding the unique name of a company, but you might have to enter the full name of a company with a common name to find the right one. Some indexes include qualifiers to distinguish between entries. For example, personal-name indexes bear qualifiers for birth and death dates, occupations, gender, and/or nationality so you can distinguish the "John Brown" that interests you over the many other "John Browns" that are indexed in the database.

Known-item searching and index browsing go hand in hand. If the search system offers browsing for the field where your desired value is likely to be filed, just do it! Choose a search system that excels at index browsing—Engineering Village and EBSCOhost are two of my favorites. Find your own favorites, and make a mental note of or record on a cheat sheet the search systems that excel at this feature. On occasion, the right database for the information you need is accessed by a search system that displays index values but doesn't let you select them. You'll see systems that do the same for their thesaurus displays. It's hard to believe that search systems would implement browsing in such a half-baked manner, but it happens. When you encounter browsing implemented in this way, your only alternative is to copy and paste or jot down relevant values on a notepad, and then follow up and enter these values directly into the system's search box using its FT searching language.

DOES THIS DATABASE SEARCH THE CONTROLLED VOCABULARY'S SYNDETIC STRUCTURE? (CV)

Chapter 6 is devoted exclusively to CV searching, so it needs no introduction here. To launch a database's CV in search of relevant index terms for a query's facets, look for a link or tab named "Thesaurus," "Thesaurus Search," "Search Tools," or bearing the words *classification*, *tree*, or *hierarchy*. When the thesaurus opens, look for a network of index-term relationships—BTs, NTs, RTs, and UFs. This is its syndetic structure. Selecting terms from this network is easy. Just make sure the system combines synonymous CV terms for each facet in a Boolean OR operation. Then it's the search system's job to add its CV searching language to your selected terms so that retrieval is limited to the database's CV fields. Chapter 6 demonstrates this simple process using the Humor query (pages 118 to 124).

Some databases have a CV with a syndetic structure, but their search systems don't let you select CV terms from displays. You have to create a work-around, such as displaying CV terms and jotting down relevant ones on a notepad. To enter these terms manually, you'll have to learn the search system's CV searching language. Chapter 6 gets you started on CV searching language and shows how to search for single words in relevant CV terms (pages 127 to 128). Other databases have a CV with a flat structure, devoid of BTs, NTs, and RTs, placing the burden on you to think of all the possible CV terms and search this flat structure to see if the terms you have in mind are CV terms. If these terms aren't selectable, then CV searching becomes doubly burdensome, requiring you to do everything manually. Personally, I avoid flat-structured CVs. I might check them for high-posted CV terms for my query's facets, but I incorporate these terms into my search statements using the system's FT searching language.

WHICH PRESEARCH QUALIFIERS ARE AVAILABLE? (QUALIFIERS)

Most Boolean systems accompany search boxes with presearch qualifiers. These qualifiers enable you to limit retrievals by subject aspects (e.g., *Age Groups, Population Groups, Regions*, etc.) or nonsubject aspects (e.g., *Date of Publication, Language, Intended Audience*, etc.) of the query at the same time you enter your search statements. CV is built into presearch qualifiers because you choose predetermined values from qualifier lists. Thus, selecting a presearch qualifier value avoids problems arising from misspelled words, embedded symbols, initials, etc.

Presearch qualifiers are database-specific, so don't expect your favorite presearch qualifiers to show up across the board. Some databases don't have presearch qualifiers, and other databases have so many qualifiers that you could use them to set up the entire search. For example, PsycINFO is especially generous, giving you twenty presearch qualifiers to choose from. Choosing its classification codes "2953 Divorce & Remarriage" and "3260 Eating Disorders" along with "Adolescence" from the *Age Groups* presearch qualifier is an exceptionally quick way to perform the Eating Disorders search. In fact, you may come to prefer selecting a database's subject presearch qualifiers over building retrieval sets using CV and FT terms because qualifiers are time savers—you select one blanket term instead of browsing and selecting multiple CV terms or manually entering multiple FT terms. Unfortunately, presearch qualifiers don't always have values that are sufficiently specific for representing every facet in a multifaceted query. By the way, you will almost always encounter a database's presearch qualifiers in the form of its postsearch clusters, so you might want to wait until you know how many sources your subject search statements retrieve before you apply them.

Your objective in known-item searches is to reduce retrievals to the one source you are seeking. Thus, consider applying a database's nonsubject presearch qualifiers to the search formulation because they may reduce retrievals to so few that you can eyeball them for the one you want. You probably know the desired source's form or genre and its language and have a vague idea about publication date, so check relevant values in your selected database's *Source Types, Language*, and *Date of Publication* presearch qualifiers, respectively.

CAN I COMBINE PREVIOUSLY CREATED SETS? (SETS)

Sets functionality is characteristic of Boolean search systems. It comes in four different flavors: (1) no sets creation; (2) sets creation and display only; (3) sets creation, display, and editing; or (4) sets creation, display, editing, and combination. Flavor 1 is hardly useful because the system provides you with no record of previously entered search terms and logic. If you want to make a record, you have to do so manually on a notepad. Flavor 2 overcomes the limitations of flavor 1, enabling you to review previously entered search terms, check your logic, and display previously retrieved sources, but you can only see what you've done. You can't change anything. Flavor 3 allows you to edit what you've done; for example, adding new search terms, deleting less-than-satisfactory search terms, correcting spelling and logic errors, or tightening up or relaxing proximity operators and truncation. Unfortunately, you're stuck with working within the constraints of your original search statement. Flavor 4 is the most flexible, allowing you to do everything flavor 3 allows you to do, plus combining previously created sets with Boolean and/or proximity operators.

To determine whether your selected database creates sets, look for a link or tab entitled "Search History," "Previous Sets," or "Previous Searches." Typically, combining sets involves clicking on the "Search History" link; checkmarking set numbers; and choosing the Boolean AND, OR, or NOT operators from a nearby pull-down menu to combine them. Alternatively, enter a Boolean expression directly into the search box with a pound sign (#) or the set abbreviation letter s appended to the set number. Examples are:

```
#1 AND #2

(s1 OR s2 OR s3) AND s4
```

WHAT IS THIS SYSTEM'S FREE TEXT SEARCHING LANGUAGE? (FT)

Chapters 7 and 8 are devoted exclusively to FT searching, so it needs no introduction here. To learn a search system's free text searching language, you really have to consult its online help. At the very least, you want to know the search system's:

- Boolean operators. Usually these operators are called AND, OR, and NOT. An alternative for NOT is AND NOT. Some systems don't offer the NOT operator.
- Bound phrase searching (also called adjacency and word order matters). Many systems accept quotes to bind word strings into phrases. Examples are "leadership training" and "school nurses."
- Proximity operators. There are two basic proximity operators, one for word order matters and a second for word order doesn't matter. These operators allow you to set a number from 0 or 1 to an upper limit that specifies how many intervening

words can separate your search words. Each search system has its own syntax for proximity operators, so check the system's online help for details.

- Truncation. Typically, search systems default to retrieving simple singular, plural, and possessive forms of your search terms but not always. At the very least, systems offer unlimited right-hand truncation so you can retrieve words and their many different endings. Variable truncation is handy, but few systems offer it. Expect each search system to have its own syntax for truncation, and don't expect them to have all of textbox 7.2's truncation functionality types.
- Nested Boolean logic. Almost all Boolean search systems accept your use of parentheses to designate which operations to perform first, second, third, and so on.

Sets, search history, and set-combination functionality aren't mandatory features for FT searching, but they sure are helpful. In their absence, you can devise such workarounds as making notes on a notepad and cutting and pasting text into reformulated search statements.

Remembering the fine details connected with a system's searching language is difficult unless you search the system on a daily basis. Consider consolidating the searching languages for the systems you search on a less-than-daily basis into cheat sheets and filing them into a print-based or electronic notebook that accompanies you to the reference desk and the information-literacy classes you teach. By the way, when search systems give you more than one approach to FT searching, record on your cheat sheets the way that is typical of the majority of the search systems you use so you'll have less to remember.

Your searches of extended-Boolean search systems are FT searches, but FT searching language isn't needed because these systems' indexing, searching, and ranking algorithms do automatically what searchers of Boolean systems must do deliberately with FT searching language. To formulate a search statement for such a system, simply enter the names of the facets, putting the most important facet name first, and hit the "Search" button. For additional retrievals, replace facet names with other words and phrases you generated for each facet, and conduct successive searches until you've accumulated enough relevant retrievals.

Associated with high recall, FT searching is embraced by expert searchers who aim to retrieve as much relevant material on a topic as they can. FT searching is the only way to retrieve information on new phenomena. Even after literary warrant kicks in and a CV is established for the phenomenon, searchers will want to search retrospectively for early material, and FT is the only way to do it.

WHICH POSTSEARCH CLUSTERS ARE AVAILABLE? (CLUSTERS)

Postsearch clusters benefit users whose search topics are unfocused, diffuse, or broad. Although clusters are discussed in conjunction with CV searching (pages 135 to 140), search systems that feature clusters produce them in response to CV searches, FT searches, or a combination of the two. Postsearch clusters are more characteristic of Boolean than extended-Boolean search systems. Cluster types and names vary from system to system. In general, subject clusters with such names as *Subjects, Controlled Vocabulary, Major Subjects, Academic Discipline, Region*, and *Classification Codes* may reveal ideas users hadn't thought of previously or describe an aspect of their topic that piques their interest. Some nonsubject clusters, such as *Document Type, Language, Year of Publication*, and *Full-Text*, may be useful for reducing high-posted searches using criteria that won't change the subject. Other nonsubject clusters, such as *Target Audience, Peer Review*, and *Document Type*, may pitch subject matter in ways that are suited to users at various levels of domain knowledge sophistication and technicality. Nonsubject clusters, such as *Author, Publication Title, Publisher*, and *Author Affiliation*, may be especially helpful in low-posted searches, revealing authors, journal titles, publishers, or research centers pursuing the research, topic, or line of inquiry that interests the user. Promote clusters to users, even to the point of demonstrating how they work to further unfocused queries.

PERFORMING A COMPREHENSIVE OR TRUNCATED TECHNICAL READING

If you have time to study a particular database's search system, be comprehensive about your technical reading, and scrutinize the availability and implementation of all nine features. You can adjust the order of the technical reading's features to suit your needs. Take each feature for a test drive using a sample search. Apply your knowledge of the search system to answer the user query at hand. Jot down notes about the system on a cheat sheet for future reference.

Most likely, you'll be rushed to use a database for the first time because the user is right there, expecting a quick response from you, so it makes sense to limit your consideration to features that enable you to answer the query. What follows are a handful of truncated technical readings based on your typecasting of the query as a subject or known-item. They don't run the gamut, so feel free to devise your own selective technical readings or revise these five to accommodate your institution's users and database collections and your personal preferences. Each selective technical reading references system features using the parenthetical word or phrase trailing each of this chapter's earlier headings, bolding it, and putting it in italics. All readings begin with **Database Relevance**, scrutinizing a database's source type, genre, selection principle, form, and editorial control to convince you of its relevance for the query at hand.

Subject Searching Using Controlled Vocabulary

Mandatory features are **Database Relevance**, **CV**, and **Qualifiers**, while keeping **Boolean, Doc Rep**, and **Sets** in mind.

When the user's query calls for a subject search in a reference or research database, check your selected database for **CV**. CV is a high-precision tool and relieves you of acquiring much knowledge of the system's searching language. On occasion, pre-search **Qualifiers** provide values that can be used to represent one or more facets of the query, and adding them to the search relieves you of acquiring much knowledge of the system's searching language. Most CV-equipped databases are **Boolean**-based, but double-check just in case. **Sets** help you store and combine intermediary search statement results into a final answer set. When searching reference databases, prefer the Can't Live Without This Facet First Strategy because their **Doc Reps** are so brief that introducing multiple facets are likely to reduce retrievals to zero. When searching research databases, you have a choice between Building Block (Buffet Edition for Boolean systems and À la Carte Edition for extended-Boolean systems), Can't Live Without This Facet First, and Pearl Growing Search Strategies.

Subject Searching Using Controlled Vocabulary Plus Clusters to Focus Unfocused Queries

Mandatory features are **Database Relevance**, **CV**, **Qualifiers**, and **Clusters**, while keeping **Boolean** and **Sets** in mind.

The only difference between this mandatory features list and the list preceding it is the inclusion of **Clusters**. When users approach you with unfocused queries, invoke **Clusters** because of their ability to give users ideas about developing their topics. Whether searching reference or research databases, prefer the Getting a Little Help from Your Friends Strategy.

Subject Searching Using Free Text

Mandatory features are **Database Relevance**, **FT**, and **Boolean**, while keeping **Doc Rep** and **Sets** in mind.

In the absence of **CV**, **FT** searching is a powerful alternative. Plus, **FT** is the only way to search for new topics for which there is no literary warrant for inclusion in a CV. Test the search system to determine its **Boolean** status. A Boolean system triggers your selection of the Building Block Search Strategy's Buffet Edition, and an extended-Boolean system triggers this strategy's À la Carte Edition. **Doc Reps** fills in your knowledge of what you are searching—surrogates, full-texts, or a combination of the two—so that you can make adjustments to the facet analysis and your use of the system's FT searching language. **Sets** are characteristic of Boolean search systems, and they enable you to store and combine intermediary search statement results into a final answer set. When searching reference databases, prefer the Can't Live Without This Facet First Strategy. When searching research databases, you have a choice between Building Block (Buffet Edition for Boolean systems and À la

Carte Edition for extended-Boolean systems), Can't Live Without This Facet First, and Pearl Growing Search Strategies.

Subject Searching Using Free Text Plus Clusters to Focus Unfocused Queries

Mandatory features are **Database Relevance**, **FT**, **Boolean**, and **Clusters**, while keeping **Doc Reps** and **Sets** in mind.

The only difference between this mandatory features list and the list preceding it is the inclusion of **Clusters**. Invoke **Clusters** when users approach you with unfocused queries because of this feature's ability to give users ideas about developing their topics. Whether searching reference or research databases, prefer the Getting a Little Help from Your Friends Strategy.

Known-Item Searching Using Browsing

Mandatory features are **Database Relevance**, **Doc Reps**, and **Browse**, while keeping **Boolean** and **FT** in mind.

Known-item searching in reference or research databases begins with **Database Relevance**. Focus on **Doc Reps** and **Browse** next to determine which fields the search system allows you to search and browse. For example, to find an author, you want to browse author fields in surrogates and bylines in full-texts, and to find author affiliations, you want to browse author-affiliation fields in surrogates or full-texts. The search system's **Boolean** status is important. In a Boolean system, study the field labels in its advanced interface, choosing the one that has the greatest promise for matching the known-item data you have in hand. Prefer **Browsing** this field's inverted index to find the desired information. In the absence of browsing, you'll have to conduct a **FT** search. In an extended-Boolean system, see if its advanced search offers index browsing. If it doesn't, you can conduct **FT** searches, entering as much known-item data as you have in hand. If **FT** searches fail, scale back on the known-item data you've entered, and try again. Prefer the Can't Live Without This Facet First Strategy for your searches of reference databases.

QUESTIONS

Accompanying each of these sample queries are a suggested database and truncated technical readings type. Choose a query that interests you to familiarize yourself with the suggested database's search system. Limit yourself to the truncated technical reading type or be comprehensive, examining how this database's search system stacks up vis-à-vis all nine features. Use the query to take the search system for a test drive. As always, conduct a facet analysis and logical combination for the query. Turn to "Answers" at the end of this chapter for a debriefing.

1. Query: How are games being used to teach information literacy? Suggested database: INSPEC. Truncated technical reading type: Subject Searching Using CV.

2. Query: Has a teacher armed with a weapon ever shot an assailant in a school? Suggested database: NewsBank. Truncated technical reading type: Subject Searching Using FT.

3. Query: You glean this information from the user: It's a new book, it's published by the University of Michigan Press, and it's about Michigan's trees and forests. In fact, she remembers that its cover shows a bunch of trees reflected in the water. Suggested database: Your library's OPAC. Truncated technical reading type: Known-Item Searching Using Browsing.

4. Query: Is the opioid crisis primarily a rural or urban problem? Suggested database: General Reference Center Gold (GRCG). Truncated technical reading type: Subject Searching Using CV.

5. Query: The social, economic, and political hopes and aspirations of African Americans after the Great War. Database: JStor. Truncated technical reading type: Subject Searching Using FT with Clusters to Focus Unfocused Queries.

6. Query: A user wants to read a biography about a woman who worked in the US Attorney General's Office during Prohibition, but she can't remember her name. Suggested database: Google. Truncated technical reading type: This appears to be a known-item search, but the user doesn't provide enough information, so you've got to put subject searching using FT to work at revealing the identity of the known-item.

7. Query: Youngsters want to know what famous people were born in their hometown for various school projects. Suggested database: Marquis's Who's Who (Wikipedia is a relevant web-based alternative). Truncated technical reading type: Known-Item Searching Using Browsing.

SUMMARY

When you've got free time to explore a database over which you want to achieve a larger measure of expertise and mastery, use chapter 13's technical reading of a database's search system to develop a comprehensive and systematic approach for familiarizing yourself with a system's most important features. Adjust the order of the technical reading's features to suit your needs.

You're more likely to be in a rush to use a database for the first time because the user is right there, expecting a quick response from you, so perform a truncated technical reading that limits your consideration to features you are most likely to use under the circumstances at hand. Chapter 13 presents five truncated technical readings, and your choice between readings is based on your typecasting of the query as a subject or known-item. Feel free to devise your own truncated technical readings or revise the five presented here to accommodate your institution's users and database collections and your personal preferences.

ANSWERS

1. **How are games being used to teach information literacy?** Facet analysis and logical combination: **Games** AND **Information Literacy**

   With respect to **Database Relevance**, INSPEC has this classification: (1) source type = source, (2) genre = text, (3) selection principle = specific disciplines in the sciences and social sciences, (4) form = research, and (5) editorial control = mediated.

   Clicking twice on "+Add a Search Field" adds search boxes separated by pull-down menus for Boolean operators and fields. These are clues that INSPEC's Engineering Village (EV) search system runs on **Boolean**. Under "Search," choose "Thesaurus" and enter games. EV responds with a thesaurus from which you can display the CV's syndetic structure, select synonymous **CV** terms, and combine them with the Boolean OR operator. Choose the two relevant **CV** terms "Computer games" and "Games of skill," making sure the Boolean OR operator is activated. Repeat the thesaurus look-up, this time for information literacy. Choose its "use" reference "Information science education." Under "Search," choose "Search History," and combine your two **Sets**, either by filling in the check box beside each set or by entering #1 AND #2 into the search box. Scanning retrievals for relevance, you notice three retrievals by *Online Searching*'s author.

2. **Has a teacher armed with a weapon ever shot an assailant in a school?** Online Searching's author. Facet analysis and logical combination: **Armed** AND **Teacher** AND **Shoot** AND **Assailant**

   With respect to **Database Relevance**, NewsBank has this classification: (1) source type = source, (2) genre = text, (3) selection principle = encyclopedic, (4) form = research, and (5) editorial control = mediated.

   Newspapers provide a daily historical record of both domestic and foreign events, so a current newspaper database is relevant for satisfying this query. News-Bank's default interface bears two search boxes with a pull-down menu set at the Boolean AND operator, obvious clues that it is a **Boolean** search system. News-Bank has no CV, so it's **FT** all the way. Use a general-purpose thesaurus and your personal experience reading newspaper stories to generate search terms for each facet. Then dress up these terms in the proximity operators ADJN (word order matters) and NEARN (word order does not matter), use quotes for bound phrases, and apply an asterisk (*) for unlimited truncation. Search statements retrieve both surrogates and full-texts. In lieu of **Sets** is NewsBank's "View History" link; click on this link to display previous search statements and retrievals; editing previous statements produces an entirely new search. Here is a sample search statement for the sample query:

```
(arm*   OR   carry*   OR   conceal*)   near3   (teacher*   OR
educator*) NEAR5 (stop* OR deter* OR kill* OR shot OR
shoot OR shooting OR injur* OR overpower* OR subdue*)
NEAR5 (assailant* OR shooter* OR attacker* OR terrorist*
OR aggressor*)
```

3. **A new book published by the University of Michigan Press about Michigan's trees and forests.** Facet analysis and logical combination: **University of Michigan Press** AND **Forests** AND **Michigan**

   With respect to ***Database Relevance***, your library's OPAC has this classification: (1) source type = surrogate, (2) genre = text, (3) selection principle = encyclopedic, (4) form = research, and (5) editorial control = mediated.

   OPACs index surrogates for the library's monograph collection (***Doc Rep***). While failing to cite the book's author or provide an exact title, the user knows its publisher and subject. Your check of the U-M's classic OPAC for a browsing capability of the publisher field comes up empty-handed. Your only option is to conduct a subject search using ***FT***. A quick glance at its advanced-search interface reveals this OPAC's ***Boolean*** status. The Can't Live Without This Facet First Strategy applies to reference queries. The **University of Michigan Press** facet is the one facet that is most concrete, but searching for it alone will produce too many retrievals. Add the **Forests** facet to the mix to reduce retrievals to a manageable size. To search the OPAC, choose "Publisher" from the fields pull-down menu and enter `university of michigan press`, and choose "Subject word(s)" from the fields pull-down menu and enter `forests OR trees`. Reordering the retrievals display by "Year" puts this promising retrieval first, with a cover showing a bunch a trees reflected in the water: Dickmann, Donald I., and Larry A. Leefers. 2016. *The Forests of Michigan*. Ann Arbor: University of Michigan Press. Show this to the user to determine if this is the desired book.

4. **Is the opioid crisis primarily a rural or urban problem?** Facet analysis and logical combination: **Opioids** AND **Rural** AND **Urban**

   With respect to ***Database Relevance***, GRCG has this classification: (1) source type = source, (2) genre = text, (3) selection principle = encyclopedic, (4) form = research, and (5) editorial control = mediated.

   Prominent on this database's basic search is a link for a "Subject Guide Search," most likely this database's source of ***CV*** terms. Testing it reveals that it is limited to the selection of one CV term at a time. Use it as a source of CV terms, but you'll have to jot down relevant terms on paper or an electronic sticky note. GRCG's **Sets** feature is type 3, allowing editing but no sets combination. More efficient than the original plan of using **CV** is a switch to **FT** searching. Opening GRCG's advanced interface reveals three search boxes with a pull-down menu set at the Boolean AND operator, obvious clues that it is a **Boolean** search system. Here's the skinny on GRCG's FT searching language: A trailing asterisk performs unlimited trunca-tion, quotes around a phrase sets up adjacency and word order matters, and use WN for word order matters and NN for word order doesn't matter. Enter FT search terms into separate search boxes and make sure the AND operator is selected from the Boolean operators pull-down menu. Mixing Boolean and proximity operators produces an error message. A source database, GRCG produces retrievals from both surrogates and full-texts (**Doc Rep**). Here are two sample search statements, one that is faithful to the Building Block Search Strategy's Buffet Edition and one to its À la Carte Edition:

- `(opioid* OR painkiller* OR oxycodone OR oxycontin OR fentanyl OR "pain killer*") AND (rural* OR countryside OR "ranch life" or "mountain life") AND (urban OR cities OR city OR "metropolitan area*" OR "suburb*")`
- `opioid* N25 rural N25 urban`

5. **The social, economic, and political hopes and aspirations of African Americans after the Great War.** Facet analysis and logical combination: **African Americans** AND **World War I**

   With respect to **Database Relevance**, JStor has this classification: (1) source type = source, (2) genre = text, (3) selection principle = social sciences, (4) form = research, and (5) editorial control = mediated.

   Checking JStor's interface for links to a thesaurus fails to reveal one. Thus, **FT** searching is the way to go. JStor's default interface is a single search box, but its advanced interface reveals two search boxes separated by a pull-down menu bearing both Boolean and proximity operators. This is evidence that JStor is a **Boolean** search system. If you test JStor using the Television Violence sample search, your conclusion would be its almost total reliance on FT searching of full-texts (**Doc Reps**). Surrogates are minimal, most restricted to citations and lacking abstracts. Thus, it will be necessary to replace Boolean operators with proximity operators for combining facets so that retrievals bear your search terms nearby, not pages away. Into the two search boxes that make up JStor's advanced inter-face, enter the two facet names as bound phrases, `"african americans"` and `"world war i,"` and pull down the Boolean operators menu, replacing the default Boolean AND with the proximity operator NEAR 5 or NEAR 10. Surprise! JStor responds with an error message telling you that it cannot combine phrases with proximity operators. After much trial and error, my students found the solution: Enter both search terms in one string, put single quotes around each phrase, enclose the string in double quotes, and add a trailing proximity operator telling JStor how close these phrases should be. Here's the string that you enter into a single search box:

```
"'african americans' 'world war i'"~15
```

JStor's lone cluster features *Subjects*. To represent the query's "social, economic, and political hopes and aspirations" component, apply such cluster values as "Business," "Economics," "Political Science," "Public Policy," and "Sociology." JStor has no *Sets*, but clicking on the "Modify Search" link displays your last search statement for editing.

6. **A biography about a woman who worked in the US Attorney General's Office during Prohibition.** Facet analysis and logical combination: **Woman** AND **Attorney General** AND **Prohibition**

    With respect to ***Database Relevance***, Google has this classification: (1) source type = source, (2) genre = text and media, (3) selection principle = encyclopedic, (4) form = reference or research, and (5) editorial control = non-mediated.

    A Web search engine, Google is powered by extended-***Boolean*** retrieval; thus, Boolean operators aren't needed. Google searches entire Web pages (***Doc Rep***), and while its advanced search allows the searcher to qualify results, there are no features for index ***Browsing*** or limiting the search to certain fields (***Qualifiers***). Your only option is a subject search using ***FT*** search terms from the user's query. Because few women were in positions of power one hundred years ago, putting the search term for the **Woman** facet first might give it greater weight beside the bound phrase for the **Attorney General** facet. Enter this search statement into Google:

```
woman "attorney general" prohibition
```

    Google tops its retrieval list with a Wikipedia entry for Mabel Walker Willebrandt. This entry includes several biographies on Willebrandt. Follow up with searches of your library's OPAC to see which ones are available for the user.

7. **Youngsters want to know what famous people were born in their hometown for various school projects.** Facet analysis and logical combination: **Birthplace**

    With respect to ***Database Relevance***, Marquis's Who's Who has this classification: (1) source type = source, (2) genre = text, (3) selection principle = encyclopedic, (4) form = reference, and (5) editorial control = mediated.

Sample searches for people's names reveals that Marquis searches biographical entries bearing over a dozen fields (***Doc Rep***) including one named "Birth Place." No index ***Browsing*** is available for this field so your only recourse is to conduct ***FT*** searches of this ***Boolean***-based system. Into the "Birth Place" search box, enter your hometown and state for a list of people born there. Qualifying by gender or political affiliation involves selecting values from a controlled list. Qualifying by occupation, company/organization, college/university, hobbies, etc., aren't controlled. For example, into the occupation field are these values to represent the educator occupation: "educator," "prof. [insert subject]," "univ. prof.," "[insert subject] professor," "coll. prof.," etc. Thus, resist the temptation to qualify searches except for ones bearing choices from pull-down menus or radio buttons.

Wikipedia reacts entirely differently to hometown searches. As you enter `list of people from [insert hometown name]`, its search system produces a drop-down list from which you can select your hometown. Then browse the entry's categories such as Artists, Authors, Bands, Composers, Musicians, etc. Note the length of the Marquis and Wikipedia lists along with unique entries and entries common to both lists.

14

Interacting with Library Users

This chapter picks up with the postsearch phases of the reference interview. Explored is system functionality that enables you to share your search results with users and to use the reference interview to alert users to the wide range of retrievals-handling functionality. This includes citation management systems (CMSs), specialized software for managing retrievals, and more.

At http://www.onlinesearching.org/p/14-interacting.html is a soup-to-nuts video that summarizes everything you need to think about when helping users find the information they want.

Beginning with sources management, this chapter walks through the seven steps of the online searching process, identifying content that is appropriate for your teaching efforts. It also suggests that you prepare for sustained teaching events, especially half- and full-semester courses and workshop series, with a syllabus, lesson plans, and teaching materials.

RETRIEVALS FOR THE LONG HAUL

At the academy, users might not perceive the benefits of saving, organizing, and reusing online sources until they commit to a discipline or decide on a career path that involves a culminating experience, such as a capstone project, portfolio, or thesis. Then they find themselves scrambling to find sources from previous projects in the folders of their personal computers or among their many Web browser bookmarks. Failing that, they backtrack, searching the open Web, Google Scholar, or their favorite licensed databases for sources they've seen before. Reuse also concerns public-library users—they want to send a friend or family member an online source that they read months ago, or they are working on a long-term project, such as a family history, invention, or patent application. In such cases, saving online sources becomes almost mandatory so that users can refer to them repeatedly during the course of their projects and long afterward. Saving sources comes in all different flavors. It varies from system to system and extends to third-party software applications called CMSs.

Saving Features in Search Systems

Saving begins with you, the reference librarian, sharing an ongoing search with a user. You get the user started, conduct an entire or partial search for him, and then send him a link to your search. In some systems (e.g., ScienceDirect), saving may be as simple as copying the URL in your Web browser's address bar and pasting it into an email message to the user. In other systems, a few extra steps may be necessary. For example, in EBSCOhost, mouse down on the system's "Share" button on the top-right side of the retrievals list, copy the URL in the rectangular box labeled "Permalink," and paste it into an email message to the user (figure 14.1). When permalinks are encoded with your institution's proxy server, clicking on the link should launch the database and restore the search so that the user can pick up where you left off.

Saving the search is also an option for the user who is searching at his own personal computer or at a public workstation. The user signs onto the search system, and if he doesn't have an account, he signs up for one right there on the spot, usually establishing a username and password. Signed onto the system, he is now able to select the "Save Search" option, name his search, and save it permanently or for a certain amount of time. The advantage of saving the search is that it resides in the search system, where links to full-texts also reside. When the user has time to resume the search, he signs onto his account, recalls the saved search, resumes the process of reviewing

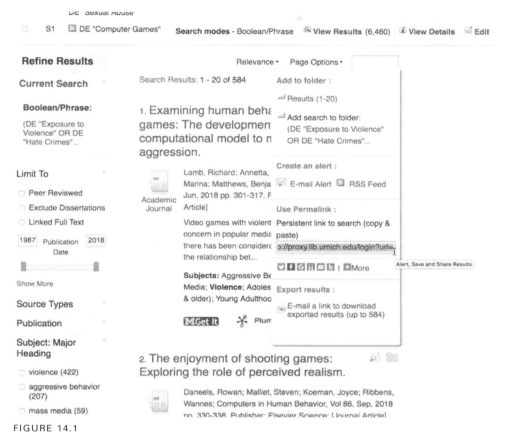

FIGURE 14.1
Copying an EBSCOhost Search's Permalink for Pasting and Sending It to a User in an email Message

retrievals, and downloads full-texts. Users should also be able to save retrievals to their accounts. In figure 14.2, the user has signed onto MyScopus, her Scopus account, where she can access saved searches, saved alerts, and saved sources (Scopus calls them lists). Because the logistics connected with saving searches and retrievals are different from system to system, familiarize yourself with how to save searches and retrievals in the systems you use and recommend to others on a regular basis.

The search alert is a special type of saved search that the search system executes per your instructions, sending you newly retrieved sources that meet your search criteria on a regular basis. Search alerts are a cinch to set up. You conduct a search and then choose the system's "Search Alert" option to save your search statements. The system responds with a form, asking you to name and describe your saved search. Figure 14.3 shows the bottom half of EBSCOhost's advanced search alert form, where you schedule how frequently and for how long you want the system to execute the saved search, how you want the system to send you newly retrieved sources (usually your choice between

FIGURE 14.2
A User's Saved Sources in the Scopus Database
Source: Scopus, a registered trademark of Elsevier, B.V., image retrieved on 17 July 2018.

email or RSS), and in what format you want to receive sources. Thereafter, sit back and wait for the system to send you retrievals.

When your reference interviews reveal users whose information needs are long-term, suggest the search alert to them. Use the search you are formulating for them as the basis for the search alert, or invite them to set up an appointment where you can set up one or more search alerts in relevant licensed and open Web databases. Even Google and Google Scholar feature search alerts. Keep a diary of the search alerts you set up for users, and message them periodically, offering to update their search alerts. Finding alerts useful, instructors may become favorably inclined to libraries generally, inviting you to brief their students on searching for information.

Managing Saved Sources in Citation Management Systems

Designed specifically to facilitate the library research process are citation management systems, which function as both libraries for the user's saved sources and suites of automated tools to help the user manage these sources and cite them in written works. For the most part, the CMS lies dormant on the user's Web browser or desktop until the user saves a source from a licensed database or the Web. The CMS senses the saved source and either acknowledges the user's saving action in a temporary pop-up message or opens its interface in a new tab or window, where CMS-based tools are available to the user to manage this source in particular or vis-à-vis the other sources that the user has saved in the CMS. Leading CMSs are EndNote, Mendeley, RefWorks, and Zotero. Using CMS-based tools, users can:

- Edit the CMS's automatically generated citations and abstracts (when available) for saved sources

Interface   EBSCOhost
Save Search As   ○ Saved Search (Permanent)
                  ○ Saved Search (Temporary, 24 hours)
                  ● Alert
                  Frequency
                  [Once a week ▾]
                  Articles published within the last
                  [No Limit ▾]
                  Run Alert for
                  [One Year ▾]
Alert Options   Alert results format
                  ○ Brief ● Detailed ○ Bibliographic Manager

                  ☑ Limit EBSCOhost access to only the articles sent
E-mail Properties ● Email all alerts and notices
                  ○ Email only creation notice
                  ○ No e-mail (RSS only)
                  E-mail Address (please separate e-mail addresses with a semicolon)
                  ┌───┐
                  │ kmarkey@umich.edu   │
                  │   │
                  │   │
                  └───┘
                  ☐ Hide addresses from recipients
                  Subject
                  ┌───┐
                  │ Does playing computer games make adolescents prone to violence or aggression? │
                  └───┘
                  Title
                  ┌───┐
                  │ EBSCOhost Alert Notification   │
                  └───┘
                  E-mail [From] address
                  ┌───┐
                  │ EPAlerts@ebsco.com   │
                  └───┘
                  E-mail Results format
                  ● Plain Text ○ HTML
                  Include in e-mail
                  ☑ Query
                  ☑ Frequency

[Save]   [Cancel]

FIGURE 14.3
Completing EBSCOhost's Advanced Search Alert Form

- Attach full-texts, read them, take notes, add tags, and file everything connected with a source together
- Create and name new folders for their projects, including nesting folders within folders
- Move saved sources between folders
- Search citations, abstracts, and even full-texts of saved sources
- Insert footnotes, endnotes, in-text citations for CMS-saved sources, and a bibliography into their paper, formatting everything in a style sheet of their choosing
- Share saved sources with friends, colleagues, or a research group

Selling Users on Citation Management Systems

Having used both RefWorks and Zotero for writing projects big and small, I am impressed with their versatility, flexibility, and time-saving potential; however, you may be hard-pressed to convince students, especially at the high school and undergraduate levels, to use a CMS because these systems assume students have a working knowledge of databases, surrogates, full-texts, cited sources, and style sheets and are comfortable using new technologies. Students might not feel the need to save sources until they undertake a major project or develop a serious and potentially long-term interest in a topic, discipline, or field of study. Conducting reference interviews with library users who are beginning major projects, you might mention to them in passing that using a CMS may streamline their efforts. If you pique their interest, then invite them to the library's CMS workshops where you and your colleagues show attendees how to use this or that CMS to save and cite sources and produce bibliographies. You could also invite them to make an appointment for one-on-one training, where you walk them through saving sources in the CMS, and then invite them back after they've saved a CMS library of relevant sources to show them how to insert references and generate a bibliography for their papers.

Many students aren't ready for a CMS. Perhaps their exposure to information-literacy concepts and skills in the grade-school levels was limited. To ramp up students in this regard is the NoodleTools research companion, ushering students through the research process while they work on their own or in groups on an actual writing assignment (NoodleTools 2018). NoodleTools isn't limited to students in schools and colleges but appeals to veteran authors who use its organizational tools to document citations, take notes, outline their written works, sequence their notes within the outline, and compose their written pieces.

TEACHING USERS DURING THE REFERENCE INTERVIEW

Reference interviews conducted via email, chat, and phone aren't necessarily naturals for the teachable moment. In the absence of visual cues, the user is left hanging on every word you say or write. Inserting an information-literacy tip that deviates significantly from answering the question may confuse the user. Thus, you may prefer to stay on topic when conducting a reference interview via these modes of communication. At the very least, you can walk the user through the steps you take to answer the question. If you sense an impatient user whose sole interest is the answer to his question, perhaps the only information-literacy tip that you leave him with is a closing that invites him to contact you or your colleagues anytime in the future.

In-person reference interviews are much more suited to teaching users about online searching and information-literacy concepts and skills generally. You will still have to judge how far afield you can go. Limiting your ability may be a host of showstoppers, such as other users who are waiting for your assistance; an impatient user who is pressed for time; or a user who is too preoccupied with a mobile device, an intimate friend, or a crying child to give you her full attention. At the very least, you can swivel your computer monitor around and walk users through what you are doing. You may find yourself giving them the keyboard more than once during the face-to-face reference interview so that they can further the search.

Introduce users to surrogate records and full-texts so that they are able to distinguish between the two in the future. Whether users don't know that the abstract serves as a brief summary of a much longer full-text or they are trying to shortcut their writing assignments, all too often, they limit their interactions with digital texts to surrogate records. Set the record straight so that users understand that securing the full-text, not the surrogate record, is their search objective.

Consider making a practice of leaving each and every user who visits you in person with one information-literacy-oriented tip above and beyond the information that satisfies their need. Here are a few ideas to get you started. Choose one or more based on your assessment of the particular situation at hand:

- Showing users how to apply clusters to explore aspects of broad topics or to put into words ideas that they may be struggling to articulate
- Limiting to quality retrievals (usually designated by the database as peer-reviewed, scholarly, or journal articles)
- Linking to full-texts
- Preferring databases at the library's website over Google and the World Wide Web
- Alerting users to a database's presearch qualifiers that map onto the big ideas (i.e., facets) in their queries
- Inviting users to revisit you and your colleagues in person or via phone, email, or chat

SUSTAINED TEACHING EVENTS

Information-literacy classes, workshops, and in-service training are sustained events that should provide you with ample opportunities for teaching attendees about online searching. Post your teaching materials online so that attendees can consult them later and refer them to their friends. Bring your business cards to one-shot workshops and workshop series, tell users that it is your business to help them, and invite them to contact you when they get stuck. Promote future information-literacy venues, and urge users to complete your evaluation forms, telling them that you and your colleagues incorporate their input into future events. Also establish a site where you and your colleagues share your teaching materials so that you can reuse content and coordinate your efforts.

Course Design and Deployment Documentation

Formalize your preparation for sustained teaching events in a course syllabus, lesson plans, and teaching materials. At the highest level of granularity is the course syllabus. It gives everyone—prospective registrants, attendees, you, and your colleagues—an overview of your workshop series or half- or full-semester course. Publish your syllabus on the open Web, and draw from its contents to generate publicity statements. At the next level of granularity are lessons plans, in which you detail what you expect attendees to learn, how you will deliver content, and what methods you will use to check for attendees' understanding (Center for Research on Learning and Teaching 2016; Milkova 2014). At the lowest level of granularity are the course materials and activities you prepare to deploy during class. Table 14.1 describes the specific contents of the syllabus, lesson plans, and teaching materials; designates their target audience; and suggests others, including yourself, who would benefit from access to your documentation.

Despite your many years of being a student on the receiving end of a teacher's instruction, you may find it daunting to be the one doing the teaching. Enroll in an information-literacy course in your library school or iSchool, where you will learn how people learn; study best practices for integrating library-user instruction with faculty partnerships; and get actual teaching experience drafting a syllabus, lesson plans, and teaching materials.

Online Searching Content

To learn about online searching, you took a for-credit, graduate-level course, and your performance, including formulating searches that retrieve relevant information, was tested. Few, if any, end users will do the same; in fact, when a select group of university professors were given the same training that you received (minus the tests), they reverted back to their original behavior within six months, querying search systems using natural-language search statements (Bates, Wilde, and Siegfried 1995). Thus, expecting end users, even those with expert knowledge in their chosen disciplines, to learn how to search the go-to database in their selected disciplines may be a

Table 14.1.   Course Design and Deployment Documentation

Target Audience	Access	Contents
Syllabus		
Your institution's library users, prospective registrants, course attendees	Your institution's library users, prospective registrants, course attendees, you, and your colleagues	Vital information: Lists course specifics (e.g., instructor's name and contact information, course name and number, etc.). Description: Describes course content and how attendees will benefit in the long term. Organization: Describes how the course will be conducted. Learning objectives: In bullet points, describes what attendees will learn as a result of taking the course. Schedule of topics: In a two-column table, schedules course content for the dates that the course meets. Materials: In a two-column table, schedules the readings, equipment, supplies, etc., that are needed on the dates that the course meets. Grading: For credit-bearing venues, describes graded assignments. Insert them in a four-column table bearing assignment names, brief descriptions, distribution dates, and due dates. Expectations: Cites your expectations of attendees (e.g., handling personal emergencies, advice about how to succeed in the course, and rules of conduct).
Lesson Plans for Each Workshop or Class Period		
You	You and your colleagues	Learning objectives: Describes what you want attendees to learn in this particular workshop or class period. Materials: Enumerates materials (e.g., lecture files, handouts, instruments, mobile devices, desktop and mobile apps, etc.). Agenda: Describes content and content-delivery methods. Time periods: Estimates how long is devoted to major agenda items. Evaluation strategies: Describes how you will check for attendees' understanding.
Teaching Materials for Each Interaction		
You and course attendees	You, course attendees, and your colleagues	A wide range of actual materials are possible (e.g., notes, outlines, PowerPoint slides, instructional videos, demonstrations, games, journals, role-playing scenarios, case studies, simulations, concept maps, LibGuides, and so on.

pipe dream. Using the seven steps of the online searching process as an outline, here is online searching content for teaching users at sustained information-literacy events.

Step 1: Conducting the Reference Interview

Almost forty years ago, the OPAC became the first information-retrieval system available to end users, and ever since, end users have preferred self-service over mediation (De Rosa et al. 2005; Mischo and Lee 1987). Reaching an impasse on satisfying their information needs, end users consult classmates, friends, parents, or someone they think has expertise on their topics of interest (Head and Eisenberg 2010; Rieh and Hilligoss 2008; Thomas, Tewell, and Willson 2017). Librarians are likely to be the last ones end users consult for help (Thomas, Tewell, and Willson 2017). In fact, many people don't think librarians are there to help them (Head and Eisenberg 2010; Ross, Nilsen, and Radford 2009; Thomas, Tewell, and Willson 2017). Tell students that you and your librarian colleagues *are* there to help them. They can reach you through their preferred medium: chat, e-mail, phone, face-to-face reference, workshops, and classes. You also want them to know that they have to be forthcoming about their queries so that you are able to develop a full understanding of what they want. Emphasize that the reference interview is a difficult task for both people. During this process, a person tries to describe for you, not something she knows, but rather something she doesn't know so that you can almost step into her shoes, seeing things from her perspective to find answers that satisfy her information needs. To quell people's anxieties, remind them that you aren't there to judge, evaluate, or gossip about their information needs; you are there to provide the right answers.

Step 2: Selecting a Database

Google is the go-to database where most everyday people get started on a research project (Asher 2011; De Rosa et al. 2005; Griffiths and Brophy 2005; Holman 2011; Lamphere 2017; Mizrachi 2010; Oxford University Press 2017; Perruso 2016). It's convenient—grab your smartphone from your purse or pocket, and launch your favorite search engine (Connaway, Dickey, and Radford 2011; Kvavik 2005). It's easy—type whatever comes to mind, and the search engine ranks relevant retrievals at the top of the list (Fast and Campbell 2004; Pan 2007). It's reassuring—what the search engine finds (and it always finds something) is pitched at an understandable reading level, neither overly technical nor too simple so that you can get an overview of your topic (Asher 2011; Lawrence 2015; Oxford University Press 2017). It's a confidence builder—you don't need anyone's help to find something useful (Head and Eisenberg 2009; Lawrence 2015). It's comprehensive—you searched the whole Internet in one fell swoop (Boss and Nelson 2005; Joint 2010). It's dependable—your favorite search engine is at your beck and call anytime of the day or night and even on holidays (Connaway, Dickey, and Radford 2011).

When it comes to selecting a database, expect end users to come to you after they have exhausted the top-ranked retrievals at their favorite search engine. Promote your library's website as *the* source of reliable and trusted information. If users want a Wikipedia-like experience that will provide them with easy-to-understand information, point out the encyclopedias at your library's website, such as World Book and Encyclopedia Britannica, or encyclopedia databases, such as Oxford Reference and the

Gale Virtual Reference Library. Qualify the sources that they'll find there, telling them that disciplinary experts have written encyclopedia entries and cited seminal sources that they should consult for more information.

Encyclopedic databases, such as Academic OneFile, General OneFile, General Reference Center Gold, ProQuest Research Library, and Reader's Guide Abstracts, may be the next step up from encyclopedias, yielding sources that don't require mastery of disciplinary knowledge to understand. News databases, such as Factiva, LexisNexis Academic, NewsBank, and ProQuest Newsstand, also have basic content.

At the academy, users are likely to receive directives from their instructors regarding the use of scholarly or peer-reviewed sources, so bring to their attention presearch qualifiers that enable them to limit content in this regard. Because users can't count on every database having such qualifiers, instruct users on how to differentiate between scholarly and nonscholarly sources. Eventually, academic instructors will require students to search for information in their discipline's go-to database for domain experts. Demonstrate your library's website, where users can search databases by subject. Show them LibGuides, your library's web-based resource pages that recommend resources on a hot topic, discipline, genre, theme, current event, and so on.

Step 3: Typecasting the User's Query

Such phrases as "I don't think I just click" and "I basically throw whatever I want into the search box and hope it comes up" have come to characterize the queries end users enter into search systems (Asher 2011; Novotny 2004). Users rush through the information-seeking process, entering successive search terms, switching databases in response to lackluster results, or giving up because they don't think the information exists (Asher 2011; Head and Eisenberg 2009).

I think it is a good idea to level with users about the emotional roller coaster they'll experience during information seeking. No one likes feeling uncomfortable, so tell users about the ISP model and its empirical evidence about the inevitability of uncomfortable feelings between spates of neutral or comfortable feelings (pages 41 to 42). If your students are working on a research-and-writing task, suggest that they keep a diary of their stages and their feelings along the way. Then let them debrief with fellow classmates after they've submitted the project for a grade. On a personal note, whenever I take on a new research-and-writing project, I experience all the ups and downs that the ISP model predicts, even after forty years of professional research and writing in our field! To lighten the burden, I check my progress vis-à-vis the ISP model because I know it explains why I feel like I do.

Introduce students to subject and known-item typecasting. For subjects, the user wants information *about* a topic, person, place, organization, and so on. For known-items, the user wants a specific source they know exists, such as a book, an article, a film, or an ad. Give users sample queries to typecast, letting them work with classmates so that they can deliberate on typecasting together. Eventually, they'll conduct subject searches or known-item searches for these queries; however, some known-items come with so little information that subject searches are necessary. Generally, subject searches are open-ended, with answers that cannot be pinned down to any one source but are answered by the user's synthesis of multiple sources. The latter are closed-ended—searches for one particular source using nonsubject attributes, such as by this author, bearing this title, or with this cover illustration.

Step 4: Conducting the Facet Analysis and Logical Combination

Google's ability to top retrieval lists with relevant sources is uncanny. It is so accurate that few people browse past the first page of retrievals (Asher 2011; Pan 2007). When researchers can experiment and switch the order of Google's ranked retrievals, putting lower-ranked retrievals atop the list and higher-ranked retrievals lower, they still prefer the top retrievals, even though they aren't as relevant (Pan 2007). Asked how Google ranks retrievals, a user replies, "Somebody that works at Google . . . comes up with the answers" (boyd 2015). Users surveyed in an Oxford University Press study suggested that systems respond with useful information because they understand their queries (Oxford University Press 2017). Another researcher concludes that users "seemed to see the keywords more as concepts rather than strings of letters to be matched" (Holman 2011, 25). Underlying such research findings is the confidence end users have in the ability of search systems to do their thinking for them, but systems *don't* think. They search for matches of user-entered search terms with indexed strings of alphanumeric characters, taking into account word proximity and many other statistical properties of words in texts. The closest search systems come to searching for concepts is controlled vocabulary (CV) searching. If users really want their searches to extend to concepts, they need to put effort into a facet analysis, then convert their facets into the database's CV or incorporate facet names into the free text (FT) search statements they enter into databases. For end users, doing the latter is probably the way to go because it requires a minimum knowledge of searching language.

Facet analysis is crucial to online searching. When users get the facet analysis "right," their chances of finding relevant information increase substantially. What prevents them from getting it right is their failure to express their interests fully. Perhaps they haven't given their topics much thought, their lack of knowledge about the discipline underlying their topics affects their ability to fully specify things, or they are self-conscious about revealing their true interests. Whatever the reason, the facet analysis is not the time for users to hold back. Emphasize to users that they must be forthcoming about their interests in the statements they enter into search systems or in the conversations they hold with librarians in reference interviews. Reading minds isn't something search systems or human beings are able to do. Users have to "let it all hang out." Failing to specify one or more facets means that retrievals aren't likely to specify the missing facet(s), and if they do, it's purely by chance.

When you talk about the facet analysis with users, you might want to substitute *big idea* or *concept* for *facet* because some users won't know what *facet* means. Use your judgment, inserting terminology you feel your users will understand. Define the facet analysis for users. A facet is a separate aspect (i.e., idea, set, notion, part, component, object, or entity) of a query. It represents one idea. It can be expressed in one word (e.g., *insurgency, automobile, ivory, norway*), or it can be expressed in a phrase that through the years has come to mean one idea (e.g., *lung cancer, zebra mussels, controlled burn*).

Advise users to conduct the facet analysis *before* they start searching. If they have trouble conducting the facet analysis, invite them to write down their queries, choose the one prompt that "feels right" to them, and complete the sentence with their query:

- I want to know whether _____.
- I am interested in _____.
- I need information on _____.
- I want to know about _____.
- I am researching _____.
- I need to find _____.

Table 14.2 shows how six users responded to these prompts, writing their queries on the blank line. Before proceeding with the next step, ask users to review what they've written. Does it really express their interests? Have they "let it all hang out," saying what's *really* on their minds? Give them a moment to revise what's there, even choosing another prompt and completing it with their queries.

Next, instruct users to dissect their queries into single words and phrases that express the big ideas that interest them. Two or three big ideas are usually enough. Five big ideas are too many. The easiest way for them to do this is to underline single words or phrases in their sentences. Table 14.3 shows such underlined words and phrases for the six queries.

Table 14.2. Using Prompts to Elicit Queries from Users

I want to know whether	genetically modifiable crops affect people's health.
I am interested in	the collapse of the Soviet Union.
I need information on	cyanobacteria as a source of alternative energy.
I want to know about	going to college. Does it change people's behavior?
I am researching	why one should not take life too seriously.
I need to find	the book *Narrow Road to the Deep North*.

Table 14.3.   Inviting Users to Dissect Their Queries into Big Ideas

I want to know whether	<u>genetically modifiable crops</u> affect people's <u>health</u>.
I am interested in	the <u>collapse</u> of the <u>Soviet Union</u>.
I need information on	<u>cyanobacteria</u> as a source of <u>alternative energy</u>.
I want to know about	going to <u>college</u>. Does it <u>change people's behavior</u>?
I am researching	why one should <u>not take life too seriously</u>.
I need to find	the <u>book</u> *Narrow Road to the Deep North*.

Finally, ask users to scrutinize their queries. If their underlined phrases exceed two words, ask them to simplify them. For example, if an underlined phrase is an adjectival phrase made up of three or more words, challenge them to reconceive it as two big ideas or reduce it to two words without losing meaning or sacrificing specificity; if one of their underlined phrases is a prepositional phrase, suggest that they consolidate their interests into a single noun or two-word adjectival phrase. In table 14.4, three users have revised their big ideas under their original underlined words and phrases: (1) breaking up "genetically modifiable crops" into "genetic modification" and "crops," (2) restating "changing people's behavior" as "behavior change," and (3) restating "not take life too seriously" as "conduct of life."

If users underline only one word or phrase, ask them to rethink their interests, dig deep inside themselves, and describe in written or spoken words what is only a vague notion inside their heads. If they still come up empty-handed, then that's fine. Their query is a candidate for the Friends Strategy and searches in a database that feature postsearch clusters. Additionally, the Conduct of Life query might benefit from clusters in a psychology, sociology, or religion database, even in an encyclopedic database.

Getting users to specify their queries, break them into facets, and transform them into search statements to which Boolean and extended-Boolean search systems respond with relevant retrievals is difficult to do. Check out the keyword generator that uses a three-step process to script user queries into Boolean search statements (University of Texas at Austin 2018).

Step 5: Representing the User's Query as Input to the Search System

Since OPACs introduced end users to online searching in the early 1980s, researchers have analyzed the queries users enter into search systems and concluded that users fail to use these systems' searching languages or fail to use them correctly (Bates,

Table 14.4.   Advising Users to Break Up or Restate Wordy Big Ideas

I want to know whether	<u>genetically modifiable crops</u> affect people's <u>health</u>.
	genetic modification crops health
I am interested in	the <u>collapse</u> of the <u>Soviet Union</u>.
I want information on	<u>cyanobacteria</u> as a source of <u>alternative energy</u>.
I need information about	going to <u>college</u>. Does it <u>change people's behavior</u>?
	college behavior change
I am researching	why one should <u>not take life too seriously</u>.
	conduct of life
I need to find	the <u>book</u> *Narrow Road to the Deep North*.

Wilde, and Siegfried 1995; Bloom and Deyrup 2012; Holman 2011; Jansen, Spink, and Saracevic 2000; Turner 2011). That end users have gleefully glommed onto Web search engines is not accidental. These systems do automatically what expert intermediary searchers have been doing all along to generate relevant retrievals—looking for search terms that are in close proximity, truncating search terms, giving more weight to title terms and index terms—while removing the burden of users having to learn and apply searching languages. Thus, your instructions to users about representing the search as input to the search system must steer clear of searching languages. We'll do exactly that now, building on our discussion of the facet analysis.

In table 14.4, users' underlined words and phrases or their restated words and phrases are the search terms that they should enter into their selected database(s). If the search system offers separate search boxes connected with the Boolean AND operator, advise the user to enter one underlined or restated word or phrase per search box. If the user runs out of search boxes, she can add a row or begin her search with what she thinks are the most important big ideas, entering the remaining big ideas only if her retrievals are too broad, too many, or a combination of the two. Even better than entering these remaining big ideas is browsing the database's clusters in search of subjects or classification captions that are satisfactory representations of one or more remaining big ideas and applying them.

In figure 14.4, the user enters the search terms `collapse` and `soviet union` into two separate search boxes in the advanced interface of the U-M Library's

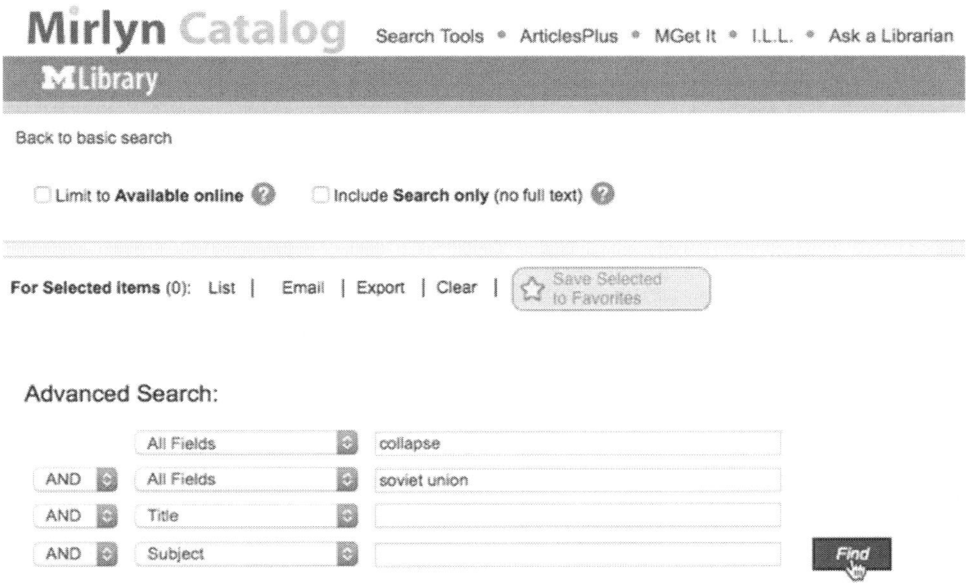

FIGURE 14.4
Entering Search Terms into Separate Search Boxes and Combining Them with the Boolean AND Operator in the University of Michigan Library's Discovery OPAC

Source: Screenshots much available under a Creative Commons Attribution license by the University of Michigan Library.

discovery OPAC. The user has to exercise her judgment, deciding whether to add quotes to phrases. Doing so may stop search systems from automatic stemming, which retrieves plural and singular forms and forms bearing different word endings (e.g., *-ed, -ing, -ation*). In this case, adding quotes to the search term `soviet union` may be warranted to limit retrieval to this particular place only. In a search for the Going to College query, it makes sense to omit quotes from the restated search term `behavior change` so that retrieval extends to such phrases as "changes in behavior," "behavioral changes," and "changing one's behavior."

If the database offers a single search box, advise the user to switch to the advanced interface. If the single search box is still there, then trial and error may be in order. The user should enter her search terms, with the most important big idea first (with or without quotes in the case of a phrase), and place the Boolean AND operator between the terms that represent each big idea:

```
genetic modification AND crops AND health
```

If retrievals are relevant, then the user should pursue them. If the system produces too few or no retrievals, then advise the user to enter her search terms minus the Boolean AND operator:

```
genetic modification crops health
```

This second search statement is for an extended-Boolean system. If it fails to produce retrievals the second time around, it is a big-time clue that the user should choose a different database.

Personally, before switching to a different database, I would browse the database's thesaurus (if it has one) and search for CV terms that are synonyms for one or more of my search terms; however, I am an expert searcher who knows how to use a database's thesaurus. Use involves several actions: spotting a database's thesaurus on the search system's interface, browsing the thesaurus for appropriate search terms, interpreting term-relationship designations, and substituting my search terms for more appropriate thesaurus terms. Furthermore, thesauri are not standard issue across all databases: They designate term relationships in different ways, and they are implemented differently in search systems. Whether to teach end users about the role of the thesaurus in online searching is a judgment call on your part because of the complexity that the thesaurus adds to the searching process. Before making a hard and fast decision, experiment in sustained interactions with upperclassmen and graduate students who are studying in a discipline with a go-to database that features a thesaurus to determine whether students glom onto the thesaurus, if it confuses them, or if they opt to ignore it.

The sixth-listed query in tables 14.2–14.4 names a known-item. Remind users about all the thinking they did to typecast their queries (step 3). Advise them that entering search terms for a query typecast as a known-item should be limited to one facet at a time, either the most specific facet or the one likely to produce fewer retrievals in a search of their selected database. The choice between `book` and `narrow road to the deep north` is simple, the former retrieving thousands of books and the latter retrieving the one book entitled *Narrow Road to the Deep North*. Show users how advanced interfaces allow them to restrict searches to certain database fields. In this case, it makes sense to restrict the search to the title field because the query bears a book's title. If the system offers a choice between browsing or searching the field that interests them, show users how browsing displays titles in the alphabetical neighborhood of their entered title, allowing them to scan for and select their desired title just in case the title they entered isn't exactly right.

Step 6: Entering the Search and Responding Strategically

Recommend the À la Carte Edition of the Building Block Search Strategy for multifaceted topics. This means entering one salient search term per facet. Because users won't know whether they are searching a Boolean or extended-Boolean search system, they might have to enter their search statements twice: the first time with Boolean AND operators between their search terms and, if retrievals aren't satisfactory, the second time without the Boolean AND operators. When you present this strategy to users, explain the analogy behind its name and use *Online Searching*'s visual representation of this strategy so that it is vivid to them (page 184), making it likely that they'll remember it and execute it in the future.

The À la Carte Edition of the Building Block Search Strategy isn't much different from how users conduct subject searches now. Calling their search terms *keywords*, users enter the first words that pop into their minds (page 321). À la Carte adds discipline and deliberation to the search-term selection and entry tasks:

- Advising users to pause and think about their interests in a systematic way instead of rushing to enter keywords into the search system at hand
- Urging users to be forthcoming about the full scope of their interests
- Expressing their interests in a sentence
- Extracting the big ideas from the sentence
- Repackaging their big ideas: Dividing complex big ideas into two facets and/or consolidating wordy ones into shorter adjectival phrases or simple nouns

The Pearl Growing Search Strategy helps users whose subject searches produce too few retrievals find additional ones. To execute this strategy, users must scrutinize the retrievals they're able to find, looking for synonyms for their search terms. For example, retrievals for the Crops and Cyanobacteria queries use the terms *transgenic plants* and *reusable energy* instead of *genetic modification* and *alternative energy*, respectively. Substituting the former for the latter is likely to increase the number of relevant retrievals because the former are the CV terms that the database uses to refer to the latter.

Three other approaches for increasing retrievals are find-like searches, backward chaining, and forward chaining. Find-like isn't available in all search systems and databases, but when it is, it requires a minimum of effort on the user's part—identifying a relevant source and clicking on the accompanying find-like link to trigger the search system to find more like it. Find a relevant source in any licensed or open Web database, switch to the Web of Science (WOS) database, and conduct a known-item search for the source. When you find it, clicking on its "N Cited References" or "M Times Cited" initiates backward or forward chaining, respectively. Scan cited references and times-cited references for relevant ones and full-texts are a click away via accompanying resolver links. This is push-button research. What could be easier?

Clusters aren't available in every database and search system, but when they are, they characterize retrievals from a variety of perspectives, providing users with a means of reducing high-posted searches using nonsubject criteria, such as date of publication, language, and genre. Helping users who are uncertain about their topics are the subject clusters that systems construct from co-occurring index terms and classification captions. Benefiting the most from subject clusters are users who have a one-facet subject query in mind. Encourage them to browse subject and classification clusters in search of interesting subtopics. For example, the user who poses the Conduct of Life query is definitely a candidate for a search in a psychology, sociology, or religion database that features clusters.

Step 7: Displaying Retrievals and Responding Tactically

Much of the information that users retrieve through their library's website has been vetted by librarians who choose the databases listed there and by publishers who decide on the content added to databases. For example, the WOS database is especially selective about the scholarly and scientific journals it indexes, choosing only those with metrics that demonstrate high impact levels, and a database, such as General Reference Center Gold, which selects general-interest journals and magazines that are understandable for readers of all ages who are unsure about their topics of interest or are exploring them for the first time. Databases are costly, so librarians consider many factors when making subscription decisions (Johnson 2018). Librarians also evaluate the books, audiobooks, films, and other materials they purchase for the library. Helping them make purchase and subscription decisions are various trade publications, such as *Publisher's Weekly*, *Choice*, *Booklist*, and *Kirkus Reviews*, that are dedicated almost entirely to reviews of newly published resources. When your library's users choose vetted resources, evaluating their credibility might take a backseat to their relevance assessments.

Asked to provide evidence why a source is relevant, users overwhelmingly point to specific subject matter that the source contains or to the overlap between their topic of interest and a particular source's contents (Markey, Leeder, and Rieh 2014, 144). When users have difficulty assessing relevance, they usually don't have a firm grasp on their topic of interest (Zhitomirsky-Geffet, Bar-Ilan, and Levene 2017). On a personal note, I recall floundering over a literature search—I just couldn't put into words what I wanted. A colleague recommended that I read a particular article, but I failed to see how this article related to my ill-defined interests. It took me over a year to firm up my topic, and when I did, that very article was the linchpin in my understanding of the topic.

That relevance is a moving target, subject to users' knowledge about a topic and their exposure to newly retrieved sources, is built into the Berrypicking Model of information retrieval (pages 40 to 41). When you discuss relevance with users, comment on this as well as on the research that demonstrates people's propensity to depend on the first few ranked retrievals to the exclusion of all other retrievals and to project relevance on them (page 322). As much as users would like there to be a "little man" inside the computer who makes intellectual decisions about the closeness of their ranked retrievals vis-à-vis the queries they have in mind (boyd 2015; Holman 2011; Oxford University Press 2017), there is no human being inside or behind the search system who does the thinking for the user. Relevance ranking is little more than a numbers game, wholly dependent on matches between a user's search terms and the terms in titles, abstracts, and index terms; their closeness in written text; their occurrences in more important fields (usually titles and index terms) over less important fields (usually full-texts); and much more. As a consequence, advise users to be circumspect about retrievals lists, going beyond the first few listed ones in pursuit of useful information and taking retrievals at face value instead of reading into them what they want them to say. Finally, talk to users about their unspoken desire to find the perfect source that matches exactly what they want to say. Rarely does such a source exist. Instead, users must synthesize the information they find and draw on qualified others for insight, knowledge, and understanding to complete an assignment, form an opinion, make a decision, or take decisive action.

Most people's starting point for information is the Internet because it's easy, convenient, reassuring, a confidence builder, comprehensive, and dependable. That *anyone* can author, sponsor, and publish information on the Internet should make users especially circumspect about the credibility of the information they find there. This is doubly important due to the problem of "fake news" that emerged during the 2016 US presidential election. *Online Searching* tables the discussion of fake news for now, treating it at length in chapter 15, where it belongs with other current trends and issues that will grow in importance in the future.

When users display retrievals, walk them through surrogate records; show them the citations that they'll use later in their written works and the titles, index terms, and abstracts that are helpful for determining a source's relevance; and convince them that securing the source's full-text is their next step. Too many users terminate their search at the surrogate—they think that the surrogate is the full-text, securing full-texts is difficult, the abstract is sufficient for their needs, or they have too many other things to do to bother with full-texts.

Demonstrate how to find full-texts. This includes artifacts from the library's physical collection, such as books, journals, and videos. Make sure users understand that the surrogate record is just that, a surrogate, and that they'll want to secure the full-text to read what the author has to say about the subject. Reading full-texts from cover to cover isn't necessary for the majority of retrievals. Instruct users on how to perform a technical reading of a lengthy text so they can invest the time they save reading full-texts for the most relevant sources (pages 276 to 277). Refer them to how-to guides on reading scientific papers (Fosmire 2015; Madooei 2014).

The sustained interaction is the right venue for introducing users to citation management systems (CMS) for managing their retrievals. Schedule the CMS workshop when users are beset with research assignments and receptive to methods for organizing their retrievals and citing them in their written works. Your workshop publicity should tell them to come to the workshop with a handful of retrievals so they can get started by populating the CMS with these retrievals and inserting footnotes, cited references, and a bibliography into a paper they are writing.

TEACHING TIPS

Going hand in hand with teaching people how to be effective online searchers is understanding how people learn. For all the detail, supplement your school's information-literacy course with elective courses on learning in your institution's education department.

Eventually, you will find yourself teaching library users in a variety of venues, and you will want to do your best. Here are teaching tips to keep in mind as you prepare for the big moment:

- *Be the epitome of organization.* Compose a syllabus for half- and semester-long classes and workshop series. Distribute an agenda that enumerates major class-period activities. If you lecture, begin with an outline that summarizes the content you expect to cover. Review your lectures in advance, making sure you haven't crammed too much into the allotted time period and your content is ordered logically.

- *Know your audience.* Do some research about your audience in advance. Here are some suggestions: When an instructor invites you to a class, interview her in advance to learn about her course, such as the assignment that is the impetus for your presentation to students and the instructor's special instructions to students about the sources and databases she expects them to use. When conducting a reference interview, ask the user tactfully about his comfort level with technical or advanced material so you can select a database that bears sources that he is likely to understand. When preparing for a workshop, check the evaluation forms that workshop attendees completed the last time the workshop was offered to see who they were and their suggestions for improvements.

- *Don't overwhelm users.* Limit your teaching objectives to what you can accomplish in the time allotted to the event, leaving ample time for questions, evaluations, and minimal deviations from your lesson plan. Librarians always want to be comprehensive, and that includes overwhelming users with too many relevant retrievals and databases. Cool it! Less is more. If faculty assign you more than you can cover, be frank with them, negotiating how much and what you can cover in the allotted time period.

- *Substitute active learning for lecturing and demonstrations.* Online searching is natural for active learning because users *do* online searching. They interact with an online system that produces results instantaneously, allowing them to experiment in a penalty-free environment and save what they do for postsearch debriefings and analyses. Whether you are teaching young people or older adults, devise situations where they experience online searching firsthand and have opportunities to share their observations about their searches and search results with others.

- *Don't jump the gun.* If you ask attendees a question or ask for a volunteer to share their online searching experiences, wait for an answer. People hesitate because they know they'll feel bad if they give a wrong answer or their participation isn't up to snuff. This is especially apparent with older learners who don't want to lose face. On a personal note, I tell students that I prefer wrong over right answers because we get to languish over a search that went awry, brainstorming what went wrong and how to improve things.

- *Admit when you don't know the answer to someone's question.* To be honest, most people's body language reveals when they don't know an answer, so don't bother faking one. Promise to follow up with the answer at the next class meeting or via email. If you don't have time to follow up, give everyone one minute to find an answer right then and there, or in a credit-bearing course, offer extra credit to the first person who messages you the right answer. Always commend the inquirer whose question has you stumped.

- *Expect the unexpected.* The database, search system, or user-authentication system goes down. The projector breaks. There's a fire drill. You go farther afield than you want to go answering a student's question. Instead of losing your cool, take a few deep breaths, and relax your shoulders, jaw, or wherever you tense up under stress. Then consider the situation, and respond accordingly. Losing too much time to unexpected events, consider a make-up class, or contact users to inform them when the class repeats in the future.
- *Be reflective about your assistance to users.* Debrief mentally about your assistance to users. Initially, this means everything—how you greet them, how you elicit what they really want, how you put your knowledge of the information universe to work to answer their questions—so you can develop a modus operandi with which you are comfortable. Then turn your attention to reference interviews that you think went really well or really badly. With regard to the latter, be honest with yourself about what you did, what you wish you would have done, and how you'll respond more effectively to a similar situation in the future. This isn't about beating yourself up; it's about learning from your experiences and priming yourself to do better in the future. Balance your debriefing with reflecting on the former so that you can build on your successes in future interactions. Revisit your modus operandi from time to time, tweaking it as needed.
- *Ask your colleagues.* It's impossible to know everything about online searching, teaching, information literacy, and library science generally. When it comes to interpersonal interactions, group dynamics, in-class policies, and the like, check with your more experienced colleagues because they've probably encountered much the same and experimented with and instituted solutions that work. When you are new on the job, your colleagues will expect you to ask questions and seek their advice. Use this initial "honeymoon" period to test your colleagues, identifying whom you can trust and take into your confidence.
- *Prepare in advance, and practice, practice, practice!* Preparing well in advance gives you the opportunity to stew over your presentation, filling in gaps, improving your original plans, and checking points that you are unsure of. Take advantage of every opportunity to make oral presentations so that you become accustomed to speaking to groups, expressing yourself extemporaneously, answering questions, handling the unexpected, and much more. Most of all, you want to overcome the jitters. It won't happen overnight, but one day, you'll notice several hours after your presentation is over that you didn't even think about getting nervous.

QUESTIONS

Questions 1 to 5 give you hands-on experience saving searches and retrievals and sharing them with another person, just like you'll have to do at the reference desk. So, with your laptop in hand, pair up with a friend or classmate, making sure that either one or both of you have signed up for a CMS account on EndNote, Mendeley, RefWorks, or Zotero. Sit side by side, choose a database, and conduct a multifaceted search for a topic of your own choosing or one of *Online Searching*'s sample topics: Television Violence, Information Literacy Games, Eating Disorders, and Child Soldiers. Use the Building Block Search Strategy's À la Carte Edition to generate a handful of relevant retrievals, and you are ready to answer these questions.

1. Often, you'll conduct a search that gets the library user started and then send him your search so he can pick up where you left off. Using the search you just conducted, share it with your friend using the system's search-sharing capability. By the way, you might have to register for an account to share searches in your chosen database's search system.
2. Alternatively, checkmark potentially relevant retrievals, and then use this system's retrievals-sharing capability to send them to your friend via email.
3. There are many reasons for saving a search. For example, you don't have time to finish the search, you aren't getting the results you expected and need to give it more time and thought, or you expect more users to approach you asking for your help with the search you just conducted. Save your ongoing search. By the way, you might have to register for an account to save searches.
4. Now that you have an account in this search system, what else can you do with your saved searches and retrievals?
5. Which CMS do you use? Demonstrate it to your friend, showing her how to save a retrieval, both its citation and its full-text, into the CMS. While the CMS is open, show your friend other retrievals you've saved. Tell her when and why you use this CMS.

Here are more questions. In addition to checking your answers with those concluding this chapter, discuss them in class with your classmates.

6. In a face-to-face reference interview, what verbal or nonverbal cues might reveal that the user would be receptive to information-literacy instruction right there and then, especially instruction that is related to but goes beyond your answers to the user's query? Do you think that there is ever an opportunity to provide information-literacy training during phone or chat interviews? Why or why not? If you've had experiences in this regard, share them with your classmates.
7. A user asks a query that snowballs into a series of unsuccessful subject searches across multiple databases, including your library's OPAC and WSD system. You are stumped. What do you do next?

8. Upon a colleague's unexpected resignation to take a new job, you are tasked with teaching her new half-semester information-literacy course. You hardly have a month to prepare. How can you streamline your preparation before the course starts?

9. How do you know that you've not only answered the user's question but also that you've gone too far, saturating him with too much information?

SUMMARY

Make the most of the reference interview, teaching users what you can sandwich into the short period of time that you have with them. You may be inclined to stay on topic when conducting such interviews via chat, email, or phone because users can't see you, and thus, they are left hanging on to every word you say or write. At the very least, you can walk users through the steps you take to answer their questions. Good listeners may catch on, able to answer comparable questions on their own in the future. Always close the interview with an invitation to contact you or your colleagues anytime in the future.

Sustained teaching events, such as the one-shot information-literacy class, the standalone workshop or workshop series, and the half- or full-semester courses, are much more suited to teaching users about online searching and information-literacy concepts and skills generally. The seven-step online searching process is the framework for this chapter's recommendations about specific online searching content for information-literacy instruction. Sustained teaching events may also warrant the preparation of a course syllabus, lesson plans, and teaching materials.

Punctuating the searching process is retrievals management. For most users, managing retrievals is a one-time event connected with the project at hand, and the save-retrievals functionality in the one system they search may be sufficient. Reusing sources may appeal to users who are close to committing to a discipline or involved in a long-term endeavor, such as a capstone project, senior thesis, book, business plan, or patent. Such users may be favorably inclined to exploring the potentials of third-party software applications called citation management systems (CMSs). Not only do CMSs enable users to save sources, but they also provide tools to help users organize, find, share, and cite their sources in written papers.

BIBLIOGRAPHY

Asher, Andrew D. 2011. "Search Magic: Discovering How Undergraduates Find Information." Paper presented at the American Anthropological Association meeting, Montreal, Canada, November. Accessed July 4, 2018. http://www.erialproject.org/wp-content/uploads/2011/11/Asher_AAA2011_Search-magic.pdf.

Bates, Marcia J., Deborah N. Wilde, and Susan Siegfried. 1995. "Research Practices of Humanities Scholars in an Online Environment: The Getty Online Searching Project Report No. 3." *Library and Information Science Research* 17 (Winter): 5–40.

Bloom, Beth S., and Marta Deyrup. 2012. "The Truth Is Out: How Students REALLY Search." Paper presented at the Charleston Library Conference, Charleston, SC, November 7–10. http://dx.doi.org/10.5703/1288284315103.

Boss, Stephen C., and Michael L. Nelson. 2005. "Federated Search Tools: The Next Step in the Quest for One-Stop-Shopping." *The Reference Librarian* 44, nos. 91–92: 139–60.

boyd, danah. 2015. "Online Reflections of Our Offline Lives." *On Being.* Podcast audio. April 9. https://onbeing.org/programs/danah-boyd-online-reflections-of-our-offline-lives/.

Center for Research on Learning and Teaching. 2016. "Sample Lesson Plans." Accessed July 4, 2018. http://www.crlt.umich.edu/gsis/p2_6.

Connaway, Lynn Sillipigni, Timothy J. Dickey, and Marie L. Radford. 2011. "If It Is Too Inconvenient I'm Not Going after It: Convenience as a Critical Factor in Information-Seeking Behaviors." *Library & Information Science Research* 33, no. 3: 179–90.

De Rosa, Cathy, Joanne Cantrell, Janet Hawk, and Alane Wilson. 2005. *College Students' Perceptions of Libraries and Information Resources: A Report to the OCLC Membership.* Dublin, OH: OCLC.

Fast, Karl V., and D. Grant Campbell. 2004. "'I Still Like Google': University Student Perceptions of Searching OPACs and the Web." *Proceedings of the ASIS Annual Meeting* 41: 138–46.

Fosmire, Michael. 2015. "Tutorials—Scientific Paper." Accessed July 4, 2018. https://www.lib .purdue.edu/help/tutorials/scientific-paper.

Griffiths, Jillian, and Peter Brophy. 2005. "Student Searching Behavior and the Web: Use of Academic Resources and Google." *Library Trends* 53, no. 4: 539–54.

Head, Allison J., and Michael B. Eisenberg. 2009. "What Today's College Students Say about Conducting Research in the Digital Age." Accessed July 4, 2018. http://www.projectinfolit .org/uploads/2/7/5/4/27541717/2009_final_report.pdf.

———. 2010. "How College Students Evaluate and Use Information in the Digital Age." Accessed July 4, 2018. http://www.projectinfolit.org/uploads/2/7/5/4/27541717/pil_ fall2010_survey_fullreport1.pdf.

Holman, Lucy. 2011. "Millennial Students' Mental Models of Search: Implications for Academic Librarians and Database Developers." *The Journal of Academic Librarianship* 37, no. 1: 19–27.

Jansen, Bernard J., Amanda Spink, and Tefko Saracevic. 2000. "Real Life, Real Users, and Real Needs: A Study and Analysis of User Queries on the Web." *Information Processing and Management* 36, no. 2: 207–27.

Johnson, Peggy. 2018. *Fundamentals of Collection Development and Management.* 4th ed. Chicago: American Library Association.

Joint, Nicholas. 2010. "The One-Stop Shop Search Engine: A Transformational Library Technology? ANTAEUS." *Library Review* 59, no. 4: 240–48.

Kvavik, Robert. 2005. "Convenience, Communications, and Control: How Students Use Technology." In *Educating the Net Generation*, edited by Diana G. Oblinger and James L. Oblinger, 7.1–7.20. Accessed July 4, 2018. https://www.educause.edu/ir/library/pdf/pub7101.pdf.

Lamphere, Carly. 2017. "Research 3.0." *Online Searcher* 41, no. 3 (May/Jun.): 30–33.

Lawrence, Kate. 2015. "Today's Students: Skimmers, Scanners and Efficiency-Seekers." *Information Services & Use* 35: 89–93.

Madooei, Ali. 2014. "The Art of Reading Research Papers." Accessed July 4, 2018. http://www.sfu.ca/~amadooei/files/ReadingAdvice.pdf.

Markey, Karen, Chris Leeder, and Soo Young Rieh. 2014. *Designing Online Information Literacy Games Students Want to Play*. Lanham, MD: Rowman & Littlefield.

Milkova, Stiliana. 2014. "Strategies for Effective Lesson Planning." Accessed July 4, 2018. http://www.crlt.umich.edu/gsis/p2_5.

Mischo, William H., and Jounghyoun Lee. 1987. "End-User Searching of Bibliographic Databases." *Annual Review of Information Science & Technology* 22: 227–63.

Mizrachi, Diane. 2010. "Undergraduates' Academic Information and Library Behaviors: Preliminary Results." *Reference Services Review* 38, no. 4: 571–80.

NoodleTools. 2018. "NoodleTools: A Research Platform, an Educational Mindset." Accessed March 9, 2018. http://www.noodletools.com.

Novotny, Eric. 2004. "I Don't Think I Click: A Protocol Analysis Study of Use of a Library Online Catalog in the Internet Age." *College & Research Libraries* 65, no. 6 (Nov.): 525–37.

Oxford University Press. 2017. "Navigating Research: How Academic Users Understand, Discover, and Utilize Reference Resources." Accessed July 4, 2018. https://global.oup.com/academic/content/pdf/navigatingresearch.pdf.

Pan, Bing. 2007. "In Google We Trust: Users' Decisions on Rank, Position, and Relevance." *Journal of Computer-Mediated Communication* 12, no. 3: 801–23.

Perruso, Carol. 2016. "Undergraduates' Use of Google vs. Library Resources: A Four-Year Cohort Study." *College & Research Libraries* 77, no. 5 (Sep.): 614–30.

Rieh, Soo Young, and Brian Hilligoss. 2008. "College Students' Credibility Judgments in the Information-Seeking Process." In *Digital Media, Youth, and Credibility*, edited by Miriam J. Metzger and Andrew J. Flanagin, 49–72. Cambridge, MA: MIT Press.

Ross, Catherine Sheldrick, Kirsti Nilsen, and Marie L. Radford. 2009. *Conducting the Reference Interview: A How-to-Do-It Manual for Librarians.* New York: Neal-Schuman.

Thomas, Susan, Eamon Tewell, and Gloria Willson. 2017. "Where Students Start and What They Do When They Get Stuck: A Qualitative Inquiry into Academic Information-Seeking and Help-Seeking Practices." *The Journal of Academic Librarianship* 43: 224–31.

Turner, Nancy B. 2011. "Librarians Do It Differently: Comparative Usability Testing with Students and Library Staff." *Journal of Web Librarianship* 5, no. 4: 286–98.

University of Texas at Austin. 2018. "How to Generate Keywords." Accessed July 4, 2018. http://legacy.lib.utexas.edu/keywords/index.php.

Zhitomirsky-Geffet, Maayan, Judit Bar-Ilan, and Mark Levene. 2017. "Analysis of Change in Users' Assessment of Search Results over Time." *Journal of the Association for Information Science and Technology* 68, no. 5: 1137–48.

SUGGESTED READING

Badke, William. 2015. "Ten Things We Really Should Teach about Searching." *Online Searcher* 39, 3 (May/Jun.): 71–73. When you teach people about online searching or help them, keep this author's words of wisdom about the hidden realities of online searching in mind.

ANSWERS

1. **Share a search with your friend using the system's search-sharing capability.** Not all systems have a search-sharing capability. "Save search/alert" is the name ProQuest uses. Mouse down on this link, choose "Get search link," copy it, and paste it into an email message addressed to your friend. If you cannot find an appropriate link, copy the search-result page's URL, paste it into an email message, and send it to your friend, asking him to make sure it works.

2. **Use this system's retrievals-sharing capability to send potentially relevant retrievals to your friend via email.** Almost all systems have a retrievals-sharing capability. One challenge is figuring out which link triggers it. Test the system's links called "email," "save," "share," and "export" with your friend until you find the right one. Your tests should reveal the many ways search systems enable you to share retrievals. A second challenge is deciding whether to send all retrievals to the user or to review them, sending only the most relevant retrievals. Time constraints may force the issue, and when they do, add a note to your email message telling the user to scan retrievals for relevance.

3. **Save your ongoing search.** Not all search systems allow users to save their searches. When they do, you have to register for an account so the system knows how to

connect you with your saved retrievals now and in the future. Use a mnemonic name for your saved searches, and make notes that tell why you saved them as a reminder in the future.

4. **What else can you do with your saved searches and retrievals in this search system?** What you can do with your account depends on the search system in which you registered. Check to see if this system allows you to do the following, and if it can do more, add to this list:

   - Edit a saved search
   - Save retrieved sources in one or more folders, name your folders, move sources between folders, copy sources into other folders, and delete sources from folders
   - Add notes to retrieved sources, and edit or delete your notes
   - Add more custom folders, nest folders within folders, and delete folders
   - Add a search alert, edit an existing one, or delete it
   - Add a journal alert, edit an existing one, or delete it

5. **Demonstrate your favorite CMS to your friend, showing her how to save a retrieval, both its citation and its full-text.** Almost all search systems have a CMS save-and-export capability. The challenge is figuring out which system link triggers it. A dead giveaway that you've found the correct link is a menu prompting you to export the retrieval into a CMS and naming specific CMSs, such as RefWorks, Mendeley, or Zotero. Give your friend a tour of the CMS you use, telling him or her what you like and don't like about it.

6. **What verbal or nonverbal cues might reveal that the user would be receptive to information-literacy instruction.**

   - Cues that users are receptive in this regard are their lingering after you've answered their questions, their follow-up questions that go beyond your answers, their return visits for assistance related to their original questions, and the depth that you're able to achieve in the course of answering their questions.
   - Of the two interview types, phone interviews have more promise. When a user asks for clarification, you may be able to back up, giving more background information or explaining in simpler terms than you intended. If the user asks a complex query, you might ask if she could visit you in the library so that she can follow along and make sure your research for her is on the right track.

7. **After a series of unsuccessful subject searches, you are stumped. What do you do next?** Admit to the user that you are having difficulty answering the question. Users facing immediate deadlines may change their topics right there and then. Users less concerned about time constraints are usually willing to give you their

email addresses so you can do some research on your own, including consulting your colleagues.

8. **How can you streamline your preparation before the course starts?**

   ▪ Before your colleague leaves, ask him to share what he has prepared to date.
   ▪ Draft a syllabus, breaking course content into smaller modules and scheduling it into each class period.
   ▪ Reuse course content from your previous courses.
   ▪ Show your syllabus to colleagues, and ask them to share their materials with you.
   ▪ Formulate lesson plans only for content that is new to you or that you feel unsure about.
   ▪ Search ERIC, Library Literature, Inspec, and other databases for course materials.

9. **How do you know that you've saturated the user with too much information?** When you notice one or more of these verbal and nonverbal cues, the user is saturated and it's time for you to stop:

   ▪ The user rustles or gathers up her laptop, papers, backpack, purse, and coat.
   ▪ The user no longer maintains eye contact with you.
   ▪ The user starts looking around the room instead of at you.
   ▪ The user keeps nodding her head in agreement with what you are saying.
   ▪ The user grabs her phone to check a text or incoming call.
   ▪ The user starts to move away.
   ▪ The user crosses her arms or moves from an open to a closed body stance.

Online Searching Now and in the Future

This final chapter discusses several important online searching issues, some probing the milieu in which expert intermediary searchers conduct their work and others speculating on the factors that are likely to shape online searching in the years to come. *Online Searching* concludes with a wish list of improvements to today's search systems and databases.

CURRENT TRENDS AND ISSUES

Seven current trends and issues are bound to play an important role in how online searching evolves over the next three to five years.

Satisficing in the Age of the Information Explosion

Beginning in the 1960s, the term *information explosion* came to be associated with the explosive growth in scholarship. Using cited references to measure scientific output, Bornmann and Mutz (2015) estimate that knowledge has doubled every nine years since World War II. This doubling is both a curse and a blessing. On the one hand, it makes it hard for domain experts to keep abreast of the latest developments in their chosen specialties and for aspiring scholars to achieve mastery of theirs. On the other hand, it means that there is plenty of information available on just about any topic under the sun. For most end users, finding what they want involves entering a few keywords into their favorite search systems, scanning the first few retrievals above the fold, and expecting them to link to relevant sources. The term *satisficing* has come to be associated with this information-seeking approach. The combination of *satisfy* and *suffice*, *satisficing* means "setting an acceptable level or aspiration level as a final criterion and simply taking the first acceptable [solution]" (Newell and Simon 1972, 681).

Satisficing is contrasted with *optimal decision making*—finding the best decision option. Marchionini (1995, 63–64) suggests that satisficing may be the only viable option available to information seekers in view of the herculean effort that would be needed to gather *all* pertinent information for an in-depth query and the time required to fully assimilate it. In short, people *satisfice* with regard to their information needs, finding information that is *good enough* and applying it to the situation at hand.

Good enough may be satisfactory for instructors who task students at the middle school, high school, and undergraduate levels with a research paper. They view the paper as a "meaningful learning experience," wanting students to find and synthesize the information, and, at the undergraduate level, to begin to ask themselves "What can I conclude from the research?" and "How do scholars work?" (Valentine 2001, 110).

Expecting end users to be comprehensive with respect to their information seeking may be more reasonable at the graduate level and beyond, when they are specializing in a discipline, becoming familiar with its most respected writers, and mastering the field's methods and techniques. The objective here should be finding sources that are seminal, central, and essential to the user's interests. Identifying such sources starts with the field's literature reviews, discipline-based dictionaries, and encyclopedias. If you are the library's subject specialist for one or more areas, identify the field's journals and annual review series that specialize in literature reviews. Backward chaining is useful for checking older sources cited repeatedly in the literature reviews of research publications. Finding the same ones cited in several such publications may mean that you've found the seminal works on the topic.

On a personal note, I needed to find research that "graded" the sources undergraduate students cited in their research papers. I found dozens of studies, and most cited three thirty-year-old papers that proposed methodologies for grading students' cited sources and/or applied them. These were *the* seminal works on the topic, and to amass more sources on the topic, I merely had to trace them forward via cited-reference searches in Google Scholar, Web of Science, and Scopus. For me, a "critical mass" meant that the new sources I was finding repeated what other sources had to say on the topic and their cited and citing sources failed to reveal new ones. Those are good rules of thumb to apply when making the decision whether to continue or stop searching for new information.

Users who want to go beyond the critical mass, striving for comprehensiveness, are likely to be conducting research for state-of-the-art, literature, or systematic reviews, doctoral dissertations, books, research proposals, patents, business plans, or encyclopedia articles. Their searches should run the gamut, enlisting all types of subject and known-item searches and feedback (see chapters 6, 7, 8, and 9) in a wide variety of discipline-based and encyclopedic databases. Of all the Boolean search strategies, the Can't Live Without This Facet First Strategy is recommended for high-recall searches because it allows the searcher to stop the searching before all facets are exhausted. Then follow up with the Pearl Growing Search Strategy, using search terms in relevant retrievals to find additional ones. Not necessarily a high-recall strategy, the À la Carte Edition of the Building Block Search Strategy will have to suffice for searching extended-Boolean systems, along with follow-up searches governed by the Pearl Growing Search Strategy.

Monitoring Changes to Database Content and Search-System Functionality

Just when you've mastered a search system, the vendor changes its interface or searching functionality. Changes are disruptive and disconcerting for everyone. Users notice and expect you to reorient them to the system and the favorite databases they search there. It's your job to bone up on the system, assessing what the vendor has done and changing what you say about the search system and its databases to users. To avoid surprises and prepare for changes in advance, keep up to date on information-industry news and developments; read trade publications, such as the monthly *Information Today*, semimonthly *Online Searcher*, and daily Search Engine Watch (http://searchenginewatch.com); attend conferences specific to online searching, such as Electronic Resources & Libraries (usually in March), Computers in Libraries (usually in April), and Internet Librarian (usually in October); participate in online discussion groups, such as ERIL-L and Liblicense-L; and share what you learn with your expert searcher colleagues via email, staff newsletter, intranet, blog, and/or a private Facebook or Google group. Use in-service training opportunities to brief your colleagues on momentous industry developments, possibly devoting entire sessions to in-depth analyses of new search systems and databases or comprehensive changes to existing ones. The availability of so many search systems and databases makes it impossible for you, your expert searcher colleagues, and users to remember all the details. Document changes on a searching language cheat sheet to which you and your colleagues can refer when they consult the search system and its databases in the future.

Track what you and your library's users are doing at the reference desk using a reference-tracking-and-reporting (RTR) application. Such applications provide forms on which you and your colleagues describe the nature and substance of your reference interviews with users. In figure 15.1, the librarian uses Gimlet for RTR, entering the duration, question, answer, and even more about the interaction (Sidecar Publications 2018).

It may seem burdensome to document every interview, but it could pay off later when you search Gimlet's entries to determine whether your colleagues have encountered the same question and how they've answered it. Gimlet's reporting capability also gives you tools to tally data on completed forms, create graphs and tables that summarize the library's reference activity, and analyze them so that you can develop an in-depth understanding of your library's reference service and fine-tune it as necessary.

Analyze COUNTER-compliant data to find out which databases your library's users are searching and which online journals they are reading. If you think better databases and journals are underused, rethink their presentation at your library's website; mount a publicity campaign to increase awareness among users most likely

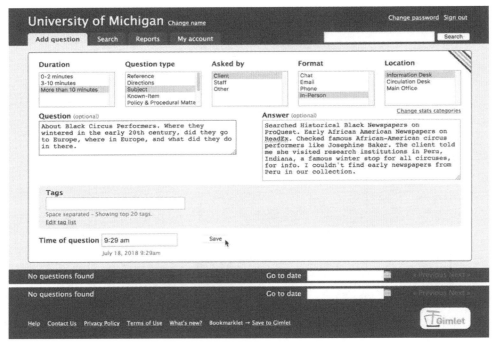

FIGURE 15.1
Characterizing a Reference Interview in Gimlet
Source: Courtesy of Sidecar Publications.

to benefit from using them; and revise your information-literacy efforts so that instructional materials, LibGuides, and your one-time and sustained interactions with users promote them. Gingerly touch base with instructors, making sure they are aware of better sources so that your recommendations don't contradict theirs. In short, you want to stay one step ahead of the game, knowing which resources your library's users gravitate toward and which questions they are likely to ask and anticipating changes to the search systems and databases you use all the time.

Disambiguating Legitimate Retrievals from Everything Else

Google and other Web search engines build a profile of your preferences based on the data-laden cookies and personal-tracking beacons they install in your Web browser and mobile apps. In response to your queries, web-based search engines routinely personalize search results, adding ads and paid content in keeping with your profile. As a result, the search engine creates a *filter bubble* around you that it fills with content biased toward your points of view, likes, and preferences (Pariser 2011). When you search for something ephemeral, trivial, and superficial, you might want Web search engines to personalize results, delivering retrievals that pertain to your personal interests and desires. When conducting research, you want search results that are immune to bias so you can take all viewpoints into consideration.

Thankfully, search systems that access licensed databases do not engage in profiling practices that give precedence to certain content. These systems do, however, perform relevance ranking, and because they don't publish specifics about their search algorithms, they leave searchers in the dark about the criteria they use to rank retrievals. Thankfully again, these search systems provide alternatives to ranked retrievals, such as listing them chronologically in ascending or descending order or alphabetically by author or title. Encourage users to experiment with different display modes. If they find relevant retrievals from other modes on a consistent basis, users might begin to question relevance ranking in search systems generally, sampling other display modes and making a habit of browsing beyond the first page of ranked retrievals.

Personally, no matter which system I search, I treat their first-listed retrievals as suspect. I pay attention to subtle cues that something is not right with their retrievals. You should be skeptical, too, making sure that the licensed online systems and services your library provides to users are free of potential bias and treat sources objectively and on their own merits. If you sense something is amiss, document what's happening with saved searches, saved retrievals, and screenshots; share your documentation with the service's customer service representative; and ask for an explanation. This is expected in return for the good money your library pays for vendor-supplied systems and services.

Subsidizing the Cost of Searching the Web

If you've ever wondered about how "free" web-based services generate revenue to remain in business, Pariser (2011, 6) sums up the secret to their success as follows: "You're getting a free service, and the cost is information about you." Your personal data are the search statements you enter into search engines, the travel dates and destinations you submit to travel aggregators, the photographs you share on image hosts, the stories you like on social news sites, the players you trade in fantasy football, and much more. Everyone who surfs the Web pays for the free services they use there with the personal data they enter into websites and the merchandise they buy there.

Here's how it works on Google. Advertisers supply Google with both ads and keywords describing their ads; in fact, they pay Google for keywords based on popularity, the most expensive keywords being those that people search most frequently. Advertisers also pay Google when people click on their ads, so they want Google to display their ads on websites where users are likely to click on them. When you enter a query into Google, it responds with ranked retrievals; some retrievals bear content likely to answer your queries and other retrievals are ads with keywords that are in keeping with your search terms and with the profile that Google has on file for you. Click on an ad and make purchases online there, and the advertiser benefits so he can stay in business and renew his advertising contract with Google. Google generates additional revenue by paying website owners to host the same ads they display on pages of ranked retrievals. Here's how it works. Website owners sign up with Google, and Google places codes on hosting websites that identify their content. When you launch a host's website, the code senses your identity, checks the profile it has on file for you, and inserts ads into the host's website that are in keeping with both your interests and the content on the host's website. If all this sounds more like advertising than Web searching, it probably is.

You can actually see this whole process unfold before your very eyes. Search for a flight at a "free" web-based travel-aggregator agency. Whether you purchase the flight or not, the agency places a cookie on your personal computer, saying, "This person wants cheap flights to [insert city name] on [insert day]." A day passes, and you launch your Web browser, going to a favorite website to check the weather, play a game, or find a recipe. The website opens bearing personalized ads from airlines, hotels, and/ or rental car companies that are in keeping with your search of the travel agency the day before. This isn't magic—it's due to your Web browser passing a cookie to the website's advertising agency, which responds with an instantaneous auction, grabbing ads from the highest-bidding travel-oriented companies and inserting them into the website you're looking at now.

If you are uncomfortable with the reach that web-based services have in what you do or think next, there are alternatives; for example, searching the DuckDuckGo search engine (https://duckduckgo.com) instead of Google, Bing, or Yahoo or entering a query via Startpage (https://startpage.com) into Google. See where your fellow classmates stand on privacy concerns by discussing these points in class:

- Cite evidence convincing you that Google and other Web services (e.g., travel, sports, social networking, shopping sites) are using your personal data.
- Have you or your friends ever avoided Google and other Web services because you knew they were tracking you? If you are willing to share, describe the information you or your friends were seeking, why you avoided certain services, and alternative strategies you employed to get the information you wanted.
- What responsibilities do you have regarding the personal data you enter into web-based services for your library's users?
- How would you advise your library's users about personal data they enter into web-based services?

The Importance of Source Credibility in the Wake of the Fake News Epidemic

Evidence of misleading, fabricated, or false reports comes from a variety of places and time periods (Batchelor 2017; Jacobson 2017):

- Europe in the Middle Ages: Catholic Church's claims over various European regions
- America in the late 1800s: yellow journalism
- Nazi Germany in the 1930s: racist propaganda
- America in 2014: buying marijuana with food stamps

A new sense of urgency regarding source credibility emerged in the wake of the fake news epidemic that accompanied the 2016 US presidential election. That the circulation of fake news stories reached a feverish pitch during this election was due to a perfect storm of factors:

- *The decline of traditional news outlets* (Quint 2017; Rochlin 2017). For the last two decades, newspapers across the country had failed due to lost revenue, and network news had been plagued by double-digit drops in believability ratings. With fewer active outlets, less news written by professionally trained journalists was reaching everyday people.
- *The rise of social-media outlets for news* (Gottfried and Shearer 2016). A Pew survey reported that, by the time of the US election, the majority (62 percent) of Americans were getting their news from social media. Social media news is easy, convenient, free, and available at any time. The news that people read on their social-media feed is a curious amalgamation, some pieces passed on to them automatically by the profile that the outlet has on file for them and other pieces passed on by friends who want to share.
- *On social-media outlets, popularity determines what's news* (Laybats and Tredinnick 2016; Ohlheiser 2018; Ojala 2017). In traditional media, headlines and story placement are indicators of a story's importance. Social media has changed all that. Algorithms detect the buzz surrounding a story, the story passes from obscurity to trending, more people see the story in their newsfeeds and pass it on to friends, and very quickly the story goes viral. That a piece reaches viral status may be due to most people's outrage and disbelief, but social media algorithms can't interpret what's behind the likes, shares, and comments that a piece receives.
- *The filter bubble that creates personalized worlds, where individuals read, see, and hear what they want* (Badke 2016; Laybats and Tredinnick 2016; Pariser 2011; Spohr 2017). People operate "in their own bubble of content created by the personalization algorithms of social media services, which feed [them] content [they] are in tune with, and filter out content that [they] might find objectionable, unpalatable, or simply uninteresting" (Spohr 2017). If things aren't going your way, you might not notice because you're only aware of what these systems' personalization algorithms are sending you.
- *The ease of monetizing websites by publishing fake news* (Kennedy 2017; Rochlin 2017; Seargeant and Tagg 2018). Making pennies per click from web-search and

advertising services might not seem like a lot, but pennies quickly become dollars when your content is clickbait, provocative content that piques people's curiosity to the extent that they *have to* click on it. Nothing is stopping website owners from posting *anything* online. When you click and share stories with your friends, website owners and advertisers make money. That a band of enterprising young Macedonians took advantage of the situation is not coincidental. They identified a lucrative marketplace (the United States during the 2016 election), populated their websites with fabricated news stories about the election that appealed to people's emotions, watched as their stories went viral, and made a fistful of cash that would go a long way in their countries (Wendling 2018).

When the 2016 US election results were final, people from both sides of the electorate emerged temporarily from their filter bubbles, seeking explanations for unexpected results. Facebook came under fire as the source of much of the fake news that grabbed headlines during the campaign's last three months (Silverman 2016; Zuckerberg 2016). The results of a Pew survey revealed that everyday Americans contributed to the fake news epidemic as a result of knowingly or unknowingly sharing a fake news story (Barthel, Mitchell, and Holcomb 2016). Suddenly, it became fashionable to refer to the present day as the post-truth era. Naming post-truth as the 2016 Word of the Year, the Oxford English Dictionary defined it as "relating to or denoting circumstances in which objective facts are less influential in shaping public opinion than personal belief" (Oxford Dictionaries). About the post-truth era, Johnson (2017) adds that "it's about picking the facts that you want to be true" (15). Laybats and Tredinnick (2016) elaborate further:

> We are living . . . in an age where politics no longer functions through rational discourse. The facts of the matter are of secondary importance to free-floating opinion. Instead, truth is replaced by demonstrative arguments that appeal to the electorate on a more visceral and emotional level. . . . It is characterized by a willful blindness to evidence, a mistrust of authority, and an appeal to emotionally based arguments often rooted in fears or anxieties. (204)

Regarding fake news as an artifact of the malaise that marks the post-truth era, pundits scrambled to offer solutions that would minimize its impact in the future:

- Establish a new government institution to deal with the natural tension between public opinion and reliable information (Lemann 2016).
- Pressure such technology firms as Facebook, Google, and Twitter to take more responsibility for fake news and misinformation, including identifying themselves as technology-media hybrids (Spohr 2017, 157).

- Appoint a government-supported inquiry into the problem of fake news and ways to combat it (Seargeant and Tagg 2018).
- Boost the strength and impact of quality journalism by supporting it financially (Kennedy 2017).
- Develop machine algorithms to detect false news (Kompella 2017; Rochlin 2017).
- Establish nonalgorithmic news segregators staffed by qualified journalists and scholars (Berghel 2017).

To get started on combatting the problem of fake news requires consensus with respect to its definition. "Sources that entirely fabricate information, disseminate deceptive content, or grossly distort actual news reports" is the definition of *fake news* that Melissa Zimdars (2016) gives in a Google document she created for her undergraduate students to help them distinguish between reliable and unreliable sources. Rochlin (2017) offers two definitions, but qualifies the first, calling it "real fake news":

> Real "fake news" (oh, the irony) can be roughly defined as a knowingly false headline and story . . . written and published on a website that is designed to look like a real news site, and is spread via social media. The intent of this sort of fake news is to have as many people like and share the fake story as possible, because the more clicks a link receives, the more money in advertising it will generate.

This definition describes clickbait. It's difficult to beat because clickbait experts make big money, get an emotional high from watching graphs of their fake stories go viral, and quickly devise new and creative ways to deceive the public (Wendling 2018).

Rochlin's (2017) second definition goes in an entirely different direction, asserting that fake news is "any story that goes against one's personal beliefs or feelings" (388). Such a definition puts agreement about what constitutes fake news entirely in the mind of the beholder. Here's a sample scenario that demonstrates how three different people interpret the same article. Adam, Baker, and Charlie search the General Reference Center Gold database and retrieve a news story with this main title, "The 'McCarthying' of Roy Moore and What He Stands For," and with this subtitle, "Judge Roy Moore, Who Ran for a Senate Seat in Alabama, was Attacked Almost Nonstop by the Media for Allegations that Wouldn't Make the Front Page if he were a Liberal Democrat." Charlie, true blue to his liberal roots, can't get past the title, dismissing the article out of hand and fuming that it is fake news that doesn't belong in a licensed database. Baker, who is a registered Republican, starts reading the article immediately, pleased that its arguments match his own. Adam treats the article as a primary source, indicative of the type of political rhetoric that has come to characterize the post-truth era. Which user reacts to this news story correctly?

To be honest, there is no correct or incorrect reaction. Charlie reacts like those who are faithful to the Democratic Party's ideological and political views, Baker reacts like a Republican, and Adam reacts like an archivist or a historian. Thus, the labeling system that Zimdars applies to sources will be entirely unacceptable to people who don't share the same ideological and political views of the classifier. For the same reason will machine algorithms, panels staffed by human beings, efforts of a new government institution, viewpoints issued by a government inquiry to study the problem, and even technology firms that coidentify as media companies, be unacceptable.

The only solution is education—digital literacy, information literacy, media literacy, and the development of critical reasoning skills. Librarians have always been leaders in the information-literacy enterprise. They can build on their existing efforts, helping people identify outright falsehoods; distinguish between advertising, opinion, and news reports; and recognize politically leaning platforms of all stripes (Jacobson 2017). Educating people about using information provides them with knowledge and skills that are theirs for a lifetime, making it possible for them to rise above the din, hear their own voices, and develop a sense of agency about their wielding information in the course of achieving personal and professional goals. Don't expect this role to be glamorous or win awards or widespread acclaim, nor will it be possible for you to reach everyone, even those who are physically present and accounted for.

Many librarians have already stepped up to the plate, and their educational efforts in this regard are hitting home runs, such as these stepwise approaches for evaluating information:

- Eight steps for spotting fake news: (1) consider the source. (2) read beyond. (3) check the author. (4) supporting sources? (5) check the date. (6) is it a joke? (7) check your biases. (8) ask the experts (International Federation of Library Associations 2018).
- CRAAP test for evaluating information (Batchelor 2017; Smith 2017).
- CARS for evaluating websites (Gardner 2017; Jacobson 2017).
- Four points: (1) Read laterally, (2) keep it nonpolitical, (3) talk about social media, (4) switch it up (Gardner 2017).
- IMVAIN: Is the material independent or self-interested? Does it have multiple sources or one? Does it verify or assert? Is it authoritative informed or uninformed? Are sources named or unnamed? (Gardner 2017).
- Three competencies for civic online reasoning: (1) Who's behind the information? (2) What's the evidence? (3) What do other sources say? (McGrew et al. 2017; Stanford History Education Group 2016).

The American Library Association's (2017) LibGuides website is a good place to start your investigation of fake news, where there are toolkits, webinars, guides, and links to fact-checking websites. Following up with Joyce Valenza's (2016) blog should triple what you find at ALA plus provide you with her explanation of the fake-news epidemic. Hernandez (2017) enlisted a systematic approach to studying fake news to build a LibGuide with four tiers that become increasingly more concrete and specific, beginning with defining fake news, applying information-literacy skills to fake-news detection, showcasing resources from other institutions, and improving information literacy generally. Batchelor (2017) lists more LibGuides, along with lists of academic and public libraries offering full-semester classes and programs dedicated to the topic, respectively. Special projects have promise for developing best practices, standards, and strategies. Examples are The Trust Project, developing transparency standards so people can easily assess the news stories they read; News Literacy Project, giving middle and high school students tips, tools, and resources to learn how to tell fact from fiction; and Project Look Sharp, providing lesson plans, materials, training, and support to help teachers integrate media literacy into their classroom curricula. Linguistics faculty at the Open University have developed animated short videos on skillful interactions with social media (Seargeant and Tagg 2018). Nonpartisan fact checkers are useful for insight on the latest trends, issues, and gone-viral sensations: FactCheck at the University of Pennsylvania; Politifact, a Pulitzer Prize–winning website of the *Tampa Bay Times*; Snopes, a regular winner of various "Best of the Web" awards and recipient of two Webby Awards; and Retraction Watch for scientific papers. Responding to calls for state-mandated media literacy at all education levels is Washington State (Batchelor 2017; Jacobson 2017; McGrew et al. 2017; Padgett 2017), and Illinois and New York State have mandated civic education at the high school level (Batchelor 2017; Colglazier 2017).

Although librarians have a treasure trove of information-literacy strategies to share with users, addressing fake news is not the occasion for business as usual. Evaluating sources is only part of the picture. It's about understanding how ranking algorithms work, what data the search system collects about people and how it uses them, which methods clickbait experts use to make their content go viral, how online advertising works, how everyday people can transform unskillful actions that exacerbate the problem of fake news into skillful ones that neutralize or mitigate the problem, and much more. To accomplish this, librarians need to join with others, such as advertising professionals, competitive intelligence specialists, fact checkers, information architects, journalists, search engine developers, search engine optimization (SEO) consultants, social-media developers, and so on, to develop a thorough understanding of the situation; broaden information literacy's scope; and combine the best of what everyone does on their own into something bold, effective, and imaginative.

The Future of Boolean Search Systems

Boolean search languages are complicated. Perhaps the only people who use the full range of a system's Boolean searching language are expert intermediary searchers, who have taken for-credit, graduate-level online searching courses and search these systems on a daily basis at the reference desk, and search system representatives, who give on-demand demonstrations and tutorials to prospective and current clients. In the mid-1980s, a National Information Standards Organization (NISO) committee defined a common command language for Boolean search systems, but the common language never really caught on (Hildreth 1986). As a result, Boolean systems are similar functionally, but their searching languages are all different, putting the burden on the searcher to learn their individual languages to use them to their full extent.

In the 1990s, the combination of graphical user interfaces (GUIs) and Web browsers simplified searching languages, replacing the formulation and entry of complicated command-bound search statements with a series of simple point-and-click actions; however, to assemble these series requires an understanding of facet analysis, indexing languages, thesaurus relationships, Boolean operators, and search strategy. Few end users have such an understanding. Thus, it should not come as a surprise that analyses of search statements entered into today's search systems conclude that these search statements are short and simple, and they rarely enlist elements of a system's formal searching language (Bloom and Deyrup 2012; Holman 2011; Park and Lee 2013).

EBSCOhost is exceptional in its ability to strike a happy medium between Boolean and extended-Boolean searching. Its Boolean functionality appeals to expert searchers who are partial to the exactitude of Boolean searching, browsing and selecting CV from a database's thesaurus, entering FT search statements directly, and choosing specific fields especially for known-item searches. EBSCOhost responds to zero-posted Boolean searches with extended-Boolean searches (EBSCOhost calls it SmartText searching), displaying relevance-ranked retrievals and clusters that users can explore to narrow their interests. Extended-Boolean searching appeals to end users because they can enter anything—a series of keywords, a rambling statement, or a title or abstract they copied and pasted from a retrieved source—into the search box and then click on "SmartText Searching" to divert EBSCOhost from its Boolean default to its extended-Boolean search.

Predicting the Demise of Licensed Databases

Researchers have predicted the demise of licensed databases (Chen 2010; Meier and Conkling 2008). Fueling their predictions are their observations that Google Scholar's coverage is comparable to this and that licensed database's coverage and that most journals post their tables of contents on the open Web, where Web search engines index their content. They suggest that libraries could save money, canceling their subscriptions to licensed databases and delegating database searching to Google, Google Scholar, Bing, and comparable "free" search services.

What these researchers fail to take into consideration is that database publishers make selection decisions about the sources they index in their databases, striving to be comprehensive about the disciplinary literature they cover, as well as covering the most respected, highly cited, and top-cited sources in the discipline—not only journals, but also the major genres in which domain experts publish their scholarship. Especially in favor of the current database search system model is the advanced functionality that search systems offer—a CV that uses domain-expert terminology; an online thesaurus for browsing, selecting, and exploding CV terms; alphabetical browsing indexes; field searching, especially for known-item searches; presearch qualifiers; postsearch clusters; and find-like searches (Bates et al. 2017; Buckland 2017). Discipline-based databases also publish lists of the sources they index to convince domain experts that they cover the most important sources in the discipline. Their search systems feature functionality so that domain experts can limit searches to one or more journals of interest. Finally, domain experts, whose searches in their discipline's go-to databases retrieve no new sources that they aren't already aware of, can rest assured that they are keeping abreast of the latest developments.

Consider the ABI/INFORM database. It specializes in business exclusively, providing full-text access not only to journals but also to dissertations, conference proceedings, working papers, and newspapers. ABI/INFORM strives to achieve comprehensiveness and depth in its coverage of the world's business literature (ProQuest 2018). Available through the ProQuest search system, ABI/INFORM provides searchers with a wide array of CV and FT searching tools. Search ABI/INFORM's online thesaurus and classification codes, limiting searches to controlled vocabulary that produce high-precision results. ProQuest searchers can browse special database fields naming companies/organizations, NAICS codes, persons, and locations; that is, criteria that are typical of user queries for business topics. Accompanying ABI/INFORM search results are clusters to help users define their interests more specifically. FT searching of full-texts is available to searchers. When displaying a full surrogate, check sources under the "Related items" for ProQuest's find-like results. A shopping analogy is appropriate here. When shopping, such specialty items as bird feeders, purses, and jeans can be found at a megadiscount retailer (e.g., Target, Walmart, or Meijer), but for quality, selection, and personal service, you'd go to a specialty store (e.g., Wild Birds Unlimited, Coach, and True Religion Brand Jeans). The same thing applies to database searching.

Web-Scale Discovery Systems: The New Google for Academic Content

If licensed databases and search systems perceive a threat, it comes from web-scale discovery (WSD) systems. The development of WSD systems is in response to library users who don't know where to start searching for scholarly, professional, and educational information, and when they do choose a database, they can't establish a foothold because searching there is complex, arcane, or unnatural.

Baffled and perplexed, users revert to what's familiar to them and what's worked in the past—Google, Wikipedia, and the open Web. To win them back, libraries have implemented WSD systems, one-stop shopping for academic information. Into a Google-like search box, users enter their search statements, and the WSD system searches a humongous index bearing content from the OPAC, licensed databases, quality open Web databases, and institutional repositories and retrieves surrogate records, many bearing abstracts, summaries, tables of contents, full-texts (when available), or links to full-texts, all ranked according to relevance.

More than a half-decade of WSD-system deployment in libraries has passed, and there are now studies that shed light on this new system's impact. At Grand Valley State University, Way (2010) attributes the dramatic decrease in the use of A&I databases and increase in full-text downloads from full-text databases to the WSD system. A study of four WSD systems across two dozen academic institutions also reports an overall increase in full-text downloads after WSD-system implementation (Levine-Clark, McDonald, and Price 2014). Korah and Cassidy (2010) surveyed Sam Houston State University (SHSU) students regarding their use of Web search engines, the library's search tools, and its federated search system (a precursor to today's WSD systems). SHSU researchers conclude that students' preference between individual databases and federated search is related to their class, starting at ratios of 1:1 for freshmen, 2:1 for upperclassmen, 4:1 for master's students, and 7:1 for doctoral students, adding that, by the time students reach graduate levels, their level of sophistication with their chosen disciplines may be more suited for their disciplines' go-to databases. Once aspiring students stake their claim to a discipline and "find" disciplinary databases, they stick with these databases, benefiting from their disciplinary specialization and their full-fledged functionality. Both graduate and undergraduate students give high satisfaction ratings to their university library's WSD system (Lundrigan, Manuel, and Yan 2016); graduate students qualify their use of the WSD system, considering its general results, to be suitable for undergraduates and prefer subject-oriented databases for their research, particularly databases bearing data, statistics, reports, and other specialized forms and genres. When subject search results from a WSD system and from subject-oriented databases are compared, the latter excel in producing high-precision results (Lee and Chung 2016); the researchers attribute this finding to the encyclopedic nature and sheer immensity of WSD-system indexes that makes specific information on topics hard to find. Two distinct trends emerge from research results: WSD systems are tools undergraduates embrace for finding relevant information, and subject-oriented databases are graduate students' tools of choice because they give disciplinary context to searches and their coverage includes discipline-specific specialized forms and genres that graduates students seek. In conclusion, these trends aren't ones that give librarians carte blanche for axing database subscriptions.

FUTURE FUNCTIONALITY WISH LIST

Search systems and databases aren't perfect. They continue to evolve. Here's my wish list for future functionality.

1. Automatic Facet Detection in Extended-Boolean Search Systems

Boolean search systems are tremendously efficient because they enable expert searchers to enter multiple synonyms for each facet, create intermediate sets for each facet, and then combine intermediate sets into a final result set. Entering a Boolean search bearing three synonyms per facet for a three-faceted query would require the direct entry of twenty-seven separate search statements in an extended-Boolean system! That's really inefficient. Some extended-Boolean systems perform automatic vocabulary control, adding synonyms to search statements, but they don't report back which synonyms they add, so searchers never know how such systems enhance their queries.

Extended-Boolean systems should be able to detect the synonyms in search statements, cluster synonyms together in facets, perform searches, and give greater weights to retrievals matching one or more synonyms for *all* facets in queries. In fact, such an enhancement could use the same technology that fuels article spinning, a black-hat SEO technique. Because this technique detects words and phrases in texts and replaces them with synonyms, it should be able to detect synonyms in a string of words and phrases and group the synonyms together for searching and relevance-retrievals ranking.

Ultimately, an extended-Boolean system enhanced with automatic facet detection has the potential to increase relevant retrievals because it has more search terms to work with. For example, today's extended-Boolean systems are satisfactory, retrieving relevant sources for the search statement `alcoholism spirituality relapse`, bearing one search term per facet that is in keeping with the À la Carte Edition of the Building Block Search Strategy. If extended-Boolean could only process this more complex search statement:

```
spirituality  alcoholism  alcoholics  anonymous  relapse
religion  intoxicants  recovery  rehabilitation  twelve
steps  sobriety
```

This bears several search terms per facet and is in keeping with the Buffet Edition of the Building Block Search Strategy. Because there are more search terms for the system to consider, it has the potential to increase relevant retrievals. Plus, sources that match two or three search terms per facet should be criteria that extended-Boolean systems with automatic facet recognition use to boost a source's ranking in retrievals lists.

2. Improved Controlled Vocabulary Tools for End Users

About the only people who use CVs are expert intermediary searchers. They put their training to work, converting user-supplied terms into a database's CV and searching for them using the search system's CV-browsing, sets-creation, and sets-combination features. CVs are a powerful tool for producing high-precision results, and it's time for search-system developers to add functionality that integrates CVs into their systems so that users take advantage of them.

Search systems that are able to perform automatic facet detection should also be able to distinguish between individual words and phrases that make up user queries. The next logical step is for these systems to match these words and phrases to the database's CV. Systems can replace user terms matching "use" references with authorized index terms to increase relevant retrievals. They could use an index term's syndetic structure to perform automatic vocabulary assistance, producing retrievals for matches of CV terms and exploding CV terms; that is, searching for a matched term's narrower terms (NTs) in low-posted searches.

That a database doesn't have a CV shouldn't be a showstopper. Developments with linked data include cross-walks between two or more CVs (Cobb 2015). Consider cross-walked CVs for a particular discipline working in concert. When a word or phrase in a user query matches an index term in one CV, cross-walks would make it possible for systems to find index terms in other CVs for the same concept or idea. Then the system represents index terms from all cross-walked CVs in its default FT searching language and performs retrievals. Search systems can do the same thing in databases bearing a CV to increase low-posted searches; that is, they'd find synonymous terms via CV cross-walks and add matching index terms to the search. I'm also confident that system designers can come up with stepwise search assistants that usher users through the process of displaying an index term's syndetic structure, inviting them to choose related terms and incorporating their selections into the ongoing search, much like how expert intermediary searchers conduct CV searches now (pages 117 to 123). All these ideas about improved CV searching hinge on automatic facet detection queries, so things aren't going to happen overnight.

3. Improved Database Selection Tools for End Users

The impetus for building WSD systems is Google-like simplicity—one search statement searches a gargantuan pool of sources. No database selection is necessary on the part of the user. To attract users to the library's licensed databases, librarians, database publishers, and search-system designers should work together to improve database-selection tools. Certainly, LibGuides and sustained instruction events are two ways to get started, but their reach is limited. Which automated tools are possible? A long time ago, searches of Dialindex, Dialog's huge index to its many databases, reported numbers of retrievals for queries across multiple databases so that searchers could follow up with in-depth searches in databases contributing the most sources. Why can't WSD systems do the same? If users notice that one or two particular databases are contributing the most sources, they may be inclined to navigate to that database specifically and benefit from its advanced features, such as discipline-specific CV, alphabetical index browsing, find-like searches, altmetrics, and more. How UIUC's Easy Search generates its suggested databases is an automated process involving its analysis of retrievals from the WorldCat database; the Library of Congress classification numbers on these retrievals; and look-up tables for databases, libraries, and subject-specialist librarians (pages 24 to 25). We need more creative solutions to the database round-up problem to make licensed databases attractive to users and responsive to their queries.

4. Automatic Source Evaluator

Most users pay lip service to source evaluation, telling anyone who asks that they recognize its importance. In practice, if they evaluate sources at all, they do so in a cursory manner. Why can't search systems that access licensed databases provide more automatic assistance in this regard? Most A&I and full-text databases already provide presearch qualifiers and postsearch clusters that enable users to limit retrievals to scholarly or peer-reviewed sources. Why not link to bibliometrics, altmetrics, and ORCID ID data so users could check author credentials and discover the latest buzz pertaining to a source?

In the wake of the fake-news epidemic, source evaluation is more important than ever before. The *ultimate challenge* is getting people to evaluate the information they find on the open Web and on social media because the information they find there is so variable. All too often, emotion and belief drive people's impulse to share what they find there with friends and family, and sharing has the unintentional consequence of drawing more attention to information than it deserves and spiraling things out of control. An automatic source evaluator could take the form of a digital-enabled coach that detects a user's sharing response, such as a tweet or Facebook post. The e-coach would interrupt users, prompting them with questions they should ask to evaluate what they are reading. Researchers are beginning to experiment with e-coaches, displaying the questions they should be asking about the source; for example, *who* wrote it, *what* did they write about, *where* was it published, *when* was it published, and *why* was it published (page 277). The e-coach would then advise users on the impact of their sharing; for example, pushing the story into trending or viral territory, making money for the originator, or guaranteeing wider distribution of the information than it deserves.

5. Intelligent Stemming in Boolean Search Systems

Intelligent stemming should be standard issue in all search systems so that searchers don't have to wonder whether their search terms retrieve singular, plural, and irregular nouns or common word endings on verbs that vary due to past, present, future, and conditional tenses. This would relieve expert searchers from having to keep track of two or three truncation symbols per system and of the subtle nuances pertaining to how a search system applies plural-singular retrieval and truncates simple word stems. When searchers need to be explicit about truncation to retrieve exactly what they want, systems should spell out the details in their online help. All too often, such help is sketchy and scant, giving few details and one obscure example. Also, give searchers controls to turn intelligent stemming on and off.

6. Automatic Technical Reader

While abstracts usually give enough information about a source for users to determine its relevance, they are vague about details that would enable users to know exactly how the source applies to their interests. Thus, such a reader would create a representation that is a middle ground between an abstract and a full-text. For research, it would draw attention to the source's title and abstract and then invite the user to read its introduction to determine the problem that the researcher is trying to solve, his objectives, and the research's importance; scan its methods section to determine how the researcher conducted the experiment; and study the source's conclusions, where the researcher states his most important findings. Nonresearch sources would be more challenging for an automatic technical reader to process because they don't have the same predictable structure as do reports of research. Because some users think that abstracts are full-texts, an automatic reader would have to present its middle-ground representation in a way that impresses on users that they still have to put effort into reading the full-texts of their most relevant retrievals.

7. Online Help

This is a no-brainer. *Every* search system should have online help that users can both browse and search. It should be called "help" on every Web page, and the link or button that opens help should be located in a conspicuous location *above the fold* on every Web page. Search systems should submit their online help to usability testing to make sure everyone understands it—end users and expert searchers alike.

8. Personalization That Users Control

Let users decide when and whether they want systems to perform personalization. Search systems should give users an on-off switch or let users regulate its strength using a slider. Personally, I like personalization when I'm traveling, wanting to know where the nearest Whole Foods, Lowe's, or Target is located, but when I'm conducting research, I would turn personalization off, wanting to see *all* retrievals, not just those that agree with my point of view.

HANDING YOU THE BATON

Okay, so expert intermediary searchers don't have batons, but they do have to orchestrate a wide array of factors to achieve their goal of helping people satisfy their information needs. So much about people is variable—their knowledge of the topic that interests them; their ability to articulate what they want to someone else; the depth of their specific knowledge of the topic they seek; their overall knowledge and ability to handle scientific, technical, and scholarly information; and the time and effort they are able (or willing) to put into solving the information problem at hand. At the library's website, the databases that your institution's budget can support to satisfy the information demands of its user base may number in the dozens, hundreds, or thousands. The search systems that access licensed databases and free open Web databases have a wide variety of searching, browsing, selecting, and retrievals-management functionality. Finally, there's you! You have prepared by taking a graduate-level course in online searching, reading *Online Searching* carefully and thoughtfully, answering its end-of-the-chapter questions, comparing your answers with its answers, and discussing them in class. To round out your knowledge, you've probably taken graduate information-literacy, reference, education, and one or more discipline-based-reference courses. You have your particular subject expertise to draw on, as well as your question-negotiation and interviewing skills. Add to the foregoing your boundless energy, extraordinary enthusiasm, and an unwavering personal commitment to the field of library and information science, and you are ready to step onto the podium, pick up the baton, and orchestrate the wide array of factors that make up the online searching enterprise in the service of helping your library's users satisfy their information needs.

BIBLIOGRAPHY

American Library Association. 2017. "Evaluating Information: Home." Accessed July 5, 2018. http://libguides.ala.org/InformationEvaluation.

Badke, William. 2016. "Evidence and the Doubter." *Online Searcher* 40, no. 2: 71–73.

Barthel, Michael, Amy Mitchell, and Jesse Holcomb. 2016. "Many Americans Believe Fake News Is Sowing Confusion." Accessed July 5, 2018. http://www.journalism.org/2016/12/15/many-americans-believe-fake-news-is-sowing-confusion/.

Batchelor, Oliver. 2017. "Getting Out the Truth: The Role of Libraries in the Fight against Fake News." *Reference Services Review* 45, no. 2: 143–48.

Bates, Jessica, Paul Best, Janice McQuilkin, and Brian Taylor. 2017. "Will Web Search Engines Replace Bibliographic Databases in the Systematic Identification of Research?" *The Journal of Academic Librarianship* 43: 8–17.

Berghel, Hal. 2017. "Lies, Damn Lies, and Fake News." *Computer* 50, no. 2: 80–85.

Bloom, Beth S., and Marta Deyrup. 2012. "The Truth Is Out: How Students REALLY Search." Paper presented at the Charleston Library Conference, Charleston, SC, November 7–10. http://dx.doi.org/10.5703/1288284315103.

Bornmann, Lutz, and Rudiger Mutz. 2015. "Growth Rates of Modern Science: A Bibliometric Analysis Based on the Number of Publications and Cited References." *Journal of the Association for Information Science and Technology* 66, no. 11 (Nov.): 2215–22.

Buckland, Michael K. 2017. "Library Technology in the Next 20 Years." *Library Hi Tech* 35, no. 1: 5–10.

Chen, Xiaotian. 2010. "The Declining Value of Subscription-Based Abstracting and Indexing Services in the New Knowledge Dissemination Era." *Serials Review* 36: 79–85.

Cobb, Joan. 2015. "The Journey to Linked Open Data: The Getty Vocabularies." *Journal of Library Metadata* 15: 142–56.

Colglazier, Will. 2017. "Real Teaching in an Era of Fake News." *American Educator* 41, no. 3: 10–11.

Gardner, Laura. 2017. "Information Literacy, a Revised Plan." *School Library Journal* 63, no. 1 (Jan.): 20.

Gottfried, Jeffrey, and Elisa Shearer. 2016. "News Use across Social Media Platforms 2016." Accessed July 5, 2018. http://www.journalism.org/2016/05/26/news-use-across-social -media-platforms-2016/.

Hernandez, Carolina. 2017. "Fake News and Information Literacy: Creating Resources to Develop Source Evaluation Skills at the University of Oregon Libraries." *OLA Quarterly* 23, no. 1: 13–15.

Hildreth, Charles. 1986. "Communicating with Online Catalogs and Other Retrieval Systems: The Need for a Standard Command Language." *Library Hi Tech* 4: 7–11.

Holman, Lucy. 2011. "Millennial Students' Mental Models of Search: Implications for Academic Librarians and Database Developers." *The Journal of Academic Librarianship* 37, no. 1: 19–27.

International Federation of Library Associations. 2018. "How to Spot Fake News." Accessed July 5, 2018. https://www.ifla.org/publications/node/11174.

Jacobson, Linda. 2017. "The Smell Test: In the Era of Fake News, Librarians Are Our Best Hope." *School Library Journal* 63, no. 1 (Jan.): 24–28.

Johnson, Ben. 2017. "Information Literacy Is Dead: The Role of Libraries in a Post-Truth World." *Computers in Libraries* 37, no. 2 (Mar.): 12–15.

Kennedy, Shirley Duglin. 2017. "How Fake News Settles into Facebook and Gets Shipped around the Web." *Information Today* 34, no. 1: 8.

Kompella, Kashyap. 2017. "Can Machine Learning Help Fight Fake News?" *EContent* 40, no. 5: 40.

Korah, Abe, and Erin Dorris Cassidy. 2010. "Students and Federated Searching: Survey of Use and Satisfaction." *Reference & User Services Quarterly* 49, no. 4: 325–32.

Laybats, Claire, and Luke Tredinnick. 2016. "Post Truth, Information, and Emotion." *Business Information Review* 33, no. 4: 204–6.

Lee, Boram, and EunKyung Chung. 2016. "An Analysis of Web-Scale Discovery Services from the Perspective of User's Relevance Judgment." *The Journal of Academic Librarianship* 42: 529–34.

Lemann, Nicholas. 2016. "Solving the Problem of Fake News." *The New Yorker*, November 30. Accessed July 5, 2018. https://www.newyorker.com/news/news-desk/solving-the -problem-of-fake-news.

Levine-Clark, Michael, John McDonald, and Jason S. Price. 2014. "The Effect of Discovery Systems on Online Journal Usage: A Longitudinal Study." *Insights* 27, no. 3: 249–56.

Lundrigan, Courtney, Kevin Manuel, and May Yan. 2016. "'Pretty Rad': Explorations in User Satisfaction with a Discovery Layer at Ryerson University." *College & Research Libraries* 76, no. 1 (Jan.): 43–62.

Marchionini, Gary. 1995. *Information Seeking in Electronic Environments*. Cambridge: Cambridge University Press.

McGrew, Sarah, Teresa Ortega, Joel Breakstone, and Sam Wineburg. 2017. "The Challenge That's Bigger than Fake News: Civic Reasoning in a Social Media Environment." *American Educator* 41, no. 3: 4–9, 39.

Meier, John J., and Thomas W. Conkling. 2008. "Google Scholar's Coverage of the Engineering Literature: An Empirical Study." *The Journal of Academic Librarianship* 34, no. 3: 196–201.

Newell, Alan, and Herbert Simon. 1972. *Human Problem Solving*. Englewood Cliffs, NJ: Prentice-Hall.

Ohlheiser, Abby. 2018. "Algorithms Are One Reason a Conspiracy Theory Goes Viral; Another Reason Is You." Intersect, *Washington Post*, February 22. https://www.wash ingtonpost.com/news/the-intersect/wp/2018/02/23/algorithms-are-one-reason-a-con spiracy-theory-goes-viral-another-reason-might-be-you/?utm_term=.af5a8e8d3310.

Ojala, Marydee. 2017. "Fake Business News." *Online Searcher* 41, no. 3 (May/Jun.): 60–62.

Oxford Dictionaries, s.v. "Post-Truth." Accessed July 5, 2018. https://en.oxforddictionaries
.com/definition/post-truth.

Padgett, Lauree. 2017. "Filtering Out Fake News: It All Starts with Media Literacy."
Information Today 34, no. 1: 6.

Pariser, Eli. 2011. *The Filter Bubble: What the Internet Is Hiding from You.* New York:
Penguin Press.

Park, Minsoo, and Tae-seok Lee. 2013. "Understanding Science and Technology Information
Users through Transaction Log Analysis." *Library High Tech* 31, no. 1: 123–40.

ProQuest. 2018. "ABI/Inform Complete." Accessed July 5, 2018. http://www.proquest.com/
products-services/abi_inform_complete.html.

Quint, Barbara. 2017. "Honesty in the Digiverse." *Online Searcher* 41, no. 2: 25–26.

Rochlin, Nick. 2017. "Fake News: Belief in Post-Truth." *Library Hi Tech* 35, no. 3: 386–92.

Seargeant, Philip, and Caroline Tagg. 2018. "The Role of Information Literacy in the Fight
against Fake News." *Information Literacy* (blog) CILIP Information Literacy Group,
February 15. Accessed July 5, 2018. https://infolit.org.uk/the-role-of-information-literacy
-in-the-fight-against-fake-news.

Sidecar Publications. 2018. "Gimlet: Simple and Refreshing." Accessed July 5, 2018. https://
gimlet.us/.

Silverman, Craig. 2016. "This Analysis Shows How Viral Fake Election News Stories
Outperformed Real News on Facebook." *Buzzfeed News.* November 16. Accessed July 5,
2018. https://www.buzzfeed.com/craigsilverman/viral-fake-election-news-outperformed
-real-news-on-facebook.

Smith, Maribeth D. 2017. "Arming Students against Bad Information." *Phi Delta Kappan* 99,
no. 3 (Nov. 1): 56–58.

Spohr, Dominic. 2017. "Fake News and Ideological Polarization: Filter Bubbles and Selective
Exposure on Social Media." *Business Information Review* 34, no. 3: 150–60.

Stanford History Education Group. 2016. "Evaluating Information: The Cornerstone
of Civic Online Reasoning." Accessed July 5, 2018. https://stacks.stanford.edu/file/
druid:fv751yt5934/SHEG%20Evaluating%20Information%20Online.pdf.

Valentine, Barbara. 2001. "The Legitimate Effort in Research Papers: Student Commitment
versus Faculty Expectations." *The Journal of Academic Librarianship* 27, no. 2: 107–15.

Valenza, Joyce. 2016. "Truth, Truthiness, Triangulation: A News Literacy Toolkit for the
Post-Truth World." *Never Ending Search* (blog). Accessed July 5, 2018. http://blogs.slj

.com/neverendingsearch/2016/11/26/truth-truthiness-triangulation-and-the-librarian
-way-a-news-literacy-toolkit-for-a-post-truth-world.

Way, Doug. 2010. "The Impact of Web-Scale Discovery on the Use of a Library Collection."
Serials Review 36, no. 4: 214–20.

Wendling, Mike. 2018. "The (Almost) Complete History of 'Fake News.'" *BBC Trending*,
January 22. Accessed July 5, 2018. http://www.bbc.com/news/blogs-trending-42724320.

Zimdars, Melissa. 2016. "False, Misleading, Clickbait-y, and/or Satirical 'News' Sources."
Accessed July 5, 2018. https://docs.google.com/document/d/10eA5-mCZLSS4MQY5QGb5e
wC3VAL6pLkT53V_81ZyitM/preview.

Zuckerberg, Mark. 2016. "I Want to Share Some Thoughts on Facebook and the Election."
Facebook. November 12. Accessed July 5, 2018. http://www.facebook.com/zuck/posts/
10103253901916271.

Glossary

A&I database. A special type of index enhanced with abstracts (also called summaries) that describe sources' contents.

abstract. A concise and accurate summary of a source's contents.

abstracting and indexing database. *See* A&I database.

adjacency operator. A proximity operator that the searcher incorporates into his search statement to retrieve texts in which the search words are adjacent to one another. The operator also specifies whether word order matters.

almanac. "A collection of facts, statistics, and lists" (Smith and Wong 2016, 477).

altmetrics. New metrics that are quantitative indicators of people's interactions with the written products of academic inquiry, scholarship, and research.

AND. The Boolean operator that searchers insert into the search statements they enter into a Boolean search system to tell the system which search terms should co-occur along with other search terms in retrievals.

article-level metric. A measure that is used to evaluate the impact of an article in scholarly journals. *See also* h-index.

author. A person, corporate body, or family responsible for creating a source.

author-bibliography search. A subject search in which users want to scan a list of sources that a particular person wrote, edited, illustrated, etc., because they like what the person does and they want to find more like it.

authority control. The editorial process used to maintain consistency in the establishment of authorized index terms for names, titles, subjects, and other phenomena.

authority file. A database of index terms, usually for names, titles, and/or subjects, that are authorized for use in the known-item and subject-heading fields of surrogate records. *See also* authority record.

authority record. An entry that displays an index term's syndetic structure and entry vocabulary, plus such related information as a scope note, the date that the index term was authorized in the CV, and a history note. *See also* authority file.

authorized term. *See* index term.

author-keywords. The subject words and phrases that journal editors ask authors to add to their manuscripts when they submit them to the journal for review. Author-supplied keywords do not comply with the rule of specific entry.

automatic vocabulary assistance. A recall-enhancing feature of search systems that searches for terms related to user-entered terms based on statistical relationships of term occurrences in text.

backward chaining. *See* bibliography scanning.

basic index. When a search statement fails to specify an index or field, the search system defaults to the system's basic index, usually made up of all fields or all subject-rich fields.

bento box. Partitioning the display of retrievals into categories by type of resource or service.

bibliographic database. *See* surrogate database.

bibliography. A systematic listing of citations, usually organized alphabetically by author name, and restricted in coverage by one or more features, such as subject, publisher, place of publication, or genre.

bibliography scanning. Finding relevant retrievals among the citations listed in a source's footnotes or bibliography. Also called backward chaining.

bibliometrics. The statistical analysis of the written products of academic inquiry, scholarship, and research, such as journal articles, books, dissertations, theses, and conference papers.

biography. An account of a person's life, often supplemented with one or more other appropriate genres (e.g., bibliography, catalog, discography, filmography, etc.) to report their accomplishments.

black hat. A computer programmer who engages in unacceptable search engine-optimization techniques.

Boolean logic. The systematic ways in which Boolean search systems produce retrievals in response to search statements bearing Boolean operators.

Boolean operators. The operators OR, AND, and NOT that searchers insert into the search statements they enter into a Boolean search system to tell the system which search terms should be present in retrievals, which search terms should co-occur along with other search terms in retrievals, and which search terms should be deliberately excluded from retrievals, respectively.

Boolean search systems. Search systems governed by Boolean logic to produce retrievals in response to user-entered search statements.

bound phrase. Enclosing a search term in quotes, parentheses, or brackets or connecting its individual elements by hyphens or underscores to indicate to the search system to process it as a phrase.

broader term (BT). A hierarchical relationship between two controlled vocabulary terms in a thesaurus that expresses either a whole–part or genus–species relationship, the broader term designating the whole or the genus.

browsing. The act of scrutinizing the system's display of indexed entries, such as an alphabetical index, classified list, cluster array, or thesaurus authority record, by a user with the intent of selecting one or more entries to further the search.

catalog. A special type of index bearing surrogate records that describe sources contained in a collection, library, or group of libraries and that are organized according to a formal scheme or plan.

cataloger. *See* indexer.

CD-ROM search system. A stand-alone, single-user search system featuring a personal computer and database on a CD-ROM (compact disk read only memory).

citation. A reference to a source that gives just enough identification information so that a person can find the source in a collection, such as a library or a database.

citation count. The number of times a person's publications have been cited in other publications.

citation management system (CMS). A library for the user's saved sources and a suite of automated tools to help the user manage these sources and cite them in written works.

citation verification search. A known-item search that verifies the citation data the user has in hand for a source or completes it for citation purposes.

cited references. Sources that the source in hand cites (usually in the form of footnotes or citations in a bibliography). Cited references go back in time. *See also* bibliography scanning.

cited-reference searches. Finding relevant retrievals among the sources that have cited an older source since its publication. Also called forward chaining.

citing references. Sources that have cited the source in hand since its publication. Citing references go forward in time. *See also* cited-reference searches.

classification. Putting sources in order, mostly by subject but sometimes by genre.

classification captions. Broad-based topical headings that make up a classification's outline. In some databases, indexers assign such captions (or codes representing the captions) to surrogates in ways that are similar to their assignment of controlled-vocabulary terms from a thesaurus so that search systems can index the captions (or their codes) to facilitate subject searching.

closed-ended questions. Questions that librarians ask users during the reference interview to elicit yes or no or short answers from them.

clusters. *See* postsearch clusters.

command-line interface. Allows users to interact with a search system by entering commands that instruct the system to perform certain operations.

controlled vocabulary. A carefully selected list of words, phrases, or codes that indexers assign to surrogate records to describe a source's intellectual contents and to facilitate online searching.

controlled vocabulary searching. Utilizing search-system features for browsing, selecting, or directly entering a database's controlled terms in the form of words, phrases, or codes, ultimately for the purpose of producing high-precision retrievals.

controlled vocabulary term. *See* index term.

corporate body. "Organizations or group of persons that are identified by a particular name and that acts or may act as an entity" (Chan and Salaba 2016, 745).

COUNTER-compliant data. Database usage statistics that conform to Project COUNTER standards.

credible. Whether the information at hand is trustworthy and written by a domain expert on the topic.

database. A systematically organized collection of data or information. A database may contain texts, media, spatial and numeric data, or a combination of these.

database aggregators. Search services that host databases from a variety of database publishers. Such services may also host databases that they themselves publish. Also called database supermarkets.

database publishers. For- and not-for-profit publishers that employ professional staff to select database content, organize it, and deposit it into the database. Some publishers index database content and add search and retrieval services, and other publishers license database aggregators to do it for them.

database supermarkets. *See* database aggregators.

descriptor. *See* index term.

dictionary. *See* discipline-based dictionary; language dictionary.

digital libraries. Research databases that provide access to actual sources across the wide range of genres—texts, media, and numeric and spatial data.

direct entry. The searcher's manual entry of search terms and searching language into the system's search box.

directory. A collection of entries for persons and organizations bearing contact information and other potentially useful information, such as age, gender, and occupation for persons and founding date, number of employees, and contact person name for organizations.

discipline-based dictionary. A collection of entries for concepts, events, objects, and overarching topics in a discipline, subject, or field of study, along with definitions and short explanations.

document representation. The information—surrogate, actual source, or both—that a search system indexes, retrieves, and displays.

domain expert. A person who has earned credentials (e.g., degree, certification, license, experience) that represent her mastery of a discipline, subject, field of study, practice, trade, or profession.

double posting. A database indexing practice in which systems index the words and phrases in surrogate record fields multiple times to maximize the searcher's chances of retrieving information.

encyclopedia. A collection of entries for concepts, events, objects, or overarching topics in a discipline, subject, or field of study that gives background information, definitions, detailed explanations, and current issues and trends and includes bibliographical references to seminal sources.

encyclopedic. A database that covers a wide range of disciplines, subjects, or fields of study.

end user. A person who uses library resources and services, excluding the library staff who provide access to library resources and services. Also known as everyday people.

entry vocabulary. Synonyms that link users to authorized index terms in a controlled vocabulary. Also called cross-references, see references, use references, and use terms. *See also* use references.

everyday people. *See* end user.

expert intermediary searcher. A person (usually a librarian) who has received special training in online searching from search-system representatives or faculty in schools of library and information science (LIS).

extended-Boolean search systems. Search systems that respond with relevance-ranked retrievals to the natural language queries end users enter into them.

facet. A word or very short phrase that describes a single concept or idea. A facet can also be a word or phrase that is a data element in a citation, such as a title or author name.

facet analysis. An analysis of the user's query in which the objective is to express it in no more than a handful of big ideas, major concepts, or facets that should or should not be present in retrievals.

facets. *See* postsearch clusters.

fact. Something that exists now or something known to have existed in the past, such as an object, event, situation, or circumstance.

fair linking. Search systems giving equal consideration to retrievals in the search and display process.

false drop. A retrieval that matches the search statement's criteria, but due to multiple meanings or the context of its matching words and phrases, it is irrelevant to the search at hand.

federated search system. A search system that dispatches the user's search statement to a set of disparate databases; merges each database's retrievals into a succinct response, with duplicates handled in an efficient manner; and presents retrievals to the user, along with functionality for sorting them in various ways.

field. A set of characters in a database that, when treated as a unit, describes a particular kind of data, like an author, title, or summary.

field label. The full or abbreviated name of a field that the user chooses from a search system's select-a-field pull-down menu or enters directly into a search statement for the purpose of restricting retrieval to this field.

fields pull-down menu. The pull-down menu in a search system's basic or advanced interface bearing field names that the user chooses for the purpose of restricting retrievals to the selected field.

filter. *See* postsearch clusters.

filter bubbles. *See* personalization.

form. The structure of a database.

forward chaining. *See* cited-reference searches.

free text (FT) searching. Using a searching language to enter natural-language words and phrases into a Boolean search system, ultimately for the purpose of producing high-recall retrievals. Free text searching that a user conducts in a full-text database is also called free text searching.

full-text. The text of the actual source itself.

full-text aggregator. *See* journal aggregator.

full-text database. A systematic organization of values (e.g., words, phrases, numbers, or codes) contained in a source database's full-text sources, along with the pointers, references, or addresses that the search system uses to retrieve the full-texts in which the values occur.

full-text fulfillment search. Finding a full-text for a desired source.

full-text publisher. *See* journal publisher.

full-text searching. *See* free text (FT) searching.

genre. The nature of the sources contained in a database—what they *are* as opposed to what they are *about*.

handbook. "A handy guide to a particular subject, with all of the critical information that one might need" consolidated into a single source (Smith and Wong 2016, 478).

high-posted searches. Searches that produce too many retrievals.

h-index. An article-level metric that is used to evaluate the impact of journal articles. An author with an index of h has published h papers, each of which has been cited by other papers h times or more.

history note. Information about an index term's representation in a CV, such as changes over the years, special instructions for searching this term online, and the range of years an unused term was in use.

hits. The number of retrievals that a search statement retrieves. Also called postings.

ILS. *See* integrated library system.

impact factor. A metric that is used to evaluate the impact of a journal. It is calculated by determining the number of times that the journal's articles are cited by other journals over a two-year period, divided by the total number of citable pieces published in the journal over the same period of time.

implicit operators. In response to a search statement, a search system inserts Boolean operators between search words, usually AND in Boolean systems and OR in extended-Boolean systems.

imposed query. A query that the user poses to a reference librarian that comes from someone else, typically a teacher, family member, boss, neighbor, friend, or colleague.

in-depth query. Negotiated queries that usually require subject searches and produce multiple retrievals from which users must synthesize an answer to their questions.

index. A systematic organization of values (e.g., words, phrases, numbers, or codes) contained in a database's surrogate records or full-text sources, along with the pointers, references, or addresses that the search system uses to retrieve the surrogates and/or full-texts in which the values occur.

index term. A controlled vocabulary term for a name, subject, or title that is authorized for indexers to assign to controlled vocabulary fields of surrogate records and for searchers to use in controlled vocabulary searches of online databases.

indexer. A human being who assigns controlled vocabulary terms to surrogate records to represent the names, subjects, or titles pertaining to sources.

indicative abstract. A summary that functions like a table of contents, describing a source's range and coverage and making general statements about the source.

indicative-informative abstract. A summary that is part indicative of the source's more significant content and part informative of its less significant content.

information explosion. The rapid increase in the amount of information that became available to people, starting at the time of the Cold War and continuing until the present day.

information need. The user's recognition that what he knows is inadequate or incomplete to satisfy an overarching goal.

information-retrieval (IR) system. *See* search system.

informative abstract. A summary that functions as a substitute for a source, detailing its quantitative or qualitative substance.

inquiry. Same as query but includes requests that do not necessarily involve online searching.

institutional repository. A combined search system and online database that a learning institution, such as a college, university, or laboratory supports, where institution members (e.g., faculty, students, researchers, or administrators) archive digital materials that are the products of their teaching, research, and/or service activities.

integrated library system. A computer-based information system that automates a library's important functional operations, such as acquisitions, cataloging, circulation, interlibrary loan, public access, and serials control, and its public services operations, such as the online public access catalog (OPAC).

intermediary searcher. *See* expert intermediary searcher.

journal aggregator. A search service that delivers full-texts for the journals that they publish and for the journals that other journal publishers outsource to them.

journal holdings record. The listing of the copies of a journal that the library has stored on its bookshelves or online. Listing journal holdings by year, volume, issue, and supplement, the record includes the names of the journal publishers or journal aggregators that supply full-texts.

journal publisher. A publisher that specializes in the publication of one or more journals. When journal publishers offer search services to their journals that include full-text-fulfillment searches, they become database publishers; however, due to costs, the majority of journal publishers outsource search services and full-text fulfillment to journal aggregators.

journal run. A subject search in which users want to scan multiple issues of a journal because it has published a relevant article(s) on the topic they seek and they want to find more like it.

keywords. The words and phrases that users enter into search systems to express their queries. The keywords users enter don't necessarily arise from a facet analysis and logical combination, and they vary in form, ranging from single words and phrases to sentences, questions, and even whole paragraphs.

known-item search. A request for an actual source that you or the user know exists. To conduct a known-item search, enter a search statement made up of words and phrases that describes an actual source's title, author, publisher, journal title, conference name, genre, date, or other publication-specific attributes. An efficient known-item search retrieves only the one desired source or puts it atop the ranked retrievals list.

language dictionary. A collection of entries for acronyms, proper nouns, phrases, or words giving definitions, etymology, foreign-language equivalents, grammar, orthography, pronunciations, regionalisms, synonyms, usage, visual imagery, and/or written-out forms.

LCNAF. *See* authority file.

lexicographer. The person who develops and maintains a thesaurus or classification.

LibGuides. An easy-to-use content-management system marketed to librarians, who use it to author web-based resource pages for users, putting users a click away from recommended resources on a hot topic, discipline, genre, theme, current event, etc.

library catalog. The physical or virtual index that users search to access a library's collection, consisting mostly of surrogate records for monographs and serial titles. *See also* OPAC.

Library of Congress Name Authority File. *See* authority file.

library website. The library's virtual services where self-service access to scholarly, professional, and educational information resides. It provides access not only to surrogate records but to the actual sources themselves in the form of digital full-texts, media, numeric and spatial data, and combinations of these. Also called database gateways, database hubs, gateway systems, information portals, scholar portals, and search tools.

licensed databases. Databases that database publishers, database aggregators, journal publishers, and journal aggregators license to libraries for a subscription fee. Because authentication is required, access to these databases is limited to a library's cardholders.

licensed Web. The online space in which licensed databases reside.

limits. *See* postsearch clusters.

link resolver. A software product that processes the citation data embedded in an openURL to determine whether the library holds or owns the actual sources itself, and when it does, it facilitates the retrieval and display of the source back to the user.

literary warrant. When enough domain experts have written on a topic, the lexicographer establishes an index term for the topic and adds it to the controlled vocabulary.

literature review. An evaluative report of what is known about a subject, theme, current event, issue, etc., that strives to be comprehensive in a certain way(s); for example, covering a certain range of years, a certain genre, or a certain methodology. *See also* systematic review.

logical combination. The addition of Boolean operators to the facet analysis to indicate to the search system how it should combine facets during retrieval.

main entry. When main entry governs the display of retrievals, the result is a retrievals list ordered alphabetically by author and, when authorship is diffuse or anonymous, by title.

major index terms. Index terms that indexers assign to surrogate records when the sources are specifically about the subjects described by the major index term.

manual. "A convenient guide to a particular procedure, typically with step-by-step instructions" (Smith and Wong 2016, 478).

media. Information packages that people experience with their visual, tactile, or auditory senses.

NAICS codes. A classification of businesses called the North American Industry Classification System.

narrower term (NT). A hierarchical relationship between two controlled vocabulary terms in a thesaurus that expresses either a whole–part or genus–species relationship, the narrower term designating the part or the species.

nearby operator. A proximity operator that the searcher incorporates into his search statement to retrieve texts in which the search words are separated by one or more intervening words and the order of the search words does not matter. Also called near operator or neighbor operator.

negotiated query. The librarian's understanding of what the user wants as a result of conducting a reference interview with the user.

nested Boolean logic. The inclusion of parentheses (or brackets) in a search statement for the same purpose that algebra uses parentheses—to designate which combinatorial operations should be done first, second, third, and so on.

NOT. The Boolean operator that searchers insert into the search statements they enter into a Boolean search system to tell the system which search terms should be deliberately excluded from retrievals.

numeric data. Data expressed in numbers.

online public access catalog. *See* OPAC.

OPAC. The online index that users search to access a library's collection, consisting mostly of surrogate records for monographs and serial titles. *See also* library catalog.

open access. Unrestricted access to peer-reviewed scholarship on the open Web.

open-ended questions. The questions that librarians ask users during the reference interview to elicit anything but a yes or no or short answer.

OpenURL. A standard for encoding citation data for actual sources into a URL that can be passed to a link resolver that processes the citation data to determine whether the library holds or owns the actual source.

open Web. The public section of the World Wide Web, where anyone with a computer, Internet connection, and Web browser can search, retrieve, display, and publish information.

OR. The Boolean operator that searchers insert into the search statements they enter into a Boolean search system to tell the system which search terms should be present in retrievals.

paywalls. The restrictions publishers levy on users who want to access their web-based sources but have no paid subscription or have not placed a firm order for a retrieved source. Paywalls operate on a soft to hard continuum, with soft allowing some access, such as the display of a retrieved source's index terms, abstract, and cited sources, and with hard restricting access almost entirely to citations.

PDF (portable document format). A file format that displays text, media, or numeric data like the printed page so that a person can read, view, print, and/or transmit the file electronically to other(s).

pearl growing. The practice of scrutinizing retrievals, both surrogates and the actual sources themselves (when available), for the purpose of finding relevant terms to incorporate in a follow-up search that retrieves additional relevant sources.

peer-review. The systematic evaluation of scholarship by domain experts in a discipline, subject, or field of study.

personalization. A relevance-enhancement technique that Web search engines perform algorithmically, using personal information that they glean from the Web to influence retrievals for a search and populating them with ones that are specific to the person's interests.

postcoordination. The searcher's deliberate combination of words into search statements *after* the search system has extracted words from texts into its searchable indexes.

postings. The number of retrievals that a search statement retrieves. Also called hits.

postsearch clusters. Nonsubject aspects, such as *date of publication* and *language*, and subject aspects, such as *regions* and *age groups*, that searchers choose after the system produces retrievals for their search statements. Also called facets, filters, limits, or refinements.

precedence of operators. Rules that govern which Boolean and proximity operators the search system processes first, second, third, and so on.

precision. A search that yields mostly relevant retrievals. Precision is calculated by dividing the total number of relevant retrievals your search retrieves by the total number of retrievals your search retrieves.

precoordination. The combination of individual concepts into complex subjects before conducting a search for them (Chan and Salaba 2016, 750).

presearch qualifiers. Nonsubject aspects, such as *date of publication* and *language*, and subject aspects, such as *regions* and *age groups*, that searchers choose to limit retrievals at the same time they enter their search statements.

proximity operator. An operator in a search system that specifies two criteria that must be met for retrieval of surrogates and/or full-texts to occur: (1) how close the words should occur in the text and (2) whether word order matters.

query. The user's immediate expression of his information need.

recall. A search that yields as many relevant retrievals as there are on the topic in the database. Recall is calculated by dividing the total number of relevant retrievals your search retrieves by the total number of relevant retrievals in the database.

reference databases. Databases filled with facts and meant for quick look-ups.

reference interview. A conversational exchange between a reference librarian and a library user, in which the user is likely to describe something she doesn't know, requiring negotiation between the two so that the librarian is able to determine what the user really wants.

refinements. *See* postsearch clusters.

related term (RT). A controlled vocabulary term in a thesaurus that is coordinate to another controlled vocabulary term. Because both terms are at the same level in the hierarchy, they are not related hierarchically. Also called an associative relationship.

relationship designator. *See* role.

relevance. The user's perception that the information at hand has the potential to answer his question or contribute to satisfying his information needs.

relevance feedback. The search system's utilization of one or more retrievals to find ones like them.

relevance-ranked retrievals. Retrievals that systems rank algorithmically in order of likely relevance using a handful to several hundreds of factors, including the number of times they match user-entered search terms in retrievals, the number of times such terms are posted in the database, and the proximity of such terms in retrievals.

research databases. Databases filled with information that doesn't provide instant answers but are meant for study, in-depth analysis, and synthesis.

resolver links. Links that trigger the release of a retrieval's citation data to link resolvers, software that automatically queries the library's other databases to determine whether they contain the actual source and, when they do, retrieves and displays the actual source to the user.

retrievals. The database's report of the number of sources it has found for a user-entered search statement that sometimes includes the display of the first dozen or so sources in the form of surrogates or the actual sources themselves. *See also* source.

role. A word or phrase that describes the part played by a person, corporate body, or family in a source's creation. Examples are author, calligrapher, editor, illustrator, photographer, and videographer.

saved search. Search-system functionality that keeps a search formulation permanently or for a specified time period. *See also* search alert.

scholarship. The process of sharing new discoveries, theories, ideas, information, and data.

scope note. In a controlled vocabulary, an index term's definition and/or explanatory information about the index term's proper usage, such as clarifying an ambiguous term or restricting the term's usage.

search alert. A special type of saved search that the search system executes per the searcher's instructions, sending him newly retrieved sources that meet his search criteria on a regular basis. *See also* saved search.

search box. Usually a single-line box into which the user enters a search statement and bearing a search button or magnifying-glass icon, on which the user clicks to submit his statement to the search system. Also called a dialog box.

search engine. *See* Web search engine.

search engine optimization (SEO). The deliberate process of effecting a higher ranking for a website.

search history. A search system's functionality for displaying the user's previous search statements, sets (when available), and number of retrievals (when available). Also for combining sets (when available).

searching language. System-provided instructions and controls that the searcher wields to tell the system which operations to perform and how to perform them.

search statement. An expression of the negotiated query that the expert intermediary searcher formulates with reference to the search system's searching language and the database's controlled- and free text vocabularies and enters into the search system, with the expectation that, on its own or in conjunction with other search statements, it will produce relevant retrievals.

search strategy. "A plan for the whole search" (Bates 1979, 206).

search system. A computer program that indexes and stores surrogates and/or the actual sources themselves, prompts people to enter search statements that represent their queries, and processes these statements in ways that enable it to respond with surrogates and/or sources that have the potential to satisfy people's queries.

search tactic. "A move to further the search" (Bates 1979, 206).

search tools. *See* library website.

see from references. *See* use from (UF) references.

see references. *See* use references.

sets. Temporary storage bins for search results.

SIC codes. *See* standard industrial codes.

source. "A distinct information or artistic creation" (Tillett 2003, 11). Also called a work. *Online Searching* uses *source* to refer in a general way to the surrogates, texts, media, and numeric and spatial data that searches produce and users scrutinize to answer user queries. *See also* retrievals.

source database. A database that both contains and searches the actual sources themselves—full-texts, media, and numeric and spatial data.

spatial data. Numeric values that reference an object, event, phenomenon, etc., to a location on the earth's surface.

specificity. A principle that governs the indexer's assignment of index terms from a controlled vocabulary to surrogates that are as specific as the source's subject matter.

standard industrial codes. A numeric code that classifies industry areas. Also called SIC codes.

stemming. The search system's retrieval of variants for words and phrases in search statements. For example, the word *argument* in a search statement retrieves such variants as *argue, argued, arguing, argument, arguments, argumentation*, and *argumentative*. Also called intelligent stemming.

subject. A topic or area of knowledge that is the content of a source or that interests a person.

subject heading. A subject word or phrase to which all material that the library has on that subject is entered in the catalog or index.

subject-rich fields. In a surrogate database, these fields are title, descriptor, identifier, author-keywords, and abstract fields. In a source database, these fields are the same as a surrogate database with the addition of the full-text.

subject search. A request for information about a topic. To conduct a subject search, enter a search statement made up of words and phrases that describes a topic, idea, object, phenomenon, person, organization, etc., and expect to retrieve several sources, none of which answers the user's query entirely but require greater scrutiny, deliberation, and synthesis on the user's part to arrive at an answer.

subject term. *See* index term.

summary. *See* abstract.

surrogate. A summary version of a source that is full-text, media, or numeric and spatial data. At a minimum, a surrogate is a citation that contains just enough information to enable a person to find the source in a collection such as a library or database. More comprehensive are surrogates bearing index terms and/or an abstract that summarizes the source's intellectual contents.

surrogate database. A database that bears summary versions of the actual sources; it does not bear the actual sources themselves.

syndetic structure. The thesaurus network of controlled-vocabulary term relationships—BTs, NTs, RTs, and UFs.

synonym. A term with the same or similar meaning as one or more other terms. In a controlled vocabulary, only one such term is authorized and the other(s) designated as use reference(s).

systematic review. A rigorous literature review, usually in the health sciences, that is based on a clearly articulated research question, identifies all relevant published and unpublished studies, assesses each study's quality, synthesizes the research, and interprets and summarizes research findings. *See also* literature review.

technical reading of a database. A methodology for searchers to quickly and efficiently familiarize themselves with a database and the system they use to search it.

technical reading of a source. Reading only those portions of a source that are the most important for understanding overall content.

texts. Written documents.

thesaurus. A controlled vocabulary that designates a subset of a natural language as authorized index terms, expresses the broader and narrower relationships between these terms, and includes related terms and cross-references from synonyms.

title. The word(s) that identify a source but are not necessarily a unique identifier for the source.

truncation. The use of a symbol, such as a question mark, asterisk, colon, or ampersand to shorten, limit, or cut off a search word so that the search system retrieves longer and/or differently spelled variants.

typecasting. Scrutinizing the user's query to determine whether a subject search or a known-item will satisfy it.

uniform resource locator (URL). An address for a website, document, or other resource on the World Wide Web.

unused synonyms. *See* use references.

URL. *See* uniform resource locator (URL).

use from (UF) references. In an authority record, a list of unused synonyms for the record's authorized name, subject, or title.

use references. In a controlled vocabulary, a synonym for or variant of a name, subject, or title that guides the user to the authorized index term. *See also* entry vocabulary.

Venn diagrams. Visual representations of Boolean expressions in which the circles are facets and the overlap between two or more circles are relationships between facets that should or shouldn't be present in search results.

web-scale discovery (WSD) system. A library's Google-like interface to much of its digital content, offering one-stop shopping for academic information. Also known as discovery system, library discovery system, single-search discovery system, single-source discovery system, or these same adjectives ending with service or tools.

Web search engine. A computer program that indexes the World Wide Web, prompts people to enter search statements that represent their queries, and processes these statements in ways that enable it to respond with surrogates for World Wide Web content that link to specific websites that have the potential to satisfy people's queries.

white hat. A computer programmer who engages in acceptable search engine optimization (SEO) techniques.

World Wide Web. *See* open Web.

WSD system. *See* web-scale discovery (WSD) system.

yearbook. A review of trends, issues, and events pertaining to a topic, place, or phenomenon in a particular year.

BIBLIOGRAPHY

Bates, Marcia J. 1979. "Information Search Tactics" *Journal of the American Society for Information Science 30*, no. 4: 205–14. Accessed February 18, 2018. http://pages.gseis.ucla .edu/faculty/bates/articles/InformationSearchTactics.html.

Chan, Lois Mai, and Athena Salaba. 2016. *Cataloging and Classification: An Introduction.* 4th ed. Lanham, MD: Rowman & Littlefield.

Smith, Linda C., and Melissa A. Wong. 2016. *Reference and Information Services: An Introduction.* 5th ed. Santa Barbara, CA: Libraries Unlimited.

Tillett, Barbara. 2003. "FRBR: Functional Requirements for Bibliographic Records." *Technicalities* 23, no. 5: 1, 11–13.

Index

Page numbers in italics refer to figures and tables.

About the Author

Karen Markey is a professor emerita in the School of Information at the University of Michigan. Her experience with online searching began with the earliest commercial systems, Dialog, Orbit, and BRS; the first end-user systems, CD-ROMs and online catalogs; and now centers on today's Web search engines and proprietary search systems for accessing surrogate and source databases of full texts, media, and numeric and spatial data. Since joining the faculty at Michigan in 1987, she has taught online searching to thousands of students in her school's library and information science program. Her research has been supported by the Council on Library Resources, Delmas Foundation, Department of Education, Institute of Museum and Library Services, National Science Foundation, and OCLC. She is the author of six books, more than a dozen major research reports, and more than 100 journal articles and conference proceedings papers.